THE PLAYS OF IBSEN
*Translated from the Norwegian
in Four Volumes by* Michael Meyer

"This, one may think, is how Ibsen might have expressed himself in English."

—*The* (London) *Times*

"Meyer does justice, both in scholarship and understanding, to one of the most fascinating creative artists ever to find the chief expression of his gifts in drama."
—*Washington Post*

"Meyer's translations of Ibsen are a major fact in one's general sense of post-war drama. Their vital pace, their unforced insistence on the poetic center of Ibsen's genius, have beaten academic versions from the field."
—George Steiner, *The New Statesman*

"Crisp and cobweb-free, purged of verbal Victoriana."
—Kenneth Tynan

"Michael Meyer's translation gives back to the lines the poetry and dignity . . . which they certainly lack in the translations we have had for so long."
—*The Listener*

"Mr. Meyer's versions should remain definitive for this generation at least."
—*The Times Educational Supplement*

The Plays of Ibsen

Published by WASHINGTON SQUARE PRESS

Most Washington Square Press Books are available at special quantity discounts for bulk purchases for sales promotions, premiums or fund raising. Special books or book excerpts can also be created to fit specific needs.

For details write the office of the Vice President of Special Markets, Pocket Books, 1230 Avenue of the Americas, New York, New York 10020.

THE PLAYS OF

IBSEN

VOLUME IV

PEER GYNT ▪ ROSMERSHOLM
THE LADY FROM THE SEA ▪ LITTLE EYOLF

Translated from the Norwegian
and Introduced by
Michael Meyer

WASHINGTON SQUARE PRESS
PUBLISHED BY POCKET BOOKS NEW YORK

Rosmersholm, The Lady from the Sea and *Little Eyolf* were first published as a collection in Great Britain in paperback in 1980 by Eyre Methuen Ltd.

Rosmersholm was first published in this translation in 1966 by Rupert Hart-Davis Ltd. Copyright © Michael Meyer 1966. Introduction copyright © Michael Meyer 1966. Revised, 1980.

The Lady from the Sea was first published in this translation in 1960 by Rupert Hart-Davis Ltd. Copyright © Michael Meyer 1960. Introduction copyright © Michael Meyer 1960. Revised, 1980.

Little Eyolf was first published in this translation in 1961 by Rupert Hart-Davis Ltd. Copyright © Michael Meyer 1961. Introduction copyright © Michael Meyer 1961. Revised, 1980.

Peer Gynt was first published in Great Britain by Rupert Hart-Davis Ltd. in 1963. Copyright © Michael Meyer 1963, 1973. First published in a paperback edition in 1973 by Eyre Methuen Ltd. Reprinted in 1980 and 1982.

WSP

A Washington Square Press Publication of
POCKET BOOKS, a division of Simon & Schuster, Inc.
1230 Avenue of the Americas, New York, N.Y. 10020

ISBN: 0-671-60767-7

First Washington Square Press printing March, 1986

10 9 8 7 6 5 4 3 2 1

WASHINGTON SQUARE PRESS, WSP and colophon are registered trademarks of Simon & Schuster, Inc.

Printed in the U.S.A.

NOTE ON THE REVISED EDITION

In this edition, I have made certain revisions to the text resulting from successive productions of these translations. Occasionally, an actor or actress or director has come up with a better line than the one I originally wrote, and I have happily made the change. I have also made certain adjustments for American usage where a word or phrase would sound out of place to an American audience.

Michael Meyer
London
1985

CONTENTS

HENRIK JOHAN IBSEN: A Chronology

1828   Born at Skien in southeast Norway on 20 March, the second child of Knud Ibsen, a merchant, and his wife Marichen, *née* Altenburg.

1834–5 Father becomes ruined. The family moves to Venstœp, a few miles outside Skien.

1844   Ibsen (aged fifteen) becomes assistant to an apothecary at Grimstad, a tiny seaport further down the coast. Stays there for six years in great poverty.

1846   Has an illegitimate son with a servant-girl, Else Sofie Jensdatter.

1849   Writes his first play, *Catiline* (in verse).

1850   Leaves Grimstad to become a student in Christiania (now Oslo). Writes second play, *The Warrior's Barrow*.

1851   Is invited to join Ole Bull's newly formed National Theatre at Bergen. Does so, and stays six years, writing, directing, designing costumes and keeping the accounts.

1852   Visits Copenhagen and Dresden to learn about the theatre. Writes *St. John's Eve*, a romantic comedy in verse and prose.

1853   *St. John's Eve* acted at Bergen. Failure.

1854   Writes *Lady Inger of Œstraat*, an historical tragedy in prose.

1855   *Lady Inger of Œstraat* acted at Bergen. Failure.
        Writes *The Feast at Solhaug,* another romantic
        verse-and-prose comedy.

1856   *The Feast at Solhaug* acted at Bergen. Small suc-
        cess. Meets Suzannah Thoresen. Writes *Olaf
        Liljekrans*, a third verse-and-prose comedy.

1857   *Olaf Liljekrans* acted at Bergen. Failure. Leaves
        Bergen to become artistic manager of the Christi-
        ania Norwegian Theatre. Writes *The Vikings at
        Helgeland*, an historical prose tragedy.

1858   Marries Suzannah Thoresen. *The Vikings at
        Helgeland* staged. Small success.

1859   His only legitimate child, Sigurd, born.

1860–1 Years of poverty and despair. Unable to write.

1862   Writes *Love's Comedy,* a modern verse satire, his
        first play for five years. It is rejected by his own
        theatre, which goes bankrupt.

1863   Ibsen gets part-time job as literary adviser to the
        Danish-controlled Christiania Theatre. Extremely
        poor. Applies unsuccessfully to Government for fi-
        nancial support. Resorts to moneylenders. Writes
        The Pretenders, another historical prose tragedy. Is
        granted a travel stipend by the Government; this is
        augmented by a collection raised by Bjœrnson and
        other friends.

1864   *The Pretenders* staged in Christiania. A success.
        He leaves Norway and settles in Rome. Remains
        resident abroad for the next twenty-seven years.
        Begins *Emperor and Galilean.*

1865   Writes *Brand,* in verse (as a play for reading, not
        acting), in Rome and Ariccia.

1866   *Brand* published. Immense success; Ibsen be-
        comes famous throughout Scandinavia (but it is not
        acted for nineteen years).

1867   Writes *Peer Gynt,* in verse (also to be read, not acted), in Rome, Ischia and Sorrento. It, too, is a great success; but is not staged for seven years.

1868   Moves from Rome and settles in Dresden.

1869   Attends opening of Suez Canal as Norwegian delegate. Completes *The League of Youth,* a modern prose comedy.

1871   Revises his shorter poems and issues them in a volume. His farewell to verse; for the rest of his life he publishes exclusively in prose.

1873   Completes (after nine years) *Emperor and Galilean,* his last historical play. Begins to be known in Germany and England.

1874   Returns briefly to Norway for first time in ten years. The students hold a torchlight procession in his honour.

1875   Leaves Dresden after seven years and settles in Munich. Begins *The Pillars of Society,* the first of his twelve great modern prose dramas.

1876   *Peer Gynt* staged for first time. *The Vikings at Helgeland* is performed in Munich, the first of his plays to be staged outside Scandinavia.

1877   Completes *The Pillars of Society.* This makes him famous in Germany, where it is widely acted.

1878   Returns to Italy for a year.

1879   Writes *A Doll's House* in Rome and Amalfi. It causes an immediate sensation, though a decade elapses before it makes Ibsen internationally famous. Returns for a year to Munich.

1880   Resettles in Italy for a further five years. First performance of an Ibsen play in England (*The Pillars of Society* for a single matinée in London).

1881   Writes *Ghosts* in Rome and Sorrento. Violently attacked; all theatres reject it, and bookshops return it to the publisher.

1882   Writes *An Enemy of the People* in Rome. Cordially
        received. *Ghosts* receives its first performance (in
        Chicago).

1884   Writes *The Wild Duck* in Rome and Gossensass. It,
        and all his subsequent plays, were regarded as ob-
        scure and were greeted with varying degrees of be-
        wilderment.

1885   Revisits Norway again, for the first time since
        1874. Leaves Rome and resettles in Munich.

1886   Writes *Rosmersholm* in Munich.

1888   Writes *The Lady from the Sea* in Munich.

1889   Meets and becomes infatuated with the eighteen-
        year-old Emilie Bardach in Gossensass. Does not
        see her again, but the experience shadows the re-
        mainder of his writing. Janet Achurch acts Nora in
        London, the first major English-speaking produc-
        tion of Ibsen.

1890   Writes *Hedda Gabler* in Munich.

1891   Returns to settle permanently in Norway.

1892   Writes *The Master Builder* in Christiania.

1894   Writes *Little Eyolf* in Christiania.

1896   Writes *John Gabriel Borkman* in Christiania.

1899   Writes *When We Dead Awaken* in Christiania.

1901   First stroke. Partly paralysed.

1903   Second stroke. Left largely helpless.

1906   Dies in Christiania on 23 May, aged seventy-eight.

Peer Gynt

ACKNOWLEDGMENTS

I gladly express my thanks to Michael Elliott for many valuable suggestions concerning the translation of *Peer Gynt;* also to the Old Vic Theatre Company for commissioning it, and to everyone concerned with that memorable production.

I also gratefully acknowledge my debt to the writings of Professor Francis Bull, the greatest of Ibsen scholars, particularly to his monograph on the play (Oslo, 1956) and his introduction in the centenary edition of Ibsen's works (Volume VI, Oslo, 1931). I have incorporated in my notes on pp. 193–98 several of William Archer's perceptive comments.

M.M.

3

Introduction

Ibsen wrote *Peer Gynt* in 1867 at the age of thirty-nine, partly in Rome, partly on the island of Ischia, and partly in Sorrento. Three years earlier, embittered by poverty and failure, he had left Norway to settle in Italy; but in the spring of 1866, the publication of *Brand* had at last brought him fame and financial security. A short while previously he had been voted the worst-clothed member of the Scandinavian community in Rome; now he began to dress with a touch of dandiness, sporting among other luxuries a velvet jacket. A new tone appears in his letters; suspicion and resentment are replaced by a buoyant confidence. Even his handwriting acquired a new assurance. For the first time in his life, he felt economically secure; more important, perhaps, he felt that his reputation was established. This mood was enhanced by the news in May 1866, that the Norwegian Government had granted him an annual pension of 400 specie-dollars (£100); to which was added 100 specie-dollars from the Society of Knowledge at Trondhjem, plus, later in the summer, a further grant of 350 specie-dollars from a scholarship travel fund. 'I have such a longing for work, such strength,' he wrote to Michael Birkeland on 4 May 1866, 'that I could kill bears!' That autumn he actually asked his publisher, Frederik Hegel of Gyldendal, not to send him certain royalties before the following summer, since he did not want to have a superfluity of cash in Italy.

For a while, however, he remained uncertain in which direction to apply his energies. Shortly after completing *Brand* he had struggled for some weeks with an historical drama about Magnus Heineson which he had planned before leaving Norway. But this came to nothing, and on 21 May 1866, he wrote to his publisher, Hegel, that he felt more inclined to settle down to the actual writing of *Emperor and Galilean,* the play about the Roman Emperor Julian the Apostate on which he had been researching for two years. On 22 July he wrote to Paul Botten-Hansen: 'Now I shall soon start to write in earnest; I am still wrestling with the material, but soon, I know, I shall have the beast under me, and then the rest will glide forward of its own volition.' But *Emperor and Galilean* still resisted him, and towards the end of August he laid it aside and set to work revising *Love's Comedy* for a new, Danish edition, removing some of the specifically Norwegian words so as to make the play more palatable to Danish readers. It is possible to discern in this deliberate deletion of Norwegian words the resentment which Ibsen still felt towards his native country, and his contempt for the campaign to purge the Norwegian language of its foreign influences—a campaign which he was shortly to castigate in a more direct and vehement fashion.

Once this work on *Love's Comedy* was finished, Ibsen thought of traveling to Greece (presumably to furnish himself with more material for *Emperor and Galilean,* which partly takes place there), and also to Paris; but both these projects fell through. On 2 November 1866, he wrote to Hegel that he was still uncertain to which of several subjects he would next turn: 'this very division of interest is proof that none of these themes has as yet sufficiently matured in my mind; but I feel confident that this will soon happen, and hope to be able to let you have the completed manuscript during the spring.'

It was around Christmas 1866, or the New Year of 1867,

that his plans for *Peer Gynt* began to clarify. On 5 January 1867, he wrote to Hegel: 'At last I am able to tell you that my new work is well under way and will, if nothing untoward happens, be ready early in the summer. It will be a long dramatic poem, having as its principal character a part-legendary, part-fictional character from Norwegian folk lore during *recent* times. It will bear no resemblance to *Brand,* and will contain no direct polemics nor anything of that kind. I have long been pondering the material for this; now the whole plan is worked out and on paper, and I have begun the first act. It grows as I work on it, and I am confident that you will be satisfied with the result.'

In point of fact, the dates inscribed by him on his manuscript show that Ibsen did not begin writing the play until nine days after this letter, on 14 January 1867; he had a tendency, not unique among authors, to tell white lies to his publisher. He completed Act One six weeks later, on 25 February. Six days later, on 3 March, he started on Act Two, which, if we are to believe a further letter to Hegel (27 March 1867), he finished in three weeks. In mid-May he moved from the heat of Rome to the island of Ischia, where he lived for three months in the little town of Casamicciola on the northern side of the island, near the extinct volcano of Epomeo. The weather was exceptionally hot, even for the natives, but Ibsen seemed to revel in it and worked throughout the day; according to Vilhelm Bergsœ, who was with him at this time, he took no siesta but spent the afternoons correcting what he had written in the mornings. He completed Act Three in as little as two and a half weeks, on 2 July. During this month the sirocco arrived and raised the temperature to above 100°F, but Ibsen continued to work both afternoon and evening, revising and fair-copying. On 8 August he was able to write to Hegel, still from Ischia:

'I have today sent you, via Consul-General Danchertsen in Naples, the manuscript of the first three acts of my new work, entitled *Peer Gynt,* a dramatic poem. This section will come to around 120 printed pages, and the remainder will add up to about the same. I hope to be able to send you Act Four towards the end of the month, and the rest not long after that. In case it should interest you, Peer Gynt was a real person who lived in Gudbrandsdal, probably around the end of the last century or the beginning of this. His name is still famous among the people up there, but not much more is known about his life than what is to be found in Asbjœrnsen's *Norwegian Fairy Tales* (in the section entitled *Stories from the Mountains).* So I haven't had much on which to base my poem, but that has meant that I have had all the more freedom with which to work on it.'

One night in mid-August there was a slight earthquake on Ischia, and although the natives treated it lightly Ibsen left the island the next day and settled in Sorrento. Here he remained for two months, writing the last two acts; there was no earthquake to trouble him, but in near-by Naples there was an outbreak of cholera, and at one time he thought his wife had caught it; but this fear proved to be unfounded.

We do not know when he began Act Four, but he completed it on 15 September, and posted the fair copy to Hegel three days later, adding: 'If the printing of the list of characters could be delayed until I have sent you the remainder of the play, I should be grateful, since I might possibly wish to add a few minor characters; but this isn't important.' The next day, 19 September, he began the final act, and completed it in twenty-five days on 14 October. Four days later he posted the fair copy of this to Hegel: 'and may luck attend it!'

Hegel was very quick to publish *Peer Gynt* after the success that had attended *Brand,* and it reached the Scandinavian bookshops on 14 November 1867, less than four weeks after he had received the final section of the manuscript. Ibsen was delighted at the book appearing in time to catch the

Christmas sales. 'Let us hope the critics will be kind to us,' he wrote to Hegel on 23 November. 'I think the book will be much read in Norway.'

Peer Gynt, however, gained a mixed reception in Scandinavia. The first omens were good; Hegel sent word that the first edition of 1,250 copies had sold out almost at once, and that a second edition of 2,000 copies was in the press. Bjœrnson, that most patriotic of poets, who more than most might have been expected to take offence at the fun poked at Norwegian nationalism, wrote Ibsen a letter full of admiration: 'I love your spleen, I love the courage with which it has armed you. I love your strength, I love your recklessness—oh, it turned all my thoughts to laughter, like the smell of the sea after the closed air of a sick-room.' He also published a review in *Norsk Folkeblad* shortly after the book appeared, praising it hugely.

Ibsen penned a letter of thanks, but before he had posted it he read an attack on the play by Clemens Petersen in the Danish magazine *Fædrelandet.* This was the leading intellectual paper in Scandinavia, having a wide circulation in Norway and Sweden as well as in Denmark, and Petersen had a considerable reputation as a literary pundit; he had written generously, though not uncritically, of *Brand,* and Ibsen had sent him a rather fulsome letter while he was preparing *Peer Gynt,* expressing the hope that Petersen would recognize that in his new work he had 'taken a marked step forward.' Petersen had some good things to say of *Peer Gynt,* but complained of 'a lack of clarity in the conception and of absolute integrity in the execution'; he also declared, somewhat obscurely, that neither *Brand* nor *Peer Gynt* was real poetry because they 'lacked idealism,' objected that the characters in *Peer Gynt* were not fully rounded or alive, and summed the play up as 'an unsuccessful allegory' which frequently degenerated into 'an intellectual swindle.'

This review so enraged Ibsen that he tore up the letter he

had written to Bjœrnson and composed another. This second letter reveals an emotional, even hysterical side to Ibsen's character such as he rarely allowed to emerge in his letters or conversation. 'Dear Bjœrnson,' he wrote on 9 December 1867, 'What is this curse that at every juncture interposes itself between us? It is as though the Devil came in person to cast his shadow over us . . . An hour ago, I read Hr. Clemens Petersen's review in *Fædrelandet* . . . If I were in Copenhagen and anyone stood as near to me as Clemens Petersen does to you, I would have struck him senseless before allowing him to commit so calculated an offence against Truth and Justice . . . My book *is* poetry; and if it isn't, it will *become* such. The conception of poetry in our country, in Norway, shall shape itself according to this book . . . He says that the Strange Passenger represents the idea of *Angst*. Were I standing on the gallows and able to save myself by confessing to such an interpretation, the thought would never have occurred to me; I never dreamed of any such thing; I merely slipped the scene in as a caprice. And is not Peer Gynt a character rounded and individual? And the Mother? . . . However, I am glad that this injustice has been flung at me; it is a sign of divine aid and dispensation; anger increases my strength. If there is to be war, then let there be war! If I am not a poet, what have I to lose? I shall try my hand as a photographer. I shall deal with my contemporaries up there, each and all of them, one by one, as I have dealt with these language reformers; I shall not spare the child in its mother's womb, nor any thought nor feeling that may have motivated the actions of any man who shall merit the honour of being my victim . . . Do you know that all my life I have turned my back on my parents, on my whole family, because I could not bear to continue a relationship based on imperfect understanding?'

He did not post the letter at once, but added a postscript the following day: 'I have slept on these words and read them through in cold blood. The mood they express is that of yesterday; I shall send them, nevertheless.' After another and equally hysterical outburst ('Do not underrate my friends and supporters in Norway; the party whose paper has allowed its pages to carry an injustice against me shall realize that I do not stand alone . . . My enemies shall learn that if I cannot build I have at least strength enough to destroy') he ended on a scarcely appeasing note: 'I reproach you merely with inactivity. It was not good of you to permit, by doing nothing, such an attempt to be made in my absence to put my literary reputation under the auctioneer's hammer.'

Bjœrnson accepted this abuse calmly, and wrote Ibsen a letter of splendid generosity and exhortation, begging him to 'be just towards us and have faith in yourself.' This reached Ibsen on Christmas Day, and so mollified him that in his next letter, on 28 December, he actually asked Bjœrnson to give Petersen* his regards. But his old feeling of resentment soon returned, and it was to be ten years before he wrote to Bjœrnson again.

Another Dane to find fault with *Peer Gynt*, and one whose condemnation must particularly have saddened Ibsen, was his old friend and admirer Georg Brandes. Writing in *Dagbladet*, he admitted that it contained great beauties and certain noble truths, but concluded: 'Beauties and Truths are far less important than Beauty and Truth in the singular, and Ibsen's poem is neither beautiful nor true; the misanthropy and self-hatred on which it is based are a poor foundation on which to build a work of art . . . What

---

*Petersen suffered swift retribution. Barely a year later, he became involved in a homosexual scandal in a school in which he had been lecturing, and was forced to leave for the United States, where he devoted himself to religious journalism among the Scandinavian-Americans—a dreadfully Ibsenish fate to befall a leading literary critic.

wormwood-tainted joy can he find in thus belittling human nature? It is time this campaign came to an end. We have had enough and the thing must stop.' Hans Andersen, too, disliked the play. 'Ibsen is repellent to him,' wrote Edvard Grieg to Bjœrnson, 'and *Peer Gynt* the worst that he has read.'

In Norway the book was better received than in Denmark, though there, too, the reception was mixed. *Morgenbladet* and *Aftenbladet* published long reviews which were on the whole laudatory; but the greatness of the play was not generally appreciated, at any rate by the critics. Apart from the anti-Norwegianism, some people were bothered by the ending, which they thought facile, and others by what seemed to them an incongruity between the young, the middle-aged and the elderly Peer. Camilla Collett, the pioneer of women's independence in Norway, was offended by the passivity of Solveig's character, declaring that a more forceful female would have shown Peer the error of his ways much earlier. And Kristofer Janson, the novelist, denounced the attack on the language reformers, of whom he was one. Ibsen, who had a long memory, used him seventeen years later as part-model for the self-pitying Hjalmar Ekdal in *The Wild Duck*.

After his first outburst of fury, Ibsen accepted these criticisms calmly. 'How goes it with *Peer Gynt?*' he wrote to Hegel on 24 February 1868. 'In Sweden, as far as I can tell from the newspaper reviews, it has been very well received; but has it sold accordingly? In Norway I gather the book has caused a great rumpus; which bothers me not in the least; but both there and in Denmark, people have discovered much more satire than I intended. Why can't people read the thing as a poem? That was what I wrote it as. The satirical sections are pretty isolated. But if, as seems to be the case, the Modern Norwegian recognizes himself in Peer Gynt, that is those good gentlemen's own funeral.'

Ibsen had no thought, when he was writing *Peer Gynt*, that it should ever be staged; he had too great a contempt for the limitations of the Norwegian theatre and of the men in charge of it. He wrote it, as he had written *Brand*, merely to be read. Five years later, however, the directorship of the Christiania Theatre passed into the hands of an enlightened Swede named Ludvig Josephson. In 1873 Josephson staged both *The Pretenders* and *Love's Comedy* in an imaginative fashion, and it occurred to Ibsen that, if suitably adapted, *Peer Gynt* might receive at the same hands a not unworthy presentation. Before approaching Josephson, however, Ibsen wrote (23 January 1874) to Edvard Grieg to ask if the latter would consider providing a musical accompaniment and to inform him of his plans regarding suitable cuts, which are sometimes surprising. 'Act I will be retained in its entirety,' he wrote, 'apart from some thinning out of the dialogue . . . The wedding scene on p. 42 can be made much more of, with the help of ballet, than appears in the text . . . In Act 2, the incident with the three peasant girls on pp. 58–59 should receive whatever musical treatment you feel appropriate; but there must be devilry in it! . . . There will have to be some kind of musical accompaniment to the scene in the troll palace, though here too the dialogue will be considerably thinned out. The scene with the Boyg, also, which will remain uncut, must have music; the Bird Voices to be sung; the church bells and psalm singing to be heard in the distance . . . Pretty well the whole of Act 4 will be omitted in performance. In its place, I thought we might have a great musical tone-picture to suggest Peer Gynt's wanderings in the wide world, with American, English and French melodies interwoven as changing and disappearing *motifs* . . . Act 5 must be shortened considerably . . . The scenes on the upturned boat and in the churchyard will have to go . . . The scenes with the Button Moulder and the Old Man of the Mountains will be trimmed down. On p. 189 the churchgoers sing on the forest path; church bells and distant psalm singing should be indicated in the music during the dialogue which follows until Solveig's song concludes the play, at which point the curtain will descend while the psalm singing is heard again clearer and louder. This is roughly how I have imagined it . . . If you agree to come in with me on this, I shall immediately approach the management of the Christiania Theatre, send them an acting script and ensure that the play is guaranteed a production. As a fee, I propose to ask 400 specie-dollars, to be shared equally between the two of us.'

Grieg did not receive this invitation with unmixed delight. 'I can't but admire,' he wrote to Bjœrnson (12 September 1874) 'the way from start to finish it splutters with wit and venom. But it will never win my sympathy. Though I think it the best thing Ibsen has written. Am I not right? But you don't imagine I had a free choice in the matter! I received the offer from Ibsen last year, and naturally baulked at the prospect of putting music to this most unmusical of subjects. But I thought of the 200 [specie-dollars] and of the voyage, and made the sacrifice. The whole thing sits on me like a nightmare.' The previous month, he had written to his friend Frantz Beyer: 'It is a dreadfully intractable subject, certain passages excepted—e.g., the part where Solveig sings—I've done that all right. And I've made something of the Old Man's palace in the mountains, which I literally can't bear to listen to, it stinks so of cow-dung and Norwegian insularity and self-sufficiency! But I think people will sense the irony behind it; especially where Peer says: "Both the dance and the music were really splendid. May the cat claw me if I lie!" '

Ludvig Josephson reacted enthusiastically to Ibsen's proposal, though he begged him not to omit the whole of Act Four, suggesting instead certain cuts to which Ibsen agreed. Grieg continued to grouse privately about his 'nightmare,' and it was not until eighteen months after he had accepted the commission, in August 1875, that he finished the music.

Peer Gynt received its first performance at the Christiania Theatre on 24 February 1876. It was the most expensive production that had yet been attempted in Norway, and was a great success; it was performed thirty-seven times, and would have continued even longer had a fire not destroyed the scenery. Despite the cuts, the play lasted for four and three-quarter hours (from 7 to 11.45 p.m.), and seems to have been produced with the accent on the lyrical rather than the satirical aspects. Ibsen did not attend the production, being still reluctant to revisit Norway; but, writing to Josephson from Munich on 5 March 1876, he declared: 'The outcome of this bold enterprise on the part of your theatre has exceeded all my expectations.'

Ibsen was still, at this time, little known outside Scandinavia, and it was not until 1880, thirteen years after the play had been published, that he received a request, from Germany, for permission to translate it. He replied to the inquirer, Ludwig Passarge (19 May 1880): 'It was a surprise to me to learn that you regard this work as suitable to be translated into German for publication there. I must confess that I at least entertain grave doubts on this score. Of all my books I regard *Peer Gynt* as the least likely to be understood outside Scandinavia. I beg you to reflect that few of your German readers will share your own capacity for understanding the poem. You yourself doubtless possess a close knowledge of the Norwegian character and the way the people live; you are acquainted with our literature and our way of speech; you know the people and the personalities one finds up there. But is not all this necessary if one is to find any real flavour in the poem? . . . I hope you will not misconstrue my voicing thus openly the considerations which would, to my mind, operate against your project. I felt it my duty not to conceal them; should they prove unfounded, I shall of course be most gratified.'

Ibsen's doubts did indeed prove unfounded, for *Peer Gynt* has become the best known of all his works outside, as inside, Scandinavia. So far from being regarded as exclusively Norwegian, Peer himself seems to have been accepted everywhere as a national prototype; a Japanese critic has described him as 'typically Japanese.' Subsequent to its première in Christiania, *Peer Gynt* was staged before the end of the century in Copenhagen (1886), Gothenburg (1892), Stockholm (1895) and Paris (1896). This last production was by Lugné-Poe, and was the subject of a perceptive notice by Bernard Shaw in the *Saturday Review*. 'Ibsen's grip of humanity,' he wrote, 'is so powerful that almost any presentable performer can count on a degree of illusion in his parts which Duse herself failed to produce when she tried Shakespeare . . . The universality of Ibsen makes his plays come home to all nations, and Peer Gynt is as good a Frenchman as a Norwegian, just as Dr. Stockmann is as intelligible in Bermondsey or Bournemouth as he is in his native town.'

The first performance of the play in England* took place on 26 February 1911 at the Rehearsal Theatre in London with, improbably, an actress, Pax Robertson, in the part of Peer. (Her mother, Catherine Lewis, ran the Ibsen Studio, which presented the production). Among the many notable interpretations of the role in this century have been those of Werner Krauss in Berlin and L. M. Leonidov in Moscow, both in 1928, Gösta Ekman in Stockholm in 1934, Ralph Richardson in London in 1944 (with Laurence Olivier as the Button Moulder), Max von Sydow in Malmö in 1957 (in a production by Ingmar Bergman), Leo McKern in London in

---

*But there had been an amateur performance in Edinburgh in 1908, by the local lodge of the Theosophical Society.

1962, Brian Cox at Birmingham in 1967 and Tom Courtenay at Manchester in 1970. *Peer Gynt* has also been filmed on no less than three occasions: in America in 1915 (directed by Oscar C. Apfel, with Cyril Maude); in Germany in 1934 (directed by Fritz Wendhausen, with Hans Albers); and again in America in 1941 (directed by David Bradley, with Charlton Heston).

Apart from what Ibsen had read in Asbjœrnsen's collection of fairy tales, the historical-legendary Peer Gynt of Gudbrandsdal may well have come to his notice five years before he wrote the play, when, having been refused a poet's stipend, he received a kind of consolatory grant to travel around the Norwegian countryside collecting folk lore. Some doubt exists as to who exactly was the original of the legend; possibly a Peder Olsen Hage who died in 1785, possibly one Peder Laurissen who lived a century earlier. William Archer noted the debts Ibsen's play owes to Asbjœrnsen: the adventure of Gudbrand Glesne on the Gjendin Edge, the encounter with the three peasant girls, the meeting with the Boyg, the devil in the nutshell, the Greenclad One and the Ugly Brat, the proposed correction of Peer's eyesight to measure up to troll standard, Soria-Moria Castle, and the threadballs (though these last recur frequently in Norwegian folk lore). The character of Peer as conceived by Ibsen, however, has little in common with that of the legendary Peer, and for this Ibsen seems to have drawn on certain of his contemporaries, including himself. Georg Brandes speaks of 'a young Dane whom Ibsen often saw on Ischia, a notably affected and pompous daydreamer and braggart. He told the young girls on Ischia and Capri that his father (a schoolmaster) was a close friend of the King of Denmark, and that he himself was a person of great distinction, who sometimes wore a suit of white satin. He called himself a poet, but had to visit wild regions in order to find inspiration . . . He died not far from Ibsen in Rome. Some traits of his character have survived in Peer Gynt.' Ibsen's old chief at Bergen, Ole Bull, is also believed to have served as part-model for Peer; soon after he had established his Norwegian Theatre there, he left it (in the spring of 1852) to go to America and found an ideal community on the model approved by the French Socialists. This was to be called Oleana, and Ibsen doubtless had this in mind when he made Peer dream of his ideal community, Gyntiana, in Act Four.

Another who lent something to Peer's character was the poet A. O. Vinje, whom Ibsen had known in his Christiania days, an incurable optimist who was always quoting his own verses and aphorisms. Vinje had written a sequence of attacks on *Brand*, and Ibsen's friends in Norway at once assumed him to have been the model for Peer. And there were several lively young Scandinavian poets in Rome during 1866–1867 who may have contributed something.

Ibsen also confessed, in a letter to Peter Hansen (28 October 1870) that he had, when creating Peer, drawn on certain traits of his own character. 'After *Brand*,' he wrote, '*Peer Gynt* followed, as it were, of its own volition. I wrote it in Southern Italy, on Ischia and in Sorrento. Thus far removed from one's readers, one loses one's inhibitions. This poem contains much that has its roots in my own childhood; my mother, with necessary exaggerations, served as the model for Aase.' Later he told Georg Brandes that he had used his contrasting memories of life in Skien before his father's bankruptcy and in Venstœp afterwards as 'a kind of model for my picture of life in "the house of rich John Gynt." '

Peer Gynt is unusual among Ibsen's plays in betraying an apparent debt to certain literary influences. Ibsen owed less to other authors than almost any other writer of comparable stature; he was an unwilling reader, at any rate of books (though he read newspapers most minutely, including the advertisements). Four works, however, all of them Danish, would seem to have left their mark on *Peer Gynt*. One was Frederik Paludan-Müller's epic poem *Adam Homo*, published some twenty years previously, which had already had its effect upon *Brand*. Adam, like Peer, is a weak character who deserts his true love, loses his grip on life, gains riches and worldly success at the cost of his soul, and finally, in the presence of death, senses the possibility of salvation through the love of the woman he had deserted. Another influence, noted by Brandes, appears to have been Œhlenschlæger's *Aladdin*. Aladdin, like Peer, is a dreamer; when contemplating suicide he says, in a phrase which has its echo in the last act of *Peer Gynt:*

> Receive this wretched, failed experiment
> Into your crucible. Melt me down again.

The phrase *at være sig selv,* to be oneself, appears in *Aladdin;* and Aladdin's mother, Morgiane, alternates like Aase between admiration and despair at her son's unpredictability. Aladdin, however, is presented as a heroic character, the apotheosis of the dreamer, where Peer is a *reductio ad absurdum* of the type. Œhlenschlæger regarded the life of the imagination as the highest form of existence; Ibsen knew its dangers.

Two other works that need to be studied by anyone interested in the origins of *Peer Gynt* are J. L. Heiberg's poem *A Soul after Death* (1840) and Hans Egede Schack's novel *The Fantasts* (1858). John Paulsen, who knew Ibsen intimately, has recorded that these were two of the few books that he ever heard Ibsen praise; and that Ibsen once told a young poet that he ought to read everything that Heiberg had written. In *A Soul after Death,* the soul, like Peer, is condemned, not for great sins, but for common bourgeois pettiness; it had lived only for material comfort, and had never tried to be itself. And there are two meetings in Heiberg's poem, one between the Actor and Death, and one between the Soul and Mephistopheles, which carry strong echoes of Peer's encounters with the Button Moulder and the Thin Person. *The Fantasts,* a remarkable psychological analysis of the danger of daydreaming, would seem to have exerted a general rather than a particular influence. It is also perhaps worth noting that Hans Andersen's story *Elverhøj,* itself an earlier satire on Norwegian nationalism, also contained a character named The Old Man of the Mountains. A sixth Dane, Søren Kierkegaard, is supposed by some to have influenced *Peer Gynt;* but the exact measure of Ibsen's debt to Kierkegaard, if any such debt existed, must remain in doubt. Ibsen once stated that he had 'read little of Kierkegaard, and understood less'; but many writers have been unconsciously influenced by authors whom they only partly understood.

Some of Ibsen's rough notes for *Peer Gynt* have survived, plus one draft and the fair copy. The notes were long assumed to have been lost, but as late as 1932 fragments of them were discovered among papers in the possession of his daughter-in-law, Bergliot Ibsen. The first 'ark' of four pages is unfortunately missing, and the manuscript begins in the middle of Act Two, where Solveig asks Aase to tell her more about Peer, and ends in the middle of Act Four. Since nearly three sides of this last four-page sheet are left blank, it would seem that Ibsen had made no further notes before beginning to write his first draft. Neither the notes nor the draft contain any very significant differences from the play as we know it. The state of the draft suggests that it was a first one; some sections were originally written in prose, others in regular trochaic and iambic metres which he later worked into a looser rhythm.

The main differences from the final version occur in the

first two acts. Originally, Peer's father was not a wastrel but a 'man of honour' whom 'Our Lord cut off in his prime,' and Peer was not an only son but had an elder brother, a very different character, who was killed in war. The troll scene as at first conceived contained a good deal of satirical matter which Ibsen later deleted; for example, it opened with the trolls irreverently singing 'For Norway, the birthplace of heroes,' presenting the anthem as a symbol of chauvinism. And there was a scene in Act Two on the mountain (after Peer's renunciation of Ingrid) between Peer and Solveig, who are later joined by Aase and Solveig's parents; her father tells Peer that he can marry her if he is prepared to go to prison as a penance for his crime, an offer which Peer refuses. Most interesting from a psychological viewpoint is the fact that as originally conceived the Boyg stands outside Aase's house and prevents Peer from returning home to his mother after he has left the troll palace. The notes for this scene read: 'He stands in pitch darkness outside Aase's house and finds his way blocked by the Great Boyg. Fights with the Great Invisible One. He wins his way in. It is empty. Fights his way out again. The Boyg is everywhere. Despair seizes him. Alone, alone! Everyone has abandoned him.'

A curious fact about these notes is that they give the lie to Ibsen's account of how he wrote the play, as described in his letter to Peter Hansen and also as reported by William Archer. On Ibsen's death in 1906, Archer wrote an article in the *Monthly Review* entitled 'Ibsen as I Knew Him,' in which he stated: 'He wrote *Brand* and *Peer Gynt* at very high pressure, amounting to nervous overstrain. He would go on writing verses all the time, even when asleep or half awake. He thought them capital for the moment; but they were the veriest nonsense. Once or twice he was so impressed with their merit that he rose in his nightshirt to write them down; but they were never of the slightest use . . . He began *Peer Gynt* at Ischia and finished it at Sorrento. He set to work on it with no definite plan, foreseeing the end, indeed, but not the intermediate details. For instance, he did not know that Peer was to go to Africa. "It is much easier," he said, "to write a piece like *Brand* or *Peer Gynt,* in which you can bring in a little of everything, than to carry through a severely logical scheme, like that of *John Gabriel Borkman,* for example." '

In fact, we know from Ibsen's letters and from the dates on his manuscript that he began the play not in Ischia but in Rome, and that he had a detailed synopsis worked out well past the opening of the African sequence. The conversations reported by Archer, however, took place long after Ibsen had written *Peer Gynt,* and it is not surprising that the old man's memory should have played him false.

As stated, Ibsen wrote *Peer Gynt* to be read, not staged; and the consequent rejection of the accepted limitations of stagecraft proved, as with *Brand,* tremendously liberating. It was not merely that he felt free to move uninhibitedly in time and space (*Peer Gynt* contains forty scenes). He had done that in *Brand.* More importantly, he felt free to ignore other frontiers, the frontiers between reality and fantasy, between (as we should now say) the conscious and the unconscious. Nobody, one hopes, any longer takes the last act of *Peer Gynt* at its face value, as the return of an old man to his youthful love; such an ending would have been, for Ibsen, most untypically banal and sentimental, two adjectives which recur frequently in contemporary criticisms of it. Whether one regards Peer as having died in the madhouse at the end of Act Four, or in the shipwreck at the beginning of Act Five, we must surely take that fifth Act as representing either the unreeling of his past life in his mind at the moment of death or (which is perhaps the same thing) as the wandering of his soul in purgatory, *'limbo patrum,* nigh to hell'. Viewed thus, the last hour of the play is Peer's life seen in a distorting mirror, just as the troll scene in Act Three is the wedding party and Peer's hopes and fears concerning it, dreamed by a drunken and confused man: the desirable yet (once he has got her) repulsive girl, the wrathful vengeance-seeking father, the conflict between lust and conscience. To present *Peer Gynt* on a purely realistic level, as still, alas, occasionally happens, is to reduce it to an amiable and confused pantomime with a facile ending, an interpretation to which Grieg's music, for all its intrinsic merits, has lent authority. Ibsen was not Freud's darling playwright, and Joyce's, for nothing; he understood, as few of their predecessors did, the power of the unconscious, the truth behind dreams and nightmares, the higher reality of what most of his contemporaries dismissed as unreality; and *Peer Gynt* may be regarded as the first prolonged exploration, whether deliberate or unconscious, of this field, to which, nearly twenty years later, he was to return with such effect in *Rosmersholm, The Lady from the Sea* and the powerful and, to his contemporaries, scarcely intelligible plays which followed. *Peer Gynt* is the direct ancestor of Strindberg's *A Dream Play*. But at the time of its appearance, as Ibsen complained, it was regarded mainly as a satire.

Yet in one sense, at least, Ibsen's critics came nearer the truth than some of the play's later admirers. They were right to find it disturbing, discordant and offensive. It is one of the most upsetting and uncomfortable plays ever written. Trolls, properly understood, are not mere goblins but, as Professor Francis Bull has written: 'the evil forces of Nature . . . embodying and symbolizing those powers of evil, hidden in the soul of man, which may at times suppress his conscious will and dominate his actions . . . By ever pandering to his evil instincts and desires they have come to be really his rulers—mysterious powers that make him afraid of himself.' This is what *Peer Gynt* is really about—the struggle between the divine purpose and our undermining passions and egocentricities, between man's deeper self and his ani-

mal, or troll, self; in Stekel's phrase: 'how the soul, oppressed by the primal passions, struggles to escape the hell
of the instincts.' The Boyg, the Greenclad One and the
Strange Passenger are, like the Thin Person, lackeys of the
Enemy; as is Peer himself, apart from the image of him
which Solveig keeps

> With the mark of destiny on his brow
> As he sprang forth in the mind of God.

Peer Gynt is an Emperor *manqué,* searching to discover
what he is Emperor of—to find at the end that the one thing
of which he was meant to be, and was not, Emperor, was
himself. The turning-point in his quest for salvation is that
moment of despair when he sees the star fall, because the
moment of despair is the moment of hope.

Twenty years after he had completed *Peer Gynt,* Ibsen
wrote a letter to its first German translator, Ludwig
Passarge, in which he seems to endorse this view that the
play is about the struggle between the troll in man and the
divine purpose. Referring specifically to *Peer Gynt,* he
stated (16 June 1890): 'Everything that I have written is
most minutely connected with what I have lived through, if
not personally experienced; every new work has had for me
the object of serving as a process of spiritual liberation and
catharsis; for every man shares the responsibility and the
guilt of the society to which he belongs. That was why I
once inscribed in a copy of one of my books the following
dedicatory lines:

> 'To live is to war with trolls in heart and soul.
> To write is to sit in judgment on oneself.'

MICHAEL MEYER

This translation of *Peer Gynt* was commissioned by the Old Vic Theatre Trust, and was first performed at the Old Vic Theatre, London, on 26 September 1962. The cast was:

AASE, a farmer's widow	Catherine Lacey
PEER GYNT, her son	Leo McKern
TWO OLD WOMEN, with sacks of corn	Ida Goldapple
	Brenda McGuinne
ASLAK, a smith	Brian Coburn
MASTER COOK	Endré Muller
SOLVEIG'S MOTHER, immigrant	Phillada Sewell
SOLVEIG'S FATHER, immigrant	Fulton Mackay
SOLVEIG	Dilys Hamlett
HELGA, her sister	June Dartnall
INGRID'S FATHER, the farmer at Heggstad	Esmond Knight
BRIDEGROOM	Trevor Peacock
BRIDEGROOM'S FATHER	Anthony Morton
BRIDEGROOM'S MOTHER	Stella Lewis
INGRID	Adrienne Corri
SÆTER GIRLS	Irene Hamilton
	Judi Bloom
	Anna Middleton
THE GREENCLAD ONE	Adrienne Corri
OLD MAN OF THE MOUNTAINS	Esmond Knight
OLDEST TROLL COURTIER	Russell Hunter
UGLY CHILD	Francis Attard
THE BOYG	Leo McKern
KARI, a cottar's wife	Ida Goldapple
MR. COTTON, a traveller	Anthony Morton
M. BALLON, a traveller	Vernon Dobtcheff

Characters

HERR VON EBERKOPF, a traveller	Esmond Knight
HERR TRUMPETERSTRAALE, a traveller	James Maxwell
OVERSEER	Jeffry Wickham
THIEF	Endré Muller
RECEIVER	Patrick Kavanagh
ANITRA, daughter of a Bedouin chieftain	Adrienne Corri
BEGRIFFENFELDT, D.Phil., director of the asylum in Cairo	James Maxwell
HUHU, a language reformer from the Malabar coast	James Kerry
FELLAH, carrying a royal mummy	Fulton Mackay
HUSSEIN, an Oriental Minister	Russell Hunter
SHIP'S CAPTAIN	Eric Thompson
BOATSWAIN	James Kerry
STEERSMAN	Eric Flynn
WATCH	Jeffry Wickham
COOK	Anthony Morton
STRANGE PASSENGER	Vernon Dobtcheff
PRIEST	Fulton Mackay
PARISH OFFICER	Russell Hunter
BUTTON MOULDER	Wilfrid Lawson
THIN PERSON	David William

Also in the cast were Peter Brookes, Roger Clissold, Robert Hewitt, Ian Hughes, Rosalind Knight, Barbara Latham, Fletcher Lightfoot, Barry Usher, Michael Wells, Fiona Walker and Rosalind Whitman.

Designed by Richard Negri
Directed by Michael Elliott

25

The action, which opens in the early years of the last century and closes about fifty years later, takes place partly in the Gudbrand Valley in Norway and on the mountains around it, partly on the Moroccan coast, partly in the Sahara Desert, the asylum in Cairo, at sea, etc.

ACT ONE

Scene One

A wooded hillside near AASE's *farm. A stream is rushing down it. On the far side is an old millhouse. It is a hot summer's day.*

> PEER GYNT, *a strongly built youth of twenty, comes down the path.* AASE, *his mother, small and frail, follows him. She is angry and is scolding him.*

AASE: Peer, you're lying!
PEER *(without stopping):* I am not!
AASE: Well, then, swear it's true!
PEER: Why swear?
AASE: Ah, you daren't! It's all rubbish.
PEER *(stops):* It's true, every word.
AASE *(squares up in front of him):*
    Aren't you ashamed?
    First you sneak off into the mountains
    For weeks on end in the busy season
    To stalk reindeer in the snow—
    Come home with your coat torn,
    Without the gun, without the meat.
    And then you look me straight in the face

And try to fool me with your hunter's lies!
Well, where did you meet the buck?

PEER: West near Gjendin.

AASE *(laughs scornfully):* Did you, now?

PEER: I suddenly smelt him on the wind.
Hidden behind an elder-bush
He was scratching in the snow for lichen—

AASE *(still scornfully):* Oh, yes!

PEER: I held my breath
And stood listening. I heard his hoof
Crunch, and saw one branching antler.
I wormed on my belly through the stones towards him.
Still hidden, I peered out.
Oh, mother, you never saw such a buck!
So sleek and fat—!

AASE: No, I'm sure!

PEER: I fired. Down he dropped, smack on the hill!
But the moment he fell, I straddled his back,
Seized his left ear, and was about
To plunge my knife into his neck—
Aah! The brute let out a scream,
Suddenly stood on all fours,
Hit the knife and sheath from my hand,
Forced its horns against my thigh,
Pinned me tight like a pair of tongs,
And shot right on to the Gjendin Edge!

AASE *(involuntarily):* In the name of Christ!

PEER: Have you seen the Gjendin Edge?
Three miles long and sharp as a scythe.
Down over glacier, slide and cliff,
[Straight down over sheer grey scree],*
You can see, on either side,
Straight into the lakes that sleep

———————
*Square brackets indicate cuts made for the 1962 Old Vic production.

28

Black and heavy, more than four thousand
Feet below. The length of the Edge
He and I cut our way through the air.
I never rode such a steed!
Before us as we thundered
It was as though there glittered suns.
Brown backs of eagles swam
In the huge and dizzy void halfway between us
And the lakes below—they fell behind
Like motes of dust. Ice-floes broke
And crashed on the shore, but we couldn't hear their
    thunder.
Only the spirits of dizziness leaped
As in dance. They sang, they swung in a ring
In my eyes and ears.

AASE *(dazed):* Ah, God preserve me!

PEER: Suddenly, on a sheer impossible spot
A great cock-ptarmigan flew into the air
Flapping, cackling, terrified,
From the crevice where it lurked
Hidden at the buck's foot on the Edge.
He swung half round, gave a high leap to heaven,
And down we both plunged into the abyss!

AASE *totters and gropes at the trunk of a tree.* PEER *continues:*

Behind us the black walls of the mountain,
Beneath a bottomless void!
First we clove sheets of mist, then a flock of gulls,
Which turned in the air and fled to every side,
Screeching. Still we fell.
But in the abyss something gleamed
Whitish, like a reindeer's belly.
Mother, it was our own reflection
In the calm water of the mountain lake,
Darting up towards the surface

With the same wild speed with which we fell.

AASE *(gasps for breath):* Peer! God help me! Tell me
    quickly—!

PEER: Buck from air and buck from deep
    In a moment smashed together,
    So that the foam rose high about us.
    We plunged, we gasped and choked.
    At long last, mother, I don't know how,
    We reached the northern shore.
    The buck swam, and I hung behind him.
    I ran home—

AASE: But the buck, Peer?

PEER: Oh, still there, I expect.
    Snaps his fingers, turns on his heel, and adds:
    If you find him, you can have him.

AASE: And you haven't broken your neck? Or both
    Your legs? Not fractured your spine? Oh, Lord,
    Praise and thanks be to Thee, who saved my son!
    Your breeches are torn, but what's that
    When one thinks what you might have suffered in such
      a fall—?
    *Stops suddenly, stares at him open-mouthed, wide-
    eyed, and speechless. At length she explodes:*
    Oh, you bloody story-teller! How you can lie!
    I remember now, I heard all this rubbish
    Before, when I was a girl of twenty.
    It happened to Gudbrand Glesne, not to you,
    You—!

PEER: To both of us.
    Such a thing can happen twice.

AASE *(hotly):*
    Yes, a lie can be stood on its head,
    Smartened up and put in new clothes,
    So its own mother wouldn't know its skinny carcase.
    [That's what you've done, letting on wild and great,

Tricking it out with eagles' backs
And all that humbug, lying right and left,
Yarning away and scaring me dumb
So I couldn't recognize a story
I'd heard in my mother's lap.]

PEER: If anyone else spoke to me like that
   I'd bash him senseless.

AASE *(weeps):*
   Oh God, I wish I was dead.
   I wish I was asleep in the black ground.
   Prayers and tears don't touch him. Peer, you're lost,
   And always will be.

PEER: Dear, beautiful, little mother,
   Every word you say is the truth.
   Calm yourself. Be happy—

AASE: Shut up!
   How can I be happy with such a pig for a son?
   Isn't it bitter for a poor, helpless
   Widow like me to be always put to shame?
   Weeps again.
   What has the family left now from the days
   When your grandfather was a wealthy man?
   Where are the sacks of silver
   Left by old Rasmus Gynt? Your father
   Gave them feet, wasted them like sand,
   Bought land in every parish, drove
   In gilded carriages! Where's what he wasted
   At the great winter feast, when every guest
   Threw glass and bottle over his shoulder
   To splinter against the wall?

PEER: Where are the snows of yesteryear?

AASE: Shut up while your mother's speaking!
   Look at the house!
   Half the window-panes stuffed with rags,
   Hedge and fence fallen down,

31

Cows and chickens exposed to wind and weather,
Fields and meadows lying fallow,
Never a month but I have the bailiffs in—
PEER: Stop that old wives' tattle!
Many's the time our luck has failed—
[And sprung again to its feet as tall as ever.]
AASE: [There's salt strewn where that grew.] Lord, you're a
    fine one!
[As proud and uppish as ever, just as bold
As when the priest that came from Copenhagen,
Asked you your name, and swore it was one
That many a prince where he came from would envy
    you,
So that your father gave him a horse and bridle
In gratitude for his civil talk.
Oh, things were fine then. The Bishop and the Captain
And all the rest of them turning up every day,
Guzzling and boozing and stuffing themselves
Till they were nearly bursting. But
It's when times are hard that a man knows his neigh-
    bour.
Empty and silent it was here the day
John Moneybags set off to tramp the roads
With a pedlar's pack on his shoulder.
Dries her eyes with her handkerchief.
You're a fine, strong lad.] You ought to be a rod
And staff for your frail old mother, work the farm,
And guard the little you've left of your inheritance.
Weeps again.
God help me, it's little use I've had of you!
Lounging all day by the hearth, poking the embers,
Frightening the girls out of the barn on dance-nights,
Making me the game of the whole county
And swapping blows with every ruffian in the parish—
PEER *(walks away from her):* Oh, let me be!

AASE *(follows him):*
    Can you deny you were the ringleader
    In that shindy at Lunde, when you fought
    Like mad dogs? Wasn't it you who broke
    The arm of Aslak the smith? Or at least
    Put one of his fingers out of joint?
PEER: Who's been filling your ears with such rubbish?
AASE *(heatedly):* The crofter's wife heard him hollering.
PEER *(rubs his elbow):* No, that was me.
AASE: You?
PEER: Yes, mother. I was the one that took the beating.
AASE: What!
PEER: He's a nimble man.
AASE: Who's nimble?
PEER: Aslak the smith. I'm telling you, I know.
AASE: Shame upon you, shame! Now I must spit!
    That loafing sot, that swaggerer,
    That boozing sponge! Did you let him beat you?
    Weeps again.
    Many's the shame I've suffered, but this is the worst.
    Nimble, is he? Need you be weak?
PEER: Whether I bash a man or get bashed,
    You start moaning. *(Laughs.)* Now cheer up, mother—
AASE: What! Have you been lying again?
PEER: Yes, just this once. So dry your tears.
    Clenches his left fist.
    This was my tongs. With this I held the smith
    Bent double; my right fist was my hammer—
AASE: Oh, you ruffian! You'll send me to my grave!
PEER: No, you're worth better. Twenty thousand times better.
    Sweet, ugly little mother, you take my word.
    The whole parish shall honour you. Just wait
    Till I do something, something really big!
AASE *(snorts):* You!

PEER: Who knows what will happen?

AASE: You'll learn to mend your breeches first!

PEER *(hotly):* I'll be King! Emperor!

AASE: God help me!
   Now he's losing the little wit he's got.

PEER: Yes, I will! Just give me time!

AASE: Oh, yes! I've heard that one before.

PEER: You'll see, mother!

AASE: Shut your gullet. You're out of your mind.
   Oh, it's true enough something might have come of you
   If you hadn't got lost in lies and twaddle.
   The Heggstad girl fancied you.
   You could have won her easily if you'd wanted—

PEER: Do you think so?

AASE: Her dad's a ninny, he'd not have argued with her.
   He's a stubborn old fool, but she gets her way in the
      end,
   And where she leads he'll follow, grumbling.
   Begins to weep again.
   Ah, Peer, my son, she's rich. The land's all hers.
   Just think. If you'd only put your mind to it
   You'd be wearing the bridegroom's coat,
   Not standing here black and tattered.

PEER *(briskly):* Come on, let's go a-wooing!

AASE: Where?

PEER: At Heggstad.

AASE: My poor boy, you'll find no bride there.

PEER: Why?

AASE: [Wait while I dry my eyes.]
   You've lost your chance, your luck's ended—

PEER: How?

AASE *(gulps):*
   While you were away
   In the western mountains, riding stags through the air,
   Mads Moen's got the girl.

34

PEER: What! That scarecrow?

AASE: Yes, now she's taking him to her bridal bed

PEER: Wait here while I harness a horse to the cart—

Turns to go.

AASE: Save your pains. The wedding's tomorrow.

PEER: Good. I'll be there tonight.

AASE: Shame on you! Haven't I grief enough?
[Without your bringing a general scorn on our heads.]

PEER: Don't worry, it'll be all right.
Shouts and laughs at the same time.
Yippee, mother! We'll do without the cart.
I can't waste time running after the mare—

Lifts her high into the air.

AASE: Put me down!

PEER: No! I'm carrying you to my wedding in my arms!

Wades out into the stream.

AASE: Help! Lord save us! We'll be drowned!

PEER: I was born for a nobler death—

AASE: Yes! You'll end by being hanged!
Seizes him by the hair.
Oh, you brute!

PEER: Keep still. The bottom's slippery here.

AASE: Donkey!

PEER: That's right; carry on. [Talk never hurt a man.]
Look, now it's getting shallow again—

AASE: Don't drop me!

PEER: Get up there now, hup! Let's play Peer and the stag.
Gallops.
You're Peer and I'm the stag.

AASE: I'm out of my wits!

PEER: There, we've made it.
Wades ashore.

Give your stag a nice kiss.
Let the driver have his fare.

AASE *(boxes his ears):* That's your fare!

PEER: Ow! That's a fine reward! Mother!

AASE: Put me down!

PEER: First to the wedding. You must speak for me.
You're clever. Talk to the old fool.
Say Mads Moen's a good-for-nothing—

AASE: Down!

PEER: And tell him what a fine fellow is Peer Gynt.

AASE: Never you fear! A grand character I'll give you!
I'll tell them all about you, I'll tell them
All your devilries—

PEER: Oh?

AASE *(kicks him angrily):*
I won't stop
Till the old man sets his dog on you like a tramp.

PEER: Hm. Then I'll have to go alone.

AASE: Yes, but I'll follow.

PEER: Dear mother, you haven't the strength—

AASE: Haven't I? The way I feel
I could crumble rocks in my bare fingers.
Ugh, I could eat flints! Put me down!

PEER: All right, if you promise—

AASE: Promise nothing! I'm coming there with you.
I'll let them know you for what you are.

PEER: You'd better stay here.

AASE: No. I want to go with you.

PEER: Sorry.

AASE: What are you going to do?

PEER: Put you on the millhouse roof.

He puts her up there. AASE *screams.*

AASE: Take me down!

PEER: Yes, if you'll listen—

AASE: Don't be a fool—

PEER: Mother dear, I beg you—

AASE *(throws a turf at him):* Peer, take me down this instant!

PEER: I would if I dared. *(Comes closer.)*
　　Remember, sit still now. Don't kick
　　Or start pulling down the tiles, or you'll hurt yourself.
　　[And maybe fall down.]

AASE: You brute!

PEER: Don't kick!

[AASE: Oh, why weren't you blown up the chimney like a
　　　changeling!*[1]

PEER: Mother, for shame!]

AASE: Grr!

PEER: Give me your blessing on my journey. Will you?
　　What?

AASE: I'll thrash you, you hulking lump!

PEER: Well, goodbye then, mother dear.
　　Be patient. I shan't be long.
　　Moves away, but turns and raises his finger warningly.
　　Remember now. No kicking. *(Goes.)*

AASE: Peer! God help me, he's going! Liar!
　　You with your tales of riding on stags!
　　Hi! Will you listen to me? No, he's gone. *(Screams.)*
　　Help! I'm getting giddy!

　　TWO OLD WOMEN *with sacks of corn on their backs
　　come down towards the mill.*

FIRST OLD WOMAN: God a'mercy, who's that screaming?

AASE: It's me!

SECOND OLD WOMAN: Aase! Look! Well, you've gone up in
　　the world!

AASE: Not far enough. Please God I'll soon be in heaven.

FIRST OLD WOMAN: Have a nice trip.

---

*For notes on the text, see p. 193ff.

AASE: Get a ladder! I must get down!
　　That devil Peer—!
SECOND OLD WOMAN: Is it your son—?
AASE: Now you can say you've seen with your own eyes
　　What he gets up to.
FIRST OLD WOMAN: We will.
AASE: Help me down! I've got to get to Heggstad—
SECOND OLD WOMAN: Is he there?
FIRST OLD WOMAN: Then you'll be revenged. The black-
　　smith's coming too.
AASE (wrings her hands): Oh, God protect the boy!
　　They'll kill him before he's through.
FIRST OLD WOMAN: Well, it's happened before.
　　Comfort yourself. [It's the ways of Providence.]
SECOND OLD WOMAN: She's out of her mind. (Shouts up the
　　hill.) Eyvind! Anders! Come down here!
MAN'S VOICE: What's the matter?
SECOND OLD WOMAN: Peer Gynt's put his mother on the
　　millhouse roof!

Scene Two

*A small hill with bushes and heather. The high road crosses
behind it, with a fence running alongside. PEER GYNT comes
along the footpath, walks briskly up to the fence, stops, and
looks out across the landscape.*

PEER: There lies Heggstad. I'll soon be there.
　　Climbs half over the fence, then stops and thinks.
　　Is Ingrid sitting there alone, I wonder?
　　Shades his eyes and peers.
　　No, the guests are swarming in like mosquitoes.
　　Hm. Perhaps I'd better turn back.
　　Swings back his leg.
　　People always snigger behind your back,
　　And whisper so that it burns right through you.

38

*Walks a few paces from the fence and absently plucks
a few leaves.*
If only I had a dram of something strong.
Or could go unnoticed. [If only they didn't know me.]
A drink'd be best. Then the laughter doesn't bite.

*Suddenly he looks round as though frightened, then
hides among the bushes. Some* GUESTS *carrying gifts of
food for the wedding walk down past him in the direction of the farm.*

A MAN *(in conversation):* His dad was a boozer and his ma's
a ninny.
A WOMAN: It's no wonder the lad's a good-for-nothing.

They pass on. A few moments later PEER GYNT *reap-
pears. He looks after them, his face red with shame.*

PEER: Were they talking about me?
With a forced toss of the head.
Well, let them talk. That won't kill me.
*Throws himself down in the heather, lies full length
on his back with his hands beneath his head and
stares at the sky.*
What a strange cloud! It's like a horse.
There's a man on it too, with saddle and bridle.
And behind him's an old woman riding a broomstick.
Chuckles to himself.
It's mother.
She's scolding and screaming: 'You brute! Stop, Peer!'
Gradually closes his eyes.
Yes, now she's afraid. Peer Gynt rides at the head
Of a mighty army. His horse has a crest
Of shining silver and four shoes of gold.
He has gloves on his hands and a sword and a scabbard,
And a trailing cloak lined with scarlet silk.
It's a fine bold body of men he has with him,

But none sits his horse as proudly as he,
Or glitters as he does against the sun.
Crowds throng below as he passes by them.
They take off their hats and their eyes gape up at him.
The women curtsey, for everyone knows
Emperor Peer Gynt and his thousand warriors.
He scatters sovereigns and shining shillings
On the roadside like pebbles. Every man
In the parish he'll make as rich as a lord.
Peer Gynt rides high over the white sea. The Prince
Of England stands on the shore and waits for him.
And all the maidens of England are with him,
The great men of England and the mighty King
Of England himself rise in homage
From their high table as Peer Gynt comes riding.
King raises his crown from his head and says—

ASLAK THE SMITH *(to several others as they walk past on the far side of the fence):* If it isn't that boozing pig Peer Gynt!

PEER *(half-raises himself):* What's that, Your Majesty?

ASLAK *(leans on the fence and grins):* Time to get up, me lad.

PEER: What the devil—?
    Is it Aslak the Smith? What the hell do you want?

ASLAK *(to the others):* He's still dopey from our last encounter.

PEER *(jumps up):* Clear off!

ASLAK: Man, where have you been?
    Six weeks away! Did the mountain trolls get you?

PEER: I've been doing strange deeds, Aslak smith.

ASLAK *(winks at the others):* Tell us, Peer.

PEER: It's my business.

ASLAK *(after a moment):* You'll be coming to Heggstad?

PEER: No.

ASLAK: They used to say the girl was keen on you.

40

PEER: Why, you black crow—!

ASLAK *(takes a step back):* Don't get angry, Peer. If Ingrid's jilted you

There are others. Think! John Gynt's son!

Come with us to the feast. There'll be juicy young lambs,

And widows too—

PEER: Go to hell!

ASLAK: You'll find someone who'll have you.

Good night. I'll give your love to the bride!

They go, laughing and whispering.

PEER *(looks after them a moment, tosses his head and half turns):*

Let her marry whom she pleases!

It's nothing to me.

Looks himself up and down.

Breeches torn. Tattered and filthy.

If only I had something new to wear—

Stamps his foot.

I'd tear the laughter out of them

Like a butcher pulling the guts from a rabbit.

Looks round suddenly.

What's that? Who was that sniggering?

I could have sworn—! I suppose it was no-one.

I'll go home to mother.

Starts up the hill again, but stops and cocks an ear towards the fence.

The dancing's begun!

Stares and listens; walks back down the hill, step by step. His eyes glitter. He rubs his thigh.

What a fine swarm of lasses!

Seven or eight to every man!

Oh, flames, I must go and join in the fun!
But mother's up on the millhouse roof.
*His eyes are drawn towards the feast again. He jumps
and laughs.*
Hey, how the dancers fly over the grass!
By God, he's a boy on the fiddle! It laughs
And splutters just like a waterfall.
And oh, what a covey of glittering girls!
Yes, flames, I must go and join in the fun!

Leaps over the fence and goes down the road.

Scene Three

*The farm at Heggstad. In the background is the farmhouse
itself. Many* GUESTS. *A dance is in lively progress on the
green. The* FIDDLER *is seated on a table. The* MASTER COOK[2]
stands in the doorway. KITCHEN WOMEN *carrying food and
drink go back and forth between the various buildings.*
OLDER PEOPLE *sit here and there chatting.*

A WOMAN *(joins a group sitting on some logs):* The bride?
Oh yes, she's crying a little,
But that's always the way.

MASTER COOK *(in another group):* Come on, good people,
empty your glasses.

A MAN: Thank you. But you never stop filling them.

A LAD *(to the* FIDDLER, *as he runs past clutching a* GIRL *by
the hand):* Play up, man! Don't spare the strings!

GIRL: Scrape till it echoes out over the meadows.

OTHER GIRLS *(in a circle around a* LAD *who is dancing):*
That's a fine leap!

A GIRL: He's a nimble leg.

THE LAD *(dancing):* It's a high roof here, and the walls are wide!

BRIDEGROOM *(comes snivelling up to his* FATHER, *who is standing talking to two or three others, and pulls his coat):* She won't, father. She's so proud.

FATHER: What won't she?

BRIDEGROOM: She's shut herself in.

FATHER: Well, find the key.

BRIDEGROOM: I don't know where.

FATHER: You dumb halfwit!

He turns back to the others. The BRIDEGROOM *wanders away across the yard.*

A LAD *(comes from behind the house):* Hey, girls! Now things'll be livening up!
    Here comes Peer Gynt!

ASLAK *(who has just joined them):* Who asked him?

MASTER COOK: Nobody. *(Goes towards the house.)*

ASLAK *(to the* GIRLS*):* If he tries to speak to you, don't listen to him.

A GIRL *(to the* OTHERS*):* No, we'll pretend we never saw him.

PEER GYNT *(enters hot and excited, stops in the middle of the* CROWD *and claps his hands):* Now, which girl's got the nimblest pair of legs?

A GIRL *(as he approaches):* Not me.

ANOTHER *(similarly):* Nor me.

A THIRD GIRL: I'm sure I haven't.

PEER *(to a* FOURTH GIRL*):* Well, let's have you, if there's no one better.

FOURTH GIRL *(turns away):* Haven't time.

PEER *(to a* FIFTH*):* You, then.

FIFTH GIRL *(walks away):* I'm going home.

PEER: Tonight? Are you out of your wits?

43

ASLAK (*after a moment, in a low voice*): Look, Peer. She's
dancing with somebody's granddad.

PEER (*turns sharply to an* OLDER MAN): Hey, you! Where are
the free ones?

MAN: Find them for yourself. (*Walks away from him.*)

PEER GYNT *falls suddenly silent. He glances shyly and
furtively at the group. They all look at him but do not
speak. He approaches other groups. As he reaches
them, they fall silent; as he walks away, they smile and
follow him with their eyes.*

[PEER (*quietly*): Their glances and smiles are needles in my
back.
My nerves grate like a sawblade under the file.]

He walks away along the fence. SOLVEIG, *holding little*
HELGA *by the hand, enters the yard with her* PARENTS.

A MAN (*to another standing near* PEER GYNT): Look. The
strangers.

SECOND MAN: The strangers from the west?

FIRST MAN: Yes, from Heydal.

SECOND MAN: Ah, yes.

PEER (*walks in front of the newcomers, points at* SOLVEIG
and asks her FATHER): May I dance with your
daughter?

SOLVEIG'S FATHER (*quietly*): You may; but first we must go
inside and greet
The people of the house.

MASTER COOK (*to* PEER, *offering him a drink*): Since you've
come, you might as well have one.

PEER (*keeps his eyes fixed on them as they go*): Thanks, I'm
going to dance. I'm not thirsty.

THE MASTER COOK *leaves him.* PEER *looks towards the
house and laughs.*

PEER: How fair she is!
   I never saw such a girl! She dropped
   Her eyes to her shoes and her white apron,
   And clutched tight to her mother's skirt,
   And carried a psalmbook wrapped in linen.
   I must look at that girl.

   Is about to enter the house.

A LAD (*comes out of the house with several others*): Why,
      Peer! Are you leaving the dance already?
PEER: No.
LAD: Then you're heading the wrong way.

   Takes him by the shoulder to turn him round.

PEER: Let me past!
LAD: Are you scared of the smith?
PEER: *I* scared?
LAD: Yes, have you forgotten what happened at Lunde?

   They all laugh and go down to the dancing-green.

SOLVEIG (*in the doorway*): Are you the boy that wanted to
      dance?
PEER: Of course I am. Don't you remember me?
   Takes her by the hand.
   Come along.
SOLVEIG: I mustn't go far, Mother said.
PEER: Mother said! Mother said! Were you born yesterday?
SOLVEIG: You're making fun—!
PEER: Well, you're almost a child. How old are you?
SOLVEIG: I was confirmed by the priest last year.
PEER: Tell me your name, girl, and we'll talk more easily.
SOLVEIG: My name's Solveig. What's yours?
PEER: Peer Gynt.
SOLVEIG (*draws her hand away*): Oh, heaven!

PEER: What is it now?

SOLVEIG: My garter's come loose. I must tie it tighter.

Leaves him.

BRIDEGROOM *(tugs at his* MOTHER*'s dress):* Mother, she won't.

BRIDEGROOM'S MOTHER: Won't? Won't what?

BRIDEGROOM: Won't, mother.

BRIDEGROOM'S MOTHER: What?

BRIDEGROOM: Unlock the door.

BRIDEGROOM'S FATHER *(quietly, angrily):* Oh, you're only fit to feed with the pigs.

BRIDEGROOM'S MOTHER: No, don't scold him. Poor lad, he'll be all right.

They walk away.

A LAD *(comes with a crowd from the dancing-green):* Have a real drink, Peer?

PEER: No.

LAD: Oh, come on, have a drop.

PEER *(scowls at him):* Have you got some?

LAD: Maybe.
Takes out a pocket flask and drinks.
Oh, how it burns! Well?

PEER: Let's have a sniff. *(Drinks.)*

SECOND LAD: Try mine too.

PEER: No.

SECOND LAD: Come on, now, don't be a fool. Drink up, Peer!

PEER: All right. *(Drinks again.)*

A GIRL *(whispers):* Come on, let's go.

PEER: Are you scared of me, lass?

A THIRD LAD: Who isn't scared of *you?*

FOURTH LAD: You showed us at Lunde what you could do.

PEER: I can do better than that, once I really cut loose.

FIRST LAD *(whispers):* Now he's off!

SEVERAL LADS *(form a circle round him):* Tell us, tell us!
   What can you do?

PEER: Tomorrow.

THE OTHER LADS: No, now, tonight!

A GIRL: Can you do black magic, Peer?

PEER: I can conjure up the Devil!

A MAN: My grandmother could do that before I was born.

PEER: Liar! There's no one else can do what I can.
   Once I conjured him into a nut.
   It was worm-eaten, you see.

LADS *(laugh):* Sure, it would be.

PEER: He swore and wept—said he'd give me whatever I
   wanted—

ONE OF THE CROWD: But he had to go in?

PEER: Of course! I plugged the hole with a peg.
   Oh, you should have heard him spluttering and skip-
   pering!

GIRL: Fancy that!

PEER: Just like a bumble-bee!

GIRL: Have you still got him there?

PEER: No, he's gone back to Hell.
   It's his fault the smith doesn't like me.

LAD: Really?

PEER: I went to Aslak and asked if he'd smash it for me.
   He swore he would; put it down on his anvil;
   But he's a clumsy lout—well, [it isn't surprising,]
   He spends all day swinging that sledgehammer—

A VOICE FROM THE CROWD: Did he kill the Devil, now?

PEER: He laid to like a man.
   But the Devil shot in a flame through the roof,
   Splitting the walls.

SEVERAL: And the smith—?

PEER: Stood there

47

With his hands fried black; since when we've not been
   friends.

They all laugh.

SEVERAL: That's a good yarn.
OTHERS: It's near his best.
PEER: You think I'm making it up?
A MAN: Oh no, you're not!
   I've heard most of it from my granddad.
PEER: That's a lie! It happened to me!
MAN: Sure, what hasn't?
PEER *(with a gesture):* I can ride through the air on horse-
   back!
   There's a lot I can do, I'm telling you!

They shout with laughter again.

ONE OF THE CROWD: Peer, ride through the air for us!
SEVERAL: Yes, dear Peer Gynt!
PEER: Oh, there's no need to beg me!
   I'll ride over the lot of you like a storm.
   The whole parish shall fall at my feet!
AN OLDER MAN: He's out of his mind.
ANOTHER: He's daft.
A THIRD: You swaggering braggart!
A FOURTH: He's a bloody liar!
PEER *(threatens them):* Just you wait! You'll see!
A MAN *(half drunk):* Just you wait. You'll get your trousers
   dusted.
OTHERS: And a tender bottom. And a fine black eye.

The CROWD *disperses, the older ones in anger, the
   younger ones laughing scornfully.*

BRIDEGROOM *(in his ear):* Peer, is it true you can ride in the
   air?

48

PEER *(brusquely):* I can do anything, Mads. I'm a man, believe me.

BRIDEGROOM: Then you've the cloak of invisibility, too?

PEER: The hat, you mean? Of course I've got it.

Turns away from him. SOLVEIG *walks across the yard leading* HELGA *by the hand.*

PEER *(approaches them. His face lights up):* Solveig! Ah, it's good you've come!

Takes her by the wrist.

Now I'll swing you fast and free!

SOLVEIG: Let me go.

PEER: Why?

SOLVEIG: You're so wild.

PEER: So is a stag when spring is dawning.

Come on, girl, don't be stubborn!

SOLVEIG *(pulls away her arm):* I daren't.

PEER: Why?

SOLVEIG: No, you've been drinking.

Goes away with HELGA.

PEER: Oh, to stick a sharp knife through them, all of them!

BRIDEGROOM *(nudges him with his elbow):* Can't you help me to get at the bride?

PEER *(absently):* The bride? Where is she?

BRIDEGROOM: In the storehouse.

PEER: Mm.

BRIDEGROOM: Oh, come on, Peer Gynt. Please try.

PEER: No, you'll have to manage without my help.

A thought occurs to him. He says quietly but sharply:

Ingrid in the storehouse!

Goes across to SOLVEIG.

Have you changed your mind?

She turns to go. He steps in front of her.

You're ashamed because I look like a tramp.

SOLVEIG *(quickly):* You don't! It isn't true!

PEER: It is. And I *have* been drinking, too.

But that was to spite you for hurting me.

Come on, then!

SOLVEIG: I daren't now, even if I wanted to.

PEER: Who are you afraid of?

SOLVEIG: Father, mostly.

PEER: Father? Oh, yes. He's one of those quiet ones.

A godly soul, eh? What? Come on, answer!

SOLVEIG: What shall I answer?

PEER: Is your father a bible man?

And you and your mother, too? Will you answer me?

SOLVEIG: Let me go in peace.

PEER: No.

Softly but sharply and menacingly.

I can turn myself into a troll!

I'll come to your bedside tonight at midnight.

If you hear something hissing and spitting

Don't think it's the cat. It's me, my dear!

I'll be drawing your blood in a cup,

And your little sister, I'll gobble her up!

For at night I'm a werewolf. I'll bite you

All over your loins and your pretty back.

Changes his tone suddenly and begs as though in anguish.

Dance with me, Solveig!

SOLVEIG *(looks darkly at him):* Now you're ugly.

She goes into the house.

BRIDEGROOM *(wanders back):* I'll give you a cow, if you'll only help me.

PEER: Come!

They go behind the house. As they do so, a large CROWD *comes from the dancing-green, most of them*

drunk. Hubbub and confusion. SOLVEIG, HELGA *and
their* PARENTS *appear in the doorway with some of the*
OLDER PEOPLE.

MASTER COOK *(to* ASLAK *the* SMITH, *who is at the head of the*
CROWD*):* Keep the peace now, will you?
ASLAK *(takes off his coat):* No. We'll settle it now.
Someone's nose must be rubbed in the dirt,
Peer Gynt's or mine.
SOME OF THE CROWD: Sure, let them fight.
OTHERS: No, let's have no violence.
ASLAK: It's fists or nothing.
[For we've come to the stage where words are useless.]
SOLVEIG'S FATHER: Control yourself, man.
HELGA: Are they going to beat him, mother?
A LAD: Let's stuff his lies down his throat.
ANOTHER: Kick him out of the feast!
A THIRD: Spit in his eye!
A FOURTH MAN *(to the* SMITH*):* Are you backing out?
ASLAK *(throws down his jacket):* I'll slaughter the pig!
SOLVEIG'S MOTHER *(to* SOLVEIG*):* You see what they think of
him?
AASE *(enters with a stick in her hand):* Is my son here? Wait
till I get his pants down!
I'll thrash the holy life out of him!
ASLAK *(rolls up his sleeves):* That stick's too puny for a fat
lout like him.
SOME OF THE CROWD: The smith'll thrash him.
OTHERS: Butcher him.
ASLAK *(spits on his hands and nods at* AASE*):* Hang him!
AASE: What! Hang my Peer? Just you try!
I've teeth and claws! Where is he?
Shouts across the yard:
Peer!

BRIDEGROOM *(enters running):* Oh, God have mercy on us all!

Mother and father, come quickly!

BRIDEGROOM'S FATHER: What's the matter?

BRIDEGROOM: Just fancy! Peer Gynt—!

AASE *(screams):* Have they killed him?

BRIDEGROOM: No, Peer Gynt—! Look up there, on the hill-side—!

CROWD: He's got the bride!

AASE *(lowers her stick):* Monster!

ASLAK *(as if thunderstruck):* By God, he's climbing like a goat!

BRIDEGROOM *(weeps):* Oh, mother, he's carrying her like a pig!

AASE *(shakes her fist up at him):* May God strike you down—!

Shrieks in terror.

Be careful!

BRIDE'S FATHER *(enters bareheaded and white with rage):* Bride-rape! I'll have his life for this!

AASE: I'll burn in Hell before you do!

ACT TWO

Scene One

A narrow path high up in the mountains. It is early morning.
PEER GYNT *is hurrying ill-temperedly along the path.*
INGRID, *still half-dressed in her bridal clothes, is trying to*
hold him back.

PEER: Get away from me!
INGRID *(weeps):* After this! Where can I go?
PEER: Anywhere you like.
INGRID *(wrings her hands):* You have betrayed me!
PEER: It's no good moaning. It's finished.
INGRID: Our crime binds us. Our double crime.
PEER: All memories belong to the Devil.
    All women belong to the Devil.
    Except one—
INGRID: Which one?
PEER: Not you.
INGRID: Who is it, then?
PEER: Go! Go back where you came from!
    Quick! To your father!
INGRID: Dear, kind—!
PEER: Oh, shut up.
INGRID: You can't mean what you say.

PEER: Can and do.

INGRID: To seduce me, and then leave me!

PEER: What wealth have you to offer me?

INGRID: Heggstad farm, and more besides.

PEER: Have you a psalmbook wrapped in linen?
Golden hair about your shoulders?
Do you drop your eyes to your apron?
Do you cling to your mother's skirt?
Tell me!

INGRID: No, but—?

PEER: Did you read with the priest last spring?

INGRID: No, but Peer—?

PEER: Is there modesty in your eyes?
When I ask, do you deny?

INGRID: Oh God—I think he's mad—

PEER: When I see you, does the sun shine?
Well!

INGRID: No, but—

PEER: What's all the rest, then? *(Turns to go.)*

INGRID *(steps in front of him):* Don't you know they'll hang
you if you leave me?

PEER: All right!

INGRID: You can have wealth and honour if you take me—

PEER: Can't afford it.

INGRID *(bursts into tears):* You raped me—!

PEER: You were willing.

INGRID: I was desperate.

PEER: I was mad.

INGRID *(threateningly):* You'll pay dearly!

PEER: The dearest payment would be cheap.

INGRID: Your mind's made up, then?

PEER: Like stone.

INGRID: Very well. We'll see who wins.

Goes down the path.

PEER *(is silent for a moment, then suddenly cries):* All memories belong to the Devil!
  All women belong to the Devil!
INGRID *(turns her head and shouts scornfully up at him):* Except one!
PEER: Yes. Except one.

  They go opposite ways.

Scene Two

By a mountain lake. The ground is soft and boggy. A storm is brewing. AASE, *in despair, is shouting and searching everywhere.* SOLVEIG *has difficulty in keeping pace with her.* SOLVEIG'S PARENTS *and* HELGA *follow a short way behind.*

AASE *(waves her arms and tears her hair):* Everything's against me. The world's angry!
  The sky, the water and the ugly mountains.
  The sky's sending down fogs to drive him crazy,
  The cunning water's waiting to rob him of his life,
  The mountains are throwing landslides and avalanches,
  And the whole parish is shouting for his blood.
  Which they shan't have, for I can't live without him.
  Oh, the fool, to let the foul fiend tempt him!
  Turns to SOLVEIG.
  Isn't it beyond belief?
  He that did nothing but lie and romance,
  That never exercised any limb but his tongue,
  That never did an honest day's work in his life—
  That—! Oh, should I laugh or cry?
  Mind, when times were tough we stuck together,
  For my man had a tongue red for drink.
  An idler he was with his bragging, wasting our wealth,
  While I and my baby sat at home

Trying to forget. What else could we do?
For I was never a one for arguing.
[It's fearful to look into the eyes of Fate,
And there isn't a woman but likes to bury her grief,
And shove her cares out of sight if she can.]
Some take to drink, others to lying,
So we took to romancing of princes and trolls
And all kinds of beasts. And stealing brides
From their white wedding-beds. But who'd have
    thought
Those daft ideas would have stuck in his head?
Frightened again.
Ow, what a screech! It's a goblin, sure,
Or a flibbertigibbet! Peer, Peer!
Up there, on that hillock—!
She runs up a little hill, looks out across the lake.
SOLVEIG'S PARENTS *come to her.*
Not a sign of him!

SOLVEIG'S FATHER *(quietly):* The worse for him.

AASE *(weeps):* Oh, my Peer! My lost lambkin!

SOLVEIG'S FATHER *(nods gently):* Yes, indeed. Lost!

AASE: No, don't speak like that!
    He's a good lad. There's nobody like him.

SOLVEIG'S FATHER: Foolish woman!

AASE: Oh, yes, yes. I'm foolish. But the boy's all right.

SOLVEIG'S FATHER *(still quiet-voiced and mild-eyed):* His
    heart is hardened. His soul is lost.

AASE *(fearfully):* No, no! Our Lord is not so hard!

SOLVEIG'S FATHER: Do you think he can sigh away his debt
    of sin?

AASE *(eagerly):* No, but he can ride through the air on a stag!

SOLVEIG'S MOTHER: Merciful heaven, are you mad?

SOLVEIG'S FATHER *(to AASE):* What do you mean, woman?

AASE: No deed's too big for him. You'll see,
    If only he lives long enough—

SOLVEIG'S FATHER: It would be best if you saw him hang on
    the gallows.

AASE *(screams):* Providence and Mercy, spare us all!

SOLVEIG'S FATHER: In the hangman's hands,
    Please God, his heart will turn to repentance.

AASE *(dazed):* Oh, you'll soon be talking me out of my
    senses.
    We must find him.

SOLVEIG'S FATHER: To save his soul.

AASE: And his body!
    If he's sitting in the bog, we must haul him out.
    If the trolls have got him, we must ring the church
    bells.

SOLVEIG'S FATHER: Hm. There's a sheep track here.

AASE: The Lord will repay you for your help.

SOLVEIG'S FATHER: It's my Christian duty.

AASE: Bah! Then the rest are heathen savages.
    There wasn't one who would come with me—

SOLVEIG'S FATHER: They know him too well.

AASE: He was too good for them. *(Wrings her hands.)*
    And to think—to think his life's at stake!

SOLVEIG'S FATHER: Here's a man's footprint.

AASE: Then it's here we must search.

SOLVEIG'S FATHER: We'll cover the ground up to our farm.

He and SOLVEIG'S MOTHER *go ahead.*

SOLVEIG *(to* AASE*):* Tell me more.

AASE *(dries her eyes):* About my son?

SOLVEIG: Yes. Everything.

AASE *(smiles and tosses her head):* Everything? You'd soon
    be weary!

SOLVEIG: You'd weary quicker of telling than I of hearing.

Scene Three

Low treeless heights at the foot of the mountain plain, with peaks visible in the distance. Long shadows fall. It is late in the day.

PEER *(runs in at full tilt and stops on the hillside):* The whole
    parish is after me in a mob!
  They've armed themselves with rifles and sticks.
  I can hear Ingrid's father hollering at their head.
  The news has spread quickly: Peer Gynt's on the loose!
  This is better sport than bashing a smith!
  This is life! I feel as strong as a bear!
  Punches around and jumps in the air.
  To smash and overturn! To dam the waterfall!
  To strike! To wrench the fir up by the root!
  This is life. It hardens and elevates.
  To hell with all bloody lies!
THREE SÆTER[3] GIRLS *(run across the hills screaming and
    singing):*
  Trond of the Valfjeld! Boord and Kaare!
  Troll-pack! Will you sleep in our arms?
PEER: Who are you calling?
GIRLS: Trolls! Trolls!
FIRST GIRL: Trond! Come gently!
SECOND GIRL: Boord! Come and rape me!
THIRD GIRL: All the beds in the hut stand empty!
FIRST GIRL: Gently means rape!
SECOND GIRL: And rape means gently!
THIRD GIRL: If there aren't any boys, we'll play with trolls!
PEER: Where are the boys, then?
ALL THREE GIRLS *(howl with laughter):* They can't come!
FIRST GIRL: Mine called me his love and called me his dar-
    ling.
  Now he's married to an old grey widow.

SECOND GIRL: Mine met a gipsy-girl north on the moor.
　　Now they're tramping the roads together.

THIRD GIRL: Mine got tired of our bastard's crying.
　　Now his head grins high on a stake.

ALL THREE: Trond of the Valfjeld! Boord and Kaare!
　　Troll-pack! Come and sleep in our arms!

PEER *(takes a sudden leap into their midst):* I'm a three-
　　headed troll, and a boy for three girls!

GIRLS: Three? Could you, lad?

PEER: Try me and see!

FIRST GIRL: To the hut! To the hut!

SECOND GIRL: We've a barrel of mead!

PEER: Let it flow!

THIRD GIRL: There'll be no bed empty this Saturday night!

SECOND GIRL *(kisses him):* He sputters and sparks like white-
　　hot iron!

THIRD GIRL *(kisses him):* Like a baby's eyes from the black
　　bottom of the lake!

PEER *(dances among them):* The heart is heavy, the head
　　plays wanton.
　　In the eyes, laughter; in the throat, tears.

THE GIRLS *(make long noses towards the mountain tops,
　　scream and sing):* Trond of the Valfjeld! Boord and
　　Kaare!
　　Troll-pack! Did you sleep in our arms?

They dance away across the mountains with PEER GYNT
among them.

Scene Four

Among the Ronde mountains. Sunset. Snow-peaks glitter around.

PEER *(enters dazed and bleary):* Castle rises on castle!
 Hey, what a shining gate!
 Stop! Will you stop? It's shrinking
 Farther and farther away!
 [The weathercock on the steeple
 Is lifting its wings to fly.
 It's all getting blue and misty,
 And the mountain's shut and barred.
 What are these trunks and roots
 That grow from the clefts in the ridge?
 It's soldiers heron-footed;
 Now *they*'re fading away!]
 It swims before me like rainbows;
 It hurts my eyes and brain.
 What's that that chimes in the distance?
 This weight pressing my eyes?
 Ugh, how it splits my forehead—
 This binding, white-hot ring!
 Oh, I cannot remember
 Who in Hell put that round my brain!
 Sinks down.
 The flight along Gjendin Edge—
 It was all a fake and a lie!
 Up the cliff with the bride—
 Then drunk for a night and a day.
 Hunted by hawks and kites,
 Threatened by trolls and the like,
 Sporting with crazy wenches—
 A bloody lie and a fake!
 Stares for a long time upwards.

There sail two brown eagles.
The wild geese fly to the south.
And I must trudge here and stumble
Knee deep in the mire and filth.
Jumps up.
I'll join them! I'll wash myself clean,
Scoured by the sharpest winds!
I shall soar! I'll wash myself pure in
The gleaming christening-font!
I'll fly high over the farmhouse,
I'll ride till my black soul shines,
Far over the salty sea
And high over England's prince!
Yes, you can stare, my pretties.
I haven't come here for you.
It's no use standing and waiting—
Well, I might take a minute or two—!
    What? Where have those eagles got to?
Oh, what the hell do I care?
There soars the crown of a gable.
It's rising up everywhere.
It's growing out of the ruins.
The gate stands open and fair.
    Ah, now I recognize it!
It's my granddad's fine new home!
The rags are gone from the windows.
The tumbledown fence is gone.
The light pours from every window.
They're feasting in the great room.
    Look, now the old Bishop's clinking
His knife on his silver cup.
The Captain has tossed back his bottle,
And broken the looking-glass up.
Let them squander away. What do we care?
Hush, mother! We don't have to stint.

The rich John Gynt gives a banquet.
Hurrah for the tree of Gynt!
But what's all this bustle and hubbub?
What can the shouting be?
The Captain's proposing the son's health!
The Bishop is calling for me!
Go in, Peer Gynt, to your judgment.
The welcoming cheers fill the room.
Peer Gynt, thou wast born to greatness,
And to greatness thou shalt come!

Takes a running jump forward, but strikes his nose against a rock, falls and remains lying on the ground.

Scene Five

A hillside, with great rustling trees. Stars twinkle through the leaves. Birds sing in the treetops. A GREENCLAD WOMAN *is walking on the hillside.* PEER GYNT *follows her, indulging in various amorous antics.*

THE GREENCLAD ONE *(stops and turns):* Is it true?
PEER *(makes a cutting gesture with his finger across his throat):* As true as my name's Peer!
   As true as you're a beautiful woman!
   Will you have me? I'll be good to you.
   You shall neither weave nor spin.
   I'll fill you with food till you're ready to burst.
   I'll never pull you by the hair—
GREENCLAD ONE: Nor beat me?
PEER: What an idea! We princes don't beat women.
GREENCLAD ONE: Are you a King's son?
PEER: Yes.
GREENCLAD ONE: My father's the King of the Ronde.
PEER: Is he? Well, that makes us two of a kind.
GREENCLAD ONE: My father's palace is inside the mountain.

PEER: My mother's is bigger, believe you me.

GREENCLAD ONE: Do you know my father? His name is
King Brose.

PEER: Do you know my mother: Her name's Queen Aase.

GREENCLAD ONE: When my father's angry, the mountains
crack.

PEER: They shake when my mother opens her mouth.

GREENCLAD ONE: When my father dances he kicks the stars.

PEER: My mother can ride through rivers in flood.

GREENCLAD ONE: Have you any other clothes beside those
rags?

PEER: Oh, you should see me in my Sunday suit!

GREENCLAD ONE: I always wear gold and silks.

PEER: They look to me more like tow and straw.

GREENCLAD ONE: Well, there's one thing you must remem-
ber.
That is the way of the mountain people.
Everything there has another meaning.
If you come to my father's house, you may easily think
You're just in an ugly heap of stones.

PEER: Well now, it's exactly the same with us.
Our gold may seem scrap to you.
You may think each crystal window-pane
Is just a fistful of socks and rags.

GREENCLAD ONE: Black seems white and ugly seems fair.

PEER: Great seems little and foul seems clean.

GREENCLAD ONE *(falls on his neck)*: O, Peer! I see it! We
were made for each other!

PEER: As the leg fits the breeches, the comb fits the hair.

GREENCLAD ONE *(calls across the hill)*: Bridal steed! Bridal
steed!
Come, my bridal steed!

*A huge pig canters in with a rope's end round its neck
as a bridle, and an old sack as a saddle.* PEER GYNT

63

swings himself astride its back and sets the GREENCLAD ONE *in front of him.*

PEER: Hup, now! We'll ride in through the Ronde gate!
    Gee-up, gee-up, my beauty!

GREENCLAD ONE *(amorously):* Just now I was feeling so sad
    and lonely.
  Who can tell what life will bring in its course?

PEER *(slaps the pig and rides away):* You can tell a great
    man by the cut of his horse!

Scene Six

The palace hall of THE OLD MAN OF THE MOUNTAINS. *A great gathering of* TROLL COURTIERS, ELVES *and* GOBLINS. THE OLD MAN OF THE MOUNTAINS *is seated on his throne, sceptred and crowned. His* CHILDREN *and* NEAREST RELATIVES *surround him.* PEER GYNT *stands in front of him. There is a great hubbub in the hall.*

TROLL COURTIERS: Kill him! Kill him! The Christian dog
    Has bewitched the Troll King's fairest daughter!

TROLL CHILD: Can I cut off his fingers?

ANOTHER: Can I pull out his hair?

A TROLL MAIDEN: Huh, ha! Let me bite his bottom!

TROLL WITCH *(with a ladle):* Shall I boil him down into
    soup?

ANOTHER WITCH *(with a carving-knife):* Shall we roast him
    on the spit or brown him in the pot?

THE OLD MAN OF THE MOUNTAINS: Calm yourselves, my
    children!
  Beckons his COUNSELLORS *nearer.*
  We can't afford to be grand.
  We've been slipping backwards in recent years.
  Our position has become precarious,

And we can't look down our noses at offers of help.
Besides, the lad has no obvious defects,
And seems well-built. True, he's only got one head,
But my daughter is no better off in that respect.
Three-headed trolls are going right out of fashion.
Even two heads are rare nowadays,
And they are not what they used to be.

To PEER GYNT:

So you want my daughter?

PEER: Your daughter, and your kingdom as her dowry.

OLD MAN: You shall have half my kingdom while I live,
    And the other half when, eventually, I die.

PEER: That suits me.

OLD MAN: Ah, but wait, my lad.
    There are certain promises you, too, must make.
    If you break one of them, the pact is broken,
    And you shall not leave this place alive.
    First, you must swear you'll never think
    Of what lies outside the kingdom of the mountain.
    Day you must shun, action, and anything touched by
        light.

PEER: Well, if I'm to be King, that's easy.

OLD MAN: Next—and this will test your wits—

Rises in his seat.

OLDEST TROLL COURTIER *(to* PEER*):* Let's see if you have a
        wisdom tooth
    To crack the nut of the Troll King's riddle.

OLD MAN: What is the difference between troll and man?

PEER: No difference, as far as I can see.
    Big trolls want to roast you, small trolls want to claw
        you.
    It's the same with us, if we dared.

OLD MAN: True. We're alike in that, and more.
    But morning is morning and night is night,

And there is a difference nevertheless.
I'll tell you what it is.
Out there, under the shining vault of heaven,
Men tell each other: 'Man, be thyself!'
But in here, among us trolls, we say:
'Man, be thyself—and to hell with the rest of the
    world!'[4]

OLDEST COURTIER *(to* PEER*):* You fathom it?

PEER: Not entirely.

OLD MAN: 'To hell with the world!' Those sharp and fateful
    words
Must be engraven on your crest, my son.

PEER *(scratches behind his ear):* Yes, but—

OLD MAN: They *must,* if you would be master here!

PEER: Oh, hell. All right. I really can't see—

OLD MAN: Next you must teach yourself to value
    Our simple and homely way of life.
    He beckons. Two TROLLS *with pigs'-heads and white*
    nightcaps bring in food and drink.
    Our cake flows from the cow, our mead from the bull.
    Don't ask yourself if it tastes sour or sweet.
    The main thing is, and this you mustn't forget,
    It's all home-made.

PEER *(pushes the things away):* To hell with your home-
    made drink!
    I'll never get used to this place.

OLD MAN: The bowl goes with it. It's gold. Who owns
    The golden bowl has my daughter's love.

PEER *(thoughtfully):* [It is written: 'Thou shalt subdue thy
    nature.']
    Well, I dare say in time it won't taste too bad.
    All right! *(Tastes.)*

OLD MAN: That's a sensible lad. Did you spit?

PEER: Taste is a question of what you're used to.

OLD MAN: Next you must throw away

Your Christian clothes. For this you must know
To the greater glory of the mountain kingdom.
Everything here is made within the mountain.
Nothing comes from the valley except
The silken bow at the tip of your tail.

PEER *(angrily):* I haven't got a tail!

OLD MAN: Well, then you must have one.
Prime Minister, tie my Sunday tail on him.

PEER: I'll be damned if you will!
Do you want to make a fool of me?

OLD MAN: You cannot court
My daughter with a bare backside.

PEER: Make a man into a beast?

OLD MAN: My son, you're wrong.
I'm only making you a respectable suitor.
You'll have a flame-yellow bow,
Which we count as the highest honour.

PEER *(thoughtfully):* Well, [they say: 'Man is but a speck of
    dust,'
And I suppose] one must toe the line of fashion.
Tie away!

OLD MAN: You're a co-operative boy.

OLDEST COURTIER: Now see how well you can flip and
    twitch it!

PEER *(angrily):* What, will you force me further yet?
Must I give up my Christian faith?

OLD MAN: No, you're welcome to keep that.
[Faith is free. We charge no tariff there.
You can tell a troll by his outside.]
As long as we agree on manners and dress
You can go on calling your freakish fancies faith.

PEER: For all your conditions, you're
A more reasonable chap than one might think.

OLD MAN: My son, we trolls are better than our reputation.
That's another difference between you and us.

But now we're through with the serious business
So let's delight our eyes and ears.
Music-girl, forth! Let the mountain-harp sound!
Dancing-girl, forth! Tread our palace floor!
Music and dance.

OLDEST COURTIER: How do you like it?

PEER: Like it? Hm—

OLD MAN: Don't be afraid to speak. What do you see?

PEER: Something horribly ugly.
A cow with a harp and a dancing sow.

TROLL COURTIERS: Eat him!

OLD MAN: Remember, his eyes and ears are human.

TROLL MAIDENS: Oh, tear off his ears! Pull out his eyes!

GREENCLAD ONE *(weeps):* Must we hear and endure such insults
While I and my sister play and dance?

PEER: Oh, is it you? Well, you know,
A joke at a feast isn't meant unkindly.

GREENCLAD ONE: Do you swear to that?

PEER: Both the dance and the music were really splendid.
May the cat claw me if I lie!

OLD MAN: That's a funny thing about human nature.
It hangs on to people a remarkable time.
[If it gets a gash in the fight with us,
It leaves a scar, but that soon heals up.]
My son-in-law was proving as pliant as any.
Willingly he's thrown off his Christian clothes,
Willingly drunk from our cup of mead,
Willingly tied a tail to his backside.
So willing, in short, to do all that we bade him,
That I really began to think the old Adam
Had been hunted out of our gate for good and all.
But now he's suddenly popped up again.
Well, well, my son, we must give you some treatment
To cure this human nature of yours.

PEER: What will you do?

OLD MAN: In your left eye
I'll make a little cut, so that you'll see awry.
But all you see will seem bright and fair.
Then I'll nip out your right window-pane—

PEER: Are you drunk?

OLD MAN *(lays several sharp instruments on the table):* Here
you see the glazier's tools.
We'll blinker you, like a surly bull.
Then you'll see that your bride is beautiful.
And there'll be an end to these illusions
Of dancing sows, and cows playing harps—

PEER: This is madman's talk!

OLDEST COURTIER: The Old Man of the Mountains speaks!
He is wise. It is you that's mad.

OLD MAN: Think how much pain and worry you'll save
yourself.
Don't forget that sight is the source
Of the bitter and searing lye of tears.

PEER: That's true. It says in the holy book:
'If thine eye offend thee, pluck it out.'
Wait! Tell me, when will my sight be healed
So that I can see again as a man?

OLD MAN: Never, my friend.

PEER: Indeed! Well, thanks very much.

OLD MAN: Where are you going?

PEER: On my way.

OLD MAN: No, wait. It's easy to get in here,
But the mountain gate doesn't open outwards.

PEER: Surely you'll not keep me by force?

OLD MAN: Now listen, Prince Peer, and be sensible.
You've a talent for trolldom. Isn't that true?
You're already shaping quite like a troll.
And you do want to become a troll?

PEER: Indeed I do.

[For a bride with a well-lined kingdom thrown in
I'd put up with losing a thing or two.]
But there's a limit to everything.
I've accepted a tail, that's true enough;
But I can remove what your Minister tied on.
I've thrown off my breeks. They were old and patched.
But I can soon button them on again.
[And I can just as quickly slip my moorings
From all your mountain way of life.]
I don't mind swearing a cow's a maiden.
A man can always swallow an oath.
But to know one can never free oneself,
Nor be able to die like a Christian soul;
To live like a mountain troll all one's days,
And never go back—that's what you want.
And that is something I'll never agree to.

OLD MAN: Now you're beginning to make me angry.
I'm not to be trifled with. You pale-faced
Pigmy! Do you know who I am?
First you take liberties with my daughter—

PEER: That's a lie!

OLD MAN: You must marry her!

PEER: You dare to accuse—?

OLD MAN: What! Can you deny
You desired and lusted after her?

PEER (snorts): Is that all? Who the hell cares about that?

OLD MAN: You human beings are always the same.
You're always ready to admit an impulse,
But won't accept the guilt for anything
Unless you've actually done it in the flesh.
So you think that lust doesn't count?
Wait. You'll soon see with your own eyes—

PEER: You won't catch me with a bait of lies.

GREENCLAD ONE: My Peer, before the year's end you'll be a
father.

PEER: Open the door! Let me out!

OLD MAN: We'll send the baby after you in a ram's skin.

PEER *(wipes the sweat from his brow):* I wish to God I could wake!

OLD MAN: Shall we send him to the palace?

PEER: Send him to the parish!

OLD MAN: Very well, Prince Peer. It's your affair.
But one thing's certain. What's done is done.
Your child will grow. And these mongrels shoot up
Indecently fast—

PEER: Old man, now don't be a stubborn ox.
Be reasonable, madam. Let's come to terms.
[Whether you measure me or weigh me]
You'll profit little by keeping me.
The truth is I'm neither a prince nor rich.

The GREENCLAD ONE *collapses and is carried out by* TROLL MAIDENS.

OLD MAN *(looks at him with deep disdain for a moment, then says):* Bash him to bits on the rocks, my children.

TROLL CHILDREN: Oh father, can't we play owl and eagle first?
The wolf game? Grey mouse and fire-eyed cat?

OLD MAN: All right, but hurry. I'm out of temper
And sleepy. Good night. *(Goes.)*

PEER *(as the* TROLL CHILDREN *chase him):* Let me go, you little beasts!
(Tries to climb up the chimney.)

TROLL CHILDREN: Goblins! Elves! Bite him in the bottom!

PEER: Yow! *(Tries to get down through the cellar-flap.)*

TROLL CHILDREN: Close every crack!

OLDEST COURTIER: What fun they're having, the little dears!

PEER *(fighting with a* TROLL CHILD *which has fastened its teeth in his ear):* Get away, you little wretch!

OLDEST COURTIER *(strikes him across the fingers):* Brute! Learn to respect a royal child.

PEER: A rat-hole! *(Runs to it.)*

TROLL CHILDREN: Block it up, brother imp!

PEER: The old man was bad, but the young ones are worse!

TROLL CHILDREN: Tear him!

PEER: Oh, why aren't I the size of a mouse? *(Runs around.)*

TROLL CHILDREN *(milling around him):* Close the circle! Close the circle!

PEER *(weeps):* Why aren't I a louse? *(Falls.)*

TROLL CHILDREN: Now for his eyes!

PEER *(buried beneath the heap of* TROLL CHILDREN*):* Help! Mother! I'm dying!

Church bells are heard tolling distantly.

TROLL CHILDREN: Bells on the mountain! The Black-Frock's cows!

The TROLLS *flee in turmoil, yelling and screaming. The hall crashes in ruins. Everything disappears.*

Scene Seven

Pitch darkness. PEER GYNT *is heard hewing and beating about with a great branch.*

PEER: Answer me! Who are you?

A VOICE IN THE DARK: Myself.

PEER: Get out of my way!

VOICE: Go round, Peer. The moor is big enough.

PEER *(tries to go through at another point, but is blocked by something):* Who are *you?*

VOICE: Myself. Can you say the same?

PEER: I can say what I like; my sword is sharp.
　Beware! Huh, hah, now it strikes and crushes!
　King Saul slew hundreds, Peer Gynt slays thousands!
　Strikes and hews.
　Who *are* you?

VOICE: Myself.

PEER: You can keep that rubbish. It doesn't help. *What* are
　you?

VOICE: The Great Boyg.

PEER: Ah! Now I begin to understand.
　Out of my way, Boyg!

VOICE: Go round, Peer.

PEER: No, through! *(Hews and slashes.)*
　He's fallen! *(Tries to advance but comes up against
　something.)*
　Oh-ho! Are there more?

VOICE: The Boyg, Peer Gynt! One, only one.
　The Boyg that's unharmed, and the Boyg that you
　wounded.
　The Boyg that's dead, and the Boyg that is alive.

PEER *(throws down his branch):* My sword is troll-smeared;
　but I have my fists!

　Fights his way forward.

VOICE: Yes, trust to your fists. Trust to your strength.
　He-he, Peer Gynt. That's the way to the top.

PEER *(tries again):* Forward or back, it's equally far.
　Outside or in, I'm still confined.
　There he is! And *there!* And round that bend!
　As soon as I'm out I'm back in the middle,
　Encircled. Name yourself! Let me see you!
　What on earth are you?

VOICE: The Boyg.

PEER *(gropes around):* Not dead. Not alive. Slimy. Misty.

And shapeless. [It's just like bumping around
In a herd of growling, half-awake bears!]
Shouts:
Hit me back!

VOICE: The Boyg is no fool.

PEER: Strike!

VOICE: The Boyg does not strike.

PEER: Fight! You shall!

VOICE: The Great Boyg wins without fighting.

PEER: If only there were a goblin to prick me,
Or even a baby troll!
Something to fight! But there's nothing.
Now he's snoring! Boyg!

VOICE: What do you want?

PEER: Use force!

VOICE: The Great Boyg wins by doing nothing.

PEER *(bites his own arms and hands):* Let me feel claws and
teeth in my flesh!
I must feel the drip of my own blood!

The wing-beats of great birds are heard.

BIRD CRIES: Is he coming, Boyg?

VOICE IN THE DARK: Yes. Step by step.

BIRD CRIES: O sisters, sisters far away!
Fly hither! The time is come!

PEER: If you're going to save me, girl, do it quickly!
Don't look at your lap, so humble and shy.
Your prayer-book! Throw it in his eyes!

BIRD CRIES: He's swaying!

VOICE IN THE DARK: We have him.

BIRD CRIES: Sisters! Come quickly!

PEER: An hour of this consuming strife
Is too dear a price to pay for life. *(Sinks to the ground.)*

BIRD CRIES: Boyg, he's fallen! Take him! Take him!

The tolling of church bells and psalm song are heard in the distance.

THE BOYG *(shrinks to nothing, and gasps):* He was too strong. There were women behind him.

Scene Eight

Sunrise. On the mountain outside AASE*'s sæter. The door is shut. Everything is still and deserted.* PEER GYNT *is lying asleep outside the sæter wall.*

PEER *(wakes and looks round dully and heavily. He spits):*
    Oh, for a salted herring![5]
    Spits again. As he does so, he sees HELGA *coming with a hamper of food.*
    Hullo, child, are you here? What do you want?

HELGA: It's Solveig—

PEER *(jumps up):* Where is she?

HELGA: Behind the wall.

SOLVEIG *(hidden):* If you come near me, I'll run away!

PEER *(stops):* Are you afraid I'll kiss you?

SOLVEIG: For shame!

PEER: Do you know where I was last night?
    The Old Man of the Mountains' daughter
    Is after me everywhere like a gadfly.

SOLVEIG: Then it was lucky they rang the bells.

PEER: They can't fool Peer Gynt. Can they?

HELGA *(starts to cry):* Oh, she's running away!
    Runs after her.
    Wait!

PEER *(seizes her by the arm):* Look what I've got in my pocket!
    A silver button, child! You shall have it—
    Only say a good word for me.

HELGA: Let me go. Let me go!

PEER: Here it is.

HELGA: Let me go. There's the basket.

PEER: God have mercy on you if you don't—!

HELGA: Oh, you're frightening me!

PEER *(quietly, lets go of her):* No, I only meant—ask her not to forget me!

HELGA *runs away.*

ACT THREE

Scene One

Deep inside the pine forest. Grey autumn weather. Snow is falling. PEER GYNT *is standing in his shirtsleeves, felling timber.*

PEER *(hacks at a large fir-tree with twisted boughs):*
  Oh yes, you're tough, old friend. But it's no use.
  You're coming down.
  Hacks at it again.
  You're wearing a chain shirt, are you?
  I'll cut through it. That's right,
  Yes, you can shake your twisted arm at me.
  I know you're angry.
  It can't be helped. I'll bring you to your knees—!
  Breaks off suddenly.
  Lies! It's only an old tree!
  Bloody lies! It was never an armoured knight!
  [It's only a fir with crevices in its bark.
  It's heavy enough hewing timber,
  But hewing *and* dreaming—it's bloody murder!]
  I'm done with it, this living in mists and dreaming.
  You're an outlaw, my lad. They've hunted you into the
      woods.

Hacks vigorously for a while.
Yes, an outlaw.
You've no mother now to look after you.
If you want to eat, you must help yourself,
[Fetch it raw from the forest and river,
Split your own wood and light your own fire.
You'll have to start doing your own work now.]
If you want a warm coat, you must shoot a deer.
If you want a house you must break stones.
If you want walls, you must fell your own wood,
And carry it there upon your back.
His axe sinks to the ground. He stares unseeingly.
It'll be a grand sight! A tower with a weathercock
I'll have on the roof-beam! And I'll carve on the gable
A mermaid, shaped like a fish from her navel!
There'll be brass on the weathercock and all the locks.
And glass! I must try to have some of that!
Strangers will stare and wonder at it
Glittering there high on the hillside—
Laughs angrily.
Bloody lies! There they are again!
You're an outlaw, my lad.
Hacks fiercely.
                    A bark-thatched hut
Will keep out the worst of the rain and frost.
[*Looks up at the tree.*
Now he's trembling. There! Just a kick
And he totters and measures his length on the ground,
The undergrowth milling and shuddering about him.
Begins to lop the branches.] *Suddenly he listens and
stands still with his axe raised.*
Someone's after me! [Is it Ingrid's father?
Old Heggstad gaffer! Ah, you'd cheat me, would you?]
Ducks behind the tree and peeps round it.
[*A boy. All alone. He seems to be frightened.*

78

He glances around. What's he got hidden there
Under his jacket? A sickle. He stops and looks round.
Lays his hand flat on the rail of the fence.
What's this, now? Why is he suddenly swaying—?]
Oh, my God! Why, he's chopped his finger off![6]
A whole finger! Right off! [He's bleeding like an ox!
Now he's running away with his hand in a clout!]
Gets up.
What a fool! An irreplaceable finger!
Right off! And of his own free will!
Ah! I see! That's the only way
To free oneself from serving the King.
That's it. They wanted to send him to the war
And the boy didn't want to go.
But to chop—? To lose for ever—?
Yes, to think—wish—to *will* it even;
But to *do* it! No, that I don't understand.

Gives a little shake of his head, then returns to his work.

Scene Two

A room down at AASE's *house. Everything is in disorder.
Boxes lie open, clothes are everywhere, a cat is on the bed.*
AASE *and* KARI, *a crofter's wife, are busy packing and putting things in order.*

AASE *(runs over to one side of the room):* Kari, come here—!
KARI: What is it?
AASE *(on the other side of the room):* Come here—!
　　Where is—? Where can I find—? Answer me! Where is
　　the—?
　　What am I looking for? I'm losing my wits.
　　Where's the key to the chest?
KARI: In the keyhole.

AASE: What's that rumbling?

KARI: The last wagon-load going off to Heggstad.

AASE *(weeps):* I wish it was me they were taking away
In a black box. Oh, the things a mortal
Has to endure! God in His mercy help me!
The whole house stripped!
What the girl's father left, the bailiff has taken.
They didn't spare the clothes on my back.
Fie! The Devil rot them for being so hard!
Sits on the edge of the bed.
The land and the house are lost to our family.
[The old man was harsh, but the law was harsher.]
There was no help and no mercy.
Peer was gone. I'd no one to save me.

KARI: At least you can stay in this room till you die.

AASE: Yes; my cat and I will be fed by the parish.

KARI: God pity you, mother. Your Peer's cost you dear.

AASE: Peer? You're out of your mind!
Ingrid came safely home in the end.
It's the Devil they ought to blame. He's the villain
And no one else. He led my boy astray.

KARI: Don't you think I'd better send for the priest?
[I'm fearing things may be worse than you know.]

AASE: The priest? Oh, yes, I almost think so.
Starts up.
But, oh God, no, I can't! I'm the lad's mother.
I must help him. It's my duty
To do what I can when the rest fail.
They've left him this coat. I must patch it up.
I wish I'd hidden the skin rug too.
Where are his stockings?

KARI: There, with the other rubbish.

AASE *(roots around):* What's this?
Oh, Kari, look! It's an old casting-ladle!
With this he played at being a button-moulder;

80

Melted and shaped and stamped.
One day at a feast, the little lad came
And asked his father for a lump of tin.
'Tin!', said John. 'No! [Good King Christian's coin!]
Silver! Let people know you're John Gynt's son!'
God forgive the poor man, he was drunk,
And then he cared neither for tin nor gold.
Here are the stockings. Oh dear, they're all holes.
We must darn them, Kari.

KARI: I'm afraid so.

AASE: When it's done, I must get to bed.
I feel weak and wretched and frail.
(Joyfully.) Look, Kari! Two woollen shirts! They've
    missed them!

KARI: Yes, so they have.

AASE: What a piece of luck! You'd better hide one.
No, wait. I think we'll take both.
The one he's wearing is worn and thin.

KARI: God forgive you, Mother Aase! It's a sin!

AASE: And if it is? What's the priest for?
He'll pardon this sin, as he pardons others.

Scene Three

Outside a newly built cabin in the forest. A reindeer's ant-
lers over the door. The snow is piled high around. It is twi-
light. PEER GYNT *is standing outside the door making fast a*
large wooden bolt.

PEER *(laughing now and then):* I must have bolts!
Bolts against trolls, and against men and women.
[I must have bolts.]
Bolts to lock out all nagging hobgoblins.
They come with the darkness. They knock and they tap.

'Let us in, Peer Gynt! We're as swift as thoughts!
We scratch under the bed, we hiss in the ashes,
We breathe down the chimney like white-hot dragons!
He-he, Peer Gynt! Do you think nails and planks
Can shut out nagging hobgoblin thoughts?'

SOLVEIG *comes over the heath on skis. She has a shawl over her head and a bundle in her hand.*

SOLVEIG: God speed your work. Don't turn me away.
　　You sent for me, and so you must take me.
PEER: Solveig! It can't be—! Yes, but it is!
　　Aren't you afraid to come so near me?
SOLVEIG: You sent me a message by little Helga.
　　Others followed, in storm and in calm.
　　All that your mother said carried a message
　　That bred each morning as I awoke.
　　The lonely nights and the empty days
　　Bore me the message that now I must come.
　　It became as though life down there had been quenched
　　I couldn't laugh or cry from my heart.
　　I didn't know how you felt about me.
　　I only knew what I had to to.
PEER: But your father?
SOLVEIG: 　　　　　In all God's earth
　　I have no one to call father or mother.
　　I have made myself free.
PEER: Solveig, my fairest—to come to me?
SOLVEIG: Yes, to you alone. You must be
　　All to me. My friend and comforter.
　　[Weeps.
　　The worst was to leave my little sister.
　　But even worse to be parted from Father.
　　But worst of all, to leave her who bore me at her breast.
　　No, God forgive me, the worst was the grief
　　At being parted from all of them—all of them.]

PEER: You know the judgment read in the spring?
  I have lost my home and my inheritance.
SOLVEIG: Do you think I left my dearest ones
  For the sake of an inheritance?
PEER: —that anyone who meets me
  Outside the forest may freely seize me?
SOLVEIG: I ran here on my skis. I asked my way.
  They said: 'Where are you going?' I answered: 'Home.'
PEER: Then to hell with nails and planks!
  Now I need no lock against hobgoblin thoughts!
  If you dare come in to live with the hunter
  I know that a blessing will fall on this house.
  Solveig! Let me look at you! Not too close!
  I just want to look at you. You're so bright and pure.
  Let me lift you. You're so delicate and light.
  Let me carry you, Solveig. I'll never get tired!
  I shall never soil you. I'll stretch out my arms
  And hold you from me, my fair, my warm one!
  Oh, who would have thought I could draw you to me?
  Oh, but I've longed for you night and day.
  Here you see I've been hewing and building.
  I must pull it down. It is mean and ugly—
SOLVEIG: Mean or fine, it is what I want.
  Here one can breathe against the wind.
  Down there it was airless. I felt shut in.
  [It was partly that that frightened me away.]
  But here where I hear the fir tree whisper—
  In stillness and song! Here I am at home!
PEER: Are you sure you want this? For the rest of your
    life?
SOLVEIG: I have chosen my path. I shall never turn back.
PEER: Then I have you! Go in! Let me see you inside!
  I'll bring pine logs to make you a fire.
  It will shine brightly and make you warm.
  You shall sit softly and never be cold.

He opens the door. SOLVEIG *goes in. He stands still for
a moment, then laughs aloud with joy and jumps in the
air.*

PEER: My princess! Now at last I've found and won her!
Hey! Now I'll build my palace on firm, true ground!

He seizes the axe and walks away. As he does so, an
OLD-LOOKING WOMAN *dressed in green rags comes out
of the trees. An* UGLY CHILD *with an ale-flagon in its
hand limps after her, clutching her by the skirt.*

WOMAN: Good evening, Peer Lightfoot!
PEER: What? Who are you?
WOMAN: Old friends, Peer Gynt.
　　My cottage lies near by. We're neighbours.
PEER: Oh? That's news to me.
WOMAN: As you built your house, mine rose beside it.
PEER *(turns):* I'm in a hurry—
WOMAN: You always were, lad.
　　But I'll trudge behind, and one day I'll catch you.
PEER: You've made a mistake, grannie.
WOMAN: I did before.
　　I did when you made such promises to me.
PEER: *I* promised—? What damned nonsense is this?
WOMAN: Have you forgotten the night you drank
　　With my father? Have you forgotten—?
PEER: [I've only forgotten what I never knew.]
　　What are you talking about? When did we meet?
WOMAN: We last met when we first met.
　　To the CHILD:
　　Give your father a drink. I dare say he's thirsty.
PEER: Father—? Are you drunk? Are you suggesting that he—?
WOMAN: Can't you tell the pig by its skin?
　　Where are your eyes? Can't you see he's crippled
　　The way you're crippled, in your soul?

PEER: Are you trying to make me believe—?

WOMAN: Are you trying to deny it?

PEER: That long-legged brat—?

WOMAN: Yes, he's shot up quickly.

PEER: You damned troll-snout, do you dare to accuse me—?

WOMAN: Wait a minute, Peer Gynt! I want none of your insults.

Weeps.

Can I help it if I'm not beautiful

As I was when you seduced me on the hillside?

Last fall, when I bore him, the Fiend gripped my back,

So it's not surprising I've become ugly.

But if you want to see me as fair as before

Just take that girl and show her the door.

Turn her out of your mind and out of your heart—

Do that, my dear, and I'll lose my snout.

PEER: Get away, you witch!

WOMAN: Yes, see if I do!

PEER: I'll split your skull—!

WOMAN: Try if you dare! Oh no, Peer Gynt.

I'm not frightened of blows. I'll come back every day.

I'll pull the door open and peer at you both.

When you're snuggling up to your girl on the hearth,

When you kiss her, Peer Gynt, when you'd pet her and play with her,

I'll sit down beside you and demand my share.

She and I will take you by turns.

Goodbye, my love. You can marry tomorrow.

PEER: You hell-born nightmare—!

WOMAN: Oh, I nearly forgot.

You must raise the brat, you lecherous devil.

Come on, baby devil, go to your father.

CHILD *(spits at him):* [You keep away from me!]

I'll hit you with my axe! Just you wait! Just you wait!

WOMAN *(kisses the* CHILD*):* [You've a wise head on those
    little shoulders.]
    You'll be the spit of your father when you grow up.
PEER *(stamps his foot):* Would God you were as far—!
WOMAN: As we are near?
PEER *(clenches his fists):* And all this—!
WOMAN: For nothing but *thinking?*
    It's bad luck on you, isn't it? Poor Peer!
PEER: It's worse for another.
    O Solveig, my taintless, my purest gold!
WOMAN: Ah, well. It's the innocent who have to suffer;
    As the Devil said when his mother hit him
    Because his father was drunk.

She trudges off into the wood with the CHILD, *who
throws the ale-flagon at* PEER.

PEER *(after a long silence):* Go round, said the Boyg. So I
    must here.
    There falls my palace in ruins about me.
    It has walled her round when I stood so near.
    Everything here is suddenly ugly.
    My joy has turned old. Go round, my lad.
    There's no way straight through to her.
    Straight? Hm, but there *should* be one.
    [There's a text, if I remember aright—]
    'If a man repent—'. How does it go?
    I've forgotten, and there's no one here to guide me.
    [Repent? It might take years to fight my way through.
    That would be a poor life;
    To smash what is pure, precious and beautiful,
    And piece it together from broken fragments.
    You can do that with a fiddle, but not with a bell.
    Where the grass would grow green, one mustn't tread.
    But anyway, the witch was lying.]
    They have gone. Gone, yes; but I can't forget them.

Tiptoeing thoughts will follow me in.
Ingrid! And those three that danced on the mountain!
Will they join me too? With cruel laughter
Demanding like her to be clasped in my arms?
To be gently lifted and lovingly laid
At arm's length? Go round, lad.
If my arm were as long as a pine tree's trunk
I fear even then I'd hold her too near
To set her down white and unstained as before.
I must find some way round, so that if I gain nothing
At least I shan't lose. One must try to forget.
Goes a few steps towards the hut, but stops again.
To go in after this? So ugly and soiled?
To take in all those black trolls with me?
To speak, yet be silent? Confess, yet conceal—?
Throws away his axe.
[It's a Sabbath evening.]
To keep tryst as I am would be sacrilege.
SOLVEIG *(in the doorway):* Are you coming?
PEER *(half to himself):* Round!
SOLVEIG: What did you say?
PEER: You must wait.
    It's dark, and I've something heavy to carry.
SOLVEIG: Wait. I'll help you. We'll share the burden.
PEER: No. Stay where you are. I must bear it alone.
SOLVEIG: Don't go too far, Peer.
PEER: Be patient.
    I may be long, but wait for me. Wait for me!
SOLVEIG *(nods after him):* Yes, I'll wait.

    PEER *goes away down the forest path.* SOLVEIG *remains
    standing in the open half-door.*

Scene Four

AASE *'s room. Evening. A log-fire is burning in the open hearth, and gives light to the room. The cat sits on a chair at the foot of the bed.* AASE *is lying in the bed, her hands moving restlessly on the coverlet.*

AASE: Oh, God! Won't he come? He's so long!
   I've no one to send and so much to say.
   There's no time to lose. It's so quick!
   Who'd have thought—? Oh, if only I knew
   I'd not been too strict with the lad—!
PEER *(enters):* Hullo!
AASE: Oh, God bless you! You've come at last, my son.
   But how dare you come down here?
   Don't you know they're after your life?
PEER: My life can look after itself. I had to come to you.
AASE: Well, Kari was wrong. Now I can go in peace.
PEER: Go? Now what are you saying?
   Where do you think you're going?
AASE: Oh, Peer, I'm near the end. I haven't much time left.
PEER *(squirms and walks up the room):* Oh, God! [I can't escape sorrow anywhere!]
   I thought I'd be free from it here—! Are your feet and hands cold?
AASE: Yes, Peer. It'll soon be over. When you see
   My eyes glaze, you must close them carefully.
   And then you must see to the coffin. Now, my dear,
   Be sure it's a fine one. Oh no, I'd forgotten—
PEER: Be quiet. There's time enough to think of that.
AASE: Yes, yes. *(Looks restlessly round the room.)*
   This is all they left me. Just like them.
PEER *(writhes):* Again! *(In a hard voice.)*
   I know it's my fault. Why remind me of that?
AASE: You? No, it's that damned liquor. [That's the cause

Of all the trouble.] My darling boy, you were drunk.
Then a man doesn't know what he's doing. Besides,
You'd been riding the stag. It's no wonder your head
    was turned.

PEER: [Yes, well, never mind that.]
Let's forget all that. Let's not be unhappy now.
Sits on the edge of the bed.
Now, mother, let's chat together,
But only of little things.
Let's forget what's ugly and crooked,
And all that's painful and sore.
Look! The old cat! So he's still alive!

AASE: He howls so at night. You know what that means.

PEER *(changes the subject):* What's the news around
    here?

AASE *(smiles):* They say there's a girl who keeps her eyes
    Turned to the mountains—

PEER *(quickly):* Mads Moen, is he happy?

AASE: [They say she won't listen to her parents' tears.]
    You ought to see them, Peer. [You might be able to
        help—]

PEER: Aslak the smith, what's happened to him?

AASE: Don't mention that rascal to me!
    I'd rather tell you *her* name—

PEER: [No, mother, let's chat together,
    But only of little things.
    We'll forget what's ugly and crooked.
    And all that's painful and sore.]
Are you thirsty? Can I fetch you a drink?
Can't you stretch your legs? This bed is short.
Let me see! Why, isn't this the bed
I slept in when I was a child?
Do you remember how often of an evening
You sat by my bedside and spread the fur rug over me
And sang me songs?

AASE: Yes, do you remember? When your father
    Was away on a journey, we'd play sledges.
    The rug was a sledge and the floor was an icebound
      fjord.

PEER: Yes, but the best of all—oh, mother,
    Do you remember that too?—was the white horses!

AASE: [Of course I do!] Do you think I've forgotten that?
    We'd borrow Kari's cat and sit it down on a chair—

PEER: To the castle west of the moon
    And the castle east of the sun,
    To Soria-Moria Castle
    The road ran high and low!
    We found a stick in a closet
    And you used that as a whip—

AASE: I sat up here on the box-seat—

PEER: Yes, yes! You threw loose the reins
    And kept turning round as we rode
    To ask me if I was cold.
    God bless you, ugly old mother!
    You were always a loving soul!
    Why are you crying?

AASE: It's my back. The hard board hurts it.

PEER: Stretch out, now. Let me settle you.
    There, now you're lying softly.

AASE (restlessly): No, Peer. I want to go.

PEER: Go?

AASE: Yes, go. It's all I want.

PEER: What nonsense! Spread the rug over you.
    Let me sit on the edge of the bed.
    There! Now we'll shorten the evening with song.

AASE: No, get the prayer-book from the closet.
    My soul's restless.

PEER: In Soria-Moria Castle[7]
    The great King's giving a feast.
    Rest there on the sledge-cushion, mother.

I'll drive you over the moor—
AASE: But Peer, have I been invited?
PEER: Yes, we both have been.

> *Throws a string round the chair on which the cat is sitting, takes a stick in his hand and sits on the foot of the bed.*

Gee-up! Will you stir yourself, Grane![8]
Now, mother, you're sure you're not cold?
Oh, yes! You can feel you're speeding
Once Grane begins to go!
AASE: Peer dear, what's that ringing?
PEER: It's the silver sleigh-bells, mother!
AASE: Oh dear, what's that hollow rumbling?
PEER: We're driving over a fjord.
AASE: I'm frightened! What's that wild sighing?
PEER: It's the pine trees, mother, whispering on the moor.
Sit still, now—
AASE: There's something winking and sparkling in the distance.
Where's that light coming from?
PEER: From the windows and doors of the Castle.
Can you hear? They're dancing.
AASE: Yes.
PEER: St. Peter's standing outside. He's asking you to step in.
AASE: Is he speaking to us?
PEER: Yes, and he's taking his hat off. He's offering his sweetest wine.
AASE: Wine? Are there cakes too?
PEER: Oh, yes! A tasty plateful!
And the Bishop's wife is offering coffee and sweets.
AASE: Oh, Lord! Am I going to meet her?
PEER: As often as you wish, and as equals.

AASE: Oh Peer, what a spree you're taking my poor old
  bones on!

PEER *(cracks his whip):* Hey! Hup! Come on, rouse yourself, Grane!

AASE: Peer dear, are you driving carefully?

PEER *(cracks his whip again):* The road's broad here.

AASE: Don't drive so fast. I feel so old and tired.

PEER: I can see the Castle towering ahead of us.
  Our journey will soon be done.

AASE: I'll lie back and close my eyes,
  And trust in you, my son.

PEER: Gee-up now, Grane, my beauty!
  By God, the excitement is great!
  They've spotted Peer Gynt and his mother,
  And they're fighting to get to the gate!
  What's that you're saying, St. Peter?
  You won't let her in? My good sir,
  You can sit on your backside till Doomsday
  And you'll find no one better than her.
  [I'm not going to boast of my virtues.
  I can turn and go back where I came.
  If you want me, I'll come in and thank you.
  If not, many thanks just the same.
  Sure, I've told as many lies as the Devil in any pulpit,
  And sworn at my mother and called her a bloody old
   hen
  Because she was always crowing and cackling at me.
  But] You see she's received with respect, mind.
  You make her feel really at home!
  She's the best soul you'll get from this parish.
  If you don't like her, go back to Rome!
  Ho-ho! Here comes God the Father!
  Now, St. Peter, we'll soon see who's who.
  In a deep voice.
  None of your bloody butler's airs, now.

Just let Mother Aase come through.
Laughs aloud and turns to his mother.
There, isn't it just as I told you?
That's made the old so-and-so run!
Frightened.
Why are you so silent, mother?
Speak to me! It's Peer, your son!
Goes to the bed-head.
Don't lie there and stare at me, mother!
Don't open your eyes so wide!
Feels her forehead and hands carefully. Then he throws the string on to the chair and says softly:
I see. You can rest now, Grane.
We've come to the end of our ride.
Thank you for all your days.
For your beatings and kisses, my dear.
But now you must thank me too.
Presses his cheek against her mouth.
So; the driver has had his fare.

KARI *(enters):* Peer! Are you here? Then the worst of our
        troubles are over.
    Dear God, how soundly she's sleeping! Or—is she—?
PEER: Hush. She is dead.

        KARI *weeps over the body.* PEER *walks round the room
        for a while. At length he stops by the bed.*

PEER: See my mother is buried with honour.
    I must get away from here.
KARI: Where are you going?
PEER: Seawards.
KARI: So far?
PEER: And far beyond.

    He goes.

ACT FOUR

Scene One

On the southwest coast of Morocco. A palm grove. A table laid for dinner, with a sun awning and rush mats. Hammocks have been hung farther back in the grove. Offshore lies a steam yacht flying the Norwegian and American flags. On the beach is a dinghy. It is towards sundown.

> PEER GYNT, *a handsome middle-aged gentleman in elegant travelling clothes, with a gold lorgnette hanging from his waistcoat, is presiding as host at the dinner-table.* MR. COTTON, M. BALLON, HERR VON EBERKOPF *and* HERR TRUMPETERSTRAALE[9] *are finishing their meal.*

PEER: Drink, gentlemen! Man was made for pleasure.
    What's done is done; what's past is past concern.
    [What can I offer you?]
TRUMPETERSTRAALE: You're a superb host, Peer.
PEER: You must allow some credit to my wealth,
    My steward and my cook.
COTTON: Here's to the four of you!
BALLON: Monsieur, you have a *goût*, a *ton*,
    Such as one seldom finds today

94

Among men living *en garçon.*
A certain—*qu'est-ce qu'on dit—?*
VON EBERKOPF:[10]   A measure
Of spiritual contemplation,
[A marvellous lack of chauvinism,
A vision that can pierce the fog
Of prejudice,] the ability
To grasp Truth in its higher aspects—
[Added to which] an *Ur-Natur,*
[An unspoilt nature, all this crowned]
With a fine wealth of worldly knowledge—
Mein herr, was that not what you meant?
BALLON: *C'est bien possible.* [It doesn't sound
Quite so *magnifique* in French.]
VON EBERKOPF: [*Ei was!* Your language is so stiff.] But if
We wish to find the cause of the phenomenon—
PEER: It's easy. I've never married.
[Why, gentlemen, it is as clear as daylight.]
What should a man be? Himself. [That's all.]
He must live for himself and himself alone.
How can he if he spends his life
[Playing the pack-camel to a wife and children.]
Carrying the woes of others?
VON EBERKOPF: But to achieve this independence
You must have had to pay a price—
PEER: Oh, yes. Indeed—when I was young.
[But I always emerged an honourable victor.]
Once I was very nearly trapped.
I was a gay and good-looking boy
And the lady to whom I lost my heart
Was of royal birth—
BALLON: Royal?
PEER *(nonchalantly):* One of those ancient mountain families—
You know—

TRUMPETERSTRAALE *(thumps the table)*: Aristocrats!

PEER *(shrugs his shoulders)*: Degenerate idiots, who count it
    their chief pride
  To keep plebeian stains from the family escutcheon.

COTTON: The romance fell through?

BALLON: Her family opposed the match?

PEER: On the contrary.

BALLON: Ah!

PEER *(forbearingly)*: Well, there were circumstances,
    You understand, that made it desirable
    That we should marry with all decent speed.
    But frankly, I found the whole business
    From first to last somewhat unappetizing.
    In certain respects I'm a fastidious man.
    [And I always like to stand on my own feet.]
    So when her father started dropping hints
    That I should change my name and my profession
    And take out a licence of nobility,
    With other suggestions that were equally
    Distasteful, not to say unacceptable,
    I [bowed my thanks, rejected his ultimatum
    And] renounced my youthful bride.
    Drums with his fingers on the table and looks pious.
    Yes, yes; there's a destiny that shapes our ends.
    [We mortals can safely put our trust in it.]
    It's a great comfort to know it.

BALLON: That was the end of the affair?

PEER: Oh, no. Far from it. [Various outsiders
    Poked in their noses and created mischief.
    Her brothers and cousins were the worst.]
    I had to fight duels with seven of them.
    [It was a time I shall never forget.]
    But I survived with honour. [It cost me blood.
    However, that same blood attests my worth.

And is a further proof that our lives are ruled
By that wise fate of which I spoke just now.]
VON EBERKOPF: You have an outlook upon life
Which entitles you to be called a Philosopher.
[Where ordinary mortals guess,
Seeing each detail separately,
For ever groping, you are able
Fully to integrate your vision.
Measuring life by an unchanging norm
You gather scattered inspirations
So that they radiate like beams
Of one supreme philosophy.]
And you've never been to University?
PEER: [As I've told you before,] I am a self-taught man.
[I've studied nothing methodically.]
But I've thought and [speculated and] read a little
About most things. I started late in life.
[And, you know, it becomes a trifle wearisome
To plough through page after page, trying to absorb
What's dull with what is lively.]
I've learned my history by fits and starts.
It was all I had time for.
And since one must have some spiritual security
[To put one's trust in when times are hard]
I read religion—intermittently.
[That way it's easier to digest.
One shouldn't read to gulp down everything.]
One must select [what one will be able to use].
COTTON: Very practical.
PEER *(lights a cigar):* My dear friends,
Consider my own career. What was I
When I came to the West? A penniless lad.
I had to sweat to earn my bread.
Believe me, things were very hard.
But life, my friends, is sweet; and death is bitter.

97

Fortune smiled upon me, as you see.
[And old man Fate was tolerant.] I prospered.
[And, since my own philosophy was elastic,
Things went from good to better.] Within ten years
The Charleston ship-owners were calling me Croesus.
My fame spread from port to port. Luck sat in my
    sails—

COTTON: What did you carry?

PEER: Mostly Negro slaves to Carolina,
And heathen images to China.

BALLON: *Fi donc!*

TRUMPETERSTRAALE: My dear sir—!

PEER: You think it was a trifle unethical?
I felt the same myself—oh, very keenly.
I may even say I hated it.
But believe me, once you've begun, it's hard to stop.
And I didn't want to create unemployment.
[In so gigantic an enterprise as this
Which keeps whole thousands in employment,
It's very hard to call things to a halt
For good. 'For good.' I can't abide those words.
On the other hand, I must confess
I've always had the healthiest respect
For what men call the consequences.
And the prospect of overstepping the mark
Has always induced a certain timidity in me.]
Well, I was beginning to grow old;
[Approaching fifty. My hair was turning grey.]
And though my health was excellent, one thought
    haunted me:
'Who knows how soon the hour of judgement will
    strike?
[And the great judgement separate sheep from goats.]'
What could I do?
To stop the China trade was impossible.

But I found a solution. [I quickly opened
Another trade with the same country.]
Each spring I sent them idols, and each autumn
Exported missionaries, generously equipped
With woollen stockings, Bibles, rice and rum—
COTTON: At a profit, I presume?
PEER: Of course. [This enterprise
Also prospered. They worked indefatigably.]
For every idol that I sold
They got a coolie honestly baptized.
Thus the effect was neutralized.
[The field of holy work never lay fallow,
The idols being countered by the missionaries.]
COTTON: But what about your African cargoes?
PEER: There too my sense of morality triumphed.
[I realized it was a foolish traffic
For one advanced in years. One never knows
When the summons to judgement may come.
Besides, there were the patrol boats
Not to mention the philanthropists
And the risks of wind and weather.
All these considerations won the day.]
'Peter,' I said, 'it's time to reef your sails.
You must right your wrongs.'
I purchased a plot of land in the South,
And kept the last cargo [which happened
To be of the primest quality,] for myself.
They flourished, and grew [sleek and] fat,
Giving the highest satisfaction
Both to themselves and me. Indeed,
I think I can say without boasting, I was
A father to them. And reaped my just reward.
[I built schools, and kept the strictest watch
To ensure the maintenance of morality].
And now I have withdrawn from the whole concern.

I've sold the plantation, with all its stock
Of hide and hair. [The day I left
I gave to every man, woman and child
Grog, *ad lib* and *gratis;* so that they all got drunk,
And every widow had an ounce of snuff.]
So surely, [if] the old saying holds true:
'Who doeth not evil worketh good'
[The follies of my past are now forgotten,
And, more than most men, I can safely claim
That my good deeds are weightier than my sins].

VON EBERKOPF *(clinks glasses with him):* It is wonderful to
    meet a man
  Who lives according to his principles.
  [Uninhibited by foggy theories,
  Immutable in the face of outward chaos.]

PEER *(who during the preceding dialogue has been helping
    himself steadily from the various bottles):*
  [We Northern warriors know how to carry a battle
  Through to its harsh conclusion.] The key to life
  Is simply this. Close your ear against
  The infiltration of a dangerous serpent.

COTTON: What serpent, my good friend?

PEER: A little one that is most seductive.
  The one that tempts you to commit yourself.
  Drinks again.
  The art of success is to stand free
  And uncommitted amid the snares of life.
  To know that the day of battle is not the day
  Of judgement. There are other days to come.
  To know that a bridge always remains open
  Behind you. That theory has shaped my whole career.
  [This theory is a national inheritance.
  I entered into it in my parents' home.

BALLON: You're Norwegian, aren't you?

PEER: By birth. But cosmopolitan by temperament.

For my success I'm indebted to America
For my book-learning to the new German schools.
From France I have acquired my waistcoat here,
My manners, and the little wit I own.
From England I have learned industriousness
And a quick eye for opportunity.
The Jew has taught me patience, and Italy
Gave me a taste for *dolce far niente*.
And once, in an awkward situation,
I lengthened the measure of my days
With the help of Swedish steel.

TRUMPETERSTRAALE *(raises his glass):* Ah! Swedish steel!]
VON EBERKOPF: Let us raise our glasses to the free man!

They clink glasses with him and drink. He begins to grow a little tipsy.

COTTON: All this is fine. Fine.
But tell me, sir, I'm curious to know
What you propose to do with all your money.
PEER: Hm! Do with it? Eh?
ALL FOUR *(edge closer):* Yes! Tell us!
PEER: Well, first of all
I want to travel. That's why I took you aboard
As travelling companions in Gibraltar,
I needed a chorus of friends to dance
Around the altar of my golden calf.
[VON EBERKOPF: Very witty.]
COTTON: But no one sails merely for pleasure.
You must have a goal. What is it?
PEER: To become Emperor.
ALL FOUR: What?
PEER *(nods):* Emperor.
ALL FOUR: Of what? Where?
PEER: Of the whole world.
BALLON: But how, my friend—?

PEER: By the power of gold. It's not a new idea.
     The thought of it has been with me all my journey.
     When I was a child, I rode in my dreams
     Far over the ocean on a cloud.
     I soared with a host of men behind me.
     [And a golden scabbard]. But I fell
     Flat on my face. But that remained my goal.
     Someone—I forget who it was—once said
     That if you gain the whole wide world
     But lose yourself, your victory
     Is but a wreath about a cloven brow.
     [Those were the words, or something similar.]
     It's the truth.

VON EBERKOPF: But who *is* your self?

PEER: The world behind my forehead's vaulted arch,
     By cause of which I am myself alone,
     [And no one else, any more than God is Satan].

TRUMPETERSTRAALE: Now I get it!

BALLON: Sublime *penseur!*

VON EBERKOPF: Most mighty poet!

PEER *(with increasing passion):* My self—it is the army
     Of wishes, appetites, desires,
     [The sea of whims, pretensions and demands,]
     All that swells here within my breast
     And by which I, myself, exist.
     But, as Our Lord has need of common clay
     To make Him omnipotent, so I need gold
     To make me Emperor.

BALLON: But you have gold.

PEER: Not enough. [Yes, perhaps for a nine days' wonder;
     As Emperor *à la* Lippe-Detmold.[11]
     But I must be myself entirely;
     Every inch a Gyntish inch,
     From top to toe, Sir Peter Gynt.

BALLON *(carried away):* Possess the loveliest woman on
        earth!
VON EBERKOPF: Your *Reich* last for a thousand years![12]
TRUMPETERSTRAALE: Stand in history with Charlemagne![13]
COTTON: Aye. But first may you find a profitable opening—
PEER: I have found it. Thanks to our anchoring here!]
        This evening we sail northward. [The newspapers
        I received on board brought tidings of importance.]
        Gets up and raises his glass.
        Dame Fortune ceaselessly assists the brave.
ALL FOUR: What? Tell us!
PEER: Greece is in revolt!
ALL FOUR *(jump up):* What? The Greeks!
PEER: They have risen against their masters.
ALL FOUR: Hurrah!
PEER: And the Turkish army is in confusion.

        Empties his glass.

BALLON: To Hellas! The gate of glory is thrown wide!
        [I'll help them with my Gallic rapier!
VON EBERKOPF: And I with fearful war-cries—from a dis-
        tance.
COTTON: I, too, with arms. On pre-payment, of course.
TRUMPETERSTRAALE: Lead on! I'll find in Bender to assist
        them
        The famous buckles of King Charles's spurs!][14]
BALLON *(falls on* PEER GYNT*'s neck):* Forgive me, *mon ami,*
        that I misjudged you!
VON EBERKOPF *(presses his hand):* Stupid dog that I am, I
        took you for a scoundrel.
COTTON: Not as bad as that. A fool, perhaps—
TRUMPETERSTRAALE *(tries to kiss him):* [I took you, Uncle,
        for an example
        Of the worst kind of rotten Yankee brood.]
        Forgive me—

[VON EBERKOPF: We have all been groping in the dark.]

PEER: What's all this?

[VON EBERKOPF: Now we see the whole Gyntish host
Of wishes, passions and desires
Most gloriously assembled—]

BALLON *(admiringly):* So *this* is being Monsieur Gynt!

VON EBERKOPF *(similarly):* This is to be Peer Gynt with honour!

PEER: But please tell me—?

BALLON: You don't understand?

PEER: No, I'll be hanged if I do.

BALLON: What! But surely you are on your way
To help the Greeks with ships and money?

PEER *(snorts):* No, thank you! I side with strength.
I am lending money to the Turk.

BALLON: Impossible!

VON EBERKOPF: Very witty. You're joking.

PEER *(is silent for a moment, then leans against a chair and
assumes a lofty mein):* Gentlemen, it is best we part
[before
The last shreds of friendship flicker away like smoke].
The empty-fisted are always rash to gamble.
[The man who scarcely owns the strip of earth
His shadow covers, is natural cannon fodder.]
But when a man is as rich as I am,
He has much to lose.
Go to Hellas. I will arm you *gratis,*
And set you safe ashore. The more you fan
The flames of patriotism, the more I have
To gain. Stand up for freedom! Fight for justice!
[Charge! Storm onwards! Stoke up hell for the Turk!]
And gloriously end your days
Upon the lances of the Janissaries!
But please excuse me. *(Slaps his pocket.)* I have gold,
And am myself, Sir Peter Gynt.

Opens his sunshade and goes into the grove, where the hammocks can be glimpsed.

TRUMPETERSTRAALE: The darned swine!

BALLON: No sense of honour!

COTTON: To hell with honour!
Think of the profit if the Greeks should win!

BALLON: [I saw myself wreathed with the victor's garland,
Surrounded by beautiful Grecian maidens.

TRUMPETERSTRAALE: I saw the spurs of Charles the Twelfth
Resting where they belong, in Swedish hands.

VON EBERKOPF: I saw my fatherland's prodigious Kultur
Spreading itself over land and sea.

COTTON: It's the material loss that bothers me.
Goddamit! I could weep real tears.
I saw myself as the master of Olympus,
And if that mountain's reputation is correct
There are copper mines to be found there
Which I could open up and work afresh.
And that river Kastale they talk so much about—
All those waterfalls must at the lowest calculation
Be worth over a thousand horse-power—]

TRUMPETERSTRAALE: I shall go, nevertheless. [My Swedish sword
Is worth twice as much as Yankee gold.

COTTON: Possibly. But if we merely join the ranks
We'll be swallowed up with the rest. And where will
our profit be then?

BALLON: *Mon Dieu!* To climb so near success—!
And then to find oneself standing by its grave!]

COTTON (*shakes his fist towards the yacht*): And that black
coffin holds all the gold
That blasted Nabob sweated from his niggers.

VON EBERKOPF: An inspiration! What are we waiting for?
His empire lies within our grasp. Hurrah!

BALLON: What are you going to do?

VON EBERKOPF: Perform a *coup!* We have only to bribe the crew,
    [Which won't be difficult] and the yacht is ours.
    Aboard!

COTTON: You mean *you—?*

VON EBERKOPF: I bag the whole caboodle. *(Goes down to the dinghy.)*

COTTON: I can't neglect my own interests.
    I'd better do the same.

TRUMPETERSTRAALE: The scoundrels!

BALLON: A bad business. *Mais enfin—(Follows the others.)*

TRUMPETERSTRAALE: I suppose I shall have to join them.
    But under protest![15] *(Follows.)*

Scene Two

Another part of the coast. Moonlight and drifting clouds. The yacht, a long way offshore, is under full steam. PEER GYNT *is running along the shore, now pinching his arm, now staring out to sea.*

PEER: I'm dreaming! It's a nightmare! I'll wake up soon.
    She's sailing away! And at full steam!
    It's a hallucination! I'm asleep! I'm drunk! I'm mad!
    Clenches his fists.
    I can't be going to die!
    Tears his hair.
    It's a dream. I insist it's a dream.
    Oh, this is dreadful! It's only too real! What monsters!
    Hear me, O Lord! You're so wise and so just! Judge!
    Stretches up his arms.
    It's me, Peter Gynt! Oh God, do pay attention!
    Protect me, Father, or I must perish!
    Make them turn the ship! Make them lower the sails!
    Stop the thieves! Make something go wrong!

Oh, listen to me! Never mind other people.
The world can take care of itself for a while.
No, he's not listening. He's deaf as usual.
That's charming! A God who won't help when you
     need him.
Waves upwards.
Psst! I've given up that nigger plantation!
I've sent missionaries all the way to China.
Surely one good turn is worth another!
Oh, please help me to get on board—!

*A jet of flame shoots into the air from the yacht, and thick
smoke belches forth. A hollow explosion is heard.* PEER
GYNT *utters a shriek and sinks down on to the sand. Gradually the smoke dissipates. The ship has vanished.*

PEER *(pale and quiet):* The sword of vengeance!
Gone to the bottom with every soul on board!
Oh, what luck, what—!
Moved.
Luck? No, it was more than that.
I was fated to be saved, and they to die.
O all thanks and praise to Thee for preserving me
In spite of all my sins!
Emits a deep breath.
What a wonderful feeling of peace and safety it gives
To know that one is under special protection!
But the desert! What about food and drink?
Oh, I'll find something. He'll see to that.
There's no need to be afraid.
Loudly and ingratiatingly.
He won't want a poor little sparrow like me
To perish. Just be humble. And give Him time.
Trust in the Lord and keep your courage up.
Gives a frightened jump.
Was that a lion growling in the reeds?

His teeth chatter.
No, it wasn't a lion.
Plucks up his courage.
[Well, what's a lion?
Those beasts know it's best to keep out of the way
And not try to mix things with their betters.
Their instinct tells them not to play with elephants.]
Still, I'd better find a tree. There's a grove
Of palms and acacias over there.
If I get up in them I'll be safe and cool.
If only I knew a psalm or two!
Climbs up into a tree.
['Morning is morning and night is night.'
That's a text that has often been weighed and sifted.
Seats himself more comfortably.
How splendid to feel so spiritually uplifted.
Noble thoughts are more than silk and pearls.]
Just trust in him. [He knows how much
Of the chalice of suffering I have strength to drink.]
He keeps a fatherly eye on me.
Throws a glance out to sea and whispers with a sigh:
But he certainly isn't economical!

Scene Three

Night. A Moroccan encampment on the edge of the desert.
Watch fires. WARRIORS *resting.*

A SLAVE *(enters, tearing his hair):* The Emperor's white
    charger is missing!
A SECOND SLAVE *(enters rending his clothes):* The Emper-
    or's sacred robes have been stolen!
AN OVERSEER *(enters):* A hundred lashes of the bastinado
    For every man who fails to catch the thief!

  THE WARRIORS *mount their horses and gallop off in all*
  directions.

108

Scene Four

Dawn. The grove of palms and acacias. PEER GYNT, *up in his tree with a broken branch in his hand, is trying to ward off a swarm of monkeys.*

PEER: Damnation! A most unpleasant night!
    Beasts around.
    Monkeys!
    You again! This is the bloody limit.
    Now they're throwing fruit. No, it isn't fruit.
    Filthy beasts! [How does the saying go?
    'Thou shalt keep watch and fight.' Well, I'm damned if
        I can.
    My eyes feel like lead.]
    They disturb him again. He says impatiently:
    I must put a stop to this. I must try to catch
    One of the brats and [hang him and] skin him
    And dress myself up in his hairy coat,
    So the others will think I'm one of them.
    What are we mortals? Just motes of dust.
    We've got to adapt ourselves a little.
    Another crowd of them. Milling and swarming!
    Be off with you! Shoo! They're acting like lunatics.
    If only I had a false tail now,
    Or something that made me a bit like an animal.
    What now? Something's rustling over my head—
    Glances up.
    It's the grandfather, with his fists full of filth—

    Huddles nervously and keeps still for a moment. The monkey makes a movement. PEER *begins coaxing him and talking to him gently as though to a dog.*

    Hullo, old boy, is that you up there?
    You're clever, aren't you? [You know what's what.]

You're not going to throw—no, of course you're not.
It's me. Pip-pip! We're good friends, aren't we?
Gives a couple of squeaks.
Do you hear, I can talk your language!
We're relatives. Tomorrow morning
I'll give you some sugar—! You filthy brute!
The whole lot down on my head! Ugh! Disgusting!
Or perhaps it was food. *(Tastes.)* I'm not sure.
But taste is a question of what you are used to.
[Who was it that said: 'One must spit and trust
In the power of habit'?] Oh, here come the young ones!
Beats around.
This is really too much, that Man, Lord of Creation,
Should be compelled to—! No, stop it! Curse!
The old one was bad, but the young ones are worse!

Scene Five

Early morning. A stony landscape, with a view over the desert. On one side a cleft in the mountain and a cave. A THIEF *and a* RECEIVER *are in the cleft with the Emperor's horse and cloak. The horse, richly caparisoned, is tied to a stone. Horsemen can be heard in the distance.*

THIEF: The tongues of the lances
　　Are licking and playing.
　　See! See!
RECEIVER: I can see my head
　　Roll in the sand!
　　Woe! Woe!
THIEF *(crosses his arms over his breast):* My father was a thief
　　So his son must steal.
RECEIVER: My father was a receiver,
　　So I must receive.

110

THIEF: Thou must bear thy lot.
   Thou must be thyself.
RECEIVER *(listens):* Footsteps [among the stones]!
   We must fly. But whither?
THIEF: The cave is deep
   And the Prophet is great.

   *They flee, leaving their loot behind them. The sound of
   horsemen dies away in the distance.*

PEER *(enters, cutting a reed pipe):* What a beautiful morn-
      ing!
   The dung-beetle's rolling his ball in the sand.
   The snail is creeping out of his house.
   Morning! Oh yes, it has gold in its mouth.
   Daylight has a wonderful power.
   One feels so safe, one's courage rises.
   I could fight a bull!
   Such silence everywhere! [Yes, these rustic pleasures!
   How extraordinary that I ever came to reject them.
   That man should choose to shut himself up in a city
   And be pestered by crowds on his doorstep.]
   The lizard darts around, snapping and thinking of noth-
      ing.
   What innocence in the life of beasts!
   Each is himself, obeying his Maker's purpose;
   [Preserving unspoiled his characteristic essence,
   And being himself, whether playing or fighting,
   As on the day when God first commanded 'Be!']
   Fixes his lorgnette on his nose.
   A toad. In the middle of a [sandstone] rock.
   [Stone all around him. Only his head is visible.]
   There he sits, staring at life as through a window;
   Being himself, and to hell with the rest of the world!
   'To hell with the world—!' Who said that?
   [I expect I read it when I was a boy,

111

In some so-called great book.] Was it the Prayer Book?
[Or Solomon? Bad.] Every year my memory gets
  worse.
Sits down in the shade.
[Here's a cool place to rest and stretch my feet.
What's this? Ferns? Edible roots.
Tastes them.
They're probably all right for animals.
But it is written: 'Subdue thy nature,'
And also: 'He that is proud shall be brought low,
And he that abaseth himself shall be exalted.'
Uneasily.
Exalted? Yes, that'll happen to me.
I can't see any other solution.
Providence will help me to escape from this country
And arrange for me to continue on my way.
This is merely a trial. Salvation will follow,
Provided only the good Lord grants me strength.

*Puts these thoughts aside.] Lights a cigar, stretches
himself and gazes out over the desert.*

What a vast and limitless waste!
Far away over there an ostrich is strutting.
What is one to believe was God's intention
In creating all this emptiness and death?
[This desert, devoid of all sources of life,
Burnt and yielding profit to no man.
This fragment of the world, for ever fallow.
This corpse that, never since the earth was born,
Has given its Creator as much as thanks.
Why was it made?] Nature is unpractical.
Is that the sea shining over there in the east?
Glittering—? No, it can't be. It's a mirage.
The sea's in the west behind me,
Dammed from the desert by a range of hills.

A thought strikes him.
Dammed? I wonder—? Those hills are narrow.
Dammed? A little dynamite, a canal,
And the waters would rush like a life-giving river
In through the gap and fill the desert.
Soon this whole white-hot grave would lie
Fresh as a dimpled sea.
The oases would rise out of it like islands.
[Atlas grow green like our mountains in the north.]
The schooners, like migrating birds,
Would cut their way southwards on the caravan routes.
[The air of life will scatter these stuffy vapours,
And dew drop from the clouds.] Towns will arise,
And grass will grow around the swaying palms.
[The land to the south behind the Sahara's wall
Will become the coastland of a vital culture.
Steam will drive factories in Timbuctoo,
Bornu will speedily be colonized,
And scientists ride in their *wagons-lit*
Through Abyssinia to the Upper Nile.]
And in the midst of my sea, on a rich oasis,
I shall personally propagate the Norwegian race.
[The blood of our Northern valleys is—well, nearly
    royal,
And a little Arab mixture will do the rest.
Around a bay on rising sand
I'll found my capital, Peeropolis.]
The world's degenerate. Now comes the turn
Of Gyntiana,[16] my new land!
Jumps to his feet.
A little money and I could do it!
A golden key to the gate of the sea!
A crusade against Death! That mean old skinflint
Shall open the sack he lies brooding on!
[In every land the cry goes up for freedom.

Like the ass in the Ark I'll send my clarion call
Across the world, and bring the baptism of liberty
To the beautiful prisoned coasts that shall be born!]
I must do it! I must find capital!
My kingdom—well, half my kingdom for a horse!
The horse neighs in the cave.
A horse! And robes! And jewels! And a sword!
Goes closer.
It can't be. [Yes, it is. But—? I have read
Somewhere, that human will can move mountains.
But a horse too—!] Well, it's a fact, here stands the horse.
[*Ab esse ad posse,* etcetera, etcetera.]
Puts on the cloak and looks himself up and down.
Sir Peter. A Turk from top to toe!
No, one never knows what fate will bring?
Gee-up now, Grane, my trusty steed!
Mounts into the saddle.
Golden stirrups! But of course!
You can tell a great man by the cut of his horse!
Gallops away into the desert.

Scene Six

The tent of an Arab chieftain, alone in an oasis. PEER GYNT,
*in Oriental costume, is reclining on cushions, drinking cof-
fee and smoking a long pipe.* ANITRA *and a group of girls
are dancing and singing for him.*

CHORUS OF GIRLS: The Prophet is come!
    The Prophet, the Master, [the Omniscient].
    To us is he come,
    [Riding across the ocean of the sand.
    The Prophet, the Master, the Infallible,
    To us, to us is he come,]
    Through the sand-ocean sailing.

114

[Let flute and drum hail him;]
The Prophet, the Prophet is come.

ANITRA: [His charger is white as the milk
That flows in the river of Paradise.]
Bend the knee! Bow the head!
His eyes are stars, shining and mild.
[But no earthborn child can endure
The brilliance of their light.]
Through the desert he came.
[Gold and pearls sprang forth on his breast.]
Where he rode, there was light.
Behind him all grew dark.
[Behind him drought and sandstorm reigned.]
He came, the Glorious One,
[Through the desert he came]
Dressed like a mortal.
[Kaba,[17] Kaba stands empty.
He himself hath proclaimed it.

CHORUS OF GIRLS: [Let flute and drum hail him.]
The Prophet, the Prophet is come.

The GIRLS *dance to soft music.*

PEER: [I have read in print, and it's perfectly true:
'No man is a prophet in his own country.']
This is the life for me! [It's much better
Than the one over there among the Charleston shippers.
There was something hollow about all that,
Something foreign to me, something fishy behind it.]
I never felt at home among those shippers.
I never felt I was one of them.
Why did I ever get on to that wagon
To root around in the garbage cans of commerce?
[Now I think about it, I can't imagine why.
It just happened that way. That's the only answer.
To be oneself by the power of gold

115

Is simply to build one's house upon sand.
If you've a gold watch and a diamond ring
People will fawn and grovel before you.
They'll raise their hats to your glittering tiepin
But the ring and the pin are not the man.]
A prophet's position is much clearer.
[You know where you are. If you're a success]
It's you that they worship and not your money.
[One is what one is, and no nonsense about it.
One isn't a debtor to Chance or Fate,
And one has no need of licence or patent.
To be a prophet. That's something for me.]
And I tumbled into it quite by chance.
Simply galloping through the desert
I stumbled upon these children of nature.
Their Messiah had come; it was clear; [there was no
    doubt about it.]
I had no intention of deceiving them.
Prophetic utterances are not lies.
Besides, I can always revise my interpretations.
[I'm not bound at all. Things aren't too bad.
It's all a perfectly private matter.]
If it comes to the worst, I can leave as I came.
My horse stands ready.
In short, I am master of the situation.

ANITRA (approaches): Prophet and Master!
PEER: What would my slave?
ANITRA: The sons of the desert wait outside.
    They beg to be allowed to see thy face.
PEER: Stop! Tell them to keep their distance.
    Tell them I shall hear their prayers from there.
    No men are allowed in here.
    Men, my child, are a most untrustworthy race.
    Miserable bastards! You can't imagine [Anitra,]
    How they have cheated—hm—sinned, my child.

116

Well, that's all over. You may dance for me, maidens.
The Prophet would forget such painful memories.

CHORUS *(dancing):* The Prophet is good. The Prophet is
    grieved
    At the evil the sons of the dust have committed.
    The Prophet is merciful. Praised be his mercy!
    He opens to sinners the portals of Paradise.

PEER *(his eyes follow* ANITRA *as she dances):* [Her legs are
    as neat and nimble as drumsticks.]
    Mm. She's a nice piece of delicatessen, that girl.
    [A trifle extravagantly moulded. Not quite
    The classical formula. But what is Beauty?
    A mere convention. It changes like coin
    From country to country and age to age.
    But a little excess is a pleasant change
    When one has drunk normality to the dregs.
    You can't get intoxicated by what's average.
    They're either too fat or too thin, or else
    Disturbingly young or disgustingly old.
    And what lies between seems insipid.]
    Her feet aren't quite clean; nor are her arms.
    Especially one. Still, that's no great defect.
    It's almost an extra qualification.
    Anitra, my child! Listen to me.

ANITRA *(approaches):* Thy handmaiden listens.

PEER: My child, you attract me. The Prophet is stirred.
    If you don't believe me, I shall give you proof.
    I'll make you a Houri in Paradise.

ANITRA: Impossible, Lord.

PEER: What? You think I'm joking?
    I mean it, as truly as I am alive.

ANITRA: But I have no soul.

PEER: That can be arranged.

ANITRA: How, Lord?

PEER: You leave that to me.

[I shall make it my personal task to educate you.
No soul! Yes, indeed, you are, as the saying goes,
Somewhat stupid. I've noticed it with distress.
But] the meanest creature has room for a soul.
Come here. Let me measure the size of your brain.
There's room, there's room. I knew I was right.
[You'll never become a profound thinker.]
Not very much room. Your soul will be small.
But what of that? You'll have enough.

ANITRA: The prophet is good—

PEER: You hesitate? Answer!

ANITRA: I'd rather—

PEER: Speak out. Don't be afraid.

ANITRA: I don't mind so much about a soul.
    I'd rather have—

PEER: What?

ANITRA (*points at his turban*): That beautiful opal.

PEER (*enraptured, hands her the jewel*): Anitra! O Thou true
    daughter of Eve!
    How can I refuse you? I am but a man.
    [And, as a distinguished author has written:
    '*Das ewig weibliche ziehet uns an!*'¹⁸]

Scene Seven

A moonlit night. A palm grove outside ANITRA'*s tent.* PEER
GYNT *is seated beneath a tree with an Arabian lute in his
hand. His hair and beard are clipped, and he looks notice-
ably younger.*

PEER (*plays and sings*): I locked the gate of Paradise
    And took away its key.
    I sailed towards the Southern Cross
    While lovely women mourned their loss
    On the salt shore of the sea.

South like a bird I sped my way
On wings of swift desire.
At last, where palm trees proudly sway
In a green wreath around the bay,
I set my ship on fire.

[I stepped aboard the desert ship,
A four-legged bold corsair.
Beneath my whip it skimmed along.
O, catch me! I'm a bird in song.
A-twittering in the air.]

Anitra, thou art the palm-tree's sap,
A wine most dear to me.
Angora goat's-milk cheese, though fare
Fit for the gods, can scarce compare,
Anitra, ah, with thee!

Hangs his lute over his shoulder and goes nearer the tent.

Silence! Is my fair one listening?
Did she hear my little song?
Is she peeping through the curtain,
Veils etcetera cast aside?
[Hush! A sound! As of a cork
From a bottle gaily springing!
Now again! And yet again!
Sighs of passion? Love's sweet song?
No, it is the sound of snoring.
Heavenly sound! Anitra sleeps!
Nightingale, O cease thy scraping.
Woe and misery befall thee
If thou darest with gulp and gurgle—
Oh well, never mind, forget it.
Nightingale, thou art a singer.
Even such a one as I.
You, like me, bewitch with music

Gentle, tender, youthful hearts.
The cool night was made for music.
Music is our common sphere.
Music makes us what we are;
Peer Gynt and the nightingale.
And the fact that she lies sleeping
Makes my passion's bliss complete.
I poise my lips above the beaker,
The rich wine as yet untasted.]
No, bless my soul, here she comes.
[Well, after all, perhaps it's best.]

ANITRA *(from within the tent):* Dost thou call in the night,
     O master?
PEER: I do indeed. The Prophet calls.
     I was wakened by the cat
     Uttering violent hunting-cries.
ANITRA: Oh, Master, those weren't hunting-cries.
     [They were something much worse.]
PEER: What?
ANITRA: I dare not tell thee.
PEER: Speak!
ANITRA: I blush—
PEER *(comes closer):* The same passion that inspired me
     When I gave you my great opal?
ANITRA *(horrified):* O treasure of the world, dost thou liken
     thyself to an old tom-cat?
PEER: Child, torn by love tom-cats and prophets
     Behave very much the same.
ANITRA: Jests flow like honey from thy lips, O Master.
PEER: My little friend, [you must not judge
     Great men by their exteriors.]
     I am at heart a jovial man,
     Especially in private audience.
     [I am bound by my position
     To assume a solemn mask.

120

Daily duties cramp my style.
My numerous worries and anxieties
Make me sometimes rather surly.
But that's just my way of speaking.
Away with all that! *En tête-à-tête*
I'm Peer—I mean—well, whoever I am.]
Come on, let's forget the Prophet.
Here you see me as myself.
Sits under a tree and pulls her over to him.
[Come, Anitra, we will rest
Beneath the palm-tree's gentle fan.
I shall whisper, you shall smile.
Then we'll change parts, and your sweet lips
Will whisper love and make me smile.]

ANITRA *(lies down at his feet)*: All thy words are sweet as
    song,
    Though I understand little. Tell me, Master,
    Can thy daughter get a soul by listening?

PEER: Soul, knowledge, spiritual enlightenment—
    You shall have them
    When in the East, on rosy streamers,
    Letters of fire proclaim the day.
    Then, my child, I'll give you lessons.
    [You'll get your education.]
    But now, in the night's sweet stillness,
    Why should I act the schoolmaster
    [With the threadbare remnants of my wisdom]?
    The soul is not the most important thing,
    The heart is what counts.

ANITRA: Speak, O Master. When thou speakest
    I see a glimmer, as of opals.

PEER: Too much wisdom leads to folly.
    [The bud of cowardice, forced to fullest bloom,
    Swells into tyranny. Truth pushed to excess
    Reads like a wise text written backwards.

121

Yes, my daughter, this world is full of people
So spiritually gorged that their eyes are blinded.
I knew such a fellow once, a pearl among men,
But he came to nothing, losing all sense in sound.
Do you see the desert surrounding this oasis?
Simply by flicking this turban, I could conjure
The seas of the world in to flood every acre.
But to create new lands and seas would be
Sheer madness.] Do you know the secret of life?

ANITRA: No, tell me.

PEER: [It is to float dry-shod down the river of time;]
To be oneself.
Only in the vigour of youth
Can I be myself, my child.
Age makes eagles lose their feathers,
Age makes old men shake and pine.
[Age makes women bald and toothless,]
Age gives misers withered hands.
Age shrinks hearts and withers souls.
Youth, ah! Youth! I shall rule
Like a Sultan, hot and strong!
Not on the shores of Gyntiana
Underneath the palms and vines,
But in the fresh and waving pastures
Of a maiden's virgin thoughts.
[So you see, my little girl, why
I have condescended to seduce you;
Why I chose your little heart
For my empire:
I shall rule your every longing,
Tyrant in my state of love!
You shall live for me alone.
I shall possess you, like a jewel.
Should we part, then life will cease—
That is, yours. So kindly note that.

Every inch and fibre of you
Must accept me as its master.
You shall have no will but mine.]
The midnight beauties of your hair,
All your rich loveliness, shall draw me
Like the Babylonian Gardens
To my royal trysting-place.
[So it's best your head is empty.
If one has a soul, one wastes so much time
In introspection. And while we're on the subject,
You can have a chain around your ankle.
Then we'll both be happy.]
My soul will do for both of us.
[In other respects, we'll maintain the *status quo*.]
ANITRA *snores.*
What? She's asleep! Has everything I've said
Been thrown away? No, that's another sign
Of my power. My talk of love bears her away
Like a river into dreamland.
Gets up and puts jewels in her lap.
Here are jewels! And here are more!
Sleep, Anitra! Dream of Peer!
Sleep. By sleeping you have set
The crown on my imperial brow.
Tonight, by force of personality,
Peer Gynt has won his greatest victory.

Scene Eight

*A caravan route. The oasis is visible far away in the back-
ground.* PEER GYNT, *on his white horse, is riding furiously
through the desert with* ANITRA *in front of him on his saddle-
bow.*

ANITRA: Let me go! I'll bite you!
PEER: You little rogue!

ANITRA: What do you want?

PEER: What do I want? To play at hawk and dove.
   To carry you off! To play mad games with you!

ANITRA: Shame on you! An old prophet—!

PEER: Oh, rubbish. The Prophet isn't old, you little goose.
   Do you think this is a sign of age?

ANITRA: Let me go! I want to go home!

PEER: Now you're being a coquette.
   Home? To Daddy? A fine idea!
   [We're two wild birds that have flown from our cage,]
   We never dare enter his sight again.
   Besides, [my dear, one should never stay too long
   In the same place. The better people know you,
   The less they respect you. Especially when you're a
      prophet
   Or anything like that. One should come and go
   Fleetingly, like a vision;] it was time I moved on.
   [They're fickle fellows, these sons of the sand.]
   I was getting no incense or prayers in the end.

ANITRA: But are you a Prophet?

PEER: I am your Emperor! *(Tries to kiss her.)*
   My little woodpecker's being coy.

ANITRA: Give me that ring you've got on your finger.

PEER: Anitra, my dearest, take all I have.

ANITRA: Your words are music. [They bewitch me.]

PEER: It's wonderful to know that you love me so dearly.
   [I'll dismount, and lead your horse like a slave.
   Hands her the whip and dismounts.
   There now, my rose, my fairest flower.
   I'll trudge beside you through the sand
   Till I'm hit by sunstroke and meet my end.]
   I'm young, Anitra! Remember that.
   [So don't be alarmed if I seem to be frivolous.
   A sense of fun is inseparable from youth.
   If you had a few more brains in your head,

124

My sweet little lily, you'd understand
My playfulness is proof that I am young.]

ANITRA: Yes, you're young. Have you any more rings?

PEER: [Of course I am!] Catch! I can jump like a stag!
If we had vine-leaves, I'd garland myself.
Yes, of course I am young! Yoo-hoo! I'm going to
dance!

Dances and sings:
I'm a happy little cock!
Come and peck me, little hen!
Yoo! Hup! Trippety-trip!
I'm a happy little cock!

ANITRA: You're sweating, Prophet. I'm afraid you'll melt.
Give me that heavy thing on your belt.

PEER: O tender care! Carry my purse for ever!
[Hearts that love are happy without gold.

Dances and sings again:
Young Peer Gynt is a naughty madcap.
He doesn't know his tummy from his toes.
'Pish!' says Peer, 'Pish! Anything goes!'
Young Peer Gynt is a naughty madcap.

ANITRA: How exalting to see the Prophet dance!

PEER: Never mind the Prophet.] Let's change clothes!
Yoo-hoo! Take them off!

ANITRA: Your cloak would be too long, your belt too wide,
And your stockings too tight.

PEER *(kneels):* Then inflict some ordeal on me!
To a heart full of love, it is sweet to suffer.
Listen. As soon as we get to my castle—

ANITRA: In Paradise. Have we far to ride?

PEER: O, a thousand miles!

ANITRA: Too far!

PEER: O listen! You shall have the soul I promised you—

ANITRA: Thanks, I'll manage without a soul.
But you asked for an ordeal—

PEER (*gets up*): Yes, by Allah! Let it be short, but hard!
  A moment of exquisite pain!
ANITRA: Anitra obeys the Prophet! Farewell!

*She hits him sharply across the fingers and gallops
back across the desert.*

PEER (*stands for a long while as though thunderstruck*):
  Well, I'll be—!

Scene Nine

The same, an hour later. PEER GYNT, *soberly and reflectively,
is removing his Turkish costume, garment by garment. Finally
he takes his little travelling-cap out of the pocket of his coat,
puts it on, and stands once again in European dress.*

PEER (*throws the turban far away*): There lies the Turk and
    here stand I!
  [This heathen life won't do at all.
  Thank goodness I only borrowed clothes
  And wasn't born to it. *Mon dieu, mon Dieu,
  Qu'allais-je faire dans cette galère?*][19]
  It's best, after all, to live as a Christian.
  [To put behind one all peacock pretensions
  And steer one's course by law and morality.
  To be oneself and get at the end
  A speech by the graveside and flowers on one's coffin.]
  Walks a few paces.
  That bitch. She was within an ace of turning my head.
  [I'm damned if I'll ever understand
  What it was that bemused me. Well, thank heavens it's
      over.]
  I nearly made a fool of myself.
  [It's lucky that joke was carried no further.
  I have erred. That's true. But it wasn't my fault.
  I was simply placed in a false situation.

It wasn't I myself who fell from grace.
This prophetic life is divorced from reality
And took its revenge with this show of bad taste.
It's a rotten profession, this being a prophet.
Its nature demands that you live in a mist.
As soon as you behave like a rational being
You're finished. I was only acting professionally
In pretending I was in love with that little goose.
All the same—
Bursts in laughter.

Just fancy!
Trying to make time stop by dancing!
Trying to swim against the current
By fluttering my feathers and wagging my tail!
Playing on the lute, and caressing and sighing,
And ending by getting properly plucked!
Such conduct is truly prophetic madness.
Plucked! Yes, she's certainly plucked me clean.
Still, I have a little left here in my pocket;
And a bit more hidden away in America.]
I'm not a beggar yet. And maybe this halfway house
Is best; to be neither rich nor poor.
I'm not dependent on coachman or horses,
And don't need to bother with trunks or carriage.
In short, I am master of the situation,
As the saying is. Which path shall I choose?
Many lie open. [And it's the choice
That distinguishes the wise man from the fool.
My business life is a finished chapter.
My love-life is a cast-off shirt.]
I don't feel inclined to retreat like a crab.
'Forward or back, it's equally far.
Outside or in, I'm still confined.'
That's how it stands in some clever book,
[I think. Something new, then. Something noble.

A goal that's worth my money and labour.]
Suppose I wrote my autobiography?
[Candidly, to show people the way
And give them a lead to imitate?]
No, wait! [I've plenty of time on my hands.]
I might become a wandering scholar
And study the decline of man.
[Yes, that is the road for me!
I loved stories when I was a child.
And I've read a good deal of them since.] Yes, that's it!
I'll trace the path of the human race,
Float like a feather on the stream of time,
Re-live man's history, as in a dream;
See the great heroes wage their battles for truth
(As a spectator, from a safe distance);
I'll see thinkers perish, and martyrs bleed,
Empires founded and empires fall,
Mighty epochs growing from small beginnings—
In short, I shall skim the cream of history.
[I must try to get hold of a copy of Becker[20]
And arrange my travels chronologically.
Admittedly my knowledge isn't very thorough,
And the inner machinery of history is complicated—
But what of that? Original conclusions
Are often reached from the most unlikely starting-point.]
How fine to set oneself a goal
And drive one's way remorselessly towards it!
Quiet, moved.
To sever the bonds that bind one to one's [home
And] friends. To say farewell to earthly riches,
And bid the sweet joys of love goodnight,
All to seek out the mystery of truth.
Wipes a tear from his eye.
That is the test of the true scientist.
Oh, I feel so happy!

Now I have fathomed the riddle of my destiny
[And shall struggle towards it, however hard the road].
It is surely pardonable to feel a little proud;
And know that I am myself, Peer Gynt,
[Also called] Emperor of the Life of Man.
I shall hold the whole of the past in my hands.
I'll never more tread in the paths of the living.
The present is worthless. Man has no faith nor courage.
His soul is earthbound, his actions meaningless.
Shrugs his shoulders.
And as for women—they're not worth one's breath.

Goes.

Scene Ten

*A summer day, far up in the North. A forest hut; the open
door has a large wooden bar on it. Reindeer's antlers over
the door. A flock of goats is grazing by the wall of the hut.*
SOLVEIG, *now a middle-aged woman, but still fair-haired
and beautiful, is sitting outside in the sunshine, spinning.*

SOLVEIG *(looks down the path and sings):* Winter may pass,
    and spring,
  And summer too, and the whole long year.
  But some time I know that you will come,
  And I shall wait, as I promised I would
  [When I saw you last, my dear.]
  *Calls the goats, then turns back to her spinning and
  singing.*
  God give you strength, wherever you may be.
  God give you joy, if you stand before His footstool.
  I shall wait here till you come back to me.
  Looks upwards.
  And if it's there you're waiting, we shall meet there, my
    friend.

129

Scene Eleven

In Egypt. Dawn. The statue of Memnon[21] stands in the sand.
PEER GYNT *enters on foot and glances briefly around.*

PEER: The statue of Memnon.
  This would be a good place to start my travels.
  Now I'll become an Egyptian for a change.
  [But firmly based upon the Gyntian self.
  Afterwards I'll move on to Assyria.]
  I don't need to begin at Genesis.
  I'll go round all that Biblical stuff.
  [I'll probably come across the odd relic of it,
  But to investigate its seams, as the saying goes,]
  That's outside my plan. [It would overtax my strength.]
  Sits on a stone.
  Now I shall rest and wait patiently
  Till the Statue has sung its usual morning song.
  After breakfast I'll climb up the Pyramid,
  And glance inside it, if I have time.
  Then I'll journey by land round the Red Sea.
  I might find King Potiphar's grave.
  Then I'll turn Asiatic! In Babylon
  I'll look for the Hanging Gardens and the Concubines—
  Hm—I mean the chief traces of ancient culture.
  Then straight on to the walls of Troy.
  From Troy I can voyage directly by sea
  To great old Athens. [And there, on the very spot,
  I'll look at the pass Leonidas defended.
  I'll acquaint myself with the better philosophers,
  And find the prison where Socrates sacrificed
  His life. Oh, no, I forgot—there's a war on there.
  Well, my Hellenic phase will have to wait.]
  Looks at his watch.
  It's too bad, how long one has to sit around

130

Before the sun rises. My time is short.
Well, after Troy—that was where I'd got to—
Gets up and listens.
What's that curious whispering sound?

Sunrise.

MEMNON STATUE *(sings):* When I died, my mother
Begged Zeus to make me immortal.
Now from my ashes there rise, youth-renewing,
Birds ever singing.
Zeus the All-Knowing
Shaped them for battle everlasting.
O Owl of Wisdom, when will they find sleep?
You must solve the riddle of my song or die.
PEER: How strange! I really thought a sound
Came from the Statue. The music of the past!
I heard a voice like stone rising and falling.
I must note that.
Writes in his notebook.
'The Statue sang. I heard the sound clearly,
But did not quite understand the words.
The whole thing was of course a hallucination.
Saw nothing else of interest today.'

He goes on

Scene Twelve

Near the village of Gizeh. The Great Sphinx carved out of the rock. In the distance can be glimpsed the spires and minarets of Cairo. PEER GYNT *enters and studies the Sphinx closely, now through his lorgnette, now through his hollowed hand.*

PEER: The Great Sphinx of Gizeh. Now where in the world
Have I met before something like this monster?

131

Something I've half forgotten. [I've met it
Somewhere.] Was it a man? And if so, who?
That statue, Memnon, it struck me later,
Looked like [that character in the fairy books,
The one they call] the Old Man of the Mountains.
[Squatting up there, so stiff and still,
With a couple of columns supporting his rump.]
But this extraordinary mongrel,
This changeling, half woman and half lion,
Did I read about it in a story book too?
Or did I actually meet it somewhere?
[A story book?] Ah yes, now I remember.
[Of course!] It's the Boyg, that I hit on the head—
I mean, I dreamed I did. I was running a fever—
Goes closer.
The same eyes. And the selfsame lips.
Not quite so torpid. And a little more cunning.
But otherwise pretty much the same.
Hullo, old Boyg. So you look like a lion
When viewed from behind in the daylight.
Do you still talk riddles? We'll try.
Let's see if you answer the same as before.
Shouts at the Sphinx:
Hi, Boyg! Who are you?

A VOICE *(from behind the Sphinx): Ach, Sfinx, wer bist du?*

PEER: What was that? An echo in German? How strange!

VOICE: *Wer bist du?*

PEER: It speaks the language fluently.
This observation is new, and mine.
Writes in his notebook.
'Echo in German. Dialect: Berlin.'

BEGRIFFENFELDT *(emerges from behind the Sphinx):* A
man!

PEER: [Oh, it was him talking.] *(Writes again.)*
'Later came to another conclusion.'

BEGRIFFENFELDT *(making all kinds of restless gestures):*
>Excuse me, *mein Herr. Eine lebensfrage—*
>What makes you come here on this particular day?

PEER: I'm just visiting an old friend of my youth.

BEGRIFFENFELDT: What? The Sphinx—?

PEER *(nods):* Yes. I used to know him well when I was younger.

BEGRIFFENFELDT: *Wunderbar!* After such a night!
>My head is throbbing. It is ready to burst.
>You know him, man? Speak! Answer!
>Can you tell me who he is?

PEER: Who he is? That's easy enough. He is *himself.*

BEGRIFFENFELDT *(gives a jump):* Ha! In a flash, the answer
>to life's riddle!
>You are sure he is himself?

PEER: Yes. Well, he says so, anyway.

BEGRIFFENFELDT: Himself! Then the hour of revolution is at
>hand!
>*Takes off his hat.*
>Your name, *mein Herr?*

PEER: I was christened Peer Gynt.

BEGRIFFENFELDT *(in hushed admiration):* Peer Gynt! Allegorical! I might have expected it!
>Peer Gynt! That means The Unknown.
>The Messiah whose coming was revealed to me!

PEER: No, really? You've come here to meet—?

BEGRIFFENFELDT: Peer Gynt! What profundity! What mystery! What penetration!
>Each word is like the voice of infinity!
>What are you?

PEER *(modestly):* I have always tried to be myself.
>Here is my passport.

BEGRIFFENFELDT: That enigmatic word again!
>*(Seizes him by the wrist.)* To Cairo.
>The Emperor of Interpreters is found!

PEER: Emperor?
BEGRIFFENFELDT: Come!
PEER: People know of me—?
BEGRIFFENFELDT *(drags him away):* The Emperor of Interpreters! The Prophet of Self!

Scene Thirteen

In Cairo. A big courtyard surrounded by high walls and buildings. Barred windows. Iron cages. THREE WARDERS *in the courtyard. A* FOURTH WARDER *enters.*

FOURTH WARDER: Hi, Schafmann, where's the director?
ANOTHER WARDER: He went out this morning before daybreak.
FOURTH WARDER: I think something must have annoyed him.
    Last night he—
OTHER WARDER: Hush! There he is!

   BEGRIFFENFELDT *enters, leading* PEER GYNT. *He locks the gate and pockets the key.*

PEER *(to himself):* This is a very clever man.
    I can hardly understand a word he says.
    Looks round.
    So this is the Philosophers' Club you spoke of?
BEGRIFFENFELDT: Yes, here they are, every man of them.
    The Circle of the Seventy Interpreters;[22]
    Recently increased by a hundred and sixty.
    Shouts at the WARDERS:
    Mikkel, Schlingelberg, Schafmann, Fuchs!
    Get into your cages at once!
WARDERS: Us?
BEGRIFFENFELDT: Who else? Get in, get in!
    When the world turns over, we must do the same.
    Forces them into a cage.

He's arrived this morning—the mighty Peer!
You can guess the rest, I need say no more.
Locks the cage and throws the key into a well.

PEER: But, my dear Doctor—director—

BEGRIFFENFELDT: Neither. I used to be—! Herr Peer,
  Can you keep a secret? I must tell someone—

PEER *(increasingly uneasy):* What is it?

BEGRIFFENFELDT: Promise you won't get frightened?

PEER: I'll try—

BEGRIFFENFELDT *(drags him into a corner and whispers):*
    Absolute Reason passed away at eleven o'clock last
      night.

PEER: God help me—!

BEGRIFFENFELDT: Yes, it's a terrible tragedy.
  And especially unpleasant for me, in my position.
  Up to now, this institution
  Has been regarded as a madhouse.

PEER: A madhouse?

BEGRIFFENFELDT: Not now, you understand.

PEER *(pale, whispers):* Yes, I understand!
  This man is mad, and no one knows it.

  He edges away.

BEGRIFFENFELDT *(follows him):* I hope you don't misunder-
      stand me?
  When I say he is dead, that isn't strictly true.
  He's beside himself. Jumped out of his skin,
  [Just like my compatriot Munchausen's fox.][23]

PEER: Excuse me a minute—

BEGRIFFENFELDT *(holds him back):* [No, not like a fox.]
  Like an eel.
  A needle through his eye, and he was squiggling on the
      wall—

PEER: How am I going to get out—?

BEGRIFFENFELDT: A razor round his neck, and pip!—out of his skin!

PEER: He's mad! A raving lunatic!

BEGRIFFENFELDT: Now it's obvious that if Reason has jumped out of his skin,

That must mean a complete revolution all over the world.

Those persons who were formerly regarded as mad

Became sane at eleven o'clock last night

[In accordance with this new phase of Reason].

Moreover, if one considers logically,

It is clear that at the hour I mentioned

The so-called sane began to rave.

PEER: You mentioned the hour. My time is rather short—

BEGRIFFENFELDT: Your time? Of course! That reminds me.
Opens a door and shouts:

Come out, my children! The promised hour has come!

Reason is dead! Long live Peer Gynt!

PEER: Now, my dear fellow—

THE LUNATICS *wander out into the courtyard.*

BEGRIFFENFELDT: Good morning! Come out here and greet the dawn

Of liberation. Your Emperor is here!

PEER: Emperor?

BEGRIFFENFELDT: Of course.

PEER: But the honour is too great. Really too much—

BEGRIFFENFELDT: Oh, this is no time for false modesty.

PEER: But at least give me time! No, I'm not worthy—
I am stupefied—

BEGRIFFENFELDT: A man who has solved the riddle of the Sphinx?

A man who is himself!

PEER: That's just it. I *am* myself in everything.

But here, as far as I can make out,

The thing is to be beside oneself.

136

BEGRIFFENFELDT: Beside oneself? No, there you're quite
    mistaken.
    Here we are ourselves with a vengeance;
    Ourselves and nothing whatever but ourselves.
    [We go full steam through life under the pressure of
      self.]
    Each one shuts himself up in the cask of self,
    Sinks to the bottom by self-fermentation,
    Seals himself in with the bung of self,
    And seasons in the well of self.
    No one here weeps for the woes of others.
    No one here listens to anyone else's ideas.
    We are ourselves, in thought and in deed,
    Ourselves to the very limit of life's springboard.
    So, if we are to have an Emperor,
    It's obvious that you are just the man.
PEER: Oh, if only—!
BEGRIFFENFELDT: Don't be depressed. Everything seems
    new at first.
    'Oneself.' Come here, you shall see an example.
    We'll choose the first that comes.
    To a melancholy figure:
    Good morning, Huhu.[24] Well, my boy,
    Still wandering round so miserably?
HUHU: What else can I do when race after race
    Dies uninterpreted?
    To PEER:
    You're a stranger here. Will you listen to me?
PEER *(bows):* Certainly.
HUHU: Then lend me your ear.
    Far in the East, like garlands round a brow
    Lie the coasts of Malabar. [The Portuguese
    And Dutch have brought their culture to the land.]
    Many Malabaris still live there.

But foreigners have messed the language up.
And now they are masters of the land.
But long ago, the orang-utang ruled.
He was the forest's lord and master;
[He was free to fight and to snarl in freedom]
Grinning and gaping as Nature created him.
He could fight and shriek in perfect freedom.
[He was master in his own kingdom.]
But then, alas, the foreigners came
And stifled the original language of the jungle.
[For four whole centuries the simian race
Brooded in darkness. And, as is well known,
Such long nights leave their mark upon a people.]
Now the voice of the jungle is silenced.
Grunts and growls are heard no more.
Now we can only express our thoughts
Through the medium of speech. How intolerably
    cramping!
[Dutchmen and Portuguese, half-castes and Malabaris
Suffer equally.] I have fought to restore
Our native tongue, the primal speech of the jungle,
Tried to resuscitate its corpse;
Fought for our right to shriek and snarl;
Have shrieked and snarled myself; [and proved the need
For shrieks and snarls if our folk literature
Is to survive] but my work has not been appreciated.
Now perhaps you understand my sorrow.
Thank you for lending me your ear.
If you have advice, let me hear it.
PEER *(to himself):* 'When surrounded by wolves it is best to
    howl.'
    (Aloud.) My friend, I seem to remember that in Mo-
    rocco
There live orang-utangs with no interpreter
[Or poet to speak for them]. Their language sounds

138

Like Malabari. Why don't you, like many great men,
Emigrate to serve your race?

HUHU: Thank you for your kind attention.
I will follow your advice.
Waves an arm impressively.
East, thou hast disowned thy singer.
Apes shall flourish in the West.

Goes.

BEGRIFFENFELDT: Well, wasn't he himself? I should have
       thought so.
[He's full of his ego; he has no room for anything else.
He is himself in everything he says
And does. Himself, because he is beside himself.]
Come here! Now I'll show you another one
Who since last night has been equally reasonable.
To a FELLAH[25] *bearing a mummy on his back:*
King Apis! How goes it, mighty Lord?

FELLAH *(wildly, to* PEER*): Am* I King Apis?

PEER *(edges behind* BEGRIFFENFELDT*):* I must admit I'm
      afraid I'm not fully acquainted
With the situation. But, to judge from your tone,
I should imagine—

FELLAH: Now you're lying, too.

BEGRIFFENFELDT: Your Majesty must explain to this gentle-
      man.

FELLAH: Yes. I'll tell him my story.
Turns to PEER GYNT.

You see this man upon my back?
King Apis was his name.
But now he's just a mummy.
He's dead, for all his fame.

He sculpted the Great Sphinx, and built
The mighty Pyramid;

139

He fought the Roman and the Turk,
And brought them low, he did.

And therefore the Egyptians
Worshipped him as divine,
And fed with sacrifices
The Bull God in his shrine.

But I am this King Apis.
It is clear as noon.
If you don't understand me now,
You'll understand me soon.

King Apis while out hunting
Was taken short, poor man,
So squatted for a minute
On my ancestor's land.

Now the earth King Apis fertilized
Nourished *me* with its corn.
And if further proof were needed,
I have invisible horns.

So isn't it a scandal
That no one calls me King?
Though I was born an Apis,
I'm just a paltry thing.

Oh sir, can't you advise me?
Help me resolve my fate;
And make these damned fools realize
I *am* King Apis the Great!

PEER: Your Majesty must build a larger Sphinx
And better Pyramids.

FELLAH: Well, that's a fine suggestion!
A fellah! A starving louse!
I haven't got the strength to keep
The rats out of my house.

Quick, think of something better.
Now tell me what I lack.
What is it that will make me like
King Apis on my back?

PEER: How if Your Majesty hanged yourself?
Wound in a shroud so grim,
And hidden in the earth's dark womb,
You'd start to look like him.

FELLAH: I'll do it! Where's a rope?
The gallows'll settle the doubt.
We won't look quite alike at first,
But time will smooth that out.

Goes off and prepares to hang himself.

BEGRIFFENFELDT: Well, there's a real personality for you!
A man of method—

PEER: Yes, yes, I see.
But he's really hanged himself! My God!
I'm feeling dizzy! I'm going out of my mind—!

BEGRIFFENFELDT: A transitional state. It'll soon pass.

PEER: Transitional? To what?
Excuse me, I must be going—

BEGRIFFENFELDT *(holds him)*: Are you mad?

PEER: Not yet. Mad? God forbid!

A commotion. HUSSEIN, *a cabinet minister, forces his way through the crowd.*

HUSSEIN: They tell me an Emperor has arrived today.
To PEER:
Is it you?

PEER *(desperately)*: Apparently.

HUSSEIN: Good! Then you must have notes to be answered?

PEER *(tears his hair)*: All right! Why not? The madder the
better!

141

HUSSEIN: Will you do me the honour of dipping me?

Bows low.

I am a pen.

PEER *(bows even lower):* And I am a piece of scrawled imperial parchment.

HUSSEIN: My story, Your Majesty, is briefly this.

People think I'm blotting paper. But I'm not. I'm a pen.

PEER: My story, Imperial Pen, is equally brief.

I'm a blank sheet of paper that no one will write on.

HUSSEIN: Nobody understands where my talent lies.

They all want to use me to soak up ink.

PEER: I was a book with a silver clasp, that a girl

Held in her hands. Whether we're called mad or sane,

It is merely a printer's error.

HUSSEIN: Can you imagine a more frustrating life

Than to be a pen, and never taste the edge of a knife?

PEER *(jumps high in the air):* Imagine being a reindeer!

To jump down from a height!

Falling and falling, and never to feel the ground under your hoof.

HUSSEIN: A knife! I am blunt! Come, cut me, slit me!

The world will perish if someone doesn't sharpen me!

PEER: Alas for the world, which our Lord thought so good!

BEGRIFFENFELDT: Here is a knife.

HUSSEIN *(seizes it):* Ah, how I shall lick up the ink!

What relief to cut oneself to a point!

Cuts his throat.

BEGRIFFENFELDT *(moves to one side):* Don't splash me.

PEER *(in increasing horror):* Hold him!

HUSSEIN: Hold me! Yes, that's the word! Hold me! Hold the pen!

Put paper on the desk—!

Falls.

I'm worn out! My postscript—! Don't forget it!

He lived and he died a pen guided by other hands!

PEER *(becomes dizzy):* What shall I—? What am I? O Great
    One! Hold me safe!

I'm whatever you wish! I'm a Turk, a sinner,

A troll! Only help me! Something has burst!

Screams.

I can't remember Your name!

O help me, Thou, O Guardian of all madmen!

    Sinks unconscious to the ground.

BEGRIFFENFELDT *(with a crown of straw in his hand, jumps
    and sits astride him):* [Ha! See him sitting enthroned
    in the mire!

Beside himself!] Crown him now!

Forces the crown on to his head and cries:

Hail, Emperor! Hail Emperor of Self!

[SCHAFMANN *(from his cage): Es lebe hoch der grosse
    Peer!*]

ACT FIVE

Scene One

On board a ship in the North Sea, off the Norwegian coast. Sunset. Stormy weather. PEER GYNT, *a vigorous old man with grizzled hair and beard, is standing aft on the poop. He is dressed partly in sailor's clothes, with a seaman's jacket and long boots. His clothes are somewhat worn, and bear the marks of hard use. He himself is weather-beaten, and his face has grown harder.*

The CAPTAIN *of the ship is at the wheel beside the* STEERSMAN. *The crew are forward.*

PEER *(leans his arms on the gunwale and gazes landward):*
There's Hallingskarv in his winter fur;
An old man pluming himself in the evening sun.
Jœkel, his brother, stands behind him,
Hooded still in his ice-green cloak.
Folgefaan lies so delicate,
Like a virgin in her white linen.
It's no use trying to turn your heads.
You'll never touch her, you old men of stone.
CAPTAIN *(shouts forward):* Another hand to the wheel, and
hoist the lantern!

144

PEER: She's blowing up hard.

CAPTAIN: We'll have a storm tonight.

PEER: Can you see the Ronde from the sea?

CAPTAIN: No, of course not. It's hidden behind the snow-
field.

PEER: And Blaahœ?

CAPTAIN: No. But in clear weather
If you go aloft you can see Galdhœpiggen.

PEER: Where is Haarteig?

CAPTAIN *(points):* Over there.

PEER: Yes, of course.

CAPTAIN: You seem to know these parts.

PEER: When I sailed from Norway, I passed this way.
The dregs of memory stay in the glass.
Spits and gazes towards the coast.
[Up there, where the clefts and scars are blue,
And the mountain valley is black and narrow
Like a ditch; and below, along the open fjords,
The people live.
Looks at the CAPTAIN.

                      In this country
They build their houses far apart.

CAPTAIN: Yes, they're pretty scattered.]

PEER: Will we be in by daybreak?

CAPTAIN: Just about. If the night's not too bad.

PEER: It's thickening in the west.

CAPTAIN: It is.

PEER: Remind me when I settle with you,
I'd like to give something to the crew.

[CAPTAIN: Thank you.

PEER: It won't be much. I made a bit
Over there, but I lost most of it.
Fate and I haven't quite hit it off.
You know what I've got on board.
Well, that's the lot. The rest—psst!

145

CAPTAIN: It's enough to make you a big man here.

PEER: I've no family.

There's no one awaiting this rich old bastard.

Well, at least I won't have to put up with any fuss on the quayside.

CAPTAIN: Here comes the storm.

PEER: Well, remember,

If any of your men are really short—

I'm not a man who looks closely at my money.]

CAPTAIN: That's generous of you. They're mostly poor men.

They've all got wives and youngsters at home.

[And their wages don't stretch far.]

If they get a little extra, they'll not forget it.

PEER: What? Wives and children? Are they married?

CAPTAIN: Married? Yes, every man. [The cook's the poorest.

There's always black hunger in his house.]

PEER: Married? Someone waiting to give them a good welcome?

CAPTAIN: Yes, as good as poor people can give.

PEER: When they come home, what'll happen?

CAPTAIN: Their wives'll give them a little extra something

For once—

PEER: A candle on the table?

CAPTAIN: Maybe two. And a dram—

PEER: And they sit there snugly round the hearth

With their children around them? All talking at once,

[No one lets anyone finish a sentence]

They're so happy—?

CAPTAIN: That's about it. So they'll bless you for your promise—

PEER (bangs the gunwale with his fist): I'll be damned if I will! Do you think I'm mad?

Why should I pay for other men's children?

I've had to work hard to earn my money.

146

There's no one waiting for old Peer Gynt.
CAPTAIN: Well, well, do as you please. It's your money.
PEER: Yes! It's mine!
Give me my bill when we cast anchor.
My fare as cabin passenger from Panama,
And a tot of rum for the crew. That's all.
[If I give any more you can knock me down the hatch-
way.
CAPTAIN: It's my job as Captain to give you a receipt,
Not a thrashing.] Excuse me. The storm's coming on.

*He goes forward. It has become dark. Lights are lit in
the cabin. The sea grows rougher. Thick mist and
heavy clouds.*

PEER: [To have a home full of children; to be their joy.
To be always in the forefront of their minds.
To be followed on one's way by the thoughts of
others—]
There's no one who ever thinks of me.
Candles on the table! I'll put out those candles!
[I'll find some way!] I'll make them all drunk!
Not one of those fools shall go ashore sober.
They'll come home drunk to their wives and children.
They'll swear, and knock them about—all their love de-
stroyed!
[They'll frighten their loved ones out of their wits.
Their wives'll scream and run from the house,
Dragging their children with them. That will be
A joyful homecoming!]
*The ship heels violently. He staggers and has difficulty
in keeping his balance.*
That was a lurch!
The sea's still itself up here in the North!
[The old devil's working as though he'd been paid for
it.

147

It's always the same up in these Northern waters.
They're sullen and churlish. Always trying to thwart
    you.]
THE WATCH *(forward):* Wreck to windward!
CAPTAIN *(amidships):* Helm hard to starboard! Keep her
    close to the wind!
STEERSMAN: Anyone on the wreck?
WATCH *(screams):* I can see three!
PEER: Quick! Lower a boat!
CAPTAIN: She'd fill before we cast off. *(Goes forward.)*
PEER: Who cares about that?
    To some of the CREW:
                If you're men, save them!
    You're not afraid of getting wet, are you?
BOATSWAIN: It's impossible in a sea like this.
PEER: They're screaming again. Look, there's a lull!
    You, cook! Will you try? I'll give you money!
COOK: Not if you gave me twenty pounds.
PEER: You dogs! You cowards! Don't you realize
    These men have wives and children at home?
    They are sitting, waiting for them—!
BOATSWAIN: Well, there's virtue in patience.
CAPTAIN: Bring her about!
STEERSMAN: The wreck's turned over.
PEER: How silent it is, suddenly!
BOATSWAIN: If they were married
    This world's the richer by three new widows.

    The storm grows. PEER GYNT *goes aft.*

PEER: There's no faith left among men any more.
    [Christianity's only preached and written;
    There's little charity and less prayer.]
    They've no respect for the powers above.
    On a night like this our Lord is dangerous.
    [These brutes should take care and remember

That it's dangerous to play with elephants.
They simply thumb their noses at Him.]
I'm guiltless. [On the Day of Judgement] I can swear
I stood ready and willing [with money in my hand].
But what good is that? [They say
An easy conscience makes the softest pillow.
That may be so on dry land, but at sea,
Where an honest man's like a fish out of water,
It's not the same.] A man can never be
Himself at sea. He must sink or swim with the rest.
If vengeance should strike the boatswain or the cook
I'll be sucked down to my death with the rest of them.
[One's individual virtues are ignored.
You're just a bit of meat for the sausage machine.]
My mistake is this. I've been too meek,
And I've had no thanks for it. If I were younger,
I'd change my style [and start acting the boss].
Well, there's still time. They shall learn in the parish
Peer Gynt has come riding back over the sea!
I'll get back our farm by hook or by crook.
I'll rebuild it. It shall shine like a palace.
But they won't be allowed to enter the door.
They shall stand at the gate and twiddle their caps;
They shall beg and grovel—that they can do—
But not one shall get a farthing out of me.
[I've had to cringe under the whip of Fate,
And they'll find that I, too, can wield the lash.]

THE STRANGE PASSENGER *(stands in the darkness at* PEER's
    side and greets him amicably): Good evening.

PEER: Good evening. What—? Who are you?

STRANGE PASSENGER: Your fellow passenger.

PEER: I thought I was the only one.

STRANGE PASSENGER: A mistaken impression, now cor-
    rected.

PEER: But it's strange I should see you for the first time tonight.

STRANGE PASSENGER: I never appear in the daytime.

PEER: [Are you ill? You're as white as a sheet—

STRANGE PASSENGER: Thank you, no. I am in excellent
   health.]

PEER: What a storm!

STRANGE PASSENGER: Yes! Beautiful!

PEER: Beautiful?

STRANGE PASSENGER: The waves are running as high as
   houses.

   It makes my mouth water. Think of the wrecks

   There will be tonight. Think of the corpses drifting
   ashore.

PEER: God preserve us!

STRANGE PASSENGER: Have you ever seen a man strangled?

   Or hanged—or drowned?

PEER: What—!

STRANGE PASSENGER: They laugh; but their laughter is
   forced.

   Most of them bite out their tongues.

PEER: Get away from me!

STRANGE PASSENGER: Just one question. Suppose we, for
   example,

   Should strike on a rock, and sink in the darkness—

PEER: You think there is a danger—?

STRANGE PASSENGER: I don't really know what I ought to
   say.

   But suppose, now, I should float and you should sink—

PEER: Oh, rubbish—!

STRANGE PASSENGER: It's just a hypothesis.

   But when a man stands with one foot in the grave

   He sometimes tends to be generous—

PEER (puts his hand in his pocket): Oh, money—

STRANGE PASSENGER: No, no. But if you would be so kind
    As to bequeath me your valuable body—
PEER: What!
STRANGE PASSENGER: Only your corpse, you understand.
    To help my researches—
PEER: Go away!
STRANGE PASSENGER: But, my dear sir, consider. It's to your
        advantage.
    I'll open you up and let in the light.
    I want to discover the source of your dreams.
    I want to find out how you're put together—
PEER: Away!
STRANGE PASSENGER: But, my dear sir! A drowned body—!
PEER: Blasphemous man!
    You're provoking the storm! Are you out of your mind?
    Look at the sea! [These waves are like mountains!]
    At any moment we may be killed.
    [And you're acting as though you can hardly wait for it.]
STRANGE PASSENGER: I see you're not in a mood for discus-
        sion.
    But time, they say, changes everything.
    Nods amicably.
    We'll meet when you're sinking, if not before.
    Perhaps you'll be more in the humour then.

    Goes into cabin.

PEER: Horrible fellows these scientists are!
    You damned freethinker!
    To the BOATSWAIN, *who is passing:*
            A word with you, friend.
    That passenger. What kind of a madman's he?
BOATSWAIN: I know of no passenger except yourself.
PEER: No passenger—? [This gets worse and worse.]
    To the CABIN BOY, *who has just come out of the cabin:*
    Who went into the cabin just now?

CABIN BOY: The ship's dog, sir. *(Goes past him.)*
WATCH *(shouts):* Land close ahead!
PEER: My trunk! My strong-box! Get my things on deck!
BOATSWAIN: We've more important things to do.
PEER: Captain—what I said just now—
    I was only joking. I'll help the cook—
CAPTAIN: The jib's blown away!
STEERSMAN: The foresail's gone!
BOATSWAIN *(shouts from forward):* Rocks under the bow!
CAPTAIN: She'll go to pieces!

The ship strikes. Alarm and confusion.

Scene Two

*Close off shore, among rocks and surf. The ship is sinking.
Through the mist can be glimpsed the dinghy, with two men
in it. A sea strikes it. It heels over, there is a scream, then
for a few moments all is silent. Soon afterwards the boat
comes to the surface bottom upwards.* PEER GYNT's *head appears close to it.*

PEER: Help! Help! A boat! Help! I'm drowning!
    O Lord, save me! [That's what the Bible says—!]
COOK *(comes up on the other side of the boat):* O Lord God!
      [For my children's sake!] Have mercy!
    Let me reach the land! *(Seizes hold of the keel.)*
PEER: Let go!
COOK: Let go!
PEER: I'll hit you!
COOK: I'll hit you!
PEER: [I'll break your bones!] I'll kick you down!
    [I'll hit you!] Let go! This boat won't take two!
COOK: No! Get off!
PEER: You get off!
COOK: No, no!

They fight. One of the COOK'*s hands is disabled, but he clings on with the other.*

PEER: Off with that hand!

COOK: Spare me, sir! Think of my children at home!

PEER: I need my life more than you. I am still childless.

COOK: Let go! You've lived. I'm young.

PEER: Get on with it! Sink! You're dragging me down!

COOK: Have pity! For God's sake! No one will mourn for you—!

His hand slips. He screams.

I'm drowning!

PEER *(grips him by the hair)*: I'll hold you by the hair. Say your prayers quickly.

COOK: I can't remember—everything's going dark—!

PEER: [Say whatever's most important.] Come on!

COOK: 'Give us this day—'

PEER: [Never mind that, cook. You'll get all you need.

COOK: 'Give us this day—']

PEER: The same old song! It's clear what you were!

The COOK *slips from his grasp.*

COOK *(sinking)*: 'Give us this day our—' *(Disappears.)*

PEER: Amen. You were yourself, to the very end.

Ah, well.

Draws himself up on to the keel.

While there's life there's hope.

STRANGE PASSENGER *(catches hold of the boat)*: Good morning.

PEER: Ugh!

STRANGE PASSENGER: I heard shouting. How nice to find you.

Well, did I prophesy correctly?

PEER: Let go! Let go! It'll barely hold one!

STRANGE PASSENGER: I'm swimming with my left leg.

I'll stay afloat
If I can just hold on with my fingers
[To this little splinter]. Now about that corpse of yours—
PEER: Shut up!
STRANGE PASSENGER: It's all you have left.
PEER: Be quiet!
STRANGE PASSENGER: Just as you please.

Silence.

PEER: What are you doing?
STRANGE PASSENGER: [I'm being quiet.
PEER: Damn your tricks! What are you up to?]
STRANGE PASSENGER: Waiting.
PEER *(tears his hair):* I'm going mad. Who are you?
STRANGE PASSENGER *(nods):* A friend.
PEER: What else? Tell me!
STRANGE PASSENGER: What do you think? Do you know no
    one else like me?
PEER: The Devil—?
STRANGE PASSENGER *(softly):* Is it his way to light the lantern
    On life's long pilgrimage of fear?
PEER: Ah! So you are a messenger of light?
STRANGE PASSENGER: My friend, have you even once a year
    Known the true anguish of the soul?
PEER: Of course one's afraid, when danger threatens—
    [But everything you say has another meaning.]
STRANGE PASSENGER: Yes, but have you once in life
    Won the victory that only defeat can bring?
PEER *(looks at him):* If you have come to open a door
    It was stupid not to come before.
    What's the good of coming now
    [When the sea's about to swallow me up]?
STRANGE PASSENGER: Would you have found that victory
    In the [warmth and] comfort of your hearthside?
PEER: Perhaps not. But I thought you were joking.

[How could you think it would open my eyes?]
STRANGE PASSENGER: Where I come from, laughter is rated
    as high as tears.
[PEER: There's a time for everything. As the proverb says:
    'The publican's meat is the bishop's poison.'
STRANGE PASSENGER: Those whose dust sleeps in funeral
    urns would tell you:
    'The tragic mask is not for everyday wear.']
PEER: Get away! [You frighten me!] Leave me! [Go!]
    I must get ashore! I will not die!
STRANGE PASSENGER: Oh, don't worry.
    You won't die in the middle of the last act.

Glides away.

PEER: [Well, at least I'm that much wiser.
    God, what a boring moralizer!]

Scene Three

*A churchyard high up in the mountains. A funeral is in prog-
ress. A* PRIEST *and* VILLAGERS. *The last verse of a psalm is
being sung.*

PEER GYNT *comes past on the road outside.*

PEER *(at the gate):* Here's one of my countrymen gone the
    way of all flesh.
    Thank God it's not me.
PRIEST *(speaks at the graveside):* Now, as his soul moves
    blindly towards its judgement
And his poor dust rests here, an empty husk,
Now, my dear friends, let me remind you
About this dead man's pilgrimage on earth.
    He was not wealthy, neither was he clever;
His bearing was unmanly, his voice was weak,
Uncertain in expressing an opinion.

[He scarce seemed master even in his home.
He slunk into church as though he sought to beg
Permission to take his place with all the rest.
  He came, as you all know, from Gudsbrandsdal,
And moved here when he was no more than a boy.]
And, you remember, till the day he died,
He always kept his right hand in his pocket.
  [That right hand in his pocket was the thing
That stamped his image sharply on our minds;
And this strange shyness, this embarrassment.
Where'er he went, he seemed to dread being seen.]
But though he chose to tread his path alone,
And lived and died a stranger in our midst,
Yet you all know, although he sought to hide it,
That hand we never saw bore but three fingers.
  I well recall one morning, years ago;
Recruiting officers had come to Lunde.
It was in time of war. [All mouths discussed
Our country's sufferings, and its likely fate.
I stood and watched. An old grey-headed Captain
Sat with the sergeants and the Burgomaster
Behind a table.] Lad after lad was measured,
Given his shilling, and sworn in as a soldier.
The room was full, and in the yard outside
The winter air was filled with young men's laughter.
Then a name was called, and a new lad stepped in,
Pale as the snow that fringes a green glacier.
They called him closer. He faltered towards the table,
His right hand swathed in a bloodstained cloth.
He gasped and swallowed, trying to find words;
[But none would come, despite the Captain's questions]
Until at length, his thin young cheeks aflame,
[Now failing to find words, now gabbling fast]
He told some tale of an accident; a sickle had slipped
And cut off one of his fingers close to the stump.

A silence filled the room.
Men looked at one another, and curled their lips,
Stoning his face with their dumb glances.
He felt their scorn although he did not see it.
Then the Captain, an old grey man, slowly rose.
He spat, pointed towards the door, and said: 'Go!'
   And as he walked, men shrank on either side,
So that he ran the gauntlet through their midst.
He reached the door, and then took to his heels
Through woods, up hills and the high tumbling screes,
Slipping and staggering.
His home lay far away among the mountains.
   Some six months later he came to live among us
[With his mother, his betrothed and a new-born child].
He leased a patch of land up in the hills
Where the waste ground slopes upwards towards Lomb.
He married, built his house, broke the hard ground.
Success attended him, as many a proud
Acre bore witness, waving tall and gold.
[In church he kept his right hand in his pocket,
But in his home I warrant those seven fingers
Toiled fully as hard as any other man's eight.]
Then the spring floods swept everything away.
   [They saved nothing except their lives.] Naked
And poor, he cleared another patch of land.
Before the autumn came, fresh wood-smoke rose
From a homestead newly built in safer lee.
[Safer? From floods, but not from avalanche.]
Two years later it lay, crushed by the snow.
   But even the avalanche could not break his spirit.
He dug, raked, carted, cleared the strangled earth.
And, ere the next winter's snows had come,
For the third time his humble home arose.
   [Three sons he had, strong and intelligent lads.
They had to go to school, but it lay far off.

157

They had to go where the mountain path could not,
Across the scar, narrow and steepling.
What did he do? The eldest had to manage
Alone, as best he might; where the slope was steepest
His father roped him to himself, and hauled him,
Bearing the second in his arms, the youngest
Upon his back. So, year by year, he toiled.
His sons grew, flourished, and in time became men.
Now he might surely look for some reward.
But three rich gentlemen in the New World
Have forgotten their father in Norway, and the slow
    journeys to school]
  His vision was narrow. Beyond the tiny circle
Of those who stood close to him, he saw nothing.
Those words that should have resounded in his heart
To him rang meaningless like tinkling cymbals.
[His race, his country, all we think great and glorious,
Were from his eyes veiled in perpetual mist.]
  But he was humble, humble was this man.
And from the day when the Captain rose, and spat,
And pointed, he carried his judgement on his brow,
[As surely as the brand of shame on his cheek]
And his three fingers hidden in his pocket.
A criminal in the eyes of the law? Perhaps.
But there is something that shines above the law
As surely as the highest mountain peak
Has clouds above it like yet loftier mountains.
This was no patriot. For Church and State
He was a barren tree. But on his mountainside,
In the narrow circle of home, where his work lay,
There he was great, because he was himself.
The metal of which God made him rang most true
Until the end. His life was as a lute
Whose strings are muted. Peace to thee, silent warrior,
Who strove and fell in thy small humble war.

It is not for us to search the heart and reins.
That is no task for dust, but for its Maker.
But freely I hope and firmly I believe
This man is not a cripple in the eyes of God.

The MOURNERS *disperse.* PEER GYNT *remains alone.*

PEER: [Now that's what I call Christianity.
There was nothing there that could distress anyone.
And the theme of the parson's sermon, that one must be
Inflexibly oneself, is edifying.]
Looks down into the grave.
Could this have been the lad who chopped off his finger
When I was felling wood that day in the forest?
Who knows? If I weren't standing here with my staff
By the graveside of this spiritual kinsman,
I could well believe it was I who lay here sleeping
And hearing, as in a vision, myself so praised.
[That's really a beautiful Christian custom
Charitably to reminisce
Over the life of the dear departed.]
I shouldn't mind accepting my judgement
At the hands of this good parish priest.
[Ah well, I've a few years yet before
The gravedigger comes and offers me lodging.
And as the Scripture says: 'What's best is best,'
And: 'Sufficient unto the day is the evil thereof.'
And: 'Don't cross your bridges before you come to them.'
Yes, the Church is the only true comforter.
I haven't fully appreciated it before.
But now I realize how good it is
To be assured by the voice of authority
'As a man sows, so shall he reap.'
One must be oneself and look after oneself
And one's own, in all things, whether great or small.
If your luck runs out, at least you've the honour

Of having lived your life in accordance with
The best principles.] Now home! Let the path
Be steep and narrow. Let Fate be spiteful to the end.
Yet old Peer Gynt will still go his own way
And remain, as always, poor but virtuous.

Goes.

Scene Four

*A hill with a dried river bed. A ruined mill stands on the
river bank. The ground is torn up, and has a waste appearance. Higher up is a large farmhouse, where an auction is
taking place. A large crowd is gathered there. There is
drinking and much noise.* PEER GYNT *is sitting on a heap of
rubbish near the mill.*

PEER: Forward or back, it's equally far.
    Outside or in, I'm still confined.
    [Time wears on and so does the river.]
    Go round, said the Boyg. I must do that here.
MAN IN MOURNING: There's only rubbish left now.
    Catches sight of PEER GYNT.
    Have we strangers, too? God save you, friend.
PEER: [Good day to you.] You're having a gay time.
    What is it, a christening or a wedding?
MAN IN MOURNING: More rightly a housewarming.
    The bride's at home to a host of worms.
PEER: And worms are fighting for what she's left.
MAN IN MOURNING: The song is over; the story's done.
PEER: Every story has the same ending,
    And every song is an old song.
    [I knew them all when I was a boy.]
A YOUTH OF TWENTY *(with a casting ladle):* Look at what
    I've bought!

160

This is the ladle Peer Gynt used
To cast his silver buttons in!
ANOTHER YOUTH: I've done better than that!
  Look! I've bought Peer Gynt's purse for a shilling!
[A THIRD: Is that all?
  Only half a dollar for the pedlar's moneybags?]
PEER GYNT: Peer Gynt? Who was he?
MAN IN MOURNING: Cuckold to Death and to Aslak the
    smith.[26]
A MAN IN GREY: You're forgetting me! Are you drunk?
MAN IN MOURNING: You're forgetting the storehouse door at
    Heggstad.
[MAN IN GREY: That's true. But you never used to be so
    particular—]
MAN IN MOURNING: As long as she doesn't put horns on
  . Death—
MAN IN GREY: Come, cousin. A dram for kinship's sake.
MAN IN MOURNING: What the hell do you mean, kinship?
    [You're drunk—]
MAN IN GREY: [Oh, nonsense. Be blood ever so thin,]
    Everyone feels he's akin to Peer Gynt.

  Wanders off with him.

PEER *(softly):* One meets old friends.
A BOY *(shouts after the* MAN IN MOURNING*):* Watch out,
    Aslak! If you get drunk
  My mother will rise from her grave and haunt you!
PEER *(gets to his feet):* They say: 'The deeper you dig, the
    better it smells.'
  Not so here.
[A LAD *(with a bearskin):* Look, the Cat of the Dovre![27]
  Or anyway his skin!
  It was he chased the trolls on Christmas Eve!]
ANOTHER LAD *(with a reindeer's antlers):* Here's the buck
    that carried Peer Gynt
  Along the crest of the Gjendin Edge!

A THIRD *(with a hammer, shouts to the* MAN IN MOURNING*)*:
>Hi, Aslak, do you recognize this hammer?
>Was it this you used when the Devil split your walls?

A FOURTH *(his hands empty)*: Mads Moen, here's the invisible cloak!
>The one Peer Gynt wore when he flew off with Ingrid!

PEER: Give me a drink, lads. I'm feeling old.
>I think I'll put up my own rubbish for auction.[28]

A LAD: What have you got?

PEER: A palace!
>It lies in the Ronde. It's got strong walls.

THE LAD: I'll bid you a button.

PEER: I'll take a dram.
>It'd be a sin to offer me less.

ANOTHER LAD: He's a funny old boy!

People gather round him.

PEER *(shouts)*: My charger, Grane! Who'll make me a bid?

ONE OF THE CROWD: Where is he?

PEER: Far away in the west!
>Towards the sunset, lads! That horse can fly
>As fast, as fast as Peer Gynt can lie!

VOICES: What else have you got?

PEER: I've gold and I've scrap.
>I bought them with ruin. I'll sell at a loss.

A LAD: Put them up!

PEER: A dream of a book with a silver clasp.
>You can have that for a placket.

THE LAD: Who wants dreams?

PEER: My Empire!
>I'll throw it among you. You can fight for it.

THE LAD: Do we get a crown too?

PEER: Of the finest straw.
>It'll fit the first man who puts it on.
>Wait a moment, here's more. A rotten egg.

A madman's grey hairs. The Prophet's beard.
I'll give them all to the one who can show me
The signpost that says: 'Here lies the way.'

PARISH OFFICER *(enters):* Look, if you go on like this you'll
      get arrested.

PEER *(hat in hand):* Maybe. But, tell me, who was Peer
      Gynt?

PARISH OFFICER: What—?

PEER: Oh, please [Your Honour]! I beg you humbly—

PARISH OFFICER: Well, they say he was a damned liar—

PEER: A liar—?

PARISH OFFICER: Yes. All the great deeds he'd ever heard of,
      He pretended he'd done them. Well, excuse me,
      I've other business—

      Goes.

PEER: And where is he now, this remarkable man?

AN OLD MAN: He went away [to some foreign land]
      Across the sea. [Things went badly for him,
      As one might have foreseen.] He was hanged many
      years ago.

PEER: Hanged? Well, well! [I guessed as much].
      Poor old Peer Gynt! He remained himself
      To the very end.
      Bows.
      Goodbye [and thank you, kind sirs].
      Goes a few steps, and then stops.
      Well, my merry lads and lasses,
      Shall I repay your kindness with a story?

SEVERAL: Yes. Do you know any?

PEER: Why, yes. I do.
      *Goes closer to them. A strange expression comes over
      his face.*
      In San Francisco, once, I was digging for gold.
      The whole city was filled with mountebanks.

163

One could play the violin with his toes.
Another danced the bolero on his knees.
[A third, they say, wrote poetry
While someone bored a hole into his brain.]
One day the Devil came and joined the circus.
[He thought he'd try his luck like all the others.]
His trick was being able to grunt like a pig.
His personality impressed them all,
Though no one recognized him.
[The house was full, and anticipation ran high.]
He stepped on to the stage in a big flowing cloak.
[*Man muss sich drappieren,* as the Germans say.]
What they didn't know was that under the cloak
He'd hidden a real pig. [At length the performance
    started.]
The Devil pinched, and the pig let out a squeal.
[People accepted it as a fantasia
On our porcine existence, with its combination
Of liberty and bondage.] Then it gave
A screech as though its throat had been cut,
At which he bowed his thanks and went.
The experts discussed the performance and dissected it.
[Some praised it, some condemned.]
Some found the tone of the squeals too thin.
Others thought the death-shriek a trifle affected.
But on one point all were agreed. The actual grunting
Had been, throughout, decidedly exaggerated.
So the Devil got his due; a just reward
For over-estimating the intelligence of his audience.

He bows and goes. An uncertain silence falls on the
CROWD.

Scene Five

Whitsun Eve. Inside the forest. Behind, in a clearing, is a cabin, with reindeer antlers above the door. PEER GYNT *is crawling in the undergrowth gathering wild onions.*

PEER: Well, I've reached one resting-place. Where's the
    next?
    One must try them all, and choose the best.
    I've tried the lot. I started as Caesar.
    And I've come right down to Nebuchadnezzar.
    [I've gone back to the Bible after all;
    The old boy's had to crawl back to his mother.]
    Well, [the Scripture says: 'Of dust thou art made,'
    And] the first thing in life is to fill one's belly.
    Onions? That won't get me far.
    I'll have to be cunning and lay some snares.
    There's a river here, so I won't go thirsty.
    [The beasts'll still regard me as their boss.]
    When I have to die, as die I must,
    I'll creep under a tree blown down by the wind.
    I'll heap leaves all over me like a bear
    And I'll carve on the bark in big bold letters:
    'Here lies Peer Gynt. A decent chap,
    Emperor of all the beasts of the forest',
    Emperor? *(Chuckles.)* You old fake!
    You're no Emperor. You're just an onion.
    Now then, little Peer, I'm going to peel you,
    And you won't escape by weeping or praying.
    Takes an onion and peels it layer by layer.
    The outermost layer is withered and torn;
    That's the shipwrecked man on the upturned keel.
    Here, mean and thin, is the passenger;
    But it still tastes a little of old Peer Gynt.
    And inside that is the digger of gold;

Its juice is all gone, if it ever had any.
[Who's this coarse fellow with calloused skin?
Ah, he's the trapper from Hudson Bay.]
This next one's shaped like a crown. No, thank you!
We'll throw that away, and ask no questions.
Here's the student of history, short and tough;
And here is the Prophet, fresh and juicy;
[Like the man in the proverb] he stinks of lies
That would blind an honest man's eyes with tears.
This layer now that curls up so softly
Is the sybarite living for ease and pleasure.
The next one looks sick; it's streaked with black
That might mean a priest; or it might mean a nigger.
Peels off several at once.
What a terrible lot of layers there are!
Surely I'll soon get down to the heart?
Pulls the whole onion to pieces.
No—there isn't one! Just a series of shells
All the way through, getting smaller and smaller!
Nature is witty!
Throws the pieces away.
[I'm thinking too much. If you start going round
With your head in the clouds, you fall flat on your face.
Well, that's a danger I needn't worry about.
I'm safe on all fours.
Scratches his head.
Life is a fox. When you think you've got her
She slips through your grasp, and you're left holding
Something different, or nothing at all.]
He has come close to the cabin. He sees it and starts.
This hut? On the moor—!
Rubs his eyes.
I feel as though I'd seen it before.
Those antlers sprouting above the doorway—
[That mermaid, shaped like a fish from her navel—

166

It's a lie! There's no mermaid. Just nails and planks
To shut out nagging hobgoblin thoughts—]
SOLVEIG *(sings in the hut):* The house is ready for Pentecost.
My love is far away.
Come back, come back to me.
If your burden is heavy,
Take your time.
I will wait for you, my love.
PEER *(gets to his feet silently, pale as death):* One who
remembered—and one who forgot.
One who kept what the other has lost.
And the game can never be played again.
Oh, here was my Empire and my crown!

Runs down the forest path.

Scene Six

*Night. A moor, with pine trees. A forest fire has ravaged it.
Charred tree-trunks can be seen for miles around. Here and
there white mist patches hug the earth.* PEER GYNT *is running across the moor.*

PEER: [Ashes, mist, and dust and wind!
That's the stuff with which to build!
Our palace shall be proud and fair
As befits a sepulchre.

Foolish dreams and stillborn wisdom
Shall be our palace's foundation.
Out of them it shall tower high.
Every stone shall be a lie!

Let fear of truth and of repentance
Flame like fire upon the summit
Sounding forth the trump of doom:
Petrus Gyntus Caesar fecit!]

What is this sound of children weeping?
Weeping but halfway to song?
Threadballs are rolling at my feet—
Kicks them.
Get away! You're blocking my path!

THREADBALLS[29] *(on the ground):* We are thoughts.
You should have thought us.
You should have given us
Little feet.

PEER *(goes round them):* I gave birth to one.
It was a monster with a twisted leg.

THREADBALLS: We should have flown
Like children's voices.
Here we roll on the ground,
Grey balls of thread.

PEER *(stumbles):* Thread! Rubbish!
Would you trip your father? *(Flees.)*

WITHERED LEAVES *(flying before the wind):* We are a trumpet-call.
You should have sounded us.
See how your sloth
Has shrunk and withered us.
The worm has gnawed us
Through and through.
We never wound
Ourselves round fruit.

PEER: You weren't born in vain.
Lie still. You'll make good manure.

A WHISPERING IN THE AIR: We are songs.
You should have sung us.
A thousand times
You have stifled and strangled us.
In the mine of your heart
We have lain and waited.

We were never summoned.
Curse you! Curse you!
PEER: Curse you, fools!
Did I have time to make up verses?

Tries to take a short cut.

DEWDROPS *(dripping from the branches):* We are tears
You never wept.
We could have melted
The sharp ice-spears.
Now they fester
Deep in your breast.
The wound has closed.
Our power has gone.
PEER: Thanks. I wept in the Troll King's palace.
But I got a tail on me just the same.
BROKEN STRAWS: We are deeds
You left undone.
The strangler Doubt
Has broken and crippled us.
On the Day of Judgement
We shall be there
To tell our story.
Take care! Take care!
PEER: Dirty tricks!
Would you damn me for what I haven't done?

Hastens away.

AASE'S VOICE *(far away):* You're a fine driver!
Look where you've thrown me
Into a snowdrift!
I'm soaking and frozen.
You've come the wrong way!
Oh, Peer, where's the castle?
The Fiend's led you astray

[With the stick from the closet].
PEER: I think I'd better be running away.
　　If I have to carry the Devil's sins
　　Upon my shoulders, I shan't get far.
　　My own are heavy enough to bear.

　Runs off.

Scene Seven

Another part of the heath.

[PEER *(sings)*: A gravedigger! A gravedigger! Where are
　　you, dogs?
　　Open your mouths and let's hear you bray!
　　Let's see you girdle your hats with crêpe.
　　I've lots of corpses to bury today!]

　THE BUTTON MOULDER *enters from a side path with his
　box of tools and a large casting-ladle.*

BUTTON MOULDER: Well met, old man.
PEER: Good evening, friend.
BUTTON MOULDER: You're in a hurry. Where are you going?
PEER: To a funeral feast.
BUTTON MOULDER: Indeed? My eyes aren't too good, but—
　　forgive me—
　　Your name isn't by any chance Peer?
PEER: Peer Gynt, they call me.
BUTTON MOULDER: Well, that's lucky!
　　You're the man I have to collect tonight.
PEER: Have to collect—? What business have you with me?
BUTTON MOULDER: As you can see, I'm a button-moulder.
　　You must go into my casting-ladle.
PEER: What for?
BUTTON MOULDER: To be melted down.
PEER: Melted?

BUTTON MOULDER: Yes. Look! It's clean and empty.
　　Your grave is dug and your coffin is ready.
　　Tonight the worms will feast in your body.
　　But I have orders from my Master
　　To collect your soul without delay.
PEER: But you can't! Without warning—!
BUTTON MOULDER: It's an ancient custom at funerals.
　　As at christenings, one chooses the day,
　　And the guest of honour receives no warning.
PEER: Yes, of course. My brain's in a whirl.
　　Then you are—?
BUTTON MOULDER: I told you. A button-moulder.
PEER: Of course.
　　[One calls a favourite child by many names.]
　　I see. So this is the end of my journey.
　　But, my good man, this is most unfair.
　　[I deserve more considerate handling than this.
　　I'm not so bad as you seem to suppose.
　　I've done quite a few good deeds in my life.
　　At the worst I may possibly have been
　　A bit of a fool.] I've never been a real sinner.
BUTTON MOULDER: [But, my dear sir!] That is just the point.
　　[By the highest standards you aren't a sinner.
　　So] you escape the horrors of torment
　　And must go with others into the casting-ladle.
PEER: What does it matter what you call it,
　　Casting-ladle or pool of fire?
　　[They're the same vintage, just different bins.
　　Get behind me, Satan!
BUTTON MOULDER: You're not so rude
　　As to suggest that my feet are shaped like hoofs?
PEER: Whether you've hoofs or pads or claws]
　　Be off with you, and take care what you do!
BUTTON MOULDER: My friend, you're labouring under a de-
　　lusion.

171

[We're both in a hurry, so to save time
I'll explain the gist of the matter to you.]
As you have told me with your own lips,
You aren't what one could call a whole-hearted
Sinner. You're scarcely even a minor one—

PEER: That's better. [Now you're beginning to talk sensibly—]

BUTTON MOULDER: Wait a moment! You are not virtuous either—

PEER: I'm not claiming that—

BUTTON MOULDER: You're [halfway between;] neither one nor the other.
[Nowadays one hardly ever meets a sinner
On the really grand scale.
There's more to that than just scrabbling around in the mud.]
A man needs strength and purpose to be a sinner.

PEER: Yes, one has to be ruthless and think of nothing else.

BUTTON MOULDER: But you weren't like that. You took your sinning lightly.

PEER: I just splashed about on the surface.

BUTTON MOULDER: Ah, we shall soon agree. The pool of fire
Is not for those who splash about on the surface.

PEER: And therefore, my friend, I can go as I came?

BUTTON MOULDER: No. Therefore, my friend, I must melt you down.

[PEER: You've learned some new tricks while I've been abroad.

BUTTON MOULDER: The custom's as old as sin. It's merely designed
To prevent waste.] You've done it yourself.
You know that one occasionally moulds a button
That's useless. For example, without a loop.
What did you do in such a case?

PEER: Throw it away.

BUTTON MOULDER: Ah, yes. I had forgotten.
John Gynt was famous for his improvidence
[As long as he had anything in his purse].
But the Master, you see, is a thrifty man.
[That's why He's remained so prosperous.]
He never rejects as worthless anything
Which He can use again as raw material.
Now you were meant to be a shining button
On the waistcoat of the world. But your loop broke.
So you must be thrown [into the rubbish bin,
And go from there] back into the great pool.

PEER: You don't intend to melt me down with other dead men?

BUTTON MOULDER: That is precisely what I intend.
[We've done it, you know, with quite a number of people.
At the Royal Mint they do the same with coins
That have got so worn you can't see the face on them.

PEER: But this is the most sordid parsimony!
Oh, come on, be a sport and let me go!
A button without a loop, a worn-out shilling—
What are they to a man in your Master's position?

BUTTON MOULDER: Oh, as long as a man has some soul left
He's always worth a little as scrap.]

PEER: No! I'll fight with all the strength I have!
Anything but this!

BUTTON MOULDER: But what else is there? Be reasonable, now.
You're hardly qualified to go to Heaven—

PEER: [Oh, I'm not aiming as high as that.] I'm easy to please.
[But I'm not going to give up a jot of myself.]
Give me the old-fashioned punishment.
Send me down [for a while] to serve [a sentence]

With Him with the Hoof—for a hundred years,
If need be—that's something a man can bear,
For they say the suffering's only spiritual.
And I think that ought to be fairly tolerable.
[It'll only be a transitional stage,
As the fox said when they started to skin him.[30]]
One will wait; then the hour of liberation
Will come, and I'll start another life,
And hope things will turn out somewhat better.
But this other business—to end one's days
As a speck of dirt in a stranger's body,
To be melted, and to be Peer Gynt no more—
It fills my soul with revulsion.

BUTTON MOULDER: But, my dear Peer, there's really no
    need
To get so upset. You have never been yourself.
What does it matter if you disappear?

PEER: I have never been—? I could almost laugh!
Have I ever been anything but myself?
No, button moulder, you're guessing blindly.
If you could look into my heart
You'd find Peer Gynt and only him;
Nobody else, nothing less nor more.

BUTTON MOULDER: It's impossible. Here are my orders.
    Look,
It is written: 'Thou shalt claim Peer Gynt.
He has defied the Master's intention;
He is waste, and must go to the casting-ladle.'

PEER: [What nonsense!] He must mean somebody else.
Does it really say Peer? Not Rasmus or John?

BUTTON MOULDER: Oh, I melted them down long ago.
Now come along quietly, and don't waste my time.

PEER: No, I'm damned if I will! It'd be a fine thing
If it turned out tomorrow He meant someone else.

174

You'd better be careful, my good man.
[Consider the responsibility—]
BUTTON MOULDER: I have it in writing—
PEER: At least give me time!
BUTTON MOULDER: What good would that do?
PEER: I'll bring you proof
    That I've been myself the whole of my life.
    [And that's what we've been arguing about.]
BUTTON MOULDER: You'll prove it? How?
PEER: Witnesses and testimonials.
BUTTON MOULDER: I'm afraid the Master won't accept them.
PEER: [Oh, surely!] He must! [However:
    'Sufficient unto the Day is the Evil thereof.']
    My good man, let me offer myself as security.
    I'll soon be back. One is only born once.
    [And one doesn't want to face oblivion.]
    Do you agree?
BUTTON MOULDER: Very well. If you wish.
    But remember. We meet at the next crossroads.

    PEER GYNT *runs away.*

Scene Eight

Another part of the moor.

PEER *(runs in frantically):* [Time is money, as the Bible
    says.]
    If I only knew where those crossroads were!
    They may be near; or they may be far.
    [The earth is burning my feet like fire.]
    A witness! A witness! Where shall I find one?
    [It's almost impossible here in the forest.
    What a mess the world is! A fine state of affairs
    When a man has to prove what's obviously his right.]

An OLD BENT MAN *plods by with a staff in his hand and
a pack on his back.*

OLD MAN *(stops):* Spare a penny, kind sir, for a homeless old
    man.

PEER: I'm sorry, I don't have any change—

OLD MAN: Prince Peer! Well, well! So we meet again!

PEER: Who are you?

OLD MAN: Don't you remember the Old Man of the Moun-
    tains?

PEER: Surely you're not—?

OLD MAN: The King of the Ronde, son.

PEER: [The King of the Ronde? Really?]
    The King of the Ronde! [Answer me!]

OLD MAN: I'm afraid I've come down in the world—

PEER: Ruined?

OLD MAN: Robbed of every penny.
    I tramp the roads, begging for food.

PEER: A witness!
    My dear sir, men like you don't grow on trees—

OLD MAN: Your Highness has also aged since last we met.

PEER: [My dear father-in-law, the years take their toll.
    But let's not waste time over private matters:
    And above all, for God's sake, no family quarrels.]
    I was a bit of a madcap in those days—

OLD MAN: Ah, well. Your Highness was young. [And youth
    will be youth.
    But you did quite right to renounce your bride.
    You saved yourself a lot of shame and bother.
    She's turned out a bad one—

PEER: Has she?

OLD MAN: Gone completely to the dogs. Would you believe
    it?
    She's gone off to live with that dreadful Trond.

PEER: Who is Trond?

OLD MAN: The troll of the Valfjeld.

PEER: Him? Oh, yes, I remember.
    I once seduced three of his girls.

OLD MAN: My grandson's grown into a fine strong lad.
- He's fathered children all over the country.
  Fine kids, too—]

PEER: Dear father-in-law, [never mind all that.
  There's something else I have on my mind.]
  I've got into rather a difficult situation.
  I need a witness [or anyway a testimonial].
  Now you can help me better than anyone.
  I might even raise you the price of a drink.

OLD MAN: You mean I can be of service to Your Highness?
  And would you give me a reference in return?

PEER: Gladly. I'm a little short of ready cash.
  [And have to economize as much as possible.]
  Now listen, and I'll explain. You remember that night
  When I came as a suitor to your palace—

OLD MAN: Of course I do, [Your Highness].

PEER: [Oh, stop this Highness business.] Now, look. You
      remember
  You wanted to slit my eye and distort my sight,
  And turn me from Peer Gynt into a troll?
  And how did I react? I resisted you.
  [I swore that I would stand on my own two feet.]
  I renounced my chances of love and power and glory
  Simply so that I could remain myself.
  Now I want you to testify to this in court—

OLD MAN: No, I can't do that.

PEER: What do you mean?

OLD MAN: You surely wouldn't force me to lie?
  You can't have forgotten. You put on troll breeches
  And sampled our mead—

PEER: [Yes, you tricked me into that.] But I refused
  To take the decisive step. And that's the test.
  [It's the final verse of the song that matters.]

OLD MAN: But it was the opposite of what you say.

PEER: What on earth do you mean?

177

OLD MAN: You left the Ronde
    With my motto branded on your brow.
PEER: What motto?
OLD MAN: Those words that divide us.
PEER: Which words?
OLD MAN: Those words that distinguish troll from man:
    'Be thyself—and to hell with the rest of the world!'
PEER *(recoils):* 'To hell with the world—?'
OLD MAN: Ever since then, with all your heart and soul,
    You have lived your life by that principle.
PEER: I? Peer Gynt?
OLD MAN *(weeps):* You're so ungrateful.
    You've lived like a troll, but have always kept it secret.
    It has made you a successful man,
    And now you turn up your nose at it.
    [At me and the motto to which you owe everything.]
PEER: Me a troll!
    [It's all absolute nonsense. I'm sure of it.
OLD MAN *(pulls out a wad of old newspapers):* I suppose you
        imagine we trolls don't have newspapers?
    Wait a second, and I'll show you in black and red
    How the *Bloksberg Express* has been lauding you to the
        skies,
    And the *Heklefjelds Pictorial,* too, ever since you left us.
    Would you care to read them, Peer? You can if you
        like.
    There's an article here with the signature 'Stallion-
        Hoof,'
    And another on 'The Importance of Troll Nationalism,'
    In which the writer emphasizes the fact
    That it isn't horns and a tail that make a troll,
    It's the spirit that matters. The hallmark, he says, of
        trolldom,
    Is really *believing:* 'To hell with the rest of the world!'
    And he ends by quoting you as an example.

178

PEER: A mountain troll? I?]

OLD MAN: Most definitely.

PEER: You mean I could have stayed where I was,
Living in peace and luxury in the Ronde?
You mean all this worry and toil has been for nothing?
Peer Gynt a troll? It's nonsense! Be off with you.
[Here's a halfpenny. Buy yourself some tobacco.

OLD MAN: Oh, dear, kind Prince Peer—!

PEER: Let go! You're mad!
Or turning senile. Go to the workhouse!

OLD MAN: That's what I'm looking for. But my grandson's
children,
As I think I told you, are influential people,
And they're going round saying I only exist in legend.
They say there's nothing as nasty as an ungrateful child,
And now I'm learning the truth of that for my sins.
It's a bit of a blow to become a myth in one's lifetime—

PEER: You're not the only person to whom that's happened.

OLD MAN: And we trolls don't have any Friendly Societies
Or Savings Banks or National Assistance.
Such institutions would never do in the Ronde.

PEER: No. The motto there was: 'Look after yourself!'

OLD MAN: Oh, Your Highness mustn't disparage that motto
of ours.
Though, if you could possibly see your way to—

PEER: My man,
You're barking up the wrong tree.] Anyway, I'm completely broke.

OLD MAN: No! Your Highness a beggar?

PEER: Yes. I've even had to pawn my [princely] self.
And that's your fault, you and your darned trolls.
[It shows the danger of keeping bad company.]

OLD MAN: Oh dear, that's another hope gone.
Well, goodbye. I'd best be moving on towards town.

PEER: What will you do there?

OLD MAN: Try to get on the stage.

[I hear they're advertising for local talent.]

PEER: The best of luck! [You can give them a kiss from me!]

If I get out of this, I'll come and join you.

[I'll write them a farce both witty and profound. I—

Yes! I think I'll call it *sic transit gloria mundi!*]

He runs off down the road. The OLD MAN *is left shouting after him.*

Scene Nine

At a crossroads.

[PEER: Well, my lad, you're really up against it now.

That 'To hell with the rest of the world' has fairly sunk you,

Your ship's a wreck; you must find some straw to cling to.

Anything rather than go into the waste bin.]

BUTTON MOULDER *(at the crossroads):* Well now, Peer.

Have you found your witnesses?

PEER: A crossroads already? That didn't take long.

BUTTON MOULDER: I can see from your face that you've failed.

[Your face is a poster telling me the news.

I don't have to ask for a paper to find what's happened.]

PEER: I got tired of the hunt. One could lose one's way—

BUTTON MOULDER: Yes. And anyway, where does it lead?

[PEER: True enough; in the forest, at nightfall—

BUTTON MOULDER:] But there's an old man trudging along.

Shall we call him?

PEER: No, let him go. He's drunk.

BUTTON MOULDER: But he might be able to—

PEER: Hush! No! Let him go!

BUTTON MOULDER: Well, shall we be off?

PEER: One question. What does it mean: 'To be oneself'?

BUTTON MOULDER: That's a strange question, from a man
Who a moment ago—

PEER: Come on, answer me!

BUTTON MOULDER: To be oneself is: to kill oneself.
But I suppose that explanation's wasted on you.
Let us say: always to serve the Master's intention.

PEER: But what of a man who never learned
What the Master intended him to be?

BUTTON MOULDER: His instinct should guide him.

PEER: But instinct can often lead you astray.
[And then you're lost before you're halfway.]

BUTTON MOULDER: Very true, Peer Gynt. And in this bad
instinct
He with the Hoof has his best angel.

PEER: [This is a damnably complicated business.]
Right. I abandon my claim of having been myself.
[It might be difficult to get proof of that.
I accept that part of my case as lost.]
But a moment ago, when I was alone on the moor,
[I felt the shoe of my conscience pinching me.]
I said to myself: 'It's true. You are a sinner—'

BUTTON MOULDER: Now we're back where we started—

PEER: No, no. I mean a great sinner.
[Not merely in deed, but also in thought and word.
When I was abroad, I behaved very badly—]

BUTTON MOULDER: Maybe. I must ask you to show me the
proof—

PEER: Yes, just give me time. I'll find a priest,
Make a confession, and bring you a certificate—

BUTTON MOULDER: Yes, if you can bring me that
You will certainly avoid the casting-ladle.
But, Peer, I have my orders—

PEER: That paper's out of date. It was made out years ago

181

[When I was leading a careless, lazy life,
Playing the Prophet, pretending to be a Fatalist].
Well, can I try?

BUTTON MOULDER: But—

PEER: Please!

Oh, please! I'm sure you can't be all that busy.
[The air round here is excellent for the health.
It lengthens people's lives considerably.
You know what the priest at Justedal[31] once said:
'Hardly anyone ever dies in this valley.']

BUTTON MOULDER: Till the next crossroads, then. But not a
    step farther.

PEER: I'll find a priest! If I have to drag him by his cassock—!

He starts running.

Scene Ten

*A hillside covered with heather. A path winds up towards
the mountains.*

[PEER: You never know what may turn out useful,
As Esben said when he found the magpie's wing.[32]
Who'd ever have guessed that a list of one's sins
Could prove a man's salvation on his last night?
Mind, the situation's still just as tricky.
Would the ladle really be worse than the fire?
Ah, well. While there's life, they say there's hope.
That's a proverb that has stood the test of time.]

*A THIN PERSON, in a priest's cassock tucked high and
with a fowling-net over his shoulder, comes running
down the path.*

PEER: What's this? A priest [with a fowling-net]!
Hurrah! I'm in luck. Good evening, your Reverence.
Awkward going, isn't it?

182

THIN PERSON: Indeed. But what wouldn't one do for a soul?

PEER: Oh, is someone about to go to heaven?

THIN PERSON: I trust not.

PEER: May I accompany your Reverence for a little of the way?

THIN PERSON: With pleasure. I am fond of company.

PEER: I should like to consult you—

THIN PERSON: Proceed.

PEER: I'm a good man. Always been law-abiding.
    Never been inside. But you know how it is,
    Sometimes a man puts his foot wrong and stumbles—

THIN PERSON: Ah, yes. That happens to the best of us.

PEER: Well, these trifles—

THIN PERSON: Trifles?

PEER: Yes, only trifles.
    [I've never done anything really wicked—]

THIN PERSON: Then, my dear sir, you're wasting my time.
    I'm not the person you seem to think me.
    What are you looking at? [You find my fingers interesting?

PEER: Your nails are somewhat strikingly developed.

THIN PERSON: And now I see you're studying my feet.]

PEER *(points):* Is that hoof natural?[33]

THIN PERSON: So I flatter myself.

PEER *(raises his hat):* I thought you were only a priest.
    And I have the honour—! Well!
    One mustn't look a gift horse in the— I mean, I'm de-
        lighted!
    [If you find the front door open, why go through the
        back?
    If the King puts his head out of the window
    You can raise your fingers at the footman.]

THIN PERSON: Give me your hand. You seem remarkably
    unbiased.

Now, my dear fellow, what can I do for you?
[Er—you mustn't ask me to give you power or money.
I couldn't do that if you put a noose round my neck.
You can't imagine how dead business has been
Lately. Trade has been completely at a standstill.
There just aren't the souls. Just the odd stray now and
    then.

PEER: Has mankind taken a turn for the better, then?

THIN PERSON: Quite the contrary. They've deteriorated dis-
    gracefully.

Most of them are only fit for the casting-ladle.

PEER: Yes, I've heard about that ladle. Actually
That was what I wanted to talk to you about.]

THIN PERSON: You may open your heart to me.

PEER: If it isn't too much to ask, I'd like—

THIN PERSON: A place of refuge? Hm?

PEER: You've guessed [before I even opened my mouth.
You said just now that business has been bad,
So I thought you might conceivably stretch a point—

THIN PERSON: But, my dear sir—]

PEER: I don't ask much.
I could even manage without a salary.
Just decent treatment—as far as circumstances permit—

THIN PERSON: A warm room?

PEER: Not too warm.
And, if possible, [freedom to come and go
As I please; and especially] the right to return
If I get the offer of anything better.

THIN PERSON: My dear friend, it pains me to say this, but
You can't imagine how many similar applications
I receive from people departing their earthly life.

PEER: But think of the wicked life I've led!
[Surely I am eminently qualified for admission?]

THIN PERSON: You said they were trifles—

PEER: Only in a sense. But, now I remember,
  I trafficked in slaves—
THIN PERSON: There are men who have trafficked in hearts
    and souls,
  [But they made a mess of the job] and failed to get in.
PEER: I shipped heathen idols to China.
THIN PERSON: Oh, [don't talk rubbish!] We laugh at such
    things!
  [There are people who set up much nastier idols
  In art and literature, and sermons for that matter;
  And even they don't get in.]
PEER: Yes, but wait a minute!
  Do you know, I once pretended to be a Prophet?
THIN PERSON: Who hasn't? [Most people's *Sehen ins Blaue*
  Ends in the casting-ladle.] No, I'm sorry.
  If you haven't any better credentials than these,
  I can't let you in [however much I might like to].
PEER: But listen! In a shipwreck
  [I was clinging to an upturned boat.
  There's a saying: 'A drowning man will clutch at a
    straw';
  But there's another: 'Charity begins at home,'
  And] I half robbed a poor cook of his life.
THIN PERSON: Would you expect me to be impressed if you
    told me
  That you'd half-robbed a kitchen-maid of something
    else?
  [Don't waste my time with all this rubbish about halves.
  I'm sorry, but] do you think I can waste expensive fuel
  On people like you in difficult times like these?
  [Now, don't get angry. It's only your sins
  That I'm disparaging. I'm sure you'll forgive me
  For speaking out so straight. So, my dear fellow,]
  Put these ideas out of your head.
  Resign yourself to the casting-ladle. What good

185

Would it be to you if I offered you board and lodging?
Think a minute. You're a sensible man.
You'd keep your memory, that's true enough,
But what have you got to remember?
I promise you, the memory of things past
Would give you little joy.
You'd find no cause for weeping or for laughter,
No cause for rejoicing or despair,
Nothing to fire your heart, or freeze your blood.
They'd merely be a source of irritation.

PEER: You may be right. [It isn't easy to know
Where the shoe pinches when one hasn't got it on.]

THIN PERSON: [That's true. I myself, thanks to Never Mind Whom,
Only need one shoe. Incidentally,
It's lucky that you happened to mention shoes.
That reminds me] I must be on my way.
I've a joint to collect; a nice, juicy roast.
[So I can't waste time exchanging pleasantries here.]

PEER: If one may ask, what sins made him grow fat?

THIN PERSON: I understand that all his life
He has been himself. [Which of course qualifies him.]

PEER: Himself? You mean such people
Are automatically your parishioners?

THIN PERSON: That depends. [The door is—left ajar.]
There are two ways in which a man can be himself.
A right way and a wrong way.
You may know that a man in Paris
Has discovered a way of taking portraits
With the help of the sun. Either one can produce
A direct picture, or else what they call a negative.
In the latter, light and dark are reversed;
And the result, to the ordinary eye, is ugly.
But the image of the original is there.
All that's required is to develop it.

186

Now if a human soul, in the course of its life,
Has created one of these negative portraits,
The plate is not destroyed. They send it to me.
[I give it treatment, and by suitable means
Effect a metamorphosis.] I develop it.
I steam it and dip it, I burn it and cleanse it
With sulphur and similar ingredients,
Till the picture appears which the plate was intended to
   give.
[I mean, the one known as the positive.]
But when a soul like you has smudged himself out,
Even sulphur and potash can achieve nothing.

PEER: Then one must come to you as black as a raven
   To be sent back as white as a dove? May I ask what name
   Is scratched beneath this particular negative
   [Which you are about to burn into a positive]?

THIN PERSON: The name is Peter Gynt.

PEER: Peter Gynt? Indeed? Is Mr. Gynt himself?

THIN PERSON: So he affirms.

PEER: Well, he's a reliable man.

THIN PERSON: You know him?

PEER: In a way.
   [You know how it is. One knows so many people.]

THIN PERSON: [My time is short.] Where did you see him
   last?

PEER: Down at the Cape.

THIN PERSON: Of Good Hope?

PEER: Yes, but I understand he's leaving very soon.

THIN PERSON: Then I must be off at once. I hope I'm in time
   To catch him. I never liked that Cape of Good Hope.
   It's always full of missionaries from Stavanger.

   Runs off southwards.

PEER: The silly bastard! Look at him,
   Running away with his tongue hanging out!

187

Well, I made a fool out of him.
[Putting on airs and acting big!]
A fat lot he's got to boast about!
[He won't get rich the way he's going.]
He'll be knocked off his perch. [And his whole show
    with him.]
Hm. I'm not too safe myself.
I've been expelled from the privileged circle;
The exclusive club of men who are themselves.
A shooting star is seen. He nods after it.
Hail, brother star! A greeting from Peer Gynt!
We flash for a moment, then our light is quenched,
And we disappear into the void for ever.
*He composes himself as though frightened, and goes
deeper into the mist. There is silence for a few mo-
ments, then he cries:*
Is there no one, no one in all the Universe—?
No one in the Abyss—no one in Heaven—?
*He comes forward again farther down, throws his hat
down on the road, and tears his hair. Gradually a
calmness comes over him.*
How unspeakably poor a soul can be
When it enters the mist and returns to nothing!
O beautiful earth, don't be angry with me
That I trod your sweet grass to no avail.
O beautiful sun, you have squandered
Your golden light upon an empty hut.
There was no one within to warm and comfort.
The owner, I know now, was never at home.
Beautiful sun and beautiful earth,
Why did you bear my mother and give her light?
The spirit is mean, and Nature is wasteful.
Life is a terrible price to pay for birth.
I want to climb, up to the highest peak.
I want to see the sun rise once again,

To gaze till I am tired at the promised land.
Then let the snow pile over me,
And let them write above: 'Here lies no one.'
And afterwards—let the world take its course.

CHURCHGOERS *(singing on the forest path):* O thrice blest
    morn, when tongues of fire
God's spirit did proclaim!
O Holy Ghost, our souls inspire
To sing in universal choir,
And praise God's glorious name!

PEER *(crouches in terror):* Never look there! That's waste
    and desert!
I was a dead man long before I died!

*He tries to slink in among the bushes, but comes upon
the crossroads.*

BUTTON MOULDER: Good morning. Where is your list of
    sins?
PEER: I've shouted and whistled all over the heath.
BUTTON MOULDER: And met no one?
PEER: Only a [travelling] photographer.
BUTTON MOULDER: Well, your time is up.
PEER: Yes. Everything's up.
    The owl smells the light. Can you hear him hooting?
BUTTON MOULDER: It's the bell for mattins.
PEER *(points):* What's that shining over there?
BUTTON MOULDER: Only the light from a hut.
PEER: What is that sound I hear like sighing?
BUTTON MOULDER: A woman singing.
PEER: There! Yes! There I'll find my sins!
BUTTON MOULDER *(grips him):* Set thy house in order!

*They have come out of the undergrowth and are stand-
ing by the cabin. Day breaks.*

PEER: My house? It's there! Away! Begone!
    If your ladle were as large as a coffin
    It would be too small for me and my sins.
BUTTON MOULDER: Well, the third crossroads, Peer. But
        then—!

Turns aside, and goes.

PEER *(approaches the cabin):* Forward or back it's equally
        far.
    Outside or in, I'm still confined.
    Stops.
    No! I hear like a wild, unending cry:
    'Go in! Go back! Go home!'
    Goes a few steps, then stops again.
    'Go round,' said the Boyg.
    Hears the song from inside the cabin.
    Ah! No! This time straight through,
    However narrow the path may be.

He runs towards the cabin. At the same moment,
SOLVEIG *appears in the doorway, dressed for church,
with a psalmbook wrapped in linen and a staff in her
hand. She stands there, erect and gentle.*

PEER *(throws himself down on the threshold):* Judge this
        sinner! O, speak!
SOLVEIG: It is he! It is he! Oh, praise be to God!

She gropes for him.

PEER: Cry out my sins!
SOLVEIG: You have sinned in nothing, my only child.

Gropes for him again, and finds him.

BUTTON MOULDER *(behind the house):* The list, Peer Gynt?
PEER: Cry out my guilt!

SOLVEIG *(sits down beside him):* You have made my life into
    a song.

Bless you for coming back to me at last.

Blessed, oh, blessed be our meeting

On this morning of Pentecost!

PEER: Then I am lost!

SOLVEIG: There is One Who rules all.

PEER *(laughs):* Lost! Unless you can solve riddles.

SOLVEIG: Tell me.

PEER: Tell you? Yes, I will!

Can you tell me where Peer Gynt has been

[Since you saw him last]?

SOLVEIG: Been?

PEER: With the mark of destiny on his brow

As he sprang forth in the mind of God!

Can you answer me that? If not, I must go

To my home, down to the land of mists.

SOLVEIG *(smiles):* Oh, that riddle is easy.

PEER: Tell me, then!

Where was my self, my whole self, my true self?

The self that bore God's stamp upon its brow?

SOLVEIG: In my faith, in my hope, and in my love.

PEER *(starts back):* What do you say? Hush! Now you speak
    in riddles!

Ah! *You* are the mother to that child?

SOLVEIG: Yes, I am. But who is its father?

It is He Who forgives when the mother prays.

PEER *(bathed in light, cries):* My mother! My wife! O, thou
    pure woman!

O hide me in your love! Hide me! Hide me!

*He clings tightly to her and buries his face in her lap. A
long silence. The sun rises.*

SOLVEIG *(sings softly):* Sleep, O sleep, my dearest boy.
I will cradle you, I will guard you.

Sleep, O sleep, my love, my joy.
Sleep now, and rest.

You've sat on my lap, we've played together.
The life-long day you've lain on my breast.
You've always been close to my heart.
Now you're tired. You can rest.
Hums.
Sleep, O sleep—

BUTTON MOULDER'S VOICE *(behind the house):* We shall
    meet at the last crossroads, Peer.

[And then we'll see if—! I'll say no more.]

SOLVEIG *(sings louder as the daylight grows):* I will cradle
    you, I will guard you.

Sleep, sleep and dream.

Notes

1. *Changeling.* There is an old Norwegian superstition that changelings left by the fairies can be blown up the chimney.

2. *Master Cook.* A kind of master of ceremonies.

3. *Sæter.* A small mountain farm where the cattle are sent to pasture in summer.

4. *Be thyself—and to hell with the rest of the world!* The phrase which Ibsen uses to formulate the philosophy of the trolls, *at være sig selv nok,* to be self-sufficient in a bad sense, was not, as many critics have assumed, created by Ibsen. The danger of self-sufficiency was a problem which was occupying people during the middle of the nineteenth century far outside the boundaries of Norway. English writers around this time were debating the reasons why the word self-sufficiency had acquired a pejorative significance; De Quincey suggested that *self-sufficingness* should be used to convey the original nobility of the Greek *autarkes* and the Latin *sibi sufficiens;* and Swinburne proposed *self-sufficience* as an alternative in, curiously enough, 1867, the very year in which Ibsen wrote *Peer Gynt.* The absence in modern English of any pejorative equivalent of self-sufficiency makes this vital phrase peculiarly difficult to translate. The usual: 'Troll, to thyself be enough' fails for this reason, apart from being deficient in any real impact.

5. *Salted herring.* The traditional remedy in Scandinavia for a hangover.

6. *Why, he's chopped his finger off!* This episode is based on a true incident of which Ibsen had read in the newspaper *Aftenbladet* on 14 June 1864. He had already used it in the epic version of *Brand,* of which he completed a considerable portion before abandoning it to treat the subject as a play. But there the boy had been a figure of shame; in *Peer Gynt* he appears as a man of honour, who had the courage to do what other men secretly wished to do. It is difficult not to believe that Ibsen's preoccupation with this matter stemmed from the sense of guilt which we know he possessed for not having taken part in the Danish-German war, about which he felt so strongly.

The lines describing this incident were cut in production because the audience was able to see it silently taking place.

7. *Soria-Moria.* The Arabic name for a group of islands beyond the Red Sea which were fabled to be the Islands of the Blest.

8. *Grane.* Sigurd Fafnirsbane's horse, descended from the god Odin's Sleipnir.

9. *Trumpeterstraale.* In the original, Herr Trumpeterstraale is a Swede, but since some of his remarks, about Charles XII's spurs and so forth, have no meaning for an English audience, we turned him, in the Old Vic production, into an American. This involved the alteration of a single line on page 103 (see footnote 13 below).

10. *A measure of spiritual contemplation . . .* This speech is deliberately obscure in the original, as a satire on the German tendency to talk abstract nonsense.

11. *Lippe-Detmold.* A tiny German principality.

12. *Your* Reich *last for a thousand years!* Literally: 'Our finest and most ancient Rhenish vintages!'

13. *Stand in history with Charlemagne!* Literally: 'And all the swords of Charles XII!'

14. *King Charles's spurs.* When King Charles XII of Sweden was fighting the Turks at Bender (in Bessarabia, on

the Dniester) in 1713, his spurs are said to have tripped him and resulted in his capture. There is also a legend that he tore with these spurs the garments of the Turkish emissary who brought him the news that the Sultan had concluded a truce with their mutual enemy Peter the Great of Russia.

15. *But under protest.* This is probably a gibe at Count Manderström, the Swedish Foreign Minister who, when Germany had attacked Denmark in 1864, had written diplomatic notes of protest but had refrained from taking any positive action. Manderström is also supposed to have been the original of the minister Hussein in the madhouse scene (see pp. 141–43). Ibsen had a particular contempt for him, and once drew a halter round his neck on a picture of him in an illustrated magazine in the Scandinavian Club in Rome. Manderström's nephew, Carl Snoilsky, later became one of Ibsen's closest friends.

16. *Gyntiana.* Ole Bull, Ibsen's old chief at the Bergen Theatre, had tried in 1852 to found an ideal Norwegian colony in Pennsylvania, on the model approved by the French Socialists. He called it Oleana; but it ended in financial disaster.

17. *Kaba.* A sacred building in Mecca, containing a black stone which pilgrims have to kiss.

18. *Das ewig weibliche ziehet uns an!* A deliberate misquotation of the last line of Goethe's *Faust.* Goethe's line reads: 'Woman eternally draws us upwards.' Peer says: 'Woman eternally draws us towards her.'

19. *Qu'allais-je faire dans cette galère?* A quotation, slightly wrong as always with Peer, from Molière's comedy, *Les Fourberies de Scapin:* 'What the devil was I doing in that boat?' Peer has already used this once, on page 115, where I have translated it: 'Why did I ever get on to that wagon?'

20. Becker. Becker's *Weltgeschichte* (1801–9) had been

translated into Danish in the middle of the nineteenth century.

21. *Memnon.* Memnon was the god of the morning. When he died, his mother Aurora begged Jupiter to honour him. Jupiter answered her prayer by turning Memnon's ashes into birds that perpetually sang, fought and played. These lines are not, as has often been supposed, meaningless, nor does their significance seem to me obscure. The statue is telling Peer that the latter has sealed up his soul, and that unless he can unseal it he will die—as indeed he does. Whether Peer dies in the madhouse, or in the shipwreck, the last scenes of the play surely show us either his soul's passage through purgatory, or the film of his life, with its failures and errors, unreeling before his eyes in the moment of death. It is interesting to note that Ibsen had written of the Memnon Statue as early as 1855 in a prologue spoken from the stage at the Bergen Theatre.

22. *The Circle of the Seventy Interpreters.* Presumably a reference to the writers of the Septuagint, the Greek version of the Old Testament said to have been made by seventy translators around 270 B.C. Various unlikely suggestions have been put forward as to the meaning of Begriffenfeldt's next sentence, 'recently increased by a hundred and sixty,' but I think this is probably merely intended as an additional example of the German's lunacy.

23. *Munchausen's fox.* Baron Munchausen claimed to have nailed a fox to a tree by its tail, cut a slit in its forehead, and whipped it so that it jumped out of its skin.

24. *Huhu.* This character is a caricature of the Norwegian *maalstrævere,* 'a party,' to quote William Archer, 'which desired to substitute a language compounded of the various local dialects for the Norwegian of the bourgeoisie and of literature, which they called Danish, and declared to be practically a foreign tongue to the peasants and lower classes generally. The peasants, they argued (like Ibsen's

orang-outangs), lived and died "uninterpreted." The movement attained no little force in the [eighteen-] sixties and
seventies, and a considerable literature sprang up in the so-
called *maal,* the work of such men as Ivar Aasen, A. O.
Vinje, and Kristofer Janson.' Janson was furious when he
read this scene and wrote a virulent attack on the play in
Aftenbladet, expressing the hope that Ibsen would soon 'tire
of spitting and scolding from his chimney corner.'

25. *Fellah.* A fellah is an Egyptian peasant. This character with the mummy on his back is an expression of a theme
frequently to be found in Ibsen's work, especially of this period: man's bondage to his past. A few years later he was to
write a poem on this theme entitled *The Corpse in the
Cargo;* and it is, of course, the central *motif* of *Ghosts.* The
Dovre kingdom and Aase's ruined farm are parallel symbols; but they should not be taken, as they have been, as
referring specifically to Norway's, or Sweden's, glorifica-
tion of her former greatness. The image of the Fellah and his
mummy may have been based on the adulation shown by the
Swedes towards the mummified body of Charles XII, and
there are references in the troll scene which are aimed at
Norwegian chauvinism; but it was humanity's bondage, not
Norway's, that troubled Ibsen more deeply.

26. *Cuckold to Death and to Aslak the smith.* Because
Aslak and, now, Death have both slept with Ingrid since
Peer seduced her on her wedding night; she is another person who has been destroyed by his greed. The Man in Grey
is, of course, Mads Moen.

27. *The Cat of the Dovre.* The white bear which Peer
Gynt took with him (in Asbjœrnsen's tale) to frighten the
trolls on Christmas Eve.

28. *I think I'll put up my own rubbish for auction.* The
word auction had painful associations for Ibsen. In a letter to
Bjœrnson (undated, but probably written in October 1866,
just before he started *Peer Gynt),* he expressed vehement in-

dignation at the fact that his belongings in Norway had been auctioned without his authorization. 'It isn't so much the loss of my furniture, etc., that grieves me, but that my private letters, papers, drafts, etc., not to speak of many things that meant far more to me than their face value, should have found their way into the hands of any Tom, Dick or Harry, is a most bitter thought.'

29. *Threadballs.* Trolls in threadballs are a common idea in Norwegian folk lore.

30. *It'll only be a transitional stage, As the fox said when they started to skin him.* A reference to the Norwegian proverb: ' "It'll be a change," as the fox said when they started to skin him.'

31. *Justedal.* Matthias Foss, a priest in Justedal in the middle of the eighteenth century, wrote in 1750 *A Short Description of Justedal,* which included the sentence: 'They [i.e., the people of Justedal] are exceedingly long-lived, so that it is seldom anyone dies there.'

32. *Esben.* Esben Askeladd is a character in a Norwegian folk tale who found a dead magpie which led to his winning the hand of a princess.

33. *Is that hoof natural?* The Devil is traditionally represented in Scandinavian folk lore as having a single hoof instead of a right foot.

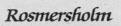

Rosmersholm

ACKNOWLEDGMENTS

The translator would like to thank Sigmund Freud Copyrights Ltd, Mr. James Strachey and The Hogarth Press Ltd for permission to quote from "Some Character-Types Met with in Psychoanalytic Work" in Volume XIV (1914–1916) of the Standard Edition of *The Complete Psychological Works of Sigmund Freud*.

Introduction

Ibsen wrote *Rosmersholm* in Munich during the summer of 1886, at the age of fifty-eight.

Two years earlier, while he was finishing *The Wild Duck* in Gossensass, his wife and son had revisited Norway for the first time in eleven years. They had sailed right up to the North Cape, and she had written to him with an infectious enthusiasm about the splendour of the landscape. That September (1884) Bjœrnson came to the Tyrol, and Ibsen met his old friend and rival for the first time in twenty years. They spent much time together, and Bjœrnson tried to persuade Ibsen to return to Norway and take over the directorship of the Christiania Theatre. Ibsen refused, but only after a struggle. "Both times you threw out the suggestion," he wrote to Bjœrnson on 29 September 1884, "a restlessness and longing filled my mind. But . . . my wife has just written to me from up there: 'I would never have believed that we were so much in the black books of the Conservatives as has, by a multitude of signs, proved to be the case.' I do not for a moment doubt that her observation is correct. When ten years ago, after a ten years absence, I sailed up the fjord, I literally felt my chest tighten with a feeling of sickness and unease. I had the same sensation during the whole of my stay there; I was no longer myself with all those cold and uncomprehending Norwegian eyes staring at me from the windows and pavements." Nevertheless, Suzannah's letters, and the meetings with Bjœrnson, had awoken a nostalgia in him.

During the winter of 1884–5 Ibsen began to lay plans for a new play. As was his custom, he pondered it for months without putting pen to paper (though his first notes may possibly date from this period). In April 1885 he wrote optimistically that he was hoping to complete it within a few months, so that it could be published in time for the Christmas sales. But he had done nothing further about it by the summer, when on an impulse he yielded to his nostalgia and decided to go back to Norway. The decision was sudden, for as late as 25 April he wrote from Rome to his publisher, Frederik Hegel of Gyldendal, that he was probably going to spend the summer in the Tyrol "where I hope to be able to work in peace and get my new play ready by the autumn." But six weeks later he was in Christiania. En route, in Copenhagen, he declared that he was thinking of spending the rest of his life in Norway, perhaps purchasing a small house on a fjord outside Christiania where he could "live in isolation, occupied exclusively with my work." In the event, however, he stayed less than four months, from the beginning of June until the end of September. His experiences in Norway during this summer of 1885 form the background to *Rosmersholm*.

Ibsen spent only a few days in Christiania before proceeding north to Trondheim, but what he saw and heard in that time left a deep and disagreeable impression on him. The previous year, 1884, there had been an important political development in Norway; and an explanation of the events that led up to this may be helpful to an understanding of *Rosmersholm*.

The King of Sweden, who was also King of Norway, ruled the country through a Cabinet, which he chose personally, and a Storthing, or Parliament; but the members of the Cabinet had no seats in the Storthing, and acknowledged no responsibility except to the King. He held a veto over the

Storthing; but this veto was suspensive, not absolute, so that a bill passed by three successive Storthings could become law despite the veto.

In the 1870's there arose the incongruous situation that the Storthing was overwhelmingly Liberal, while the Cabinet remained Conservative. In 1872, accordingly, the Storthing passed a bill enacting that Cabinet ministers should sit in the Storthing. King Oscar vetoed this. It was passed twice more by successive Storthings, and so should have become law; but the King now declared that on matters affecting the constitution his veto was absolute and permanent. Faced with this apparent impasse, the Storthing took the extreme measure of impeaching the members of the Cabinet before the Supreme Court, and one by one the ministers were dismissed and fined. The King selected a new and equally Conservative ministry; the Storthing dug in its heels; the King refused to yield, and it was rumoured that he was considering a *coup d'état;* but eventually, on 26 June 1884, he sent for the leading Liberal statesman, Johan Sverdrup, and invited him to form a ministry. The conflict thus ended in a complete victory for the Liberals.*

Such was the situation which greeted Ibsen when he arrived in Christiania in June 1885. "Since he had last been home," noted Henrik Jæger in his early biography (I quote Archer's admirable translation), "the great political battle had been fought out, and had left behind it a fanaticism and bitterness of spirit which astounded him. He was struck by the brutality of the prevailing tone; he felt himself painfully affected by the rancorous and vulgar personalities which drowned all rational discussion of the principles at stake; and he observed with sorrow the many enmities to which the contest had given rise. Men who had hitherto been the clos-

---

*For a detailed account of these happenings, see William Archer's article in the *Fortnightly Review* of September 1885.

est friends were now the bitterest foes; and this although they had done each other no personal wrong, but had merely arrived at different views of life. On the whole, he received the impression—as he later remarked in conversation—that Norway was inhabited, not by two million human beings, but by two million cats and dogs. This impression has recorded itself in the picture of party divisions presented in *Rosmersholm.* The bitterness of the vanquished is admirably embodied in Rector Kroll; while the victors' reluctance to speak out their whole hearts is excellently characterized in the freethinker and opportunist, Mortensgaard."

Ibsen's disillusionment at this evidence of pettiness and party strife is apparent from a statement he made at Trondhjem on 14 June. The local Workers' Association had organized a procession with banners in his honour, and Ibsen made a speech of thanks. In it, he declared: "There is still much to be done in this country before we can be said to have achieved full freedom. But our present democracy scarcely has the power to accomplish that task. An element of nobility must enter into our political life, our government, our members of parliament and our press. I am of course not thinking of nobility of wealth, of learning, or even of ability or talent. I am thinking of nobility of character, of mind and of will. That alone can make us free.* And this nobility, which I hope may be granted to our people, will come to us from two sources, the only two sections of society which have not as yet been corrupted by party pressure. It will come to us from our women and our working men. The reshaping of social conditions which is now being under-

---

*Ibsen had already adumbrated this idea in *An Enemy of the People* (1882); and in his notes for *The Wild Duck* he had written: "A new aristocracy will arise. It will not be the aristocracy of birth or of wealth, of talent or knowledge. The aristocracy of the future will be the aristocracy of the mind and of the will."

taken in Europe is principally concerned with the future status of the workers and of women. That is what I am hoping and waiting for, and what I shall work for, all I can.''

These inter-party bitternesses affected Ibsen personally. The right-wingers, as Suzannah had noted, regarded him as an apostate; several of his former friends in Christiania held aloof from him, or so he felt, and the respectable citizens of Trondhjem did not acclaim him as the workers did. Seventeen months later, on 10 November 1886, shortly after he had finished *Rosmersholm*, Ibsen summed up his feelings about Norway in a letter to Georg Brandes. ''The impressions, experiences and observations which I brought back from my trip to Norway in the summer of last year,'' he wrote, ''had for a long while a confusing effect on me. . . . Never have I felt so foreign to my Norwegian fellow-countrymen's activities as after the lessons which this past year has taught me. Never so repelled. Never so nauseated.''

There had, however, been one compensation. From Trondhjem he had, in June 1885, gone on to Molde, a pretty seaside town on the north-west coast, which so pleased him that he spent two months there.* In Molde he met a former acquaintance, the Swedish poet Count Carl Snoilsky. Snoilsky, at forty-four, was thirteen years younger than Ibsen, and had first met him in Rome over twenty years earlier in 1864. They had met again in Sweden in 1869 and 1877, when Ibsen had been disappointed at Snoilsky's apparent movement towards a more Conservative outlook (he had taken a position in the Swedish Foreign Office), and at the withering of his creative talent.

In his youth Snoilsky had been a fertile and gifted poet but after he had married, and become a civil servant, his creative springs dried up, and for ten years he found himself scarcely able to write a line. ''I have wasted my life,'' he

---

*He was later to use it as the setting for *The Lady from the Sea*.

noted sadly in 1874, "and it is too late to change things now." But in 1879, at the age of thirty-eight, he left the Foreign Office, divorced his wife, married one of her relatives, and went abroad into voluntary exile. At once he found himself able to write again, and published one volume after another. But the kind of poetry he was writing now was very different from the charming lyrics that had made his name. He, the refined nobleman, had become absorbed by the class struggle and the spirit of revolution. He longed to enter into contact with the common people; but his own upbringing and aristocratic heritage inhibited him. In 1883, two years before he met Ibsen at Molde, Snoilsky wrote: "Certainly creative literature can have an enormous influence, as Ibsen has shown, in the debating of social problems. . . . [But] my powers do not suffice for so lofty a task, and so broad a public. I dare not aim so high. I am, moreover, conscious of my main handicap—that I have not, from childhood, lived the life of the *people*—my education and upbringing in the narrow classical tradition have unfitted me, like the vast majority of our *litterateurs,* to address the humbler strata of society in a language they understand. Unlike my colleagues, however, I am often painfully conscious of this barrier, this limitation, and do my best to transcend it."

Three years after their divorce, Snoilsky's first wife died of consumption, and many people blamed him for her death. But Ibsen, during the four days he spent with Snoilsky at Molde, took a great liking both to him and to his new wife; he thought her sensitivity and strength of character largely responsible for Snoilsky's regeneration as a person. He was deeply interested in Snoilsky's conviction that poetry should not deal merely with the "beautiful", but should be connected with contemporary thought and ideas (he had boldly and outspokenly defended *Ghosts);* and also in the temperamental difficulty which Snoilsky found in accepting this intellectual conviction. Snoilsky had expressed this difficulty in a poem, *The White Lady,* about the sixteenth-century Duke Charles of Sweden, later King Charles IX, the brother and co-deposer of Erik XIV. Snoilsky portrayed Duke Charles as a man nagged by an uneasy conscience, in contrast to his son, the great Gustav II Adolf, who had no fear of such ghosts. Ibsen had depicted a similar contrast in *The Pretenders,* between Earl Skule and Haakon Haakonsson; and Snoilsky found himself in the same predicament as Earl Skule and Duke Charles—he could not shake off his inherited instincts and identify himself with the people. Gradually Snoilsky had resigned himself to the idea that he really belonged among the medieval troubadours rather than among the socially-conscious poets of the eighteen-eighties.* Ibsen was to base the character of John Rosmer very recognizably on Snoilsky; and Rebecca bears certain resemblances, though she is not to be identified with her, to Snoilsky's second wife.

Ibsen left Norway towards the end of September 1885, and returned to Munich. He took some time to sort out his impressions of his visit. "Ever since my return here," he was later to write to Georg Brandes in the letter already quoted (10 November 1886), "I have been plagued by a new play which absolutely demanded to be written. But only when I had completely clarified my experiences, and drawn my conclusions from them, could I think about translating the fruit thereof into a creative work."

He pondered the play all winter and spring. On 4 Decem-

---

*On 4 April 1886 Snoilsky wrote to Ibsen that he was "written out" *(utsjungen);* that he had learned from Ibsen "the untenability of a purely aesthetic appreciation of life," and had come to look on "all poetry that failed to deal with major contemporary problems as something superfluous." He therefore regarded himself as superfluous, and had decided to "retire." Fortunately he did not; and one of his later poems, *Ibsen at Molde,* provides a memorable portrait of Ibsen which should act as a corrective to the common conception of him.

ber 1885 he wrote to Frederik Hegel: "I am now pretty well in the clear with my plan for my new play, and shall be starting to write it in a few days. It will be in four acts, and interests me greatly." Two and a half months later, on 14 February 1886, he wrote to Snoilsky that he was "fully occupied with a new play, which has long been in my thoughts and for which I made some close studies during my trip to Norway during the summer." But still it would not come, and on 20 February he informed Edvard Fallesen, the director of the Royal Theatre in Copenhagen, that it "cannot be expected before the autumn."

Some time during this period, we do not know when, he made some brief notes and began a draft, of which he completed less than an act. The notes contain the following:

WHITE HORSES

He, the refined, aristocratic character, who has changed to a liberal viewpoint and been ostracized by all his former friends and acquaintances. A widower; has been unhappily married to a half-mad melancholic, who ended by drowning herself.

She, the governess of his two daughters, emancipated, hot-blooded, somewhat ruthless beneath a refined exterior. Is regarded by their acquaintances as the evil spirit of the house; an object of suspicion and gossip.

Eldest (sic) *daughter;* is in danger of succumbing to inactivity and loneliness. She has rich talents which are lying unused.

Younger daughter; sharply observant; passions beginning to dawn.

The journalist; genius, tramp.

In the living-room of the vicarage. S. and Miss B. in conversation. The student enters from a walk. Old retired apothecary on business; goes. The family assembled. The Captain. The magistrate with daughter on a visit and with an invitation; it is accepted; then the change of heart is to be revealed. The family alone; the talk turns to the white horses.*

The few pages which exist of the first draft open with a former priest, aristocratically named Boldt-Rœmer, talking to his children's governess, Miss Radeck. Thanks to her, he has seen the light of liberalism and renounced the priesthood; it is hinted that his former wife was drowned in the mill-pool. The local schoolmaster, Hekman, enters, and tries to persuade Boldt-Rœmer, whose name now changes to Rosenhjelm, to champion the Conservative cause against Mortensgaard. Rosenhjelm is protesting that he is unfitted for such a task when the fragment ends.

On 25 May 1886 Ibsen scrapped what he had written and began an entirely new draft. The title page shows that it was still to be called *The White Horses,* and that it was now to be in five acts. It progressed swiftly; Act 1 was ready by 1 June, and Act 2 by 8 June. This draft opens similarly to the final version as we know it; the two principals are now named Rebecca and Rosmer, but Rebecca is Rosmer's second wife. Dr. Gylling (Kroll) enters; it is established that the Rosmers are newly married. Rosmer's first name is Eilert and his dead wife was Agate (later Agnete); they had a son, Alfred, is who also dead. We learn that the Rosmers have always, by tradition, been alternately soldiers and priests; Rosmer's father, formidably named Eilert Hanibal *(sic)* Rosmer, was a soldier, so his son had to be a priest. ''Thus it

---

*This final paragraph is separate to the rest, and may have been jotted down at an earlier date.

has been for more than two hundred years.'' The tutor, Ulrik Rosenhjelm, enters (Ibsen often, when he abandoned a name, transferred it to some other character), and makes the references to Rebecca as ''the pastor's wife'' which are effectively retained in the final version. After he has gone, Gylling wonders whether to get him to write (''anonymously, of course'') for the new paper which he (Gylling) is founding as a counterblast to Mortensgaard. Rebecca tells Rosmer that she has given Rosenhjelm an introduction to Mortensgaard; Rosmer observes that Rosenhjelm will now be receiving invitations from both editors. It is established that Rosmer is to reveal his change of heart tomorrow. Rebecca refers to the white horses, and gets Mrs. Helset *(sic)* to tell the legend of them. The act ends with Rebecca saying: ''All the free people I have known—all the ones who thought they were free—they've all had some kind of white horse that they never cease to believe in.'' ROSMER: ''You mean that full freedom is to—?'' REBECCA: ''Is to get rid of one's white horses.''

In Act 2, Rosmer reveals to Rebecca that he has shirked revealing his change of heart to his friends. She persuades him to go to Gylling and make a clean breast of it; but Gylling is now announced. Gylling tells of Sejerhjelm's *(sic)* bad behaviour in town. Now at last Rosmer reveals his change of heart, and abandonment of his religious beliefs. Gylling is shocked, and reveals that Beate *(sic)* told him before she killed herself that Rosmer and Rebecca loved each other (though she did not, in this draft, say that they ''had'' to marry). Rebecca has now become Miss Dankert.

On 10 June Ibsen began Act 3; it is set, as in the final version, in Rosmer's study, and Rebecca has now become Miss West. But five days later, in the middle of the Mortensgaard scene, he scrapped this draft completely, throwing out the title *White Horses* (which he may have thought too reminis-

cent of *Ghosts*),* and renaming it *Rosmersholm*. This draft
he completed in a day over seven weeks; Act 1 took from
15–28 June, Act 2 from 1–12 July, Act 3 from 15–24 July,
and Act 4 from 26 July to 4 August.

This draft is essentially the play as we know it, though Ibsen made an unusual number of small corrections when he
came to fair copy it, continuing, among other things, to alter
the names of the supporting characters. It contains, however, one or two interesting variations. Rebecca tells Rosmer and Gylling that when she came to the district from
Finnmark with Dr. West, aged a little over twenty, she was
"not what people call an—an innocent woman." Rosmer
asks who the man was; she replies: "Someone who had absolute power over me. He had taught me everything. Everything I knew about life then." This description, which may
or may not be intended to refer to Dr. West (we do not know
whether Ibsen had yet conceived the idea of making him Rebecca's lover) strongly foreshadows the Stranger in Ibsen's
next play, *The Lady from the Sea,* into which he was also to
put the two daughters of his first notes for *Rosmersholm*.
(The Stranger, like Dr. West and Rebecca, came from
Finnmark, the extreme north of Norway, a region associated
by Norwegians with trolls and strange magic; Rebecca lik-
ens herself in the final version to a sea-troll hanging on to the
ship of Rosmer's life to hold it back, and it is Rosmer's need
to feel clean and pure, without which he cannot feel free,
that leaves Rebecca powerless, as church bells take the
power from trolls). And in the last act of this draft, it is Het-

---

*Eight weeks before, on 14 April, he had seen *Ghosts* on the stage for the
first time, at Augsburg. This may possibly account for the obvious similari-
ties between the two plays. Both have as their theme the influence of the
dead over the living. In both, the action is dominated by a dead person,
Captain Alving and Beata Rosmer. And Rosmer, like Oswald Alving, is the
last, unhappy member of his line.

man (Brendel), not Rosmer, who gives Rebecca the idea of killing herself to show her love:

HETMAN: Is she leaving?

ROSMER: Tonight.

REBECCA: In half an hour.

HETMAN: You don't understand how to keep your women. The first one left you too.

ROSMER: Yes, she did.

HETMAN: Brave woman. She went freely—to smooth your path . . . That woman must have had some kind of wings, I reckon.

REBECCA: Wings? Why wings?

HETMAN: Didn't she raise herself so high that she was able to die for her love? . . . I could have sworn no living soul could do that.

ROSMER: To resort to death—to prove one's love?

REBECCA: I shall not leave tonight.

ROSMER *(in anguish):* Yes, go! Go!

HETMAN: Stay, my pretty lady. There's no danger for you. He won't tempt you down under the water. Farewell!

When Ibsen fair-copied the play, he altered this, and instead gave Brendel the speech about the necessity of a woman cutting off her finger and ear to show her love for a man. Dr. Arne Duve, in his Book *Symbolikken i Henrik Ibsens Skuespill,* points out what Ibsen cannot of course have known, that finger and ear are common symbols for the male and female sexual organs; though I have never heard this speech spoken in a way that suggested that either the Brendel or the Rebecca had the faintest idea what it implied. Dr. Duve also observes that Beata means "the happy one", and that the word "west" commonly suggests defeat and death; though I think that here it probably possesses its other symbolic significance of "the unknown," as in the idea, found in so many national mythologies, of mysterious "islands of the west."*

On 6 August Ibsen began his fair copy but, as stated, he made a great number of small revisions, and did not finish it until 27 September. "This play," he told Hegel in a letter on 2 October, "is to be regarded as the fruit of studies and observations which I had cause to make during my stay in Norway during the summer of last year. It cannot, as far as I can surmise, offer grounds for attack from any quarter. I hope, though, that it may provoke a lively debate. I especially anticipate one in Sweden."

Rosmersholm was published by Gyldendal of Copenhagen on 23 November 1886, in an edition of 8,000 copies, and received its premiere at the National Theatre in Bergen on 17 January 1887. Even more than its predecessor, *The Wild Duck,* it baffled the critics and public, and, like *The Wild Duck*—and, for that matter, all the plays that Ibsen subsequently wrote—won nothing like the contemporary acclaim that had greeted *Brand, Peer Gynt, The Pillars of Society, A Doll's House* and *An Enemy of the People.* It had a cool welcome when it was staged in Christiania on 12 April, and ran for only ten performances. No more than six further performances of it were given in Christiania during the next two years, and it was not produced there again before 1900. Its first performance in Germany, at Augsburg on 16 April 1887, with Ibsen present, was a disaster, and reaction to the first London production on 23 February 1891, with Florence Farr and F. R. Benson, was equally hostile.

---

*But a witch named Rebecca West had been burned in Worcestershire during the seventeenth century (the case is mentioned in Margaret Murray's *The God of the Witches),* and it is conceivable that Ibsen had read of this case somewhere and, consciously or unconsciously, borrowed the name.

England was, of course, particularly backward in its appreciation of Ibsen; but the general reaction, even among Ibsen's admirers, was that the play was obscure, and that the characters were abstractions rather than credible human beings. One of the few people to appreciate it was Strindberg who, in the spring following the publication of *Rosmersholm*, wrote an appreciation of it in an essay entitled *Soul-Murder (Själamord)*. In this, he declared that *Rosmersholm* was "unintelligible to the theatre public, mystical to the semi-educated, but crystal-clear to anyone with a knowledge of modern psychology"—one of the very few occasions on which he ever paid public tribute to Ibsen. One can understand the attraction that *Rosmersholm* held for Strindberg, for he, too, was deeply interested in "magnetism" and "hypnosis," the ability of one person to gain control over the mind of another. He had treated this theme himself in *The Father*, which he began only two months after *Rosmersholm* appeared, and was to do so again the following year in *Creditors*: while the degenerating effect of an aristocratic heritage was to be the theme, also the following year, of *Miss Julie*.

Gradually, *Rosmersholm* came to be appreciated. Bernard Shaw, reviewing Lugné-Poe's Paris production when it visited London in 1895, described the play as "this most enthralling of all Ibsen's works." In Italy, Eleonora Duse made Rebecca one of her most famous roles; Edward Gordon Craig did the décor for her—"one scene only—a vast room of great beauty"—and composed an eloquent programme note. "There is the powerful impression of unseen forces closing in upon the place," he wrote. "We hear continually the long drawn out note of the horn of death." The first American production took place on 28 March 1904 at the Princess Theatre in New York, when Florence Kahn, later the wife of Max Beerbohm, played Rebecca to the Rosmer of William Morris. It was ill received. "The presentation was in almost every respect a disappointment," commented the *Dramatic Mirror*. "Not only did the players murder the play; they buried its meaning so deep that many of the scenes were unintelligible." Three years later, however, Minnie Fiske presented *Rosmersholm* at New Haven, Connecticut, with herself as Rebecca, on, if we are to believe the records, Christmas Day, 1907, bringing it to the Lyric Theatre in New York five days later. It ran there for four weeks, and was then toured for 199 consecutive performances, reaching as far west as San Francisco. The cast included Bruce McRae as Rosmer, George Arliss as Ulrik Brendel and Florence Montgomery as Mrs. Helseth. The best English Rebecca to date was probably the young Edith Evans in 1926, though the part was also finely acted by Flora Robson in 1930 (at Cambridge, with Robert Donat as Rosmer), and Jean Forbes Robertson in 1936. Peggy Ashcroft gave a performance in 1959 which was widely praised, though I found it deeply disappointing; admirably accomplished, it suggested none of the passionate overtones of Rebecca's character. There was no earthly reason why this woman should have killed herself. But she was handicapped by a horribly flattened and truncated text. The play and its ending only make sense if Rebecca is played (as she is written) as a deeply passionate woman; just as Rosmer, beneath his inhibitions and frightened at the suggestion of it, is a deeply passionate man. If Rebecca is played as an intellectual bluestocking and Rosmer as a sexless parson, the ending makes nonsense. Why should such a couple kill themselves for love? It is only Rebecca's enemy, Dr. Kroll, who calls her an intellectual. Of course she had an intellect, but that is another thing. Ibsen, like Geroge Eliot, knew well the predicament of the woman of intellect whose passions can find no outlet. Rebecca and Dorothea Brook of *Middlemarch* have a good deal in common.

As recently as October 1964, a number of previously unpublished letters of Ibsen were privately printed in a limited edition,* and among them are two of particular interest in which Ibsen discusses the characters of *Rosmersholm*. Hans Schrœder, the director of the Christiania Theatre who had rejected *Ghosts*—a memory which the unfortunate man was to carry round his neck like an albatross for the rest of his days—had written to Ibsen asking for permission to stage *Rosmersholm,* and telling him of his plans for casting. On 2 January 1887, replying to Schrœder's suggestions, Ibsen delivered himself of some pungent comments on the latter's taste. "You think Mrs. Gundersen was born to play Rebecca. I don't agree. Mrs. Gundersen's strength is for the big declamatory line, and there are none of those in my play. How could she manage these seemingly light but exceedingly pregnant dialogues? Dual personalities, complex characters, are not her forte. Then you want Gundersen to play Rosmer. Permit me to ask what the effect is likely to be when Rebecca tells how she has been gripped by 'a wild and sensual longing' for him? Or when Brendel calls him 'my boy,' etc.? Or when Dr. Kroll hectors and browbeats him? Is G's personality compatible with this and much else? For Rosmer you must choose the most delicate and sensitive personality that your theatre can lay its hands on. . . . That the role of Dr. Kroll, that pedagogic autocrat, should be entrusted to Mr. Bjœrnson† is, I trust, a joke on which I need waste no further ink. Is it, though, conceivable that this monstrous idea is seriously being harboured? If the artistic direction of the theatre is so totally lacking in critical and self-critical ability, I fear that I can await the production only with the direst misgivings."

Henrik Ibsens Brevveksling med Christiania Theater 1878–1899, edited with a commentary by Œyvind Anker (Gyldendal Norsk Forlag, Oslo, 1964).
†Bjœrn Bjœrnson, the son of Bjœrnstjerne Bjœrnson.

Schrœder yielded, with a fair grace, and the cast was altered in accordance with Ibsen's wishes. A month later, Ibsen addressed to him some further advice about the characters. "Dr. Kroll," he wrote from Munich on 5 February 1887, "is an authoritarian with a passion for domineering, as is so often the case with headmasters. He is of course of good family; Major Rosmer's son married his sister. The Doctor's manner is therefore that of a well-born government official. Despite a certain asperity which now and then manifests itself, his behaviour in general is friendly and agreeable. He can be lovable when he pleases, or when he is with people he likes. But it is to be noted that he only likes those people who share his opinions. The rest irritate him, and with them he easily becomes ruthless and reveals a tendency towards malice. His appearance is distinguished; he is handsomely dressed, in black. Coat almost down to his knees, but no lower. He wears a white cravat, large and old-fashioned, which goes twice round his neck. i.e., no tie. His dress explains why Ulrik Brendel at first takes him for Pastor Rosmer and then for a 'brother of the cloth.' In Act One Rosmer also wears a black coat, but grey trousers and a tie or cravat of the same colour. In Acts Three and Four, however, he is dressed entirely in black.*

"Rebecca's manner must on no account carry any hint of imperiousness or masculinity. She does not *force* Rosmer forward. She *lures* him. A controlled power, a quiet determination, are of the essence of her character."

During rehearsals for the Christiania production, Constance Bruun, the young actress who had been chosen instead of Laura Gundersen to play Rebecca, was taken ill, and the part was given to another young actress, Sofie

---

*Œyvind Anker well observes that Ibsen's minute instructions regarding dress remind one of the meticulous costume designs he had made during his employment at the Bergen Theatre from 1851 to 1857.

Reimers. She wrote to Ibsen in Munich asking his advice; he gave it briefly (25 March 1887). "No declamation. No theatricalities. No grand mannerisms! Express every mood in a manner that will seem credible and natural. Never think of this or that actress whom you may have seen. Observe the life that is going on around you, and present a real and living human being."

Rosmersholm baffles readers and audiences, to say nothing of directors and actors, even today, and few Rebeccas indeed have ever made convincing either her refusal to marry Rosmer, when that has been her principal aim all along, or her ultimate suicide. By far the most penetrating analysis of the play, and of the secret motives which impel the characters, was made by Sigmund Freud in his essay *Character-Types,* which he wrote during the 1914 war. In the second section of this essay, sub-titled "Those wrecked by success," he deals with the common and disturbing psychological phenomenon of people who, when what they most want at last lies within their grasp, find themselves unable to seize hold of it. After an illuminating consideration of Lady Macbeth, Freud moves on to *Rosmersholm,* and makes the following analysis of Rebecca:

"Ibsen has made it clear," writes Freud, "by small touches of masterly subtlety that Rebecca does not actually tell lies but is never entirely straightforward. Just as, in spite of her freedom from prejudice, she has understated her age by a year, so her confession to the two men [Rosmer and Kroll] is incomplete, and as a result of Kroll's insistence it is supplemented on some important points. Hence it is open to us to suppose that her explanation of her renunciation exposes one motive only to conceal another. . . . Rosmer's influence may only have been a cloak, which concealed another influence that was operative, and a remarkable indication points in this direction."

When, Freud continues, in the final scene, after her confession about herself and Beata, Rosmer again asks Rebecca to become his wife, by implication forgiving her; "she does not answer, as she should, that no forgiveness can rid her of the feeling of guilt she has incurred from her malignant deception of poor Beata; but she charges herself with another reproach which affects us as coming strangely from this free-thinking woman, and is far from deserving the importance which Rebecca attaches to it. . . . She has had sexual relations with another man; and we do not fail to observe that these relations, which occurred at a time when she was free and accountable to nobody, seem to her a greater hindrance to the union with Rosmer than her truly criminal behaviour to his wife. . . .

"After she has learnt that she has been the mistress of her own father, she surrenders herself wholly to her now overmastering sense of guilt.* She makes the confession to Rosmer and Kroll which stamps her as a murderess; she rejects forever the happiness to which she has paved the way by crime, and prepares for departure. But the true motive of her sense of guilt, which results in her being wrecked by success, remains a secret. As we have seen, it is something quite other than the atmosphere of Rosmersholm and the refining influence of Rosmer. . . .

"Rebecca's feeling of guilt has its source in the reproach of incest, even before Kroll, with analytical perspicacity, has made her conscious of it. If we reconstruct her past, expanding and filling in the author's hints, we may feel sure that she cannot have been without some inkling of the intimate relation between her mother and Dr. West. It must have made a great impression on her when she became her

---

*Because the consciousness of incest makes her feel irretrievably tainted, as though she had discovered that she was suffering from venereal disease—M.M.

mother's successor with this man. She stood under the domination of the Oedipus complex, even though she did not
know that this universal phantasy had in her case become a
reality. When she came to Rosmersholm, the inner force of
this first experience drove her into bringing about, by vigorous action, the same situation which had been realized in the
original instance through no doing of hers—into getting rid
of the wife and mother, so that she might take her place with
the husband and father. She describes with a convincing insistence how, against her will, she was obliged to proceed,
step by step, to the removal of Beata. . . . Everything that
happened to her at Rosmersholm, her falling in love with
Rosmer and her hostility to his wife, was from the first a
consequence of the Oedipus complex—an inevitable replica
of her relations with her mother and Dr. West.

"And so the sense of guilt which first causes her to reject
Rosmer's proposal is at bottom no different from the greater
one which drives her to her confession after Kroll has
opened her eyes. But just as under the influence of Dr. West
she had become a freethinker and despiser of religious morality, so she is transformed by her love for Rosmer into a
being of conscience and nobility. This much of the mental
process within her she understands, and so she is justified
in describing Rosmer's influence as the motive for the
change—the motive that had become accessible to her.

"The practising psycho-analytical physician knows how
frequently, or how invariably, a girl who enters a household
as servant, companion or governess, will consciously or unconsciously weave a daydream, which derives from the
Oedipus complex, of the mistress of the house disappearing
and the master taking the newcomer as his wife in her place.
Rosmersholm is the greatest work of art of the class that
treats of this common phantasy in girls. What makes it into a
tragic drama is the extra circumstance that the heroine's day-

dream had been preceded in her childhood by a precisely corresponding reality.''

Rosmersholm marks Ibsen's final withdrawal as a playwright from the polemical field. A year after writing it, on 12 September 1887, he declared in a speech at Gothenburg that his political interests were waning and, with them, his eagerness for battle. He may have based the character of Rosmer principally on Snoilsky; but he put a good deal of himself into it too. Although he enjoyed writing and making speeches on controversial subjects, he disliked embroiling himself; and what he had seen of the results of party strife in Norway in 1885 determined him to withdraw still further from the battle. *Rosmersholm* is the last of his plays which introduces public or local politics as a decisive factor in shaping people's characters and destinies. In *The League of Youth, The Pillars of Society, Ghosts*, and *An Enemy of the People*, such politics had played an important part; the actions of Stensgaard, Bernick, Manders and Peter Stockmann are, at critical moments, influenced by a fear of offending local political opinion. Gregers Werle in *The Wild Duck* is very much a political animal; and *A Doll's House*, though politics do not enter directly into it, struck at the heart of one of the most controversial issues of the day. But in the six plays which follow *Rosmersholm*, the battle is out of earshot. It is the trolls within, not the trolls without, that determine the destinies of Ellida and Hilde Wangel, Hedda Gabler, Halvard Solness, the Allmers, the Borkmans and Arnold Rubek. They are conscious of strange, sick passions which direct their lives; and *Rosmersholm* provides a link between Ibsen's old method and his new. Rosmer is the last of his characters to be caught up in and undermined by local politics; and Rebecca is the first of those passionate but inhibited lovers who dominate the dark plays of his final period.

His disillusionment with politics, arising from his experiences in Norway in 1885, was complete. In a speech in Stockholm on 24 September 1887, he declared his belief that the present age was the end of an era, and that a new age was dawning, a third kingdom in which "current political and social conceptions will cease to exist." As Professor Francis Bull has put it, in Trondhjem in 1885 he had a programme, in Stockholm in 1887 a dream vision. In 1885 he had identified himself with the age; in 1887 and afterwards, he cherished only a vague hope for an unguessable future.

MICHAEL MEYER

CHARACTERS

JOHN ROSMER, owner of Rosmersholm; a former parish priest

REBECCA WEST, living at Rosmersholm

DR. KROLL, a headmaster; brother-in-law to Rosmer

ULRIK BRENDEL

PETER MORTENSGAARD

MRS. HELSETH, housekeeper at Rosmersholm

The action takes place at Rosmersholm, an old country seat in the neighbourhood of a small town by a fjord in western Norway.

This translation of *Rosmersholm* was first performed in London on 17 May 1973 at the Greenwich Theatre. The cast was:

JOHN ROSMER	Jeremy Brett
REBECCA WEST	Joan Plowright
DR. KROLL	John Nettleton
ULRIK BRENDEL	John Bailey
PETER MORTENSGAARD	John Warner
MRS. HELSETH	Margery Mason

Directed by Robin Phillips

ACT ONE

The living-room at Rosmersholm; spacious, old-fashioned and comfortable. Downstage on the right-hand wall is a tiled stove decorated with fresh birch-branches and wild flowers. Upstage of this, a door. In the rear wall, folding doors to the hall. In the left-hand wall, a window. Downstage of this, a stand with flowers and plants. By the stove, a table with a sofa and easy chairs. Around the walls hang portraits, some old, some comparatively new, of priests, officers and court officials in uniform. The window is open, as are the door to the hall and the front door beyond. Outside, an avenue of old trees is visible, leading to the estate. A summer evening. The sun has set.

> REBECCA WEST *is seated in an armchair by the window, crocheting a large white woollen shawl, which is almost completed. Now and then she glances out enquiringly from behind the flowers. After a few moments,* MRS. HELSETH *enters right.*

MRS. HELSETH: I'd better start laying the table soon, hadn't I, miss?

REBECCA: Yes, would you? I'm sure the Pastor will be back soon.

MRS. HELSETH: Isn't it draughty there, miss?

REBECCA: A little. Would you close it, please?

226

MRS. HELSETH *goes over and shuts the door leading to the hall. Then she crosses to the window.*

MRS. HELSETH *(about to close it, looks out):* Why, isn't that the Pastor coming now?

REBECCA *(quickly):* Where? *(Gets up.)* Yes, that's him. *(Behind the curtain.)* Get back. Don't let him see us.

MRS. HELSETH *(moves back into the room):* Oh, look, miss! Fancy that! He's beginning to use the mill path again.

REBECCA: He did the day before yesterday, too. *(Peers out between the curtain and the window-frame.)* But now we'll see whether—

MRS. HELSETH: Will he dare take the footbridge?

REBECCA: That's what I want to find out. *(After a pause.)* No. He's turning. He's going round the top today too. *(Leaves the window.)* The long way round.

MRS. HELSETH: Ah well, miss. It must be hard for the Pastor to cross that bridge. After what happened there—

REBECCA *(gathers her crocheting):* They cling to their dead here at Rosmersholm.

MRS. HELSETH: If you want my opinion, miss, it's the dead who cling to Rosmersholm.

REBECCA *(looks at her):* The dead?

MRS. HELSETH: Yes. It's almost as though they couldn't free themselves from the ones they left behind.

REBECCA: What makes you say that?

MRS. HELSETH: Well, otherwise this white horse wouldn't keep on appearing.

REBECCA: Mrs. Helseth, what exactly is all this about this white horse?

MRS. HELSETH: Oh, nothing. You wouldn't believe such things, anyway.

REBECCA: Do you believe in it, then?

MRS. HELSETH *(goes across and shuts the window):* Ah,

you'd only laugh at me, miss. (*Looks out.*) Why—isn't that the Pastor on the mill-path again—?

REBECCA (*looks out*): That? (*Goes to the window.*) No, that's—why, it's Dr. Kroll!

MRS. HELSETH: Yes, so it is!

REBECCA: Well, that's a pleasant surprise. He must be coming to call on us.

MRS. HELSETH: He walks straight over the bridge, he does. Though she was his sister, and his own flesh and blood. Well, I'll go in and lay then, miss.

She goes out right. REBECCA *stands for a moment at the window; then she waves, smiles and nods towards the newcomer. Dusk is beginning to fall.*

REBECCA (*walks over and speaks through the door, right*): Mrs. Helseth, do you think you could give us something a little extra tonight? I expect you know what the headmaster likes best.

MRS. HELSETH (*offstage*): Very good, miss. You leave it to me.

REBECCA (*opens the door to the hall*): Well, at last—! Dear Dr. Kroll, how good to see you!

DR. KROLL (*in the hall, puts down his stick*): Thank you. I trust I don't call at an inconvenient moment?

REBECCA: You? Don't be absurd.

KROLL (*enters*): Enchanting as ever! (*Looks around.*) Is Rosmer up in his study?

REBECCA: No, he's taking a walk. He's been a little longer than usual. But he'll be back any minute now. (*Indicates the sofa.*) Do please sit down until he comes.

KROLL (*puts down his hat*): Thank you, thank you. (*Sits and looks around.*) Well, how very attractive you've made this old room look! Flowers everywhere.

REBECCA: Mr. Rosmer loves to have fresh flowers around.

KROLL: So do you, I imagine.

REBECCA: Yes. I find them so beautifully soothing. In the old days we had to deny ourselves that pleasure.

KROLL *(nods sadly):* Poor Beata couldn't stand their perfume.

REBECCA: Nor their colours. They—confused her.

KROLL: Yes. I remember. *(More lightly.)* Well, how are things out here?

REBECCA: Oh, life goes on. Quiet and peaceful. One day very like another. And how are things with you? Your wife—?

KROLL: Ah, my dear Miss West, let's not talk about me. Every family has its troubles. Especially in such times as we live in now.

REBECCA *(after a moment, sits in an armchair by the sofa):* Why haven't you come out to see us? You haven't been once these holidays.

KROLL: Well, one doesn't like to bother people—

REBECCA: If you knew how we've missed you—

KROLL: And anyway, I've been away—

REBECCA: So I've heard. I gather you've been addressing public meetings.

KROLL *(nods):* Yes, what do you say to that? Never thought I'd turn political agitator in my old age, did you?

REBECCA *(smiles):* You've always been a bit of an agitator, Dr. Kroll.

KROLL: For my own amusement, yes. But now I'm taking it seriously. Do you ever see these radical newspapers?

REBECCA: Well, yes, I can't deny—

KROLL: My dear Miss West, there's no earthly reason why you shouldn't. A person such as yourself—

REBECCA: That's what I think. I have to keep up with things. Keep informed about what's going on—

KROLL: Of course I suppose one can't expect you as a woman to take active sides in this civil dispute—I nearly said civil war—that's raging here. But then, you must have read all this mud that's been thrown at me by these so-called representatives of the people? It's really infamous the crudities that they indulge in.

REBECCA: I thought you gave them a pretty good nip or two.

KROLL: I did. I say it myself. Yes, I've tasted blood now! They'll learn I'm not the cheek-turning kind—! *(Breaks off.)* But let's not discuss this distressing subject this evening.

REBECCA: No, dear Dr. Kroll, I'd rather not.

KROLL: Tell me, how are you finding life at Rosmersholm now that you're alone here? Since our poor Beata—?

REBECCA: Oh, thank you, I'm quite happy. Of course it seems empty without her. And sad—I miss her terribly. But apart from that—

KROLL: Do you plan to stay? Permanently, I mean?

RÉBECCA: Dear Dr. Kroll, I don't really think about it one way or the other. I've grown so used to the place now, I almost feel I belong here.

KROLL: But of course. So I should hope.

REBECCA: And as long as Mr. Rosmer feels I can be of any use and comfort to him—well, I think I'll stay.

KROLL *(looks at her, moved):* You know, it's a pretty noble thing for a woman to sacrifice her youth for other people.

REBECCA: What else would I have had to live for?

KROLL: First you had that foster-father of yours to look after—I know how unreasonable he was, once he got paralysed, and what a strain that must have been—

REBECCA: Oh, he wasn't so—unreasonable in the old days, when we were living up in the north. It was those dreadful sea voyages that broke him. But once we'd moved down here—yes, we did have one or two difficult years before his troubles ended.

KROLL: Weren't the years that followed even more difficult for you?

REBECCA: No, how can you say such a thing! I loved Beata—
and she so needed care and affection, the poor darling.

KROLL: Bless you for remembering her so charitably.

REBECCA *(moves a little closer to him):* Dear Dr. Kroll, you
say that so kindly and sincerely—I'm sure you have no
bad feeling about this.

KROLL: Bad feeling? What do you mean?

REBECCA: Well, it wouldn't be so strange if you found it
rather painful to see a stranger like me running Rosmersholm.

KROLL: Great heavens alive, how—?

REBECCA: But you don't. *(Gives him her hand.)* Thank you,
dear Dr. Kroll! Thank you, thank you!

KROLL: But how in heaven's name could such an idea enter
your head?

REBECCA: I began to worry a little because you so seldom
visited us.

KROLL: Then you've been barking up the wrong tree, Miss
West. And besides—nothing has really changed here. I
mean, it was you, and you alone, who ran Rosmersholm
during those last unhappy months of poor Beata's life.

REBECCA: I was only a substitute for Mrs. Rosmer.

KROLL: Yes, well— You know what, Miss West? For my
own part, I shouldn't be at all sorry to see you—but one
mustn't speak of such things yet.

REBECCA: What do you mean?

KROLL: If things should so turn out that you should fill the
place left by—

REBECCA: I have the place I want, Dr. Kroll.

KROLL: Materially, perhaps; but not—

REBECCA *(interrupts earnestly):* Shame on you, Dr. Kroll!
How can you sit here joking about such things?

KROLL: Ah well, our good John Rosmer probably feels he's
had his share of matrimony. All the same—

REBECCA: The whole idea is ridiculous.

KROLL: All the same—! Tell me, Miss West—if it isn't an impertinent question—how old are you?

REBECCA: I'm ashamed to admit I am already twenty-nine, Dr. Kroll. Coming up to thirty.

KROLL: Really. And Rosmer—how old is he? Let me see. He's five years younger than I am—well then, he must be forty-three. I think that would be highly suitable.

REBECCA *(rises):* Indeed, yes. Most suitable. Will you take tea with us this evening?

KROLL: Thank you—yes, I had thought of staying. There's something I want to discuss with our friend. And, by the way, Miss West—just in case you should start having any further foolish thoughts, I intend to visit you both regularly—just like in the old days.

REBECCA: Oh yes, please do! *(Presses his hands.)* Thank you, thank you! You're so good and kind!

KROLL *(a little growlishly):* Am I? That's more than I ever hear at home.

JOHN ROSMER *enters right.*

REBECCA: Mr. Rosmer—do you see who's sitting here?

ROSMER: Mrs. Helseth told me.

DR. KROLL *has got up.*

ROSMER *(softly, emotionally, clasps* KROLL's *hands):* Welcome back to Rosmersholm, my dear Kroll! *(Puts his hands on* KROLL's *shoulders and looks him in the eyes.)* My dear old friend! I knew everything would be all right between us again.

KROLL: But, my dear fellow—have you, too, had this foolish delusion that there was something wrong?

REBECCA *(to* ROSMER*):* What a blessing it was only a foolish delusion!

ROSMER: Was it really, Kroll? But then, why did you never come to see us?

KROLL *(earnestly, softly):* Because I didn't want to be a living reminder of your years of unhappiness—and of—of her who ended in the millrace.

ROSMER: That was very kind of you. You're always so considerate. But I promise you it was quite unnecessary. Come [Kroll. Let's sit down on the sofa.]* *(They sit.)* No, I don't find it painful to be reminded of Beata. We speak about her every day.

KROLL: Do you really?

REBECCA *(lights the lamp):* Indeed we do.

ROSMER: But it stands to reason. We both loved her so dearly. And Rebec—Miss West and I both know we did all we could to help the poor darling. We have nothing with which to reproach ourselves. Our memory of Beata is purely a happy one.

KROLL: You dear, good people! From now on I shall come and visit you every day.

REBECCA *(sits in an armchair):* Well, let's see if you keep your word.

ROSMER *(somewhat hesitantly):* Kroll—I'm deeply grieved that our friendship was ever interrupted. I've always greatly valued your advice, all the years we've known each other. Ever since I left school.

KROLL: Well, yes, and I'm proud of it. Is there something particular at the moment that—?

ROSMER: There's so much I want to discuss with you heart-to-heart.

REBECCA: Yes. It must be such a comfort to have an old friend one can—

KROLL: Oh, believe me, there's even more that I want to discuss with you. I suppose you know I've now become an active politician?

ROSMER: Yes, so you have. How did that happen?

---

*Brackets indicate suggested cuts for performance.

KROLL: I had to, Rosmer. Couldn't help it—though I put up a pretty stiff fight against it! One can't just go on being an idle observer. Now that these dreadful radicals have gained power, I feel the moment has come. So I've persuaded our little circle of friends in town to close their ranks. The moment has come, I tell you!

REBECCA *(with a gentle smile):* Isn't it a little late, now?

KROLL: Well, I won't deny it would have been better if we could have stemmed the tide earlier. But who could have foreseen what was going to happen? Not I, at any rate. *(Gets up and walks round the room.)* But now my eyes have been opened. Would you believe it, the spirit of anarchy has forced its way into the school itself!

ROSMER: The school? Surely not your school?

KROLL: Indeed it has. My own school. I have discovered that for over six months the boys in the Sixth Form—some of them, anyway—have been running a secret society! And they've taken out a subscription to that damned paper of Mortensgaard's!

REBECCA: The *Morning Star?*

KROLL: Yes—fine mental sustenance for the future leaders of our country, eh? But the worst of the matter is that it's not the idlers and dunces who have banded together in this conspiracy against me. It's all my best pupils.

REBECCA: Does this hurt you so deeply, Dr. Kroll?

KROLL: Hurt me! To see my whole life's work obstructed and threatened! But that's not the worst. There's something else. *(Looks around.)* There isn't anyone listening?

REBECCA: No, of course not.

KROLL: Well, then—you will hardly credit it, but this discord and subversion have penetrated into my own house—into the calm and peace of my very home! They have destroyed my family life.

ROSMER *(rises):* What! Your own home—!

REBECCA *(goes over to* KROLL*):* But, my dear Dr. Kroll, what on earth has happened?

KROLL: Would you believe it—my own children—! Well, to cut a long story short, Lauritz is the ringleader of the conspiracy. And Hilda has embroidered a red cover to hide the *Morning Star* in.

ROSMER: That I'd never have imagined! In your own home—!

KROLL: Who'd have dreamed it was possible! In my own home, where obedience and order have always reigned— where, until now all voices have spoken as one—!

REBECCA: How does your wife take all this?

KROLL: That's the most incredible thing of all. All her life, in great things and small, she's shared my opinions and supported everything I've said—and now even she's started taking the children's side. And she blames *me* for what has happened. Says I've repressed them. As though it weren't necessary to give them an occasional—! Well, so I've had trouble at home, too. But of course I don't talk about it. Such things are best kept quiet. *(Walks across the room.)* Oh dear, oh dear, oh dear! *(Stops by the window with his hands behind his back and looks out.)*

REBECCA *(has gone over to* ROSMER *and, unnoticed by* KROLL, *whispers quickly):* Tell him!

ROSMER *(similarly):* Not tonight.

REBECCA *(as before):* Yes, now.

She goes over and attends to the lamp.

KROLL *(comes across the room):* Well, my dear Rosmer, so now you know how the spirit of the age has cast its shadow over my domestic as well as my official life. These decadent, cankerous, demoralizing heresies—must I not fight them with all the weapons I can muster? Yes, Rosmer, that is what I intend to do. [Not only with my tongue, but with my pen!]

ROSMER: Do you think you'll be able to achieve anything?

KROLL: I shall at any rate have performed my duty as a citizen. And I regard it as the duty of every right-minded and patriotic Norwegian to do the same. Actually, that's the chief reason I came out to see you this evening.

ROSMER: But, my dear fellow, what could I—?

KROLL: You must rally to our cause. Help your old friends, lend us all your strength.

REBECCA: But, Dr. Kroll, you know how Mr. Rosmer dislikes that kind of public activity.

KROLL: He must overcome his dislike. You're too passive, Rosmer. You sit here walled in by your books—oh, heaven knows I've every respect for research and scholarship. But this is no time for such indulgences, more's the pity. You don't seem to realize what the situation in our country is. [Practically every single accepted idea has been turned topsy-turvy.] It's going to be a battle to get these vicious heresies rooted out.

ROSMER: I agree. But that kind of work is hardly in my line.

REBECCA: And I think Mr. Rosmer has come to look at life from a more liberal viewpoint than before.

KROLL *(starts):* More liberal—!

REBECCA: More open-minded. Less prejudiced.

KROLL: What on earth do you mean? Rosmer—surely you couldn't be so feeble as to imagine that these demagogues have won anything more than a temporary victory?

ROSMER: My dear Kroll, you know how little I understand politics. But I believe that in recent years people have perhaps begun to think more independently.

KROLL: And you regard that as a good thing? Anyway, you're quite wrong, my friend. Just you find out for yourself the opinions that these radicals are propagating! It's hardly any different from the wisdom that's preached in the pages of the *Morning Star*.

REBECCA: Yes, Mortensgaard has a lot of influence over people around here.

KROLL: Isn't it incredible! A man with a past like that! Thrown out of his teaching job for an immoral relationship! A man like that setting himself up as a leader of the people! And he's succeeding! He's actually succeeding! I hear he's now planning to expand his newspaper. I'm told on good authority that he's looking for a partner.

REBECCA: Why don't you and your friends start a rival newspaper?

KROLL: That's exactly what we're doing. This very day we have bought the *County Telegraph*. [The financial aspect presented no difficulties.] But— *(Turns to* ROSMER.*)* Well, this is really what I came to speak to you about. It's the running of the paper—the editorial side—that is our problem, you see. Tell me, Rosmer—remembering the issues at stake, couldn't you see your way to helping us out?

ROSMER *(almost as though frightened):* I?

REBECCA: How could you imagine such a thing?

KROLL: I know you hate public meetings and don't want to expose yourself to the kind of rough stuff that goes on there. But the more secluded work of an editor, or what I might rather call the—

ROSMER: No, no, my dear chap, you mustn't ask me to do this.

KROLL: I'd gladly have a shot at it myself. But I couldn't possibly manage it. I'm already so overburdened with obligations. You, on the other hand, no longer have any professional commitments. Of course the rest of us will give you all the help we can—

ROSMER: I can't, Kroll. I'm not the right man for it.

KROLL: Not the right man? That's what you said when your father procured this living for you—

ROSMER: I was right. That was why I went my own way.

KROLL: Oh, if you're only as good an editor as you were a man of God, we shan't complain.

ROSMER: Look, Kroll. I'm telling you once and for all. I won't do it.

KROLL: Well, at least you'll let us use your name.

ROSMER: My name?

KROLL: Yes, the mere name of John Rosmer will be a great asset to our paper. The rest of us are known to be politically committed. I gather that I myself am already branded as a furious fanatic. [So our names aren't likely to make any converts among the misguided masses.] But you—you've always stood outside the battle. Your goodness and incorruptibility, your sensitivity and intellect, your unimpeachable integrity, are known and prized by everyone throughout the county. To say nothing of the honour and respect which you command as a former man of God! And, last but by no means least, there's your family name.

ROSMER: Oh, my family name—

KROLL (points to the portraits): The Rosmers of Rosmersholm. Men of God and men of war. Respected servants of their country. Every one of them a man of honour who knew his duty. A family that for nigh on two hundred years has been venerated and looked up to as the first in the county. (Puts a hand on ROSMER's shoulder.) Rosmer—you owe it to yourself and to the traditions of your family to defend and protect everything that has hitherto been held sacred in our society. (Turns.) Well, what do you say, Miss West?

REBECCA (with a soft, quiet laugh): Dear Dr. Kroll! I find all this unspeakably funny.

KROLL: What! Funny!

REBECCA: Yes. You might as well know—

ROSMER (quickly): No, no—please! Not now!

KROLL *(looks from one to the other):* My dear friends, what on earth—? *(Breaks off.)* Hm!

MRS. HELSETH *enters through the door right.*

MRS. HELSETH *(to* ROSMER*):* There's a man at the servants' entrance. He says he wants to speak with you, sir.

ROSMER *(relieved):* Is there? Well, tell him to come in.

MRS. HELSETH: Here? Into the drawing room?

ROSMER: Of course.

MRS. HELSETH: But he doesn't look the type to bring in here.

REBECCA: How does he look, Mrs. Helseth?

MRS. HELSETH: Oh, not at all respectable, miss.

ROSMER: Didn't he say who he was?

MRS. HELSETH: Yes, I think he said he was called Hekman or something.

ROSMER: I don't know anyone of that name.

MRS. HELSETH: He said something about being called Uldrik too.

ROSMER *(starts):* Ulrik—Hetman! Was that it?

MRS. HELSETH: Hetman—yes, that was it.

KROLL: I'm sure I've heard that name before—

REBECCA: Wasn't that the name he used to write under—you remember, that strange old—?

ROSMER *(to* KROLL*):* It is Ulrik Brendel's pen-name, Kroll.

KROLL: Ulrik Brendel! That charlatan. Yes, I remember him.

REBECCA: So, he's still alive.

ROSMER: The last I heard of him, he'd joined up with a troupe of strolling players.

KROLL: The last *I* heard of him, he was in the workhouse.

ROSMER: Please ask him to come in, Mrs. Helseth.

MRS. HELSETH: As you say, sir. *(She goes.)*

KROLL: Are you really going to allow that man into your drawing room?

ROSMER: Surely you remember? He used to be my tutor.

KROLL: I remember he used to come here and stuff your head full of radical nonsense, until your father chased him out of the door with a horsewhip.

ROSMER *(a little bitterly):* Father always acted the major, even in his own house.

KROLL: Thank him in his grave for it, my dear Rosmer. Ha!

> MRS. HELSETH *opens the door on the right for* ULRIK BRENDEL, *exits and closes it behind him. He is an imposing figure, somewhat emaciated, but brisk and lively, with grey hair and beard. He is dressed like a common tramp, in a worn frock coat and bad shoes; no shirt is visible. Old black gloves; a soft, dirty hat beneath his arm; and a walking stick in his hand.*

ULRIK BRENDEL *(hesitates at first, then walks briskly over to* KROLL *and holds out his hands):* Good evening, John!

KROLL: I beg your pardon—

BRENDEL: Did you think you'd see my face again? Within these hated walls?

KROLL: I beg your pardon. *(Points.) That* is—

BRENDEL *(turns):* But of course! *Le voilà!* John—my boy—my best beloved!

ROSMER *(shakes his hand):* My dear old tutor!

BRENDEL: Certain memories notwithstanding, I was loth to pass this ancient seat without paying a fleeting visit.

ROSMER: You are most heartily welcome here now. Never fear that.

BRENDEL: And this charming lady—? *(Bows.)* Your wife, of course.

ROSMER: Miss West.

BRENDEL: A close relative, no doubt. And yon stranger—? A brother of the cloth, I see.

KROLL: My name is Kroll, sir. I am the local headmaster.

BRENDEL: Kroll? Kroll? *Momento!* Had you, sir, in your salad days, pretensions towards philology?

KROLL: Naturally I read the subject.

BRENDEL: Why, *Donnerwetter,* then I used to know you!

KROLL *(deprecatingly):* I'm sorry—

BRENDEL: Weren't you—?

KROLL *(as before):* I'm sorry—

BRENDEL: —one of those crusading moralizers who got me expelled from the University Debating Society?

KROLL: Possibly. But I must disclaim any closer relationship.

BRENDEL: Ah, well. *Comme vous voulez,* Herr Doctor! What boots it? Ulrik Brendel remains the man he is.

REBECCA: Are you making for town, Mr. Brendel?

BRENDEL: A hit, madam—a palpable hit! At intervals I find myself impelled to strike a blow for existence. Against the grain; but, *enfin!*—needs must—!

ROSMER: But, my dear Mr. Brendel, won't you let me help you? Somehow or other—?

BRENDEL: Ha? What a suggestion! [Wouldst thou profane the bond that binds us?] Never, John—never!

ROSMER: But what are you planning to do in town? Believe me, you won't find it easy to—

BRENDEL: Leave that to me, my boy. The die is cast. You see me at the outset of a great campaign, that dwarfs all my previous reconnoitrings. *(To* KROLL.*)* Dare I ask the Herr Professor—*unter uns*—is there a reasonably respectable and capacious lecture hall in your esteemed town?

KROLL: I suppose the largest is the Workers' Union—

BRENDEL: And has Your Honour any influence in this no doubt most useful organization?

KROLL: I have nothing whatever to do with them.

REBECCA *(to* BRENDEL*):* You ought to get in touch with Peter Mortensgaard.

BRENDEL: *Pardon, madame!* What kind of an idiot is that?

ROSMER: What makes you think he's an idiot?

BRENDEL: The very name proves him an upstart.

KROLL: I hadn't expected that answer.

BRENDEL: But I will conquer my nausea. [I have no choice.] When a man such as myself stands at a crossroads in his life— Right! I shall contact this individual—open negotiations—

ROSMER: Are you seriously at a crossroads?

BRENDEL: My own dear boy, don't you know that Ulrik Brendel is always serious? Yes, John! I intend to become a new man. To abandon the role of modest onlooker which I have hitherto assumed.

ROSMER: But how do you—?

BRENDEL: I now descend into the arena of life! We live at the crossroads of a storm-wracked age. I shall lay my mite upon the altar of liberation!

KROLL: You too—?

BRENDEL *(to them all):* Is the company acquainted with my *obiter scripta?*

KROLL: No, to be frank, I—

REBECCA: I've read several. My guardian used to have them.

BRENDEL: Then, fair lady, you have wasted your time. It is all bunk. Take my word for it.

REBECCA: Oh?

BRENDEL: What you have read. My major works remain unknown. Save to myself.

REBECCA: Why is that?

BRENDEL: Because they have not yet been written.

ROSMER: But, my dear Mr. Brendel—

BRENDEL: My dear boy, you know I'm a bit of a sybarite. A gourmet. Always have been. I like to savour things in solitude. Then I enjoy them doubly—nay, tenfold! When golden dreams descended on me, enveloping me in mist—when new and dazzling ideas were born in me, and wafted me heavenwards on their swift pinions—I fashioned them into poems, visions, images! In my head, you understand—

ROSMER: Yes, yes.

BRENDEL: Ah, John! I have drunk deep of pleasure! The blissful mystery of creation—in my head, as I explained—the applause, the eulogies, the fame, the laurels—I have garnered them all with hands that shook with joy. I have sated my self in secret dreams with a rapture that drugged my senses—

KROLL: Hm!

ROSMER: But you never wrote any of it down?

BRENDEL: Not a word. The dull toil of the scribe has always repelled me. And why should I profane my own ideals when I can enjoy them pure and undisturbed? But now I offer them up. I feel like a mother about to deliver her unspotted daughters into the rough arms of their husbands. But I offer them, notwithstanding—a sacrifice upon the altar of liberation. A sequence of closely argued lectures—throughout the country—!

REBECCA *(animatedly):* This is a noble gesture, Mr. Brendel! You are sacrificing the dearest thing you possess.

ROSMER: The only thing.

REBECCA *(looks meaningly at* ROSMER*):* How many other men would do this? Would have the courage to do it?

ROSMER *(returns her glance):* Who knows?

BRENDEL: My audience is moved. That quickens my heart—and strengthens my will. I shall proceed to action. One thing, though— *(To* KROLL.*)* Can Your Reverence tell me—is there a Temperance Association in this town? A Society of Total Abstinence? Doubtless there is.

KROLL: Indeed, yes. I myself am its president, at your service.

BRENDEL: I knew it by your face! Well, then, it is not impossible that I may look in on you and enrol for a week.

KROLL: I am sorry. We do not enrol members by the week.

BRENDEL: *A la bonheur,* Herr Pedagogue. Ulrik Brendel has never forced his presence on such institutions. *(Turns.)*

But I must not linger in this house, so rich in memories. I must press to town, and select a suitable abode. There is, I trust, a decent inn?

REBECCA: Won't you have a drink to warm you before you go?

BRENDEL: How do you mean, "warm" me, gracious lady?

REBECCA: A cup of tea or—

BRENDEL: Thanks, bountiful hostess. I never presume on private hospitality. *(Makes a farewell gesture to them all with his hand.) Auf Wiedersehen, mein Herrschaft! (Goes towards the door, but turns.)* Ah, true, I had forgotten. John—Pastor Rosmer—will you, for auld lang syne, do your old tutor a small service?

ROSMER: With all my heart.

BRENDEL: *Bon!* Then lend me—just for a day or two—a well pressed evening shirt.

ROSMER: Is that all?

BRENDEL: For once I march on foot. My luggage is being sent after me.

ROSMER: Of course. But isn't there anything else—?

BRENDEL: Well—since you mention it—could you conceivably spare an old, used, summer overcoat?

ROSMER: Yes, yes, of course.

BRENDEL: And if you should chance to have a decent pair of boots to match the coat—

ROSMER: I'm sure that can be arranged. As soon as we know your address I'll have them all sent on.

BRENDEL: No, no! I wish no inconvenience to be caused. I'll take these trifles with me.

ROSMER: Very well. Come upstairs with me, then.

REBECCA: No, let me. Mrs. Helseth and I can see to it.

BRENDEL: Never could I permit this *belle madame*—

REBECCA: Oh, nonsense. Now just you come with me, Mr. Brendel. *(Goes out right.)*

ROSMER *(detains him):* Tell me—isn't there any other way I can help you?

BRENDEL: Other way? I really can't imagine—yes, damn it—now I think of it—! John—you haven't by any chance five shillings on you?

ROSMER: We'll see. *(Opens his purse.)* I've a couple of ten shilling notes—

BRENDEL: Don't bother. I can always get them changed in town. You shall have the change shortly. Don't forget—two ten shilling notes. *Guten nacht,* my own, dear boy! Worshipful Sir, good night. *(He goes right, where* ROSMER *takes leave of him and closes the door behind him.)*

KROLL: Merciful heaven! So that was the Ulrik Brendel who people once believed would reshape the world!

ROSMER *(quietly):* At least he has had the courage to live life the way he thought it should be lived. I don't think that's so small an achievement.

KROLL: What! A life like his! Don't tell me he's turning your head again.

ROSMER: Oh, no, Kroll. Now I see my way clearly.

KROLL: Let us hope so, my dear Rosmer. You're so impressionable.

ROSMER: [Come and sit down.] I want to talk to you.

KROLL: By all means. *(They sit on the sofa.)*

ROSMER *(after a few moments):* We've made it pleasant and comfortable here, don't you think?

KROLL: Yes. It is very pleasant and comfortable here now. And peaceful. Yes, you've found yourself a home, Rosmer. And I have lost mine.

ROSMER: Don't say that, Kroll. Things will come right.

KROLL: Never. Never. The memory will always rankle. Things will never be as they were.

ROSMER: [Now listen, Kroll.] We two have been very close

for so many years. Do you think anything could happen that could ever make us cease to be friends?

KROLL: I can't imagine anything that could make us enemies. Why do you ask?

ROSMER: You mind so violently if people don't share your opinions.

KROLL: Well, possibly—but you and I agree on pretty well everything. In essentials, anyway.

ROSMER *(quietly):* No. Not any longer.

KROLL *(moves to rise):* What do you mean?

ROSMER *(puts a hand to restrain him):* No, you must sit still. Please, Kroll. I beg you.

KROLL: What is this? I don't understand you.

ROSMER: In my mind a new spring has dawned. A new youth, a new way of thought. So that—now I stand—

KROLL: Where? Where do you stand?

ROSMER: Where your children stand.

KROLL: You? You! But that's impossible! Where do you say you stand?

ROSMER: On the same side as Lauritz and Hilda.

KROLL *(bows his head):* An apostate! John Rosmer an apostate!

ROSMER: I ought to have felt a sense of joy at what you call my apostasy. But it grieved me. Because I knew it would grieve you deeply.

KROLL: Rosmer—Rosmer! I shall never recover from this. *(Looks sadly at him.)* To think that you can ally yourself with the forces of evil that are seeking to destroy our unhappy country.

ROSMER: I want to ally myself with the forces of emancipation.

KROLL: Yes, I know. That is the name given to it by the seducers, and by the victims they lead astray. But do you really believe that there is any emancipation to be hoped for from this spirit that is doing its best to poison our whole communal life?

ROSMER: I am not identifying myself with that spirit. Nor with either of the contending parties. I want to bring together men from all sides in a spirit of unity. As many as possible, and as urgently as possible. I want to devote my life and all my strength to this one end, of creating a responsible public opinion in our country.

KROLL: Don't you think we've had enough of public opinions? Personally, I think we're all well on the way to being dragged down into the gutter where only the common people can thrive.

ROSMER: That is exactly where I feel the task of public opinion lies.

KROLL: Task? What task?

ROSMER: To make all the people in this country noblemen.

KROLL: All the people—?

ROSMER: As many as possible, anyway.

KROLL: How?

ROSMER: By emancipating their minds and purifying their wills.

KROLL: You're a dreamer, Rosmer. Will *you* emancipate them? Will *you* purify them?

ROSMER: No, my dear friend. I can only try to open their eyes to the need for it. They must do it themselves.

KROLL: And you think they can?

ROSMER: Yes.

KROLL: By their own strength?

ROSMER: Yes, by their own strength. There is no other.

KROLL *(gets up):* Is this proper language from a man of God?

ROSMER: I am no longer a man of God.

KROLL: Yes, but—the faith you were brought up in—?

ROSMER: I no longer have it.

KROLL: No longer—!

ROSMER *(gets up):* I have given it up. I *had* to give it up, Kroll.

KROLL *(controls his emotion):* I see. Yes, yes, yes. The one follows the other. Was that why you left the Church?

ROSMER: Yes. When I saw things clearly—when I knew for sure that it was not a passing temptation, but something that I never could nor would escape from—then I left.

KROLL: So it has been fermenting inside you all this time. And we—your friends—were told nothing about it. Rosmer, Rosmer—how could you hide this dreadful truth from us?

ROSMER: Because I thought it was something that concerned only me. Besides, I didn't want to cause you and my other friends unnecessary distress. I thought I could go on living here as before, quiet and peaceful and happy. I wanted to read, to bury myself in those fields of thought that had hitherto been closed to me. To find my way into the great world of truth and freedom to which my eyes have now been opened.

KROLL: Apostate! Every word proves it. But why are you confessing all this? And why just now?

ROSMER: You have forced me to, Kroll.

KROLL: I? *I* forced you—!

ROSMER: When I heard about your violent conduct at those meetings—when I read about all the cruel speeches you made there—those hateful outbursts against your opponents [—your scornful condemnation of everything they stood for—]! Oh, Kroll! That you, you, could become like that! Then I saw my duty plainly. This strife that is being waged makes people evil. Their hearts must be filled with peace and joy and understanding. That is why I now stand forth to declare myself openly. I, too, want to test my strength. Couldn't you—from your side—help me, Kroll?

KROLL: Never while I draw breath shall I compromise with the forces that are seeking to destroy our society.

ROSMER: Then if we must fight, at least let us fight with honourable weapons.

KROLL: Whoever is not with me in such issues, him I no longer know. And I owe him no consideration.

ROSMER: Does that apply to me too?

KROLL: It's you who have broken with me, Rosmer.

ROSMER: Is this a breach, then?

KROLL: Yes! It is a breach with all those who have hitherto been your friends. Now you must face the consequences.

REBECCA WEST *enters right, and throws the door wide open.*

REBECCA: There! Now he's off to his sacrificial orgy. And now we can go and eat. Dr. Kroll!

KROLL *(takes his hat):* Good night, Miss West. I have no further business in this house.

REBECCA *(tensely):* What is it? *(Shuts the door and comes closer.)* Have you told him—?

ROSMER: Yes, he knows now.

KROLL: We won't let you go, Rosmer. We'll force you to come back to us.

ROSMER: I shall never do that.

KROLL: We'll see. You are not the kind of man who can stand alone.

ROSMER: I shall not be alone. There are two of us to bear the solitude together.

KROLL: Ah—! *(A suspicion crosses his mind.)* That too! Beata's words—!

ROSMER: Beata—?

KROLL *(dismisses the thought):* No, no. That was vile. Forgive me.

ROSMER: What? What do you mean?

249

KROLL: Please forget it. No, it's unthinkable! Forgive me. Goodbye. *(Goes towards the door leading to the hall.)*

ROSMER *(goes after him):* Kroll! We can't part like this. I'll come and see you tomorrow.

KROLL *(in the hall, turns):* You shall not set foot in my house! *(Takes his stick and goes.)*

ROSMER *stands for a second in the open doorway. Then he closes the door and walks across to the table.*

ROSMER: It doesn't matter, Rebecca. We shall manage. We two loyal friends. You and I.

REBECCA: What do you think he meant when he said: "It's unthinkable"?

ROSMER: Oh, don't bother about that, my dear. Whatever it was, he didn't believe it. Tomorrow I'll go in and see him. Good night.

REBECCA: Are you going to bed so early again tonight? After this?

ROSMER: Tonight as always. I feel so at peace now that it's over. You see—I am quite calm, Rebecca. You must take it calmly too, my dear. Good night.

REBECCA: Good night, my dearest. And sleep well.

ROSMER *goes out through the hall door. We hear him mount the stairs.* REBECCA *walks over and pulls a bellrope by the stove. After a few moments* MRS. HELSETH *enters right.*

REBECCA: You can clear the table again, Mrs. Helseth. The Pastor doesn't want anything. And the Doctor has gone home.

MRS. HELSETH: The Doctor gone? What's wrong with him?

REBECCA *(takes her crochet-work):* He thought a storm was blowing up—

MRS. HELSETH: That's strange. There isn't a cloud in the sky this evening.

250

REBECCA: As long as he doesn't see the white horse. I'm afraid we may soon be hearing from one of these ghosts of yours.

MRS. HELSETH: God forgive you, Miss West! Don't say such wicked things!

REBECCA: All right, all right—

MRS. HELSETH *(lowers her voice):* Do you really think someone's going to go soon, miss?

REBECCA: No, of course not. But there are so many kinds of white horses in this world, Mrs. Helseth. Well, good night. I'm going to my room.

MRS. HELSETH: Good night, miss.

REBECCA *goes out right with her crochet-work.*

MRS. HELSETH *(turns down the lamp, shakes her head and mumbles to herself):* Blessed Jesus! That Miss West. The way she talks sometimes.

ACT TWO

JOHN ROSMER's *study. In the left-hand wall is the entrance door. In the rear wall, a doorway with a curtain drawn aside from it, leading into his bedroom. Right, a window. In front of it, a desk, covered with books and papers. Bookshelves and cupboards around the walls. Frugally furnished. Downstage left, an old-fashioned couch with a table by it.*

> JOHN ROSMER, *wearing a smoking jacket, is seated in a high-backed chair at the desk. He is cutting a pamphlet and glancing through it, pausing now and then to dwell on it. There is a knock on the door left.*

ROSMER *(without turning):* Come in.

> REBECCA WEST *enters in a house coat.*

REBECCA: Good morning.

ROSMER *(turning the pages):* Good morning, my dear. Is there something you want?

REBECCA: I only wanted to ask if you've slept well.

ROSMER: Oh, yes. So deeply and peacefully. No dreams— *(Turns.)* And you?

REBECCA: Oh—yes, thank you. Towards morning.

ROSMER: I don't know when I last felt as easy in my heart as I do now. Oh, I'm so thankful I got that off my chest.

252

REBECCA: Yes, you shouldn't have kept it to yourself for so long, John.

ROSMER: I can't understand how I could have been such a coward.

REBECCA: It isn't a question of cowardice—

ROSMER: Oh, yes it was. When I think about it honestly, there was a good deal of cowardice in it.

REBECCA: All the more credit to you, then, for managing to overcome it. *(Sits down beside him on a chair by the desk.)* But now I want to tell you about something I've done—you mustn't be angry with me—

ROSMER: Angry? My dear, how could you imagine—?

REBECCA: Well, it was perhaps a little high-handed of me, but—

ROSMER: Well, tell me what it was.

REBECCA: Last night, when that Ulrik Brendel was leaving—I wrote him a few lines to take to Mortensgaard.

ROSMER *(a little doubtfully):* But, my dear Rebecca—! Well, what did you write?

REBECCA: I said he'd be doing you a service if he took care of that unfortunate man and gave him all the help he could.

ROSMER: My dear, you shouldn't have done that. That'll only have done Brendel harm. Besides, I'd much rather not have anything to do with Mortensgaard. You know the trouble I had with him once.

REBECCA: Don't you think it might be a good idea if you made things up with him?

ROSMER: I? With Mortensgaard? Why do you say that?

REBECCA: Well, you can't really feel safe now—now that you've quarrelled with your friends.

ROSMER *(looks at her and shakes his head):* Surely you don't imagine that Kroll or any of the others would want to be vindictive? That they might be thinking of—?

REBECCA: First reactions, you know—one can't be sure. I think possibly—after the way he took it—

ROSMER: Oh, you ought to know him better than that. Kroll's nothing if not a gentleman. I'll go along this evening and have a word with him. I'll talk to all of them. You'll see, everything'll be all right—

MRS. HELSETH *enters through the door left.*

REBECCA *(rises):* What is it, Mrs. Helseth?

MRS. HELSETH: Dr. Kroll's downstairs in the hall.

ROSMER *(gets up quickly):* Kroll!

REBECCA: Do you think he—?

MRS. HELSETH: He asks if he can come up and speak with you, sir.

ROSMER *(to* REBECCA*):* What did I tell you! Yes, of course he can. *(Goes to the door and calls down the stairs.)* Come up, my dear fellow. I'm delighted to see you.

ROSMER *stands holding the door open.* MRS. HELSETH *goes.* REBECCA *draws the curtain across the open doorway. Then she begins tidying here and there.* DR. KROLL *enters, hat in hand.*

ROSMER *(quiet, moved):* I knew it couldn't be the last time we'd—

KROLL: Today I see things in a different light from yesterday.

ROSMER: I knew you would. Now you've had time to think the matter over—

KROLL: You completely misunderstand me. *(Puts his hat on the table by the couch.)* It is imperative that I speak with you privately.

ROSMER: Surely Miss West—?

REBECCA: No, no, Mr. Rosmer. I'll go.

KROLL *(looks her up and down):* I must ask you to excuse

me, Miss West, for calling so early, and catching you before you have had time to—

REBECCA *(surprised)*: What do you mean? Do you find it improper that I should walk around at home dressed like this?

KROLL: Heaven forbid. I don't pretend to know what is regarded as proper nowadays at Rosmersholm.

ROSMER: Kroll—what on earth's come over you today?

REBECCA: Good morning, Dr. Kroll. *(She goes out left.)*

KROLL: By your leave— *(Sits on the couch.)*

ROSMER: [Yes, my dear fellow, let's sit down and have a frank talk about this.] *(Sits on a chair opposite KROLL.)*

KROLL: I haven't closed my eyes since I left this house. I lay awake all night, thinking and thinking.

ROSMER: And what have you come to tell me?

KROLL: [It'll take a long time, Rosmer.] Let me begin by telling you a little about Ulrik Brendel.

ROSMER: Has he been to see you?

KROLL: No. He got himself settled in some low tavern. In the worst possible company, naturally. He drank and stood drinks as long as his pockets were full. Then he started abusing them, called them scum and riff-raff. Which of course they were. Then they beat him up and threw him in the gutter.

ROSMER: I'm afraid he's quite incorrigible.

KROLL: He'd pawned your coat, too. But it seems he's managed to get that redeemed. Can you guess by whom?

ROSMER: You?

KROLL: No. The gallant Mr. Mortensgaard.

ROSMER: I see.

KROLL: I gather the first call Mr. Brendel made was upon that "idiot" and "upstart."

ROSMER: It seems to have turned out well for him—

KROLL: Very. *(Leans over the table, a little closer to ROSMER.)* But that brings me to something about which—

for the sake of our old—our former friendship—I feel it my duty to warn you.

ROSMER: What on earth do you mean, Kroll?

KROLL: I mean that there's some game being played in this house behind your back.

ROSMER: How can you say that? Are you referring to Reb—to Miss West?

KROLL: I am. I can well understand her point of view. She's been accustomed for so long to having her own way here. None the less—

ROSMER: My dear chap, you're completely mistaken. She and I have no secrets from each other. On any subject.

KROLL: Do her confessions to you include the fact that she's been corresponding with the editor of the *Morning Star?*

ROSMER: Oh, you mean that note she gave Ulrik Brendel.

KROLL: You know about it, then. And do you approve of her starting a relationship with this scandalmonger who seeks every week to make a laughing-stock of me [both professionally and in my public life]?

ROSMER: My dear Kroll, I'm sure that aspect of the matter hasn't even occurred to her. In any case, she is perfectly free to act as she chooses, just as I am.

KROLL: Indeed? Yes, I suppose that's all part of this new philosophy you've become so enamoured of. I assume Miss West shares your standpoint?

ROSMER: She does. The two of us have worked towards it together.

KROLL *(looks at him and slowly shakes his head):* Oh, you poor, blind dupe!

ROSMER: I? What makes you say that?

KROLL: Because I dare not—*will* not think the worst. No, no! Let me finish! You do value my friendship, Rosmer? And my respect? Or perhaps you don't?

ROSMER: I surely don't need to answer that question.

KROLL: Very well. But there are other questions that do demand an answer—a full explanation on your part. Will you allow me to submit you to a kind of—cross-examination?

ROSMER: Cross-examination?

KROLL: Yes. I want to question you on certain matters which you may find it painful to be reminded of. You see—this business of your apostasy—your emancipation, as you call it—ties up with much else about which, for your own sake, I want you to speak frankly to me.

ROSMER: My dear fellow, ask anything you like. I've nothing to hide.

KROLL: Tell me, then. What do you really think was the main reason Beata killed herself?

ROSMER: Have you any doubts? Or rather—can anyone ever hope to know why a poor, irresponsible mental invalid decides to end her misery?

KROLL: Are you so sure that Beata was insane? The doctors were by no means certain.

ROSMER: If the doctors had seen her as I so often saw her, they would have had no doubts.

KROLL: I had none—at the time.

ROSMER: How could one? Those uncontrollable, sick fits of sensuality—and the way she expected me to reciprocate them. She—frightened me. And then that illogical and remorseless way she reproached herself during those last years.

KROLL: Yes, when she learned she'd never be able to have any children.

ROSMER: Yes, well, I mean—! To feel such appalling and inescapable anguish about something that was in no way her fault! Is that sanity?

KROLL: Hm—! Do you happen to recall whether you had any books in the house that dealt with the—purpose of marriage—from the so-called "progressive," modern viewpoint?

ROSMER: I remember Miss West lent me a book about that. She'd inherited her guardian's library, as you know. But, my dear Kroll, you surely don't imagine we were so careless as to mention anything like that to poor Beata? I assure you on my honour, we are completely innocent in this matter. It was her own deranged imagination that gave her these wild ideas.

KROLL: I can tell you one thing, anyway. That poor, tormented, overstrung woman ended her life in order that you might be happy—and free to live—the life you wanted to.

ROSMER (half-rises from his chair): What do you mean by that?

KROLL: You must listen calmly to me now, Rosmer, because now at last I can tell you this. During the year before she died, Beata twice visited me to tell me how desperate and frightened she was.

ROSMER: About this?

KROLL: No. The first time she came and said she feared you were in danger of becoming an apostate. That you were thinking of abandoning your ancestral faith.

ROSMER (eagerly): That's impossible, Kroll! Quite impossible! You must be mistaken about this.

KROLL: Why?

ROSMER: Because as long as Beata was alive, I was still in doubt—still battling with myself. And I fought that battle alone. I didn't speak of it to a soul. I don't think even Rebecca—

KROLL: Rebecca?

ROSMER: I mean—Miss West. I call her Rebecca for convenience.

KROLL: So I have noticed.

ROSMER: So I can't imagine how Beata could ever have got that idea. And why didn't she talk to me about it? She never did. She never said a word.

KROLL: Poor creature. She begged and prayed *me* to speak to you.

ROSMER: Then why didn't you?

KROLL: I naturally assumed she was distraught. Making an accusation like that against a man like you! Well, then she came again—about a month later. She seemed calmer then. But as she was leaving, she said: "Soon now they can expect to see the white horse at Rosmersholm."

ROSMER: Yes, yes. The white horse. She spoke so often about that.

KROLL: And when I tried to persuade her to stop having such morbid ideas, she simply replied: "I haven't much time left. John must marry Rebecca now—at once."

ROSMER *(almost speechless):* What did you say? *I* marry—?

KROLL: It was a Thursday afternoon. On the Saturday evening, she threw herself off the bridge into the millrace.

ROSMER: And you never warned us—!

KROLL: You know yourself how often she used to say she hadn't long to live.

ROSMER: Yes, I know. All the same—you should have warned us!

KROLL: I thought of it. But by then it was too late.

ROSMER: But why haven't you mentioned it since? Why have you kept quiet about all this?

KROLL: What good would it have done to come here and cause you still further suffering? I naturally supposed it was just some crazy delusion. Until last night.

ROSMER: And now you don't?

KROLL: Was Beata deluded when she said you were going to abandon your childhood faith?

ROSMER *(stares unseeingly):* Yes. That I can't understand. That's the most incredible thing—

KROLL: Incredible or not, she proved right. And now I ask you, Rosmer—how much truth is there in her other accusation? Her final one, I mean?

ROSMER: Accusation? How was that an accusation?

KROLL: You don't seem to have noticed the way she phrased it. She had to go, she said. Why? Well?

ROSMER: So that I could marry Rebecca—

KROLL: Those weren't quite her words. Beata used a different expression. She said: "I haven't much time left. John *must* marry Rebecca now—at once."

ROSMER (*looks at him for a moment, then rises*): Now I understand you, Kroll.

KROLL: Well? What is your answer?

ROSMER (*quite calm and controlled the whole time*): To such a question—? The only proper answer would be to show you the door.

KROLL (*gets up*): As you wish.

ROSMER (*moves in front of him*): Now you listen to me. For over a year—ever since Beata died—Rebecca West and I have lived alone together here at Rosmersholm. All that time you have known of Beata's accusation against us. But never for a single moment have I noticed that you objected to Rebecca and me living here together.

KROLL: I didn't know until last night that this was an association between an apostate and a—an emancipated woman.

ROSMER: Oh—! Then you think there is no purity of spirit to be found in apostates and emancipated people? You don't believe they can have any sense of morality?

KROLL: I have little faith in any morality that is not rooted in Christian faith.

ROSMER: And you assume that this applies to Rebecca and me, too? To our relationship—!

KROLL: With all deference to both of you, I cannot shrug off the opinion that there is no great gulf between free thought and—hm!

ROSMER: And what?

KROLL: And free love—since you force me to use the words.

ROSMER *(quietly):* And you aren't ashamed to say that to me! You, who have known me ever since I was a child.

KROLL: That is precisely the reason. I know how easily you let yourself be influenced by the people you associate with. And this Rebecca of yours—well, this Miss West—we don't know so very much about her. In short, Rosmer—I am not giving you up. And you—for God's sake try to save yourself while there's still time.

ROSMER: Save myself? How—?

MRS. HELSETH *looks in through the door left.*

ROSMER: What is it?

MRS. HELSETH: I wanted to ask Miss West if she could come down.

ROSMER: Miss West is not up here.

MRS. HELSETH: Oh? *(Looks round.)* That's strange. *(Goes.)*

ROSMER: You were saying—?

KROLL: Now listen. I'm not going to ask what went on here in secret while Beata was alive—or what may still be going on here now. I know you were deeply unhappy in your marriage. And that must to some degree excuse your conduct.

ROSMER: Oh, how little you really know me—!

KROLL: Don't interrupt me. What I wish to say is—that if this liaison with Miss West is to continue, it is absolutely essential that this change of heart, this dreadful apostasy into which she has lured you, be hushed up. Let me speak! Let me speak! I say that if you must be mad, then in God's name think and believe anything you wish—one way or the other. But keep your opinions to yourself. This is after all a purely personal matter. You don't have to shout these things from every street corner.

ROSMER: I do have to abandon a position which is both false and ambiguous.

KROLL: But you have a duty to your family traditions, Rosmer. Remember that! Since time immemorial Rosmersholm has been a stronghold of order and morality [—of respect and reverence for everything that is accepted and upheld by the best elements in our society.] The whole county has always taken its tone from Rosmersholm. Should the rumour become current that you yourself have broken with what I may call the Rosmer tradition, it will cause the most fatal and irreparable confusion.

ROSMER: My dear Kroll, I can't see it like that. I feel I have a bounden duty to create a little light and happiness in those places where for so many years the Rosmer family has created nothing but darkness and misery.

KROLL *(looks sternly at him):* A worthy ambition for a man who is to be the last of his line! Let sleeping dogs lie, Rosmer. That is no task for you. You were born to live peacefully among your books.

ROSMER: Possibly. But now I too want to take part in the battle of life, at least once.

KROLL: The battle of life! Do you know what that will mean for you? It will mean a battle to the death with all your friends.

ROSMER *(quietly):* They are not all as fanatical as you.

KROLL: You're an ingenuous fool, Rosmer. You've no experience of life. You don't realize what a storm is about to break over you.

MRS. HELSETH *peers in through the door.*

MRS. HELSETH: Miss West asked me to say—

ROSMER: What is it?

MRS. HELSETH: There's a man downstairs who wants a word with you, sir.

ROSMER: Is it the one who was here last night?

MRS. HELSETH: No, it's that Mortensgaard.

ROSMER: Mortensgaard!

KROLL: Aha! So it's come to that, has it? It's come to that already!

ROSMER: What does he want with me? Why didn't you tell him to go away?

MRS. HELSETH: Miss West said I was to ask if he might come up.

ROSMER: Tell him I'm engaged—

KROLL *(to* MRS. HELSETH*):* Ask him to come up, Mrs. Helseth.

> MRS. HELSETH *goes.*

KROLL *(takes his hat):* I quit the field—for the moment. But the main battle has still to be fought.

ROSMER: As truly as I live, Kroll—I have nothing whatever to do with Mortensgaard.

KROLL: I no longer believe you. In anything. From now on I can never believe you. Now it is war to the knife. We'll see if we can't clip your wings.

ROSMER: Oh, Kroll! How can you sink so low?

KROLL: That comes well from you. Have you forgotten Beata?

ROSMER: Are you going to start all that again?

KROLL: No. The riddle of the millrace I leave to you, and to your conscience. If you still have any.

> PETER MORTENSGAARD *softly and quietly enters the room left. He is a slightly built little man with thinning reddish hair and beard.*

KROLL *(throws a look of hatred at him):* So! The *Morning Star!* Standing sentinel over Rosmersholm! *(Buttons his coat.)* Well, that leaves me in no doubt which course I must steer.

MORTENSGAARD *(quietly, to* KROLL*):* The *Morning Star* will always shine to guide you on your path.

KROLL: Yes, you've long shown your goodwill towards me.

I seem to remember a Commandment which says: "Thou shalt not bear false witness against thy neighbour."

MORTENSGAARD: You don't need to school me in the Commandments, Dr. Kroll.

KROLL: Not the Seventh?

ROSMER: Kroll—!

MORTENSGAARD: If I should need instruction, the Pastor is surely the most appropriate person.

KROLL *(with suppressed scorn):* The Pastor? Yes—Pastor Rosmer is unquestionably the best informed authority on that subject. Well, gentlemen—I wish you a fruitful conversation. *(Goes, banging the door behind him.)*

ROSMER *(stands staring at the door, and says to himself):* Well, well—so be it. *(Turns.)* Tell me, Mr. Mortensgaard, what brings you out here to visit me?

MORTENSGAARD: It was actually Miss West I came to see. I felt I had to thank her for the kind letter she sent me yesterday.

ROSMER: I know she wrote to you. Have you spoken with her?

MORTENSGAARD: For a moment. *(With a slight smile.)* I hear there has been a change of heart regarding certain matters here at Rosmersholm.

ROSMER: My attitude has changed towards many things. I might almost say—everything.

MORTENSGAARD: So Miss West gave me to understand. She thought it might be a good idea if I came up and had a little chat with you about this.

ROSMER: About what, Mr. Mortensgaard?

MORTENSGAARD: May I have your permission to announce in the *Morning Star* that you have changed your views— and that you are devoting yourself to the cause of liberalism and progress?

ROSMER: Certainly you may. Indeed, I beg you to.

MORTENSGAARD: Then I shall publish it tomorrow morning.

This will be a sensational item of news, that Pastor Rosmer of Rosmersholm now feels he can fight the good fight under our banner.

ROSMER: I don't quite follow you.

MORTENSGAARD: Well, I mean, it gives our party a strong moral boost every time we win a devout Christian to our cause.

ROSMER *(somewhat surprised):* Then you don't know—? Didn't Miss West tell you about that too?

MORTENSGAARD: What, Pastor? Miss West seemed in rather a hurry. She said I should come upstairs and hear the rest from you.

ROSMER: Well then, I must tell you that I have [emancipated myself in more senses than one. In every direction. I have] completely renounced the teaching of the Church.

MORTENSGAARD *(looks at him amazed):* Well, strike me dumb! *You* renounce the—!

ROSMER: Yes, I now stand where you yourself have stood for so long. You can publish that in the *Morning Star* tomorrow, too.

MORTENSGAARD: Publish that? No, my dear Pastor. I'm sorry, but I think we'd best turn a blind eye to that.

ROSMER: Turn a blind eye—?

MORTENSGAARD: To begin with, I mean.

ROSMER: But I don't understand—

MORTENSGAARD: Well, you see, Pastor—you probably don't know the ins and outs of things the way I do. But since you've come over to the liberal way of thinking—and since, as Miss West said, you want to lend a hand in the movement—then I take it you want to help us in every way you possibly can.

ROSMER: Indeed I do.

MORTENSGAARD: Well, I only want to let you know, Pastor, that if you come into the daylight about this business of your leaving the Church, you tie your hands from the start.

ROSMER: You think so?

MORTENSGAARD: Yes, don't you deceive yourself. There won't be much you'll be able to achieve then, not in this part of the country. Besides—we've enough freethinkers in the movement already, Pastor. I had it on the tip of my tongue to say "too many"! What the party needs is good Christians—that's something everyone has to respect. And that's what we're so short of. So it'd be best if you could keep mum about everything that the public don't need to know. That's only my opinion.

ROSMER: I see. In other words, you daren't associate yourself with me if I openly declare my apostasy?

MORTENSGAARD *(shakes his head)*: I couldn't risk it, Pastor. I've made it a rule of late never to support anyone or anything that's anti-Church.

ROSMER: Have you rejoined the Church?

MORTENSGAARD: That's another matter.

ROSMER: I see. Yes, I follow you.

MORTENSGAARD: Pastor—you must remember that my hands, more than most people's, aren't completely free.

ROSMER: What binds them?

MORTENSGAARD: The fact that I am a marked man.

ROSMER: Ah—I see.

MORTENSGAARD: A marked man, Pastor. You of all people ought to remember that. It was you who put the mark on me.

ROSMER: If I had felt then as I do now, I would have dealt less harshly with your misdemeanour.

MORTENSGAARD: I don't doubt it. But now it's too late. You've branded me once and for all. Branded me for my whole life. I don't suppose you fully realize what a thing like that means. But now you may soon be feeling the pinch yourself, Pastor.

ROSMER: I?

MORTENSGAARD: Yes. Surely you don't suppose Dr. Kroll and his cronies are going to forgive you for what you've done to them? And the *County Telegraph* is going to be pretty rough from now on, I hear. You may find yourself a marked man, too.

ROSMER: I don't think they'll be able to hurt me. My conscience is clean.

MORTENSGAARD *(with a quiet smile):* That's a bold claim to make, Pastor.

ROSMER: Maybe. But I have the right to make it.

MORTENSGAARD: Even if you examine your own conduct as closely as you once examined mine?

ROSMER: You say that very strangely. What are you driving at? Have you something special in mind?

MORTENSGAARD: Yes, there is one thing. Only one. But it'd be enough, if any nasty-minded enemy of yours happened to hear about it.

ROSMER: Will you be good enough to let me know what this might be?

MORTENSGAARD: Can't you guess, Pastor?

ROSMER: No, I can't. I haven't the faintest idea.

MORTENSGAARD: Well, then, I'd better tell you. I have in my possession an odd letter that was once written here at Rosmersholm.

ROSMER: Miss West's letter, you mean? Is there anything odd about that?

MORTENSGAARD: No, not about that. But I did once get another letter from this house.

ROSMER: Also from Miss West?

MORTENSGAARD: No, Pastor.

ROSMER: Well, from whom, then? From whom?

MORTENSGAARD: From the late Mrs. Rosmer.

ROSMER: From my wife? *You* received a letter from my wife?

MORTENSGAARD: I did.

ROSMER: When?

MORTENSGAARD: Shortly before the poor lady's death. It'd be about eighteen months ago now. And it struck me as very odd.

ROSMER: You know that my wife was mentally ill at that time.

MORTENSGAARD: I know many people thought that. But I don't think you'd notice it from this letter. When I say it was odd, I mean in another way.

ROSMER: What in heaven's name did my poor wife find to write to you about?

MORTENSGAARD: I have the letter at home. She starts by saying that she is living in great fear and trembling. There are so many wicked people around here, she writes. And these people only think of causing you mischief and injury.

ROSMER: Me?

MORTENSGAARD: So she says. And then there comes the really odd thing. Shall I tell you, Pastor?

ROSMER: Yes! Tell me everything! Everything!

MORTENSGAARD: The poor lady begs and beseeches me to be magnanimous. She says she knows it was the Pastor that got me sacked from my school. But she begs me with all her heart not to take my revenge.

ROSMER: How did she think you could take revenge?

MORTENSGAARD: She says in the letter that if I should happen to hear any rumours about sinful goings-on at Rosmersholm, I mustn't pay any attention to them, because it was only bad people spreading such things around to make you unhappy.

ROSMER: Does it say that in the letter?

MORTENSGAARD: You can read it yourself, Pastor, any time that's convenient.

ROSMER: But I don't understand—! What did she think these wicked rumours referred to?

MORTENSGAARD: Firstly, that you'd abandoned the faith you'd been brought up in. Mrs. Rosmer said that was quite untrue. Secondly—hm—

ROSMER: Secondly?

MORTENSGAARD: Well, secondly she writes—it's a bit confused, this part—that she knows nothing whatever of any immoral relationship at Rosmersholm. That no wrong has ever been done to her as a wife—and if such rumours should come to my ears, she begs me not to mention them in the *Morning Star*.

ROSMER: Did she name anyone?

MORTENSGAARD: No.

ROSMER: Who brought you this letter?

MORTENSGAARD: I've promised not to tell. It was brought to me one evening after dark.

ROSMER: If you had bothered to enquire, you would have learned that my poor unhappy wife was not completely in her right mind.

MORTENSGAARD: I did enquire, Pastor. But I must say that wasn't exactly the impression I received.

ROSMER: No? But why do you choose to warn me now about this old and confused letter?

MORTENSGAARD: To warn you to be very careful, Pastor Rosmer.

ROSMER: Personally, you mean?

MORTENSGAARD: Yes. You must remember that, from now on, you are no longer sacrosanct.

ROSMER: You seem convinced I have something I ought to hide.

MORTENSGAARD: I can't see myself why a man who's found emancipation shouldn't be allowed to live his life to the full. But, as I said, from now on you'd best be careful. If any rumour should get about that might offend people's sense of right and wrong, you can be sure the whole of our progressive movement will suffer for it. Goodbye, Pastor Rosmer.

ROSMER: Goodbye.

MORTENSGAARD: And I'll go straight down to the press and print the great news in the *Morning Star*.

ROSMER: Print everything.

MORTENSGAARD: I'll print everything that our good readers need to know.

He bows and leaves. ROSMER *remains standing in the doorway while* MORTENSGAARD *goes down the stairs. The front door is heard to close.*

ROSMER *(in the doorway, calls softly):* Rebecca! Reb—! Hm. *(Louder.)* Mrs. Helseth—isn't Miss West down there?

MRS. HELSETH *(from the hall):* No, Pastor. She's not here.

The curtain backstage is drawn aside, and REBECCA *is revealed in the doorway.*

REBECCA: John!

ROSMER: *(turns):* What! Were you in my bedroom? My dear, what were you doing there?

REBECCA *(goes over to him):* I was listening.

ROSMER: But Rebecca—how could you do such a thing?

REBECCA: Yes, I could. He said it so horribly, that thing about the way I was dressed—

ROSMER: Ah, so you were there already when Kroll—?

REBECCA: Yes. I wanted to know what he was up to.

ROSMER: I would have told you.

REBECCA: You wouldn't have told me everything. And certainly not in his words.

ROSMER: Did you hear everything, then?

REBECCA: Most of it. I had to go downstairs for a moment when Mortensgaard came.

ROSMER: And then you came back—

REBECCA: Please don't be angry with me, my dear.

ROSMER: You must do whatever you think right. You are a free woman. But what do you think about all this, Rebecca? I've never felt I needed you as I do now.

REBECCA: We both knew this would happen some time.

ROSMER: No, no. Not this.

REBECCA: Not this?

ROSMER: I always feared that sooner or later our pure and beautiful friendship might be misinterpreted and reviled. Not by Kroll. I'd never imagined anything like this of him. But by all those others, with their foul minds and their ignoble eyes. Oh yes, Rebecca—I was right to keep our relationship so jealously to ourselves. It was a dangerous secret.

REBECCA: Oh, what does it matter what other people think? *We* know that we are guiltless.

ROSMER: I? Guiltless? Yes, I used to think that—until today. But now—now, Rebecca—

REBECCA: Well, now what?

ROSMER: How am I to explain that terrible accusation of Beata's?

REBECCA (*vehemently*): Oh, don't talk about Beata! Don't think about Beata any more. You've managed to free yourself from her at last. She's dead.

ROSMER: Since I learned this, she has become hideously alive again.

REBECCA: No, no! You mustn't, John! You mustn't!

ROSMER: Yes, I tell you. We must try to get to the bottom of this. How can she have got this mad idea into her head?

REBECCA: Surely you aren't beginning to doubt that she was—mad?

ROSMER: Yes, Rebecca—that's just what I can't be so sure of any longer. And besides—even if she was—

REBECCA: If she was—? Yes, what then?

ROSMER: I mean—what was it that drove her sick mind over the edge into madness?

REBECCA: Oh, what good can it do to go on brooding about it?

ROSMER: I can't help it, Rebecca. I can't stop these doubts nagging at me, even if I wanted to.

REBECCA: But it can be dangerous—to circle and circle around one morbid thought.

ROSMER *(paces around restlessly, pondering)*: I must have betrayed my feelings somehow. She must have noticed how happy I began to feel after *you* came here.

REBECCA: But, my dear, even if this is true—

ROSMER: Think . . . She must have noticed that we read the same books. That we loved to be together, and to talk about all these new ideas. But—I don't understand! I was so careful not to let her suspect anything. When I think back, why, it was almost as though my life depended on it, the way I kept her apart from us, and from everything that concerned us. Didn't I, Rebecca?

REBECCA: Yes, yes, of course you did.

ROSMER: And you did too. And yet—! [Oh, it's too dreadful to think of! So] she was going round here, in her sick love for me—always silent, silent—watching us—noting everything—and misinterpreting everything.

REBECCA *(clasps her hands)*: Oh, I should never have come to Rosmersholm!

ROSMER: To think what she must have suffered in silence! All the dreadful fantasies her sick brain must have built up around us! Did she never say anything to you that led you to suspect anything?

REBECCA *(seems startled)*: To me! Do you suppose I'd have stayed here a day longer?

ROSMER: No, no, of course not. Oh, what a struggle it must have been for her! And she fought it alone, Rebecca. In despair, and quite alone. And then, in the end, that terrible accusing victory—in the millrace.

He throws himself down in the chair at the desk, puts his elbows on it and covers his face with his hands.

REBECCA *(approaches him cautiously from behind):* Now, listen, John. If it lay in your power to call Beata back—to you—to Rosmersholm—would you do it?

ROSMER: Oh, how can I tell what I would or wouldn't do? I can think of nothing but this one thing—that can never be undone.

REBECCA: You were just beginning to live, John. You *had* already begun. You had made yourself free—free in every way. You felt so relieved and happy—

ROSMER: Oh, yes, Rebecca, I did, I did. And now this dreadful discovery—

REBECCA *(behind him, her arms on the back of his chair):* How beautiful it was when we used to sit downstairs in the drawing room in the dusk. Helping each other to plan our lives anew. You were going to lay hold of life—the living life of today, you called it! You wanted to go like a liberating angel from home to home winning people's hearts and souls. Creating nobility all around you—in wider and ever wider circles.

ROSMER: Happy, noble men.

REBECCA: Yes—happy.

ROSMER: Because it is happiness that makes men noble, Rebecca.

REBECCA: Don't you think—suffering, too? Deep suffering?

ROSMER: Yes—if one manages to survive it. Conquer it. Leave it behind.

REBECCA: That is what you must do.

ROSMER *(shakes his head sadly):* I shall never conquer this—not completely. There will always remain a doubt. A question. I shall never again be able to enjoy the one thing that makes life so wonderful to live.

REBECCA *(over the back of the chair, more quietly):* What is that, John?

ROSMER *(looks up at her):* The sense of calm and happy innocence.

REBECCA *(takes a step back):* Yes. Innocence.

Short pause.

ROSMER *(with his elbow on the desk, leans his head on his hand and looks straight ahead of him):* And the way she managed to work it all out. How systematically she must have pieced it all together! First she begins to doubt my faith. How could she have suspected that? But she did. And then her suspicion increased to certainty. And then— yes, of course, then it was easy for her to imagine all the rest. *(Sits up in his chair and runs his hands through his hair.)* Oh, all these dreadful speculations! I shall never be free from them. I feel it. I know it. They will always haunt me, and remind me of the dead.

REBECCA: Like the white horse of Rosmersholm.

ROSMER: Yes. Rushing out from the darkness. From the silence.

REBECCA: And for the sake of this wretched superstition you are prepared to turn your back upon life—which you had begun to live?

ROSMER: Yes, it is hard. Hard, Rebecca. But I have no choice. How could I possibly forget all this?

REBECCA *(behind the chair):* By starting a new life.

ROSMER *(starts and looks up):* A new life?

REBECCA: Yes. A new relationship to the world outside. Live, work, act. Don't sit here brooding over insoluble riddles.

ROSMER *(gets up):* A new life? *(Walks across the room, stops by the door, then comes back.)* One question occurs to me. Haven't *you* asked yourself that question, Rebecca?

REBECCA *(catches her breath):* I don't—know—what you mean.

ROSMER: How do you suppose our relationship is going to shape itself after today?

REBECCA: I think our friendship will continue—whatever happens.

ROSMER: That's not quite what I meant. What first brought us together—and binds us so closely—our belief that man and woman can live together in pure comradeship—

REBECCA: Yes, yes—well?

ROSMER: I mean, such a relationship—like ours—doesn't it demand a life led in peace and serenity?

REBECCA: Go on.

ROSMER: But what I see lying ahead of me is a life of strife and unrest, and emotional tumult. I want to live, Rebecca! I'm not going to let myself be beaten by fear. I'm not going to let my life be dictated, either by the living or by—anyone else.

REBECCA: No, no, you mustn't. Be free, John! You must be free!

ROSMER: Then can't you guess what I'm thinking? Don't you know? Can't you see that the only way I can free myself from all these nagging memories—from the horror of the past—?

REBECCA: Yes?

ROSMER: —is to confront it with something new, and living, and real?

REBECCA *(catches at the back of the chair):* What do you mean?

ROSMER *(comes closer):* Rebecca—if I were now to ask you—will you be my second wife?

REBECCA *(is speechless for a moment, then cries in joy):* Your wife! Your—! I!

ROSMER: Yes. Let us try. We two shall be one. The place left here by the dead must not stand empty.

REBECCA: I—take Beata's place—?

ROSMER: Then her part in the saga of Rosmersholm will be finished. Completely finished. For ever and ever.

REBECCA *(quietly, trembling):* Do you believe that, John?

ROSMER: It must be so. It must! I can't—I *will* not go through life with a corpse on my back. Help me to throw it off, Rebecca. And then let us lay all memories to rest in freedom, and joy, and love. You shall be my wife—the only wife I have ever had.

REBECCA *(controlled):* Don't ever speak of this again. I shall never be your wife.

ROSMER: What! Never? But—don't you think you could come to love me? Isn't there already—something of love—in our friendship?

REBECCA *(puts her hands to her ears as though in terror):* Don't talk like that, John! Don't say such things!

ROSMER *(grasps her arm):* Yes, yes. It could happen. I can see from your face, you feel it too. Don't you, Rebecca?

REBECCA *(again calm and composed):* Listen, now. I tell you—if ever you speak of this again, I shall leave Rosmersholm.

ROSMER: Leave! You? You couldn't. It's impossible.

REBECCA: It is even more impossible that I should become your wife. That I can never be. Never in this world.

ROSMER *(looks surprised at her):* "Can't," you said? And you said it so strangely. Why can't you?

REBECCA *(clasps both his hands):* My dear—for both our sakes—don't ask me why. *(Lets go of him.)* No, John. *(She goes towards the door, left.)*

ROSMER: From now on, I can ask no other question but "Why?"

REBECCA *(turns and looks at him):* Then it is finished.

ROSMER: Between you and me?

REBECCA: Yes.

ROSMER: It will never be finished between us. You will never leave Rosmersholm.

REBECCA *(her hand on the door-knob):* No, perhaps I won't. But if you ever ask me that again—it will be finished none the less, John.

ROSMER: Finished none the less? How?

REBECCA: Because then I shall go the way Beata went. Now you know, John.

ROSMER: Rebecca!

REBECCA *(in the doorway, nods slowly):* Now you know. *(Goes.)*

ROSMER *(stares as though lost at the closed door):* Rebecca!

ACT THREE

The living room at Rosmersholm. The window and the hall door stand open. Morning sunshine outside.

REBECCA WEST, *dressed as in Act One, is standing at the window, watering and arranging the flowers. Her crochet-work is lying in the armchair.* MRS. HELSETH *is going around with a feather mop, dusting the furniture.*

REBECCA *(after a brief silence):* The Pastor's very late down this morning.

MRS. HELSETH: Oh, he's often like that. He'll be here soon.

REBECCA: Have you seen him at all?

MRS. HELSETH: Only for a moment. When I came up with the coffee, he went into his bedroom and started dressing.

REBECCA: I ask because yesterday he wasn't very well.

MRS. HELSETH: Yes, he looked poorly. I wonder if there isn't something the matter between him and his brother-in-law.

REBECCA: What could that be?

MRS. HELSETH: I wouldn't know. Perhaps that Mortensgaard's set them against each other.

REBECCA: That's quite possible. Do you know this Peter Mortensgaard?

MRS. HELSETH: I do not. The idea, miss! A man like that!

REBECCA: You mean, because he edits that nasty paper?

MRS. HELSETH: Oh, it isn't just that. Surely you heard, miss. He had a child with some married woman whose husband had left her.

REBECCA: Yes, I did hear that. But that must have been long before I came here.

MRS. HELSETH: Oh goodness, yes, miss. He was quite a young man. I reckon she ought to have known better. He wanted to marry her. But they put a stop to that. And they made him suffer for it, all right. But since then, my word, he's done all right for himself. There's plenty of people as aren't ashamed to run after him now.

REBECCA: Yes, most of the poorer people turn to him when they need help.

MRS. HELSETH: Oh, it isn't only the poor ones—

REBECCA *(gives her a furtive glance):* Oh?

MRS. HELSETH *(by the sofa, dusting busily):* The kind of people you'd least expect, so I've heard say, miss.

REBECCA *(arranging the flowers):* That's just an idea you've got, Mrs. Helseth. *You* couldn't know about a thing like that.

MRS. HELSETH: You think I couldn't know, miss? Oh yes, I know all right. If you want the truth, I once took a letter to Mortensgaard myself.

REBECCA *(turns):* No—did you?

MRS. HELSETH: Indeed I did. And that letter was written here at Rosmersholm.

REBECCA: Really, Mrs. Helseth?

MRS. HELSETH: As I stand here. And written on fine paper it was, too. With fine red wax on the envelope.

REBECCA: And it was entrusted to you? Well then, Mrs. Helseth, it isn't difficult to guess who sent it.

MRS. HELSETH: Oh?

REBECCA: Obviously poor Mrs. Rosmer, when she was ill—

MRS. HELSETH: It's you that say so, miss, not me.

REBECCA: But what was in the letter? No, of course—you can't know.

MRS. HELSETH: Hm—maybe I do, for all that.

REBECCA: Did she tell you what she'd written?

MRS. HELSETH: No, she didn't do that. But when he, that Mortensgaard, had read it, he started asking me all kinds of questions, sly-like, so that I soon knew what was in it.

REBECCA: What do you think she said? Oh, dear Mrs. Helseth, do please tell me!

MRS. HELSETH: No, I won't, miss. Not for all the money in the world.

REBECCA: Oh, you can tell me. You and I are such good friends.

MRS. HELSETH: God forbid I should ever let on to you about that, miss. I can't say more than that it was some awful thing they'd gone and put into that poor woman's sick mind.

REBECCA: Who had?

MRS. HELSETH: Wicked people, Miss West. Wicked people.

REBECCA: Wicked—?

MRS. HELSETH: That's the word I used. Really wicked people, they must have been.

REBECCA: Who do you think it could have been?

MRS. HELSETH: Oh, I know what I think. But heaven forbid I should open *my* mouth. There's a certain lady in town—hm—!

REBECCA: I can see you mean Mrs. Kroll.

MRS. HELSETH: Yes, she's a fine one. Always been snooty to me, she has. And she's never had any liking for you.

REBECCA: Do you think Mrs. Rosmer was in her right mind when she wrote that letter to Mortensgaard?

MRS. HELSETH: Depends what you mean by right mind, miss. I wouldn't say she was out of it.

REBECCA: But she became so distressed when she learned

she could never have any children. That was when the madness started.

MRS. HELSETH: Yes, she took that badly, poor thing.

REBECCA *(takes her crochet-work and sits in the chair by the window):* Actually—don't you think that was a good thing for the Pastor, Mrs. Helseth?

MRS. HELSETH: What, miss?

REBECCA: That there weren't any children. Mm?

MRS. HELSETH: Well, I don't know what I ought to answer to that.

REBECCA: Yes, believe you me. It was the best thing for him. Pastor Rosmer wasn't made to sit here listening to little children crying.

MRS. HELSETH: Little children don't cry at Rosmersholm, miss.

REBECCA *(looks at her):* Don't cry?

MRS. HELSETH: No. Little children have never cried in this house, not as long as anyone can remember.

REBECCA: That's strange.

MRS. HELSETH: Yes, isn't it, miss? But it's part of the Rosmers. And there's another strange thing. When they grow up, they never laugh. Never laugh until the day they die.

REBECCA: That's most extraordinary—

MRS. HELSETH: Have you ever heard or seen the Pastor laugh?

REBECCA: No—now I think of it, I almost believe you're right. But people in general don't laugh much around here, I think.

MRS. HELSETH: That they don't. It started at Rosmersholm, people say. And then it spread around like a kind of plague, I shouldn't wonder.

REBECCA: You're a deep woman, Mrs. Helseth.

MRS. HELSETH: Ah, you mustn't sit there making fun of me, miss— *(Listens.)* Sssh, ssh! Here's the Pastor coming down. He doesn't like seeing mops about.

She goes out through the door right. JOHN ROSMER, *stick and hat in hand, enters from the hall.*

ROSMER: Good morning, Rebecca.

REBECCA: Good morning, my dear. *(After a moment, crocheting.)* Are you going out?

ROSMER: Yes.

REBECCA: It's a lovely day.

ROSMER: You didn't come up to see me this morning.

REBECCA: No—I didn't. Not today.

ROSMER: Aren't you going to from now on?

REBECCA: Oh, I don't know yet.

ROSMER: Is there anything for me?

REBECCA: The *County Telegraph* has come.

ROSMER: The *County Telegraph*—!

REBECCA: It's lying there on the table.

ROSMER *(puts down his hat and stick):* Is there anything in it about—?

REBECCA: Yes.

ROSMER: And you didn't bring it up to me—?

REBECCA: You'll read it soon enough.

ROSMER: I see. *(Takes the paper and reads it standing at the table.)* What! ". . . secret traitors . . . we cannot warn our readers sufficiently against irresponsible renegades . . ." *(Looks at her.)* They call me a renegade, Rebecca.

REBECCA: They mention no names.

ROSMER: What difference does that make? *(Reads on.)* ["Secret traitors against justice and morality"]—"Judases who have the impertinence to blazon their apostasy as soon as they think that the most [appropriate—and most] profitable moment has come." "A monstrous outrage on the good name of a revered family"—["in the hope that those temporarily in power will not omit suitably to reward . . ."] *(Puts the paper down on the table.)* And they write this about me. These people who have known me so long and so well. They don't believe it, they know there isn't a word of truth in it, but they write it, all the same.

REBECCA: There's more to come.

ROSMER *(takes up the paper again):* "Immaturity of judgement the only possible excuse . . . corrupting influence possibly extending also to fields of personal conduct which we do not at present wish to make the subject of public discussion or complaint . . ." *(Looks at her.)* What does that mean?

REBECCA: That's a reference to me.

ROSMER *(puts down the paper):* Rebecca—this is the action of dishonourable men.

REBECCA: Yes, I hardly think they're the ones to complain about Mortensgaard.

ROSMER *(walks up and down):* Something must be done. Everything that is good in men will be destroyed if this kind of thing is allowed to continue. But it shall not! Oh, how happy—how happy I would feel if I could bring a little light into all this gloom and ugliness!

REBECCA *(rises):* Yes, John, yes! That would be something great and noble to live for!

ROSMER: If only I could awake them to self-knowledge. Bring them to a feeling of shame and repentance. Teach them to approach one another in tolerance and love, Rebecca.

REBECCA: Yes! Only put all your energies into that, and you'll see. You will win!

ROSMER: I think it could be done. If I could succeed, what a joy it would be to be alive! No more hateful strife. Only emulation. Every eye directed towards the same goal. Every will, every mind, striving forwards—upwards— each by its own natural and predestined path. Happiness for all—created by all. *(Chances to look out through the window, starts and says sadly):* Ah! Not through me.

REBECCA: Not—? Not through you?

ROSMER: And not *for* me, either.

REBECCA: Oh, John, you mustn't let such doubts get the better of you.

ROSMER: Happiness—my dear Rebecca—happiness consists above all else in a calm and happy sense of innocence. Freedom from guilt—

REBECCA *(stares straight ahead):* Oh, can't you ever stop thinking about guilt?

ROSMER: You don't know how it feels. But I—

REBECCA: You least of all.

ROSMER *(points out through the window):* The millrace—

REBECCA: Oh, John—!

MRS. HELSETH *looks in through the door right.*

MRS. HELSETH: Miss!

REBECCA: Later, later. Not now.

MRS. HELSETH: Just a word, miss.

REBECCA *goes over to the door.* MRS. HELSETH *tells her something. They whisper together for a moment.* MRS. HELSETH *nods and goes.*

ROSMER *(uneasily):* Was it for me?

REBECCA: No, only something about the housekeeping. You ought to go out and get some fresh air, John. Take a good long walk.

ROSMER *(takes his hat):* Yes, come along. We'll go together.

REBECCA: No, my dear, I can't just now. You go on your own. But stop brooding about these things. Promise me that.

ROSMER: I'm afraid I shall never be able to forget them.

REBECCA: But how can you let anything so groundless have such power over you—?

ROSMER: Is it so groundless, Rebecca? I've been lying

awake all night thinking about it. Wasn't Beata perhaps right after all?

REBECCA: What do you mean?

ROSMER: In believing that I was in love with you, Rebecca.

REBECCA: Wasn't—she—right?

ROSMER *(puts his hat on the table):* This is the question I keep asking myself. Have we two been deceiving ourselves in calling our relationship a friendship?

REBECCA: You mean we ought to have called it—?

ROSMER: Love. Yes, Rebecca, I mean that. Even when Beata was alive, I thought only of you. You were the one I yearned for. With you I found a happiness that was calm and joyful and not merely based on sensuality. When you really think about it, Rebecca—we were like two children falling sweetly and secretly in love. We made no demands, we dreamed no dreams. Wasn't that how you felt too? Tell me.

REBECCA *(torn within herself):* Oh—I don't know what to reply to that.

ROSMER: And this life we lived so passionately—with each other and for each other—we mistook for friendship. No, Rebecca—our relationship has been a spiritual marriage—perhaps from the first moment we knew each other. So that I *am* guilty. I had no right to do this—no right, for Beata's sake.

REBECCA: No right to live in happiness? Do you believe that, John?

ROSMER: She saw our relationship through the eyes of *her* love. Condemned it by the measure of *her* love. She had to. Beata couldn't have judged us in any other way than she did.

REBECCA: But then how can you blame yourself for what finally happened?

ROSMER: It was her love for me that threw her into the millrace. That fact remains inescapable, Rebecca. And it is useless for me to try to escape from it.

REBECCA: Don't think about it! Think only of the great and noble task to which you have dedicated your life!

ROSMER *(shakes his head):* That can never be accomplished, Rebecca. Not by me. Not after what I know now.

REBECCA: Why not by you?

ROSMER: Because there can never be victory for a cause that is rooted in guilt.

REBECCA *(bursts out):* Oh, these doubts, these fears, these scruples—they're all inherited! They talk at Rosmersholm about the dead haunting the living in the shape of white horses. I think this is just one of them.

ROSMER: Perhaps it is. But what help is that if I cannot escape from it? You must believe me, Rebecca. What I say is true. For a cause to win a lasting victory, it must be led by a man whose soul is joyful and free from guilt.

REBECCA: Does joy mean so much to you, John?

ROSMER: Joy? Yes, Rebecca. It does.

REBECCA: You, who can never laugh?

ROSMER: Yes, in spite of that. Oh, Rebecca—believe me—I could be the most joyful man on earth.

REBECCA: You must go for your walk now, my dear. Take a good, long one. You hear? Look, here's your hat. And your stick.

ROSMER *(takes them):* Thank you. You won't come with me?

REBECCA: No, no. I can't just now.

ROSMER: Very well. I shall feel you're with me, though. As I always do.

He goes out through the hall. After a few moments RE-BECCA *glances out after him through the open door. Then she walks towards the door right.*

REBECCA *(opens it and calls softly):* All right, Mrs. Helseth. You can let him in now.

> *She goes over towards the window. Shortly afterwards* DR. KROLL *enters right. He bows silently and formally, and keeps his hat in his hand.*

KROLL: Has he gone?

REBECCA: Yes.

KROLL: Does he usually stay out long?

REBECCA: Usually, yes. But today I wouldn't be sure. [So if you don't want to meet him—

KROLL: No, no. I want to talk to you. Alone.

REBECCA: Then we'd better start. Please sit down.]

> *She sits in an armchair by the window.* DR. KROLL *sits in a chair beside her.*

KROLL: Miss West—you can hardly imagine how deeply this hurts me—this change that has taken place in John Rosmer.

REBECCA: We expected it would—at first.

KROLL: Only at first?

REBECCA: Mr. Rosmer was sure that sooner or later you would come to feel as he does.

KROLL: I?

REBECCA: You and all his friends.

KROLL: Well, there you see what poor judgement he has where life and human nature are concerned.

REBECCA: In any case—since he now feels bound to free himself from all former ties—

KROLL: Ah but, you see, that's exactly what I don't believe.

REBECCA: What do you believe, then?

KROLL: I think you're the one who's behind all this.

REBECCA: Your wife gave you that idea, Dr. Kroll.

KROLL: Never mind where I got it from. The point is that I feel strong doubts—overwhelmingly strong doubts—

when I consider the sum of your conduct since first you came here.

REBECCA *(looks at him):* I seem to remember there was a time when you felt an overwhelmingly strong belief in me, dear Dr. Kroll. A passionate belief in me, I might almost have said.

KROLL *(lowers his voice):* Whom could you not bewitch—if you put your mind to it?

REBECCA: Are you suggesting that—?

KROLL: Yes, you did. I'm not any longer so foolish as to suppose that you felt anything for me. You merely wanted to gain admittance to Rosmersholm. Get a footing here. [And you wanted me to help you. Yes, I see it all now.]

REBECCA: You seem to have forgotten that it was Beata herself who begged and prayed me to come here.

KROLL: Yes, after you'd bewitched her too. Or would you call that friendship, what she came to feel for you? She began to worship you, to idolize you, and in the end it developed into a—what shall I call it?—into a kind of desperate infatuation. Yes, that's the word for it.

REBECCA: You must please remember your sister's state of mind. I don't really think *I* can be described as emotionally unstable.

KROLL: No, indeed you are not. But that makes you all the more dangerous to people you want to get into your clutches. You find it so easy to act remorselessly and ruthlessly, simply because you are so cold-blooded.

REBECCA: Cold-blooded? Are you so sure of that?

KROLL: Quite sure, now. Otherwise you couldn't have gone on here year after year pursuing your end so calculatedly. Yes, yes—you've got what you wanted. You have him in your power—and Rosmersholm too. But to achieve all this, you didn't shrink from sacrificing his personal happiness.

REBECCA: That's not true! It isn't I, it's you who have made him unhappy.

KROLL: I?

REBECCA: Yes, when you led him to believe that he was to blame for the dreadful thing that happened to Beata.

KROLL: So he feels deeply about that?

REBECCA: Of course he does. You know how sensitive he is—

KROLL: I thought these so-called emancipated men were able to set themselves above such scruples. But that's how it is, eh? Ah well—I knew it really. The descendant of these men who look down on us here can't find it so easy to tear himself free from something that's been handed down in his family from generation to generation.

REBECCA *(drops her eyes thoughtfully):* John Rosmer is deeply rooted in the traditions of his family. That is certainly true.

KROLL: Yes, and you ought to have remembered it if you'd had any real feeling for him. But of course you couldn't have that kind of feeling. Your background is so vastly different from his.

REBECCA: What do you mean, my background?

KROLL: I mean your family background. Your—origins, Miss West.

REBECCA: I see. Yes, that's quite true. My background is very humble. All the same—

KROLL: I don't mean socially. I was thinking of your moral background.

REBECCA: I don't understand.

KROLL: The circumstances of your birth.

REBECCA: I beg your pardon?

KROLL: I say this merely because it explains your whole conduct.

REBECCA: I don't follow you. Kindly explain what you mean.

289

KROLL: I assumed you knew. Otherwise one would hardly see why you were adopted by Dr. West—

REBECCA *(rises):* Ah. Now I understand.

KROLL: And took his name. Your mother's name was Gamvik.

REBECCA *(walks across the room):* My father's name was Gamvik, Dr. Kroll.

KROLL: Your mother's occupation must of course have brought her into frequent contact with the district physician.

REBECCA: It did.

KROLL: And as soon as your mother dies, he takes you into his own home. He treats you harshly. Yet you stay with him. You know he won't leave you a penny—all you got was a case of books. Yet you stay with him. Put up with his tantrums—look after him until the day he dies.

REBECCA *(over by the table, looks scornfully at him):* And all this you can only explain by the suggestion that there was something immoral—something criminal—about my birth?

KROLL: What you did for him I attribute to an unconscious filial instinct. Your whole conduct seems to me irrefutable evidence of your birth.

REBECCA *(vehemently):* There isn't a word of truth in anything you say! Dr. West hadn't even arrived in the district when I was born.

KROLL: I beg your pardon, Miss West. He came there the previous year. I have done a little research into the matter.

REBECCA: You're wrong, I tell you! Completely wrong!

KROLL: You said the day before yesterday that you were twenty-nine. Coming up to thirty.

REBECCA: Oh? Did I say that?

KROLL: You did. From which I calculate—

REBECCA: Stop. There's no need to calculate anything. I

may as well tell you at once: I am a year older than I admitted.

KROLL *(smiles disbelievingly):* This is something new. What is the explanation?

REBECCA: When I reached twenty-five I thought I was a little old to be unmarried. So I subtracted a year.

KROLL: You? An emancipated woman? Do you have old-fashioned prejudices regarding the right age for marriage?

REBECCA: Yes. It was silly of me—laughable, even. But one always has some little prejudice clinging to one that one can't shake off. That's human nature.

KROLL: Possibly. But my calculation may be correct all the same. Because Dr. West paid your district a brief visit the year before he became employed there.

REBECCA *(cries):* That's a lie!

KROLL: Is it?

REBECCA: Yes. My mother never mentioned that.

KROLL: Didn't she?

REBECCA: No. Never. Nor Dr. West. Not a word.

KROLL: Might that not have been because they both had reason to forget a year? Just as you have done, Miss West. Perhaps it's a family trait.

REBECCA *(walks around, twisting and untwisting her hands):* It isn't possible. It's only something you're trying to make me imagine. It can't be true. It can't! Not possibly—!

KROLL *(gets up):* But my dear—why in heaven's name are you taking it so to heart? You quite frighten me. What am I to imagine—?

REBECCA: Nothing. You are to imagine nothing.

KROLL: Then you really must explain to me why this fact— this possibility, if you like—so alarms you?

REBECCA *(composes herself):* It's quite simple, Dr. Kroll. I just don't want people here to think of me as illegitimate.

KROLL: I see. Well, let's settle for that explanation—for the moment. So you have retained a certain—prejudice on that issue too?

REBECCA: Yes, I have.

KROLL: Well, I suppose it's the same with most of this so-called emancipation of yours. You've read books that have given you a whole lot of new ideas and opinions. You've picked up a smattering of new-fangled theories about this and that—theories that seem to upset much of what has hitherto been regarded as gospel and unchallengeable. But you've only accepted all this intellectually, Miss West. You don't really feel it in your blood.

REBECCA *(thoughtfully)*: You may be right about that.

KROLL: Yes, just ask yourself honestly, and you'll see! And if it's like that with you, then it's easy to guess how John Rosmer must feel about it. It's pure and absolute madness—it's—why, it's suicide for him even to think of standing forth publicly and claiming to be an apostate! We know what a shy and reticent man he is. Imagine him being [repudiated and persecuted by his old associates,] exposed to the contempt and ridicule of all the best people in society! He's never the kind of man to endure that.

REBECCA: He must. It's too late for him to draw back now.

KROLL: It is certainly not too late. By no means. The whole matter can be hushed up—or at least explained away as a temporary, if regrettable, aberration. But—one condition is absolutely imperative.

REBECCA: And what is that?

KROLL: You must get him to legalize the relationship, Miss West.

REBECCA: His relationship with me?

KROLL: Yes. You must make him do that.

REBECCA: You can't rid yourself of the conviction that our relationship is of the kind that requires to be—legalized [as you put it]?

292

KROLL: I have no wish to get involved in the matter personally. But I have observed in the past that the prejudices, as you would call them, which people find it easiest to overcome—hm—!

REBECCA: Concern the relationship between man and woman?

KROLL: Yes—to speak frankly—that is my experience.

REBECCA *(wanders across the room and looks out through the window):* It was on the tip of my tongue to say—I wish you were right, Dr. Kroll.

KROLL: What do you mean by that? [You said it so strangely.]

REBECCA: Oh, nothing. Let's not talk any more about it. Ah—here he is.

KROLL: Already! Then I'll be off.

REBECCA *(goes over to him):* No—wait. There's something I'd like you to hear.

KROLL: Not now. I don't think I could bear to see him.

REBECCA: Please stay, I beg you. Do. Or you'll regret it later. This is the last time I shall beg anything of you.

KROLL *(looks at her amazed, and puts down his hat):* Very well, Miss West. So be it.

A moment's silence. Then JOHN ROSMER *enters from the hall.*

ROSMER *(sees* KROLL *and stops in the doorway):* What! *You* here?

REBECCA: He didn't want to meet you, John.

KROLL *(involuntarily):* John!

REBECCA: Yes, Dr. Kroll. Mr. Rosmer and I call each other by our Christian names. [Our relationship has led to that excess.]

KROLL: Was that what you wanted me to hear?

REBECCA: That—and other things too.

ROSMER *(comes closer):* Why have you come here?

KROLL: I wanted to make one last effort to stop you, and to win you back.

ROSMER *(points to the newspaper):* After what I have read here?

KROLL: I did not write that.

ROSMER: Did you do anything to stop it?

KROLL: That would have been a betrayal of the cause I stand for. And anyway, it did not lie within my power.

REBECCA *(tears the newspaper into pieces, crumples them and throws them behind the stove):* There. Now they're out of sight. Let them be out of mind, too. There's going to be nothing more like that, John.

[KROLL: Not if you can persuade him to see sense—

REBECCA: Come, my dear, let's sit down—all three of us. I want to tell you everything.]

ROSMER *(sits unwillingly):* What's come over you, Rebecca? [You're so—dreadfully calm.] What is it?

REBECCA: [The calmness of decision.] *(Sits.)* [You sit down too, Dr. Kroll.]

KROLL *sits on the sofa.*

[ROSMER: Of decision, you say. What decision?]

REBECCA: I want to give you back what you need to be able to live. You shall have your joyful innocence returned to you, my dear.

ROSMER: What on earth is all this?

[REBECCA: I just want to tell you something. That's all that's necessary.

ROSMER: Well, tell me.]

REBECCA: When I came down here from the north—with Dr. West—I felt that a great new world was opening up for me. The Doctor had taught me so many things. Everything I knew about life—then. *(With difficulty, and scarcely audibly.)* But then—

KROLL: Yes?

294

ROSMER: But, Rebecca—I know all this.

REBECCA *(composes herself):* Yes, yes—you're right really. I suppose you do know all this.

KROLL *(looks closely at her):* I think perhaps I should go.

REBECCA: No, stay where you are, Dr. Kroll. *(To* ROSMER.*)* Yes, that was it, you see—I wanted to be part of this new age that was dawning. To share in all these new discoveries—! Dr. Kroll told me one day that Ulrik Brendel had had a great influence over you when you were young. I thought it must surely be possible for me to carry on what he had begun.

ROSMER: Did you come here with that purpose—?

REBECCA: I wanted us two to go forward together into freedom. Onward—always onward. But between you and full freedom there was always this dreadful and insuperable barrier.

ROSMER: What barrier?

REBECCA: I mean, John, that you could only blossom into freedom outside in the bright sunshine. But you stayed here, ailing and sickening in the darkness of that dreadful marriage.

ROSMER: You never spoke of my marriage like that before.

REBECCA: No, I didn't dare. I was afraid you might hate me for it.

KROLL *(nods to* ROSMER*):* You hear that!

REBECCA *(continues):* But I knew well where your salvation lay. Your only hope of salvation. So I took action.

ROSMER: What do you mean, took action?

KROLL: Are you saying that you—!

REBECCA: Yes, John. *(Rises.)* Please don't move. Nor you, Dr. Kroll. It wasn't you, John. You are innocent. It was I who lured—who ended by luring Beata into the labyrinth.

ROSMER *(jumps up):* Rebecca!

KROLL *(rises from the sofa):* The labyrinth!

REBECCA: The labyrinth—that led to the millrace. Now you know, both of you.

ROSMER *(stunned):* But I don't understand—! What is she saying? I don't understand a word—!

KROLL: Oh, yes, Rosmer. I am beginning to understand.

ROSMER: But what did you do? What could you have said to her? There was nothing. Absolutely nothing.

REBECCA: She learned that you were emancipating yourself from your old-fashioned prejudices.

ROSMER: But I wasn't, not then.

REBECCA: I knew you soon would.

KROLL *(nods to* ROSMER*):* Aha!

ROSMER: Go on. What else? I want to know the rest, too.

REBECCA: Not long afterwards—I begged and prayed her to let me leave Rosmersholm.

ROSMER: Why did you want to leave then?

REBECCA: I didn't want to leave. I wanted to stay here. But I told her I felt it would be best for us all—if I went away for a while. I let her understand that if I stayed any longer—something might—something might happen—

ROSMER: You said that? You did that?

REBECCA: Yes, John.

ROSMER: And—that is what you meant when you said you "took action"?

REBECCA *(in a broken voice):* Yes.

ROSMER *(after a moment):* Have you confessed everything now, Rebecca?

REBECCA: Yes.

KROLL: Not everything.

REBECCA *(looks at him, frightened):* What else could there be?

KROLL: Didn't you, in the end, make Beata understand that it was necessary—not merely that it was best, but that it was necessary—for your sake and for Rosmer's—that you should go away somewhere—as quickly as possible? Well?

REBECCA *(softly and barely audibly):* I may perhaps have said something like that.

ROSMER *(sinks into the armchair by the window):* And she [—poor, sick creature—]went around here believing in this web of lies and treachery! Believing in it implicitly! Unquestioningly! *(Looks up at* REBECCA.*)* And she never turned to me. Never said a word— Oh, Rebecca, I see it now. *You* dissuaded her!

REBECCA: She had got it into her head that because she was a barren wife she had no right to be here. And then she got it into her head that it was her duty to you to make room for someone else.

ROSMER: And you—you did nothing to put this idea out of her head?

REBECCA: No.

KROLL: Perhaps you even encouraged it? Answer! Did you?

REBECCA: She may have understood me so.

ROSMER: Yes, yes! She always bowed to you in everything. And so she made room. *(Jumps up.)* How could you— how could you play this ghastly game?

REBECCA: I thought it was a choice between two lives, John.

KROLL *(sternly and magisterially):* You had no right to make such a choice.

REBECCA *(vehemently):* But do you think I did all this calculatedly and in cold blood? No, I was different then from what I am now—standing here and talking about it. And besides—I think a person can have two wills. I wanted to be rid of Beata. Somehow or other. But I never thought it would happen. Every step that I ventured forward, I felt as though a voice cried within me: "No further! Not an inch further!" But I *couldn't* stop! I had to venture another inch. Just one. And then another—just one more. And then it happened. That's how such things do happen.

Short silence.

ROSMER *(to* REBECCA*):* And what do you suppose will happen to you now? When this becomes known?

REBECCA: I don't care what happens to me. It doesn't much matter.

KROLL: No word of remorse. Perhaps you feel none?

REBECCA *(coldly aloof):* I'm sorry, Dr. Kroll, but that is something which concerns no one but myself. I shall settle that matter alone.

KROLL *(to* ROSMER*):* And this is the woman with whom you share your roof. In an intimate relationship! *(Looks around at the portraits.)* Oh, if those who are gone had eyes to see you now!

ROSMER: Are you going back to town?

KROLL *(takes his hat):* Yes. As quickly as possible.

ROSMER *(takes his hat likewise):* Then I shall accompany you.

KROLL: You will! Yes, I knew we hadn't lost you for good.

ROSMER: Come then, Kroll. Come!

They go out through the hall without looking at RE-BECCA. *After a few moments, she goes cautiously over to the window and peers out through the flowers.*

REBECCA *(speaks half-aloud to herself):* Not over the bridge today, either. Round. Never past the millrace. Never. *(Leaves the window.)* Ah, well. *(Goes over and pulls the bellrope. After a few seconds* MRS. HELSETH *enters right.)*

MRS. HELSETH: What is it, miss?

REBECCA: Mrs. Helseth, will you be so kind as to have my trunk brought down from the attic?

MRS. HELSETH: Trunk?

REBECCA: Yes, the brown sealskin trunk. You know.

MRS. HELSETH: Yes, I know. But good heavens, miss—surely you're not going on a journey?

REBECCA: Yes, Mrs. Helseth. I am going on a journey.

MRS. HELSETH: Not at once?

REBECCA: As soon as I've packed.

MRS. HELSETH: Well, I never heard the like! But you'll soon be back, of course, miss?

REBECCA: No, I shall never come back here again.

MRS. HELSETH: Never! But, blessed Jesus, what's to become of Rosmersholm once you've left? Just when the poor Pastor was beginning to be so happy and comfortable.

REBECCA: Yes. But today something frightened me, Mrs. Helseth.

MRS. HELSETH: Frightened you? Mercy on us, what?

REBECCA: I thought I caught a glimpse of white horses.

MRS. HELSETH: White horses! In broad daylight?

REBECCA: Oh, they never sleep, the white horses of Rosmersholm. *(Changes her tone.)* Well—my trunk then, please, Mrs. Helseth.

MRS. HELSETH: Very good, Miss West. Your trunk.

They both go out right.

ACT FOUR

The living room at Rosmersholm. It is late evening. The lamp, beneath its shade, is burning on the table. REBECCA WEST *is standing by the table packing some small belongings in a valise. Her cloak, hat and the white crocheted shawl are hanging over the back of the sofa.*

MRS. HELSETH *enters right.*

MRS. HELSETH *(speaks softly and seems uneasy):* All your things are down now, miss. They're inside the back door.

REBECCA: Good. You've ordered the coachman?

MRS. HELSETH: Yes. He asks what time you'll be requiring him.

REBECCA: I should think about eleven. The steamer leaves at midnight.

MRS. HELSETH *(hesitates a little):* But the Pastor? Suppose he isn't back by then?

REBECCA: I shall leave in any case. If I don't see him, you can tell him I'll write. A long letter. Tell him that.

MRS. HELSETH: Well, that's all very well, writing. But— poor Miss West—I think you ought to try and speak with him once more.

REBECCA: Perhaps. And perhaps not.

MRS. HELSETH: Dear oh dear, that I should live to see this day! I'd never have believed it.

REBECCA: Wouldn't have believed what, Mrs. Helseth?

MRS. HELSETH: Well, I really thought Pastor Rosmer had more in him than this.

REBECCA: More in him?

MRS. HELSETH: Indeed yes, miss.

REBECCA: But, my dear Mrs. Helseth, what do you mean by that?

MRS. HELSETH: I mean what's right and proper, miss. He oughtn't to run away from things like that.

REBECCA *(looks at her):* Now, listen, Mrs. Helseth. Tell me honestly. Why do you think I'm going away?

MRS. HELSETH: Bless you, miss, you've no choice! Oh dear, oh dear, oh dear. But I don't think the Pastor's acted rightly. That Mortensgaard had some excuse—*she* still had her husband alive. So they couldn't have married, however much they wanted. But the Pastor—well!

REBECCA *(with a faint smile):* Could you have imagined anything like that between me and Pastor Rosmer?

MRS. HELSETH: Never. I mean—not until today.

REBECCA: But today—?

MRS. HELSETH: Well—after all those terrible things people say they've written about the Pastor in the newspapers—

REBECCA: Aha.

MRS. HELSETH: A man as can go over to Mortensgaard's way of thinking—well, he's capable of anything. That's my opinion.

REBECCA: Perhaps. But what about me, then? What do you say about me?

MRS. HELSETH: God bless you, miss—I don't see as how anyone can blame you. It isn't so easy for a single woman to hold out on her own. I mean, we're all human, Miss West.

REBECCA: That's very true, Mrs. Helseth. We are all human. What are you listening for?

MRS. HELSETH *(quietly):* Blessed Jesus, miss, I do believe that's him.

REBECCA *(starts):* Then he's—! *(Resolutely.)* Very well. So be it.

JOHN ROSMER *enters from the hall.*

ROSMER *(sees her clothes and valise, turns to* REBECCA *and asks):* What does this mean?

REBECCA: I am leaving.

ROSMER: Now?

REBECCA: Yes. *(To* MRS. HELSETH.*)* Eleven o'clock, then.

MRS. HELSETH: Very good, miss. *(Goes out right.)*

ROSMER *(after a short pause):* Where are you going, Rebecca?

REBECCA: North with the steamer.

ROSMER: North? Why there?

REBECCA: That's where I came from.

ROSMER: But you have nothing to do up there now.

REBECCA: I've nothing here either.

ROSMER: What do you intend to do?

REBECCA: I don't know. I just want to be finished with it all.

ROSMER: Be finished with it?

REBECCA: Rosmersholm has broken me.

ROSMER *(suddenly alert):* What?

REBECCA: Broken me completely. When I first came here, I was so alive and fearless. Now I am a slave to a strange and foreign law. After today I don't think I shall ever dare attempt anything again.

ROSMER: Why not? What is this law you say you—?

REBECCA: Oh, my dear, let's not talk about that now. What happened between you and Dr. Kroll?

ROSMER: We have settled our differences.

REBECCA: I see. So that's how it ended.

ROSMER: He gathered all our old friends together at his house. They made me realize that the task of making the

302

world noble is not for me. And anyway, it's such a hopeless idea, Rebecca. I shall forget about it.

REBECCA: Ah, well. Perhaps it's best that way.

ROSMER: You say that now? Do you believe that?

REBECCA: I have come to believe it. During the past few
days.

ROSMER: You are lying, Rebecca.

REBECCA: Lying—?

ROSMER: Yes, you are lying. You have never believed in
me. You have never believed that I was the man to carry
that cause to victory.

REBECCA: I believed we two might do it together.

ROSMER: That isn't true. You believed that *you* might be able
to achieve something in life. And that you could use me to
that end. That I could serve your purpose. That's what
you believed.

REBECCA: Now listen, John—

ROSMER *(sits sadly on the sofa):* Oh, never mind. I see the
whole thing clearly now. You've used me like a kind of
glove.

REBECCA: Now listen, John. [Let's talk about this. It will be
for the last time.] *(Sits in a chair by the sofa.)* I was going
to write to you about it, when I had got back to the north.
But perhaps you'd better hear it now.

ROSMER: Have you something more to confess?

REBECCA: Yes. The most important thing of all.

ROSMER: The most important thing?

REBECCA: The thing you've never guessed. The thing that
both excuses and condemns all the rest.

ROSMER *(shakes his head):* I don't understand any of this.

REBECCA: It's quite true that I once intrigued to gain admittance to Rosmersholm. I thought I might manage to find
success and happiness here. One way or another—you understand.

ROSMER: Then you achieved what you wanted.

303

REBECCA: I think I could have achieved anything—then. Because I feared nothing. I still had a free will. I had no inhibitions. I wasn't afraid of human relationships. But then it started—this thing that broke my will—and frightened me for ever.

ROSMER: What started? Speak so that I can understand you.

REBECCA: It came over me—this blinding, uncontrollable passion—! Oh, John—!

ROSMER: Passion? You—! For what?

REBECCA: For you.

ROSMER *(tries to spring up):* What!

REBECCA *(restrains him):* [Sit still, my dear. There's something else you have to hear.]

ROSMER: Are you trying to say—that you've loved me—in that way!

REBECCA: I thought it was love—then. Yes, I thought it was love. But it wasn't. It was what I tell you. A blinding, uncontrollable passion.

ROSMER *(with difficulty):* Rebecca—is this really *you—you—* that you're talking about?

REBECCA: Yes, John. Whom else?

ROSMER: Then it was this that—it was this that made you "take action," as you call it.

REBECCA: It swept over me like a storm at sea. Like one of those storms we sometimes get in the winter, far up in the north. It seizes you—and carries you with it, John— whithersoever it will. It's useless even to try to resist it.

ROSMER: And it swept poor Beata into the millrace.

REBECCA: Yes. It was a fight for survival. Between Beata and me.

ROSMER: You were always the strongest at Rosmersholm. Stronger than Beata and me together.

REBECCA: I knew you so well, John. I knew I could never reach you until you'd been set free. Physically and mentally.

ROSMER: But I don't understand you, Rebecca. You—you and everything you've done—it's all an insoluble riddle to me. Now I *am* free—physically and mentally. Now you stand at the goal you set yourself from the beginning. And yet—

REBECCA: I have never been further from my goal than now.

ROSMER: And yet—when I asked you yesterday—when I begged you: "Be my wife!"—you cried out in terror that it could never happen.

REBECCA: I was crying in despair, John.

ROSMER: Why?

REBECCA: Because Rosmersholm has drained my strength. It has broken my courage and paralysed my will. The time is past when I was afraid of nothing. I have lost the power to take action, John.

ROSMER: Tell me how this has happened.

REBECCA: It has happened through living with you.

ROSMER: But how? How?

REBECCA: When I found myself alone here with you—and you had found yourself—

ROSMER: Yes, yes?

REBECCA: —because you were never really yourself, as long as Beata was alive—

ROSMER: I'm afraid you're right there—

REBECCA: But then, when I began living here with you—alone in peace, just the two of us—when you shared all your thoughts with me, unreservedly—every mood and feeling, just as it came to you—then the great change happened. To me, I mean. Gradually, you understand. Almost imperceptibly—but irresistibly. To the very depths of my soul.

ROSMER: Rebecca!

REBECCA: All the rest—that blinding, sickening passion—faded away from me. All my tormenting furies fell silent and still. A calm came over me—the kind of calm you

305

find on a bird-cliff up in the far north, under the midnight sun.

[ROSMER: Go on. Tell me all you can.

REBECCA: There isn't much else, John. Only that—] It was then that I began to love. The great and selfless love that asks for nothing more than companionship. The way it's been between us.

ROSMER: Oh, if only I'd had any inkling of all this—!

REBECCA: It's best the way it is. Yesterday—when you asked me if I would be your wife—my heart cried aloud with joy—

ROSMER: Yes, Rebecca. I sensed it.

REBECCA: Just for a moment, I was able to forget myself. My old spirit and will were crying out for their freedom. But now they no longer have any power or strength.

ROSMER: How do you explain what has happened to you?

REBECCA: It's the Rosmer view of life—or yours, anyway. It has infected my will.

ROSMER: Infected—?

REBECCA: And poisoned it. Enslaved it to a law which I had not previously recognized. You—being with you—has ennobled my soul—

ROSMER: Oh, if I could only believe that!

REBECCA: You can believe it all right. The Rosmer view of life ennobles. But— (*Shakes her head.*) —but—but—

ROSMER: But—? Well?

REBECCA: But it kills happiness, John.

ROSMER: How can you say that, Rebecca?

REBECCA: For me, anyway.

ROSMER: Can you be so sure of that? If I were to ask you again now—if I were to go on my knees and beg you—?

REBECCA: Oh, my dearest—please don't ever speak of that again. It's impossible—! You'd better know, John. Before I came to Rosmersholm—something happened to me—

ROSMER: More than you've told me?

REBECCA: Yes. Something else. Something more terrible—

ROSMER *(with a faint smile):* Isn't it strange, Rebecca? Do you know, once or twice I'd wondered about that.

REBECCA: Did you? And yet—? In spite of that—?

ROSMER: I never believed it. I just—played with the thought, you know.

REBECCA: If you want me to, I'll tell you about that too.

ROSMER: No, no! I don't want to hear a word about it. Whatever it may be—I can forget it.

REBECCA: But I can't.

ROSMER: Oh, Rebecca—

REBECCA: Yes, John. That's what's so dreadful—that now, when all life's happiness is offered to me with open hands—now I've become the kind of person whose conscience about the past makes it impossible for me to accept it.

ROSMER: Your past is dead, Rebecca. It no longer has any hold on you. It has nothing to do with you. All that happened to someone else.

REBECCA: Oh, my dearest, those are just words. What about that sense of innocence you spoke about? Where shall I find that innocence?

ROSMER *(sadly):* Innocence.

REBECCA: [Yes, innocence.] The secret of joy and happiness. Wasn't that the lesson you wanted to teach your new generation of happy, noble men?

ROSMER: Oh, don't remind me of that. That was only a hopeless dream, Rebecca. A wild delusion that I no longer believe in. People cannot be ennobled from without, Rebecca.

REBECCA *(quietly):* Not even by love, don't you think?

ROSMER *(thoughtfully):* Ah, that would be the thing! The

307

greatest thing that life could have to offer. If it were true. *(Restlessly.)* But how can I find the answer to that question? The real answer?

REBECCA: Don't you believe me, John?

ROSMER: Oh, Rebecca—how can I believe you in anything now? You've hidden so much from me. Now you come forward with this new idea. If you've some hidden purpose behind all this, for God's sake tell me straight out what it is! If there's anything you want, I'll willingly do anything I can for you.

REBECCA *(twists her hands):* Oh, this killing doubt—! John, John!

ROSMER: Yes, isn't it terrible, Rebecca? But I can't help it. I shall never be able to free myself from this doubt. Never be sure that you really love me, purely and with all your heart.

REBECCA: But doesn't something deep inside you tell you that a change has taken place in me? And that this change has been caused by you, and by you alone?

ROSMER: Oh, Rebecca—I no longer believe in my ability to change people. I no longer have any faith in myself. Neither in myself nor in you.

REBECCA *(looks sadly at him):* How will you be able to live then, John?

ROSMER: I don't know. I don't know at all. I don't think I can live. In any case, I don't know anything worth living for.

REBECCA: Oh, life—life is its own renewer. Let us hold fast to it, John. We leave it soon enough.

ROSMER *(jumps up restlessly):* Then give me back my faith! My faith in you, Rebecca! My faith in your love! I want proof! Proof!

REBECCA: Proof? But how can I give you proof—?

ROSMER: You must. *(Walks across the room):* I can't stand this desolation—this emptiness—this—this—

308

There is a loud knock on the door leading from the hall.

REBECCA *(jumps up from her chair):* Ah—did you hear that?

The door opens. ULRIK BRENDEL *enters. He is wearing a stiff shirt, a black coat, and good boots outside his trousers. Otherwise he is dressed as before. He looks confused.*

ROSMER: Oh, is it you, Mr. Brendel?

BRENDEL: John, my boy! Hail—and farewell!

ROSMER: Where are you going so late?

BRENDEL: Downhill.

ROSMER: What do you—?

BRENDEL: I am homeward bound, *mon cher élève!* My heart is homesick for the great void.

ROSMER: Something has happened to you, Mr. Brendel. What is it?

BRENDEL: You perceive the transformation? Ah—well you may. When I last set foot in this room, I stood before you as a man of substance, slapping my breast pocket.

ROSMER: Oh? I don't quite understand—

BRENDEL: But tonight you see a deposed monarch standing in the ashes of his incinerated palace.

ROSMER: If there's any way I can help you—

BRENDEL: You have retained the heart of a child, my dear John. Can you spare me a loan?

ROSMER: Yes, yes, of course.

BRENDEL: Could you possibly stretch to an ideal or two?

ROSMER: What did you say?

BRENDEL: A few cast-off ideals. You'd be doing a good deed. I'm cleaned out, dear boy. Absolutely stripped.

REBECCA: Didn't you give your lecture?

BRENDEL: No, seductive lady. Would you believe it! As I raised my hand to empty the horn of plenty, I made the distressing discovery that I was bankrupt.

REBECCA: But all those unwritten works you spoke about?

BRENDEL: For five and twenty years I have squatted like a miser on his padlocked money-bags. And then yesterday, when I opened them to bring my riches forth—there was nothing! The mills of time had ground everything into dust. *Nichts*—nothing!

ROSMER: But are you sure of this?

BRENDEL: No room for doubt, my duck. The President convinced me of that.

ROSMER: The President?

BRENDEL: His Excellency, if you prefer. *Comme vous voulez.*

ROSMER: Whom do you mean?

BRENDEL: Peter Mortensgaard, of course.

ROSMER: What!

BRENDEL *(confidentially):* Ssh, ssh, ssh! Peter Mortensgaard is the lord and master of the future! Never have I encountered so superior a presence. Peter Mortensgaard possesses the secret of omnipotence. He can do anything he sets his mind to.

ROSMER: Don't you believe that.

BRENDEL: Yes, my boy! Because Peter Mortensgaard never wants to do more than lies within his power. Peter Mortensgaard knows how to live life without ideals. And *that,* you see—*that* is precisely the secret of action and of victory. It is the sum of all the world's wisdom. *Basta!*

ROSMER *(softly):* Now I understand. Yes, you are leaving here poorer than you came.

BRENDEL: *Bien!* And now learn a lesson from your old tutor. Blot out everything he ever imprinted on your mind. Build not on shifting sand. And take care—proceed warily—before you build on this charming creature who now sweetens your existence.

REBECCA: Do you mean me?

BRENDEL: I do, bewitching lady from the sea.

REBECCA: Why should I be nothing for a man to build his life on?

BRENDEL *(takes a step closer):* I gather that my former pupil has a cause which he wishes to carry to victory.

REBECCA: Well?

BRENDEL: His victory is assured. But—mark this well—on one inescapable condition.

REBECCA: What is that?

BRENDEL *(takes her gently by the wrist):* That the woman who loves him shall, with a light heart, go out into the kitchen and chop off her delicate rosy-white finger— *here*—just *here* at the middle of the joint. *Item,* that the aforesaid adoring woman—equally gladly—shall snip off her incomparably formed left ear. *(Lets go of her and turns to* ROSMER.*)* Farewell, Johannes! My victorious disciple!

ROSMER: Are you going now? It's such a dark night.

BRENDEL: Night and darkness are best. Peace be with you. *(He goes.)*

There is a moment's silence in the room.

REBECCA *(takes a deep breath):* Oh, how close and suffocating it is in here!

She goes to the window, opens it, and remains standing there.

ROSMER *(sits in the armchair by the stove):* There's no other way, Rebecca. I see it now. You *must* leave.

REBECCA: Yes. I see no choice.

ROSMER: Let us make the most of these last moments. Come over here and sit beside me.

REBECCA *(goes over and sits on the sofa):* What is it, John?

ROSMER: First I want to tell you that you have no need to worry about your future.

REBECCA *(smiles):* Hm. *My* future.

ROSMER: I prepared for all contingencies a long time ago. Whatever may happen, you are provided for.

REBECCA: That too, my dear?

ROSMER: Surely you must have known—?

REBECCA: It's a long time since I thought of anything like that.

ROSMER: Yes, yes—you must have imagined things could never be different between us from the way they were.

REBECCA: Yes, I did feel that.

ROSMER: So did I. But if I were to go—

REBECCA: Oh, John. You will live longer than I.

ROSMER: This wretched life is my own to do what I wish with.

REBECCA: What do you mean? You aren't thinking of—?

ROSMER: Would it be so strange? After the humiliating defeat I have suffered? I, who was to carry my cause to victory—! And now I have fled the field—before the battle has even begun!

REBECCA: Take up the fight again, John! Only try, and you'll see! You will win! You will ennoble hundreds of souls—thousands! Only try!

ROSMER: Oh, Rebecca! I no longer have any faith in that cause.

REBECCA: But it has already stood the test. You have ennobled one human being at least. Me, for as long as I live.

ROSMER: If only I could believe you.

REBECCA (clasps her hands): Oh, John! Is there nothing—nothing that could make you believe it?

ROSMER (starts as though in fear): Don't say that, Rebecca! Please! Don't ever talk about that!

REBECCA: Yes, we must talk about it. Do you know of anything that could dispel your doubt? I can't think of a way.

ROSMER: Thank God that you can't. Thank God for us both.

REBECCA: No, no, no—I can't rest satisfied with that! If you know of anything that can acquit me in your eyes, I demand it as my right that you name it.

ROSMER *(as though forced to speak against his will):* Let's see, then. You say you have discovered the true meaning of love. That through me your soul has been ennobled. Is this true? Have you calculated correctly, Rebecca? Shall we check your calculation?

REBECCA: I am ready.

ROSMER: When?

REBECCA: Any time. The sooner the better.

ROSMER: Then show me, Rebecca—if you—for my sake—this very night—! *(Breaks off.)* Oh, no, no, no!

REBECCA: Yes, John! Yes, yes! Tell me, and you'll see!

ROSMER: Have you the courage—and the will—with a light heart, as Ulrik Brendel said—for my sake, now, tonight—freely and willingly—to go the way that Beata went?

REBECCA *(draws herself up from the sofa and says almost speechlessly):* John!

ROSMER: Yes, Rebecca. This is the question I shall never be able to escape from—after you are gone. Every hour of the day it will haunt me. Oh—I seem to see you there before my eyes. You are standing on the bridge. In the middle of it. Now you are leaning out over the parapet. You sway as the rushing water draws you down. No. Then you shrink back. You have not the courage to do as she did.

REBECCA: But if I had the courage? And the will, to do it gladly? What then?

ROSMER: Then I would have to believe you. I would regain my faith in my life's work. Faith in my ability to ennoble humanity. Faith in the capacity of man to be ennobled.

REBECCA *(slowly takes her shawl, throws it over her head and says calmly):* You shall have your faith back.

ROSMER: Have you the courage—and the will—to do this, Rebecca?

REBECCA: That you will be able to judge tomorrow—or later—when they drag me out.

ROSMER *(clutches at his forehead):* There's a—hideous fascination—in this—!

REBECCA: I don't want to stay lying down there. Longer than necessary. You must see that they find me.

ROSMER *(jumps up):* But all this—is madness! Go—or stay. I will believe you—I will take your word for it. This time too.

REBECCA: Words, John! Let's have no more cowardice and running away. How can you take my word for anything after today?

ROSMER: But I don't want to see you defeated, Rebecca.

REBECCA: There will be no defeat.

ROSMER: There will be. You will never have the courage to go Beata's way.

REBECCA: You think not?

ROSMER: Never. You are not like Beata. You don't see life through distorted eyes.

REBECCA: But I see it through Rosmer eyes. The crime that I have committed—demands atonement.

ROSMER *(looks fixedly at her):* Is that what you believe in your heart?

REBECCA: Yes.

ROSMER *(with decision):* Very well. Then I kneel to our emancipated view of life, Rebecca. We acknowledge no judge over us. Therefore we must pass judgement upon ourselves.

REBECCA *(misunderstands him):* Yes, John, yes. If I go, it will save what is best in you.

ROSMER: There is nothing left in me to save.

REBECCA: There is. But I—after today I would be like a sea troll, hanging on to the ship that is to carry you forward and holding it back. I must be cast overboard. Would you have me linger on up here in the world, dragging my life along like a cripple? [I must retire from the game, John.]

ROSMER: If you go—then I shall go with you.

REBECCA *(smiles almost imperceptibly, looks at him and says more quietly):* Yes, John. Come with me—and witness—

ROSMER: I shall go with you, I said.

REBECCA: To the bridge, yes. You will never dare walk on it.

ROSMER: You have noticed that?

REBECCA *(sadly, brokenly):* Yes. That was what made my love hopeless.

ROSMER: Rebecca, now I place my hand on your head. *(He does as he says.)* And take you in marriage as my lawful wife.

REBECCA *(clasps both his hands and bows her head against his breast):* Thank you, John. *(Lets go of him.)* And now I go gladly.

ROSMER: Man and wife should go together.

REBECCA: Only as far as the bridge, John.

ROSMER: And on to it. As far as you go, I shall go with you. Now I am no longer afraid.

REBECCA: Are you so completely sure—that this way is the best one for you?

ROSMER: I know it is the only one.

REBECCA: Suppose you are wrong? Suppose it is only an illusion? One of those white horses of Rosmersholm?

ROSMER: That may be. We shall never escape them—we who live in this house.

REBECCA: Then stay, John!

ROSMER: The husband shall go with his wife, as the wife with her husband.

REBECCA: But first tell me this. Is it you who go with me? Or I with you?

ROSMER: That we shall never know.

REBECCA: I should like to know.

ROSMER: We go together, Rebecca. I with you, and you with me.

REBECCA: Yes. I think you are right.

ROSMER: For now we two are one.

REBECCA: Yes. Now we are one. Come! Let us go gladly!

They go out hand in hand through the hall, and turn to the left. The door remains open behind them. For a few moments the room is empty. Then MRS. HELSETH *opens the door right.*

MRS. HELSETH: Miss—the carriage is—! *(Looks round.)* Not here? Out together at this hour? Well, I must say! Hm! *(Goes out into the hall, looks round and comes back again.)* They're not on the seat. Well, well. *(Goes to the window and looks out.)* Blessed Jesus! What's that white thing over there—? Upon my soul, if they're not both standing on the bridge! God forgive the sinful creatures! If they're not putting their arms round each other—! *(Screams aloud.)* Ah! They've fallen—both of them! Into the millrace! Help! Help! *(Her knees tremble; she holds, shaking, on to the back of the chair, hardly able to speak.)* No. No help. The dead mistress has taken them.

The Lady from the Sea

Introduction

The Lady from the Sea represents an important turning-point in Ibsen's work. He wrote it in 1888, at the age of sixty; it was the twenty-first of his twenty-six completed plays.

Twenty years before, having explored the possibilities of poetic drama in *Brand* (1865) and *Peer Gynt* (1867), and of historical drama in a string of early plays culminating in *Emperor and Galilean* (begun in 1864 and finished in 1873), he had turned to the business of exposing the vanities and weaknesses of contemporary society. *The League of Youth* (1869) attacked the hollowness of radical politicians; *The Pillars of Society* (1877) attacked with equal vehemence the hollowness of conservatism. Then, turning his attention from the hypocrisy of politicians to the hypocrisy of social conventions, he wrote *A Doll's House* (1879), *Ghosts* (1881) and *An Enemy of the People* (1882). The three plays that followed, *The Wild Duck* (1884), *Rosmersholm* (1886) and *The Lady from the Sea* (1888) were less studies of social problems than of the sickness of the individual; and this is also true of the five mighty dramas of his old age, *Hedda Gabler* (1890), *The Master Builder* (1892), *Little Eyolf* (1894), *John Gabriel Borkman* (1896) and *When We Dead Awaken* (1899).

The Lady from the Sea, more than any other of his plays, impressed Ibsen's contemporaries as signifying a change of heart. Within a few days of its publication Ibsen's earliest champion in England, Edmund Gosse, wrote: "There is thrown over the whole play a glamour of romance, of mystery, of landscape beauty, which has not appeared in Ibsen's work to anything like the same extent since *Peer Gynt*. And moreover, after so many tragedies, this is a comedy. . . . *The Lady from the Sea* is connected with the previous plays by its emphatic defence of individuality and its statement of the imperative necessity of developing it; but the tone is quite unusually sunny, and without a tinge of pessimism. It is in some respects the reverse of *Rosmersholm;* the bitterness of restrained and baulked individuality, which ends in death, being contrasted with the sweetness of emancipated and gratified individuality, which leads to health and peace."

Later, in a speech delivered in Norway in 1906, the year of Ibsen's death, the Danish critic, Georg Brandes, recalled a conversation he had had with Ibsen shortly before he began to write *The Lady from the Sea.* "I remember that, after Ibsen had written *Rosmersholm,* he said to me one day: 'Now I shan't write any more polemical plays.' Good God, I thought, what will become of the man? But, as we know, he kept his word. His last plays are not polemical, but are plays about families and the individual. The difference between these two groups of (prose) plays is shown by the fact that of the first six (*The Pillars of Society, A Doll's House, Ghosts, An Enemy of the People, The Wild Duck* and *Rosmersholm*), only one, *An Enemy of the People,* is named after its chief character, while all the plays in the group beginning with *The Lady from the Sea,* except the last (*When We Dead Awaken*), have as their title the name or nickname of a person."

To understand the reasons for this change of heart, we must go back three years from the time Ibsen wrote *The Lady from the Sea,* to 1885.

In the summer of that year he had returned to Norway

from his self-imposed exile in Italy and Germany for only the second time in twenty-one years. His previous visit (to Christiania in 1874) had not been altogether happy; but on this occasion he travelled beyond the capital to the little seaside town of Molde, high up on the north-west coast. Although he had been born by the sea, in the port of Skien, and had spent all his youth and early manhood within sight of it, he had since 1864 been living in Rome, Dresden and Munich and, apart from that one brief visit to Christiania, had not seen the ocean; for he did not count the quiet waters of the Mediterranean as such. Molde brought back to him memories of Grimstad and Bergen, and it is related that he stood for hour after hour gazing down into the fjord, or out at the rough waters of the Atlantic.

People in Molde told him strange stories about the sea, and the power it had over those who lived near it. Two tales in particular remained in his mind. One, told him by a lady, was of a Finn who, by means of the troll-power in his eyes, had induced a clergyman's wife to leave husband, children and home, and go away with him. The other was of a seaman who left home and stayed away for many years, so that his family believed him dead; suddenly he returned, and found his wife married to another man.

The first story must have reminded Ibsen of his own mother-in-law, Magdalene Thoresen, who had fled from her native Denmark to escape from a love affair with an Icelandic poet, and had married a widowed clergyman seventeen years her senior. In one of her letters she has left a vivid account of what happened. "While I was studying in Copenhagen I met a young man, a wild, strange, elemental creature. We studied together, and I had to yield before his monstrous and demonic will. With him I could have found passion and fulfilment; I still believe that. . . . Now I have never regretted that he let me go, for as a result I met a better person, and have lived a better life. But I have always been conscious that he could have nurtured into flower that love of which my spirit was capable. So I have lived my life oppressed by a feeling of want and longing.'' Of her husband she said: ''Thoresen was my friend, my father and my brother, and I was his friend, his child. . . . He was a man to whom I could openly and unhesitatingly say anything and be understood.'' She had already told him of ''a tragic incident in my restless life. But I bade him regard the past, those years when I had been ignorant, helpless and unprotected, years which I found it impossible to explain either to myself or to anyone else, as a closed book. I begged him to accept me as I was as the result of that struggle and, if he thought me worthy of it, to let the rest be blotted out. He accepted me.''

Magdalene Thoresen was powerfully affected by the sea, and could hardly live away from it. Even in old age she had to go down every day to bathe in the surf. ''People in Norway,'' Ibsen said to a German friend while he was writing *The Lady from the Sea*, ''are spiritually under the domination of the sea. I do not believe other people can fully understand it.''

During the winter of 1885, after his return from Molde, Ibsen was occupied with planning *Rosmersholm*. As usual, he did not put pen to paper until the summer, and completed the play in September 1886. Certain traits in the character of Rebecca West in *Rosmersholm* are plainly influenced by Ibsen's stay in Molde. She is obsessed by the sea; Ulrik Brendel calls her ''a mermaid,'' and she compares herself to the sea-trolls which, according to legend, clung to ships and hindered their sailing.

Ibsen had determined to revisit the northern sea again the following summer, but in the meantime there occurred a chain of events which, though unconnected with the sea, were also to leave their mark on his next play.

In December 1886, shortly after he had completed *Ros-*

mersholm, Ibsen was invited by Duke George II of Saxe-Meiningen to visit Liebenstein for a theatrical festival, in the course of which, among other plays, *Ghosts* was to be performed. Duke George was the patron and inspirer of the famous Meiningen troupe which, under its director Chronegk, so influenced theatrical managers all over Europe during the eighteen-eighties (including Antoine, Otto Brahm, Stanislavsky and Henry Irving, who was much impressed by their lighting and grouping when he saw them in London in 1881). It was not the first time Ibsen had been a guest of the Duke, for as long ago as 1876 he had visited Meiningen to see a performance of *The Pretenders*—a performance which may possibly have influenced his subsequent writing. This time, however, the Duke showed Ibsen signs of especial favour which evidently left a deep impression on him. In his letter of thanks Ibsen speaks of "a long and deeply cherished dream" having been fulfilled, and says that the memories of his stay at Liebenstein will remain with him to enrich his remaining days. During the next few months his plays were performed with success in town after town throughout Germany; he was repeatedly feted, three books were published about him, and eminent German authors praised him and wrote poems in his honour. In France, too, and even England, people were beginning to take serious notice of him at last. He had attracted attention in these countries through *A Doll's House* and *Ghosts,* but hitherto his reputation outside Scandinavia had still largely been that of a revolutionary. Now he was beginning to be looked upon as an altogether larger and more permanent figure; and Ibsen, like most revolutionary writers, was much gratified at being at last accepted by what is nowadays known as "the Establishment."

Next summer (1887) Ibsen returned again to the north; but this time he chose, not Norway, but Denmark. At first he went to Frederikshavn, but "I was frightened away from that town, which has become a colony for artistic coteries,'' and he moved after ten days to the little town of Sæby, on the east coast of north Jutland. He found this much more to his liking and, as at Molde two years before, spent hours each day gazing out to sea. A nineteen-year-old Danish girl named Engelke Wulff, who was also staying at Sæby, noted on the beach "a little, broad-shouldered man, with grey side-whiskers and eyebrows. He stood staring out across the water, with his hand shading his eyes. He had a stick with him with which he supported himself while he took a book out and wrote something in it. From where I sat and watched him, I supposed him to be drawing the sea." Ibsen saw her, too, as she sat doing her handiwork, and after a time got into conversation with her. She told him of her longing to see the world, and of her love of the theatre, and he promised that he would put her into his next play. One thinks immediately of Bolette; but in fact, when they met by chance in a street in Christiania some years later, he called her "my Hilde," and one must assume that some of Hilde's lines in *The Lady from the Sea*, if not her character, stemmed from his conversations with Engelke Wulff on the beach at Sæby.

Another young lady from Sæby imprinted herself on Ibsen's memory, though he never met her, for the good reason that since 1883 she had been lying in Sæby churchyard. Her name was Adda Ravnkilde; she was a talented young writer who had killed herself at the age of twenty-one, leaving behind her several stories and a novel, which was later published with a foreword by Georg Brandes. One theme recurs throughout her writings; the unsuccessful efforts of a young girl to free herself of her obsession for a man who she knows is not worthy of her. Ibsen read her writings, and visited her home and her grave. Her story, like the one he had heard in Molde, must have made him think of Magdalene Thoresen; Magdalene had succeeded in escaping from her obsession, but if she had not she might have suffered the same fate as this young girl.

On 12 September 1887 Ibsen made a speech at Gothenburg, in the course of which he said that his polemical interests were waning and, with them, his eagerness for battle. Twelve days later, in a speech in Stockholm, he startled his audience by describing himself as an "optimist," declaring that he believed the world was entering a new epoch in which old differences would be reconciled and humanity would find happiness. On 5 October he attended a dinner in the Copenhagen home of his publisher, Hegel. In his address of thanks Ibsen said that this summer, in Denmark, he had discovered the sea; that the smooth and pleasant Danish sea, which one could come close to without feeling that mountains cut off the approach, had given his soul rest and peace, and that he was carrying away memories of the sea which would hold significance for his life and his writing.

In addition to his rediscovery of the sea, and the international recognition that was now being accorded him, a third mollifying influence should be mentioned. During the eighteen months that elapsed between the completion of *Rosmersholm* and the beginning of *The Lady from the Sea*, Ibsen held a number of conversations with Henrik Jæger, who was preparing the first authorised biography for publication in 1888, in honour of Ibsen's sixtieth birthday. In the course of these conversations Ibsen recalled many old memories, to help Jæger with the early chapters. These memories included some which Ibsen had tried to forget; but now, when he dragged them out into the daylight, he found that they no longer had the power to frighten him. Consequently, as Professor Francis Bull has observed, Ibsen must have felt impelled to ask himself whether it did not lie within a man's power to drive away "ghosts" and "white horses," of whatever kind, provided he had the courage to look his past in the face and make his choice between the past and the present, a choice taken "in freedom and full responsibility." In *Rosmersholm* a potentially happy relationship between two people is destroyed by the power of the past; in *The Lady from the Sea* Wangel and Ellida overcome that power, and it may be that Ibsen's conversations with Jæger gave him a new confidence, if only a temporary one, in man's ability to escape from the terror of his own history.

A fourth influence, though scarcely a mollifying one, was the increasing interest of scientists during the eighteen-eighties in the phenomena of hypnosis and suggestion. Throughout Europe during this decade writers were being infected with this interest; Ibsen's preliminary jottings for *The Wild Duck* in 1884 contain references to "the sixth sense" and "magnetic influence," and Strindberg's *Creditors*, written in the same year as *The Lady from the Sea*, is closely concerned with "magnetism" and hypnosis.

It was Ibsen's practice to allow eighteen months to elapse after the completion of a play before beginning to write another; he would meditate long on a theme before putting pen to paper. Consequently it was not until 5 June 1888 that he made the first rough notes for *Rosmersholm*'s successor, which he provisionally entitled *The Mermaid*. Five days later he began the actual writing. It took him nine weeks to complete his first draft, and since in his manuscript he dated each act we can tell exactly how long the various stages of the play took him. Act I is dated 10–16 June; Act II, 21–28 June; Act III, 2–7 July; Act IV, 12–22 July; and Act V, 24–31 July. Early in August he began to revise the play, and by 18 August he had corrected the first two acts to his satisfaction. Two days later he began to revise the third act, and on 31 August he started on the fourth. We do not know when he finished his revision, but on 25 September he posted his final manuscript to Hegel, and on 28 November 1888 the play was published by Gyldendal in Copenhagen under the new title of *The Lady from the Sea,* in a first printing of 10,000 copies. It was first performed on 12 February 1889, simultaneously at the Christiania Theatre, Christiania, and at the Hoftheater, Weimar.

When *The Lady from the Sea* first appeared, most of the critics were puzzled, especially in Norway, and apart from a production at the Schauspielhaus in Berlin in 1889 the play seems never fully to have succeeded in Ibsen's lifetime. Its psychology struck his contemporaries as fanciful and unconvincing, although Kierkegaard had long ago asserted, as Freud was shortly to assert, the importance of allowing someone who is psychologically sick to be faced with some kind of choice and to make his own decision. When, however, *The Lady from the Sea* was revived in Oslo in 1928, on the centenary of Ibsen's birth, Halvdan Koht wrote: "It was a surprise to find how fresh the play seemed. . . . What especially impressed everyone was how closely the whole conception of the play was related to the very latest scientific psychology, both that which Pierre Janet had originated in the nineties, and the 'psycho-analysis' which Sigmund Freud had founded at the same time, and which became universally known shortly after the beginning of the twentieth century. *The Lady from the Sea* instantly acquired a new meaning and new life. Science had in the meantime seized on all morbid activities of the soul, had penetrated into all its borderlands, and had tried to follow all the suppressed impulses in their subconscious effect, the strife between original, suppressed will or desire, and acquired, thought-directed will. With poetic insight Ibsen had seemed to foresee all this. He envisaged a woman who felt hampered and bound in her marriage because she had married, not for love, but for material support, and in whom there consequently arose a series of distorted imaginings which gripped her mind like witchcraft. She needed a doctor, so Ibsen made her husband one—he had at first intended to make him a lawyer. Moreover, Ibsen discovered the remedy for Ellida; he gave her back her full sense of freedom. . . . As early as *Love's Comedy* (1862) he had declared war on all marriage which was not built upon full freedom, and now he wished to picture a marriage which, from being a business arrangement, became a free and generous exchange. Ellida was to experience what Nora (in *A Doll's House*) missed— 'the miracle'.''

Ibsen's rough notes and draft of *The Lady from the Sea* provide some interesting revelations of the dramatist's mind at work. At first, as already explained, he intended to make Wangel a lawyer, "refined, well-born, bitter. His past stained by a rash affair. In consequence, his future career is blocked." But he abandoned this conception, and Wangel became instead a kindly and understanding doctor. His wife first appears as Thora (perhaps after Magdalene Thoresen), but Ibsen changed this to Ellida. In the *Saga of Frithiof the Bold* there is a ship named *Ellide,* "which," Halvdan Koht points out in his biography of Ibsen, "there means something like 'the storm-goer.' Such a name gave a stronger suggestion of storm and mysterious troll-powers; the ship *Ellide* in the saga was almost like a living person fighting its way against evil spirits that tried to drag it down." Ibsen originally intended that Ellida should have broken her engagement with the seaman because of social and moral prejudices derived from his upbringing; but, significantly, he discarded this motive, and the conflict between Wangel and the Stranger became instead a struggle to gain control over the subconscious powers of her soul. Ibsen also planned at first to have an extra group of characters who would represent the outside world and be contrasted with the inhabitants of the little town, but he scrapped this idea, presumably to achieve stronger dramatic concentration.

328

Lyngstrand, the consumptive sculptor, had made a phantom appearance four years earlier in Ibsen's first notes for *The Wild Duck*. Bolette and Hilde seem to have been present in Ibsen's mind while he was planning *Rosmersholm*, since his early notes for that play contain mention of Rosmer's two daughters by his dead wife, the elder of whom "is in danger of succumbing to inactivity and loneliness. She has rich talents, which are lying unused," while the younger daughter 'is "sharply observant; passions beginning to dawn." Among the characters Ibsen considered putting into *The Lady from the Sea*, but subsequently discarded, was "an old married clerk. In his youth wrote a play, which was performed once. Is continually touching it up, and lives in the illusion of getting it published and becoming famous." This character, who appears to have been based on a friend of Ibsen's youth named Vilhelm Foss, turned up four plays later as Vilhelm Foldal in *John Gabriel Borkman*. Hilde Wangel was to reappear formidably in *The Master Builder*.

The early notes for *The Lady from the Sea* also contain mention of a "strange passenger," visiting with the steamer, who "once felt a deep attachment to her [Ellida] when she was engaged to the young sailor." This character was clarified into Hesler, a civil servant; then Ibsen altered his name to Arenholdt, Askeholm and, finally, Arnholm, and turned him from a civil servant into a schoolmaster.

The "young sailor" does not figure in Ibsen's first cast list, and Ibsen seems to have intended that he should not appear; then he hit on the notion of making him, and not Arnholm, "the strange passenger" or, as he finally called him, "the Stranger." The Stranger is (unless one reckons Ulrik Brendel in *Rosmersholm* as such) the predecessor of those intruders from the Outside World who enter so importantly into Ibsen's later plays: Hilde in *The Master Builder,* The Rat Wife in *Little Eyolf,* Mrs. Wilton in *John Gabriel Borkman*, the Nun in *When We Dead Awaken*. After several

THE LADY FROM THE SEA

productions had failed to portray the Stranger satisfactorily, Ibsen issued a directive that this character "shall always stand in the background, half concealed by the bushes; only the upper half of his body visible, against the moonlight." In a letter to Julius Hoffory he stressed that the Stranger "has come as a passenger on a tourist steamer. He does not belong to the crew. He wears tourist dress, not travelling clothes. No-one knows what he is, or who he is, or what his real name is." At Weimar, where he thought the production "quite admirable," though Wangel and Lyngstrand were disappointing, he allowed himself an unusual luxury in the way of praise. "I cannot wish for, and can hardly imagine, a better representation of the Stranger than the one I saw here. A long, lean figure, with a hawk face, black, piercing eyes, and a splendid deep, quiet voice."

The incident of the rings which Ellida and the Stranger throw into the sea as a token of betrothal was borrowed from Ibsen's own experience. Thirty-five years before, in his early days as an apprentice at the theatre in Bergen, he had fallen in love with a fifteen-year-old girl named Rikke Holst, and they had betrothed themselves to each other in just this way. Rikke's father had broken off the match and, three years before he wrote *The Lady from the Sea,* Ibsen had re-encountered his former fiancée, now married to a rich business man and surrounded by numerous children. That meeting, too, left its mark on the play.

The objection most commonly raised against *The Lady from the Sea* is the difficulty of making the climactical moment of Ellida's choice seem convincing. In this connection Dr. Gunnar Ollén has written: "No one who saw the production in Vienna in the spring of 1950, with Attila Hörbiger as Wangel and Paula Wessely as Ellida, will share the opinion that Ellida's choice is implausible. The way Hörbiger played the scene in which he gives Ellida her freedom, her choice seemed utterly natural. He became red in the face, and had difficulty in enunciating his words, standing absolutely motionless and upright, with tears streaming down his cheeks. Quite simply, a stronger emotional power emanated from her husband than from the sailor. She . . . stared at Wangel as though seeing him for the first time, and then walked slowly across to him as though magnetically drawn. It was as if two hypnotists were fighting to gain control of a medium.''

Pirandello particularly admired *The Lady from the Sea*, and Ellida was Eleonora Duse's favourite role among the many of Ibsen's in which she excelled. She chose it both for her ''farewell performance'' in 1909, and for her come-back twelve years later. In 1923 she played it in London, at the New Oxford Theatre, and James Agate has left a memorable description of her performance:

''This play is a godsend to a great artist whose forte is not so much doing as suffering that which Fate has done to her. With Duse, speech is silver and silence golden. . . . The long second act was a symphony for the voice, but to me the scene of greatest marvel was the third act. In this Duse scaled incredible heights. There was one moment when, drawn by every fibre of her being to the unknown irresistible of the Stranger and the sea, she blotted herself behind her husband and took comfort and courage from his hand. Here terror and ecstasy sweep over her face with that curious effect which this actress alone knows—as though this were not present stress, but havoc remembered of past time. Her features have the placidity of long grief; so many storms have broken over them that nothing can disturb again this sea of calm distress. If there be in acting such a thing as pure passion divorced from the body yet expressed in terms of the body, it is here. Now and again in this strange play Duse would seem to pass beyond our ken, and where she has been

331

there is only a fragrance and a sound in our ears like water flowing under the stars.''

Duse's interpretation remained unchallenged for over half a century. Then, in 1976, Vanessa Redgrave played Ellida in a production of *The Lady from the Sea* by Tony Richardson at the Circle in the Square, New York. Her performance was unanimously admired. ''There is,'' wrote Clive Barnes in the *New York Times*, ''a divine contradiction in almost everything she does—she is at once girlish and womanly, and gauche and graceful . . . Both she and Mr. Richardson see Ellida's story as the exorcism of the bewitched, and the manner in which Miss Redgrave plots that course is masterly . . . What a lovely play this is! Sea-green, passionate, but quiet.'' Two years later, she acted the part again in a new and even better production by Michael Elliott at the Royal Exchange Theatre, Manchester, transferring (16 May 1979) to the Round House in London where her interpretation, and the play, were again rightly acclaimed: ''She combines,'' wrote Michael Coveney in the *Financial Times*, ''animal passion and suffocating doubt in a marvellous expression of Ellida's inner struggle''; and Francis King prophesied in the *Sunday Telegraph:* ''I suspect that one day we shall be reminiscing about Miss Redgrave's Ellida as fondly as gaffers now reminisce about Duse.'' It was indeed one of the great Ibsen performances and productions.

MICHAEL MEYER

CHARACTERS

DR. WANGEL, a country doctor
ELLIDA, his second wife
BOLETTE
HILDE } his daughters by a previous marriage
ARNHOLM, a schoolmaster
LYNGSTRAND
BALLESTED
A STRANGER
YOUNG PEOPLE FROM THE TOWN
TOURISTS and VISITORS

The action takes place during the summer in a small town by a fjord in northern Norway.

This translation of *The Lady from the Sea* was performed at The Circle in the Square, New York, on 18 March 1976, with the following cast:

DR. WANGEL	Pat Hingle
ELLIDA	Vanessa Redgrave
BOLETTE	Kimberly Farr
HILDE	Allison Argo
ARNHOLM	John Heffernan
LYNGSTRAND	Kipp Osborne
BALLESTED	George Ede
A STRANGER	Richard Lynch

Directed by Tony Richardson

It was first performed in London on 16 May 1979, at the Round House, in a production by the Royal Exchange Theatre, Manchester. The cast was:

DR. WANGEL	Graham Crowden
ELLIDA	Vanessa Redgrave
BOLETTE	Sherrie Hewson
HILDE	Lynsey Baxter
ARNHOLM	John Franklyn-Robbins
LYNGSTRAND	Christopher Good
BALLESTED	Ronald Herdman
A STRANGER	Terence Stamp

Directed by Michael Elliott

ACT ONE

DR. WANGEL's *house. On the left is a large verandah, roofed. In the foreground, and surrounding the house, is a garden. Below the verandah, a flagstaff. On the right, in the garden, an arbour, with a table and chairs. In the background is a hedge, containing a small gate. Behind the hedge, a path along the shore, shaded by trees. Through the trees we can see the fjord, with high mountain ranges rising to peaks in the distance. It is a hot and brilliantly clear summer morning.*

BALLESTED, *middle-aged, dressed in an old velvet jacket and a broad-brimmed artist's hat, is standing beneath the flagstaff busying himself with the line. The flag itself is lying on the ground. A short distance away stands an easel with a canvas on it. Beside it is a folding chair, on which lie brushes, a palette and a paint-box.*

BOLETTE WANGEL *comes out through the open doors leading on to the verandah. She is carrying a big vase of flowers, which she puts on the table.*

BOLETTE: Hullo, Ballested. Can you manage all right with that?

BALLESTED: Oh yes, Miss Bolette. It's quite a simple matter

really. If I may be so bold as to ask—are you expecting visitors today?

BOLETTE: Yes, we're expecting Dr. Arnholm this morning. You know, the schoolmaster.

BALLESTED: Arnholm? Wait a moment! Wasn't there a gentleman called Arnholm who used to be—ah—tutor here a few years ago?

BOLETTE: That's right, my old tutor. He arrived in town last night.

BALLESTED: So he's in these parts again?

BOLETTE: Yes, that's why we want the flag up.

BALLESTED: Very proper.

> BOLETTE *goes back into the garden room. A few moments later* LYNGSTRAND *comes up the path from the right, and stops, interested, on catching sight of the easel and painting materials. He is a thin young man, shabbily but decently dressed and of delicate appearance.*

LYNGSTRAND *(from the other side of the hedge):* Good morning.

BALLESTED *(turns):* Oh! Good morning. *(Hoists the flag.)* There now! Up she goes! *(Makes the line fast and gets busy at the easel.)* Good morning, sir. I don't think I've had the pleasure—

LYNGSTRAND: You're a painter, are you?

BALLESTED: Er—conceivably. Why not a painter, inter alia?

LYNGSTRAND: Why not indeed? Can I come inside for a moment?

BALLESTED: You wish to look at my work?

LYNGSTRAND: Yes, I'd like to very much.

BALLESTED: There's nothing much to see yet. Still, if you'd really like to. Pray step in.

LYNGSTRAND: Thank you. *(He comes in through the gate.)*

BALLESTED *(painting):* Just now I'm working on the stretch of the fjord—there, you see, between the islands.

LYNGSTRAND: Yes, I know.

BALLESTED: I haven't begun on the figure yet, though. It's impossible to secure a model in this town.

LYNGSTRAND: Are you going to have a figure as well?

BALLESTED: Yes. On this rock—here in the foreground. I'm going to have a mermaid. Half-dead.

LYNGSTRAND: Why half-dead?

BALLESTED: She's wandered in from the sea, and can't find her way back. So here she lies, dying in the brackish waters of the fjord. You follow me?

LYNGSTRAND: Yes, I see.

BALLESTED: It was the lady of the house here who put the idea into my head.

LYNGSTRAND: What are you going to call this picture when you've finished it?

BALLESTED: I'm thinking of calling it "The Death of the Mermaid."

LYNGSTRAND: Very appropriate. You should be able to make something really good out of this.

BALLESTED *(looks at him):* A—ah—fellow-forager, perhaps?

LYNGSTRAND: Er—painter, you mean?

BALLESTED: Yes.

LYNGSTRAND: No, I'm not a painter. I'm going to be a sculptor, actually. My name is Lyngstrand. Hans Lyngstrand.

BALLESTED: So you're going to be a sculptor? Yes, yes—sculpture's a fine art too—very fine. I think I've seen you in the town once or twice. Have you been around here long?

LYNGSTRAND: No, only a fortnight. But I'm going to stay the whole summer, if I can manage to.

BALLESTED: And enjoy the bathing amenities, no doubt?

LYNGSTRAND: Yes, that's why I came. To regain my strength.

BALLESTED: Oh? You don't look—ah—infirm.

LYNGSTRAND: I am a little—infirm, as you say. Nothing dangerous. My chest, you know. Just a shortness of breath now and then.

BALLESTED: That's nothing. Er—perhaps you should consult a doctor all the same—a good doctor.

LYNGSTRAND: I thought—Dr. Wangel—if I get an opportunity.

BALLESTED: Yes, I should. *(Glances left.)* There's another steamer coming in. Bursting with passengers. It's quite phenomenal how the tourist traffic has increased here these last few years.

LYNGSTRAND: Yes, I've noticed you get a lot of trippers.

BALLESTED: Ah, and a lot of people come for the whole summer too. I often fear our little town may lose its character with all these strangers coming here.

LYNGSTRAND: Were you born here?

BALLESTED: No, but I've accli—acclimatised myself. I've been here so long and got so much into the ways of the place that I feel like one of the natives.

LYNGSTRAND: Then you've been here a long time?

BALLESTED: Seventeen years. No—eighteen! I came with a theatrical company. But we got into financial difficulties, so the company broke up. Scattered to the four winds.

LYNGSTRAND: But you stayed.

BALLESTED: Yes, I stayed. And did quite nicely, really. My forte in those days used to be decoration and design.

   BOLETTE *comes out with a rocking chair, which she sets down on the verandah.*

BOLETTE *(talking to someone in the garden room):* Hilde, see if you can find that embroidered footstool for father, will you?

338

LYNGSTRAND *(goes to the verandah and greets her):* Good
morning, Miss Wangel.

BOLETTE *(leaning over the rail):* Why, hullo, Mr. Lyngstrand, is it you? Good morning. Forgive me a moment, I
must just— *(Goes back into the house.)*

BALLESTED: You know the family then?

LYNGSTRAND: Not really. I've just met the young ladies
once or twice here and there. And exchanged a few words
with Mrs. Wangel the last time they had a concert up on
the hill. She suggested I should come and see them some
time.

BALLESTED: You must cultivate their acquaintance.

LYNGSTRAND: I thought I'd pay them a call. A visit, as they
say in England. I've been trying to think up some
excuse—

BALLESTED: Excuse! Pah! *(Glances away left.)* Oh, confound
it! The steamer's almost alongside now. I must get along
to the hotel. The new arrivals may need my services. I run
a little line as haircutter and friseur, I must tell you.

LYNGSTRAND: You're very versatile.

BALLESTED: Well, one's got to accli—acclimatise oneself.
One's got to learn to do a bit of everything in a little place
like this. If you should ever need anything in that line—
pomade, or suchlike—just ask for Monsieur Ballested,
the dancing master.

LYNGSTRAND: Dancing master?

BALLESTED: Chairman of the Horn Society, if you like.
We're giving a concert up on the Prospect this evening.
Goodbye, goodbye!

*He goes out through the garden gate with his painting
materials and disappears left.* HILDE *comes out of the
house with the footstool.* BOLETTE *follows her with
more flowers.* LYNGSTRAND, *down in the garden,
raises his hat.*

HILDE *(comes to the verandah railing—she does not acknowledge his greeting):* Bolette tells me you've actually ventured into the garden today.

LYNGSTRAND: Yes, I have taken that liberty.

HILDE: Been walking all morning?

LYNGSTRAND: No, actually, I've just—

HILDE: You've been swimming, then, I suppose?

LYNGSTRAND: Yes, I had a little dip. I saw your mother down there. She was just going into her bathing-hut.

HILDE: Who, do you say?

LYNGSTRAND: Your mother.

HILDE: Oh, I see what you mean. *(She puts the footstool down in front of the rocking-chair.)*

BOLETTE *(quickly):* Did you see anything of father's boat out on the fjord?

LYNGSTRAND: Yes, I thought I saw a boat sailing this way.

BOLETTE: That would be father. He's been visiting some patients on the islands. *(She busies herself at the table.)*

LYNGSTRAND *(climbs on to the first step of the stairs to the verandah):* How splendid you're making it look with all these flowers.

BOLETTE: Yes, it looks rather nice, don't you think?

LYNGSTRAND: Wonderful. As though you were celebrating some sort of red letter day.

HILDE: We are.

LYNGSTRAND: I guessed as much. Your father's birthday, I presume?

BOLETTE *(warningly to HILDE):* Ssh!

HILDE *(ignoring her):* No, mother's.

LYNGSTRAND: Really? Your mother's?

BOLETTE *(softly, but angrily):* Hilde—!

HILDE: Leave me alone. *(To LYNGSTRAND)* Well, I suppose you'll be going back to your hotel for lunch now?

LYNGSTRAND *(steps down):* Yes, I ought to be getting a bite of something.

HILDE: I suppose the food up there seems wonderful to you?

LYNGSTRAND: I don't live at the hotel any longer. I found it too expensive.

HILDE: Where do you live now, then?

LYNGSTRAND: Up at Mrs. Jensen's.

HILDE: Which Mrs. Jensen?

LYNGSTRAND: The midwife.

HILDE: Really, Mr. Lyngstrand, I have better things to do—

LYNGSTRAND: Ah, of course. I ought not to have said that.

HILDE: Said what?

LYNGSTRAND: What I said just now.

HILDE: I haven't the faintest idea what you're talking about.

LYNGSTRAND: No, no. Well I'd better say au revoir to you and Miss Bolette.

BOLETTE *(comes down the steps):* Goodbye, Mr. Lyngstrand, goodbye! Do please excuse us today. Some other time—when you have nothing to do—you must come and look round the house and see father and—the rest of us.

LYNGSTRAND: Yes, thank you very much. I should love to. *(He raises his hat and goes out through the garden gate. As he goes down the path to the left, he raises his hat again up towards the verandah.)*

HILDE *(half aloud):* Au revoir, monsieur! Give my love to Mother Jensen.

BOLETTE *(quietly, shaking her by the arm):* Hilde, you little beast! Are you mad? He could easily have heard you.

HILDE: Do you think I care if he did?

BOLETTE *(glances right):* Here's father.

DR. WANGEL, *in travelling clothes, with a small bag in his hand, comes up the path from the right.*

WANGEL: Well, young ladies, here I am again. *(Enters through garden gate.)*

BOLETTE *(goes down into the garden to meet him):* Oh, father! It's good to have you back!

341

HILDE *(also runs down to him)*: Are you free for the day now, father?

WANGEL: Oh no, I shall have to go down to the surgery for an hour or two. Tell me, has Arnholm arrived yet?

BOLETTE: Yes, he got into town last night. We heard from the hotel.

WANGEL: You haven't seen him, then?

BOLETTE: No. But I expect he'll come here this morning.

WANGEL: Yes, I'm sure he will.

HILDE *(pulls his arm)*: Father! Look!

WANGEL *(looks up at the verandah)*: Why yes, child. I see. How very nice.

BOLETTE: Don't you think we've made it look pretty?

WANGEL: I should say you have. Is your—are there just the three of us at home now?

HILDE: Yes, she's gone down to—

BOLETTE *(quickly)*: Mother's gone down to bathe.

WANGEL *(gives BOLETTE an affectionate glance, and pats her head. Then he says awkwardly)*: But tell me, young ladies, are you going to have the house looking like this for the rest of the day? With the flag flying and everything?

HILDE: Father! Of course!

WANGEL: I see. But—

BOLETTE *(with a wink)*: Of course, you know we've really done all this for Dr. Arnholm. When such an old friend comes to pay his first—

HILDE *(shakes his arm playfully)*: He used to be Bolette's tutor, father!

WANGEL *(with a half smile)*: What a couple of rogues you are! Ah, well! I suppose it's only natural that we should spare a thought now and then for her who is no longer with us. All the same— Here, Hilde! *(Gives her the bag.)* Run down with that to the surgery, there's a good girl.

No, children, I don't like this—the way you—every
year— Ah, well, I suppose it must be so.

HILDE *(about to go through the garden with* WANGEL'*s bag,
stops, turns and points):* Isn't that Dr. Arnholm?

BOLETTE *(looks in the same direction):* That? *(Laughs.)*
Silly! He's much too old for Arnholm.

WANGEL: Upon my soul, I think it is he! Yes, it is, yes!

BOLETTE *(stares, amazed):* Good heavens, I think you're
right.

> DR. ARNHOLM, *the schoolmaster, elegantly dressed in
> morning clothes, with gold spectacles and a slender
> cane, comes up the path from the left. He looks over-
> worked. He glances into the garden, gives a friendly
> wave and comes in through the gate.*

WANGEL *(going to greet him):* Welcome, my dear fellow!
(Warmly.) Welcome home!

ARNHOLM: Thank you, Dr. Wangel, thank you. You are too
kind. *(They shake hands warmly and go together across
the garden.)* And here are the children! *(Holds out his
hands and looks at them.)* I should hardly have recognised
them.

WANGEL: No—I don't suppose you would.

ARNHOLM: Except—Bolette perhaps. Yes, I think I should
have known Bolette.

WANGEL: Really? It must be eight or nine years since you
last saw her. Ah, yes. A great deal has changed here in
that time.

ARNHOLM *(looking round):* I was just thinking the opposite.
Except that the trees are a little taller—and that arbour—

WANGEL: Ah, yes, externally—

ARNHOLM *(smiles):* And now you have two eligible
grown-up daughters.

WANGEL: Well—one.

HILDE: Oh, father!

WANGEL: Shall we go and sit on the verandah? It's cooler there. *(Indicates to* ARNHOLM *to precede him up the steps.)*

ARNHOLM: Thank you, my dear doctor, thank you.

They go up. WANGEL *waves* ARNHOLM *into the rocking chair.*

WANGEL: There, now. Just sit back and take things easy. You look quite exhausted after your long journey.

ARNHOLM: Oh, that's nothing. The air here is so—

BOLETTE *(to* WANGEL*):* Shall we bring some seltzer and some lemonade into the garden room? It'll soon be too hot to sit out here.

WANGEL: Yes, do that, will you, children? Bring us some seltzer and some lemonade. And some brandy, too, perhaps.

BOLETTE: You want some brandy, too?

WANGEL: Just a drop. In case anyone should feel like it.

BOLETTE: Yes, of course. Hilde, take father's bag to the surgery, will you?

BOLETTE goes into the garden room and closes the door behind her. HILDE *takes the bag and walks through the garden and out behind the house, to the left.*

ARNHOLM *(who has watched* BOLETTE *go out):* What a lovely girl—er—your daughters have grown into.

WANGEL *(sits):* Yes, they have, haven't they?

ARNHOLM: Yes. I'm amazed at Bolette—and Hilde too. But now, tell me about yourself, my dear doctor. Have you decided to settle here for good?

WANGEL: Oh yes, I think so. I was born and bred here, as they say. And here I spent those unbelievably happy years with her—the few years we were allowed. You met her when you were here before, Arnholm.

ARNHOLM: Yes. Yes.

WANGEL: And now I have found a new happiness here with—my new wife. Yes, all in all I must confess that fate has been kind to me.

ARNHOLM: You have had no children by your second marriage?

WANGEL: We had a little boy two, no, two and a half years ago. But we didn't keep him long. He died when he was four or five months old.

ARNHOLM: Is your wife not at home today?

WANGEL: Yes, she'll be here soon. She's down at the fjord bathing. She goes every day now. Whatever the weather.

ARNHOLM: You speak as if there was—something the matter with her.

WANGEL: There's nothing exactly the matter with her. She's been very nervous these past few years. Off and on, you know. I can't make up my mind what's behind it. Bathing in the sea has become a—a kind of passion with her.

ARNHOLM: Yes. I remember she used to be like that.

WANGEL *(with an almost imperceptible smile):* Of course, you knew Ellida when you taught out at Skjoldviken.

ARNHOLM: Yes. She used to come to the vicarage. And I met her quite often when I went out to the lighthouse to see her father.

WANGEL: The life out there has never loosed its hold on her. The people here can't fathom her. They call her: "The Lady from the Sea."

ARNHOLM: Do they really?

WANGEL: Yes. That's why— Talk to her about the old days, Arnholm. It will do her so much good.

ARNHOLM *(glancing uncertainly at him):* You have some special reason for thinking that?

WANGEL: Yes.

ELLIDA'S VOICE *(from the garden, offstage right):* Is that you, Wangel?

WANGEL *(getting up):* Yes, my dear.

345

ELLIDA WANGEL *comes through the trees by the arbour, wearing a large, lightweight bathing wrap, her hair wet and spread over her shoulders.* DR. ARNHOLM *gets to his feet.*

WANGEL *(smiles and stretches out his hands to her):* Well, here she is, our Lady from the Sea.

ELLIDA *(goes quickly up to the verandah and clasps his hands):* Thank heaven you're back. When did you arrive?

WANGEL: Just now—a few minutes ago. *(Indicates ARNHOLM.)* Well, aren't you going to greet an old friend?

ELLIDA *(holding out her hand to ARNHOLM):* You've come then. Welcome! Forgive me for not being here when you—

ARNHOLM: Please. You mustn't put yourself to any trouble—

WANGEL: How was the water today? Fresh and clean?

ELLIDA: Fresh? Dear God, the water here is never fresh. It's lifeless and stale. Ugh! The water is sick here in the fjord.

ARNHOLM: Sick?

ELLIDA: Yes—sick. I mean I think it makes one sick. Poisonous, too.

WANGEL *(smiles):* Well, you're certainly doing your best to recommend the amenities of the place.

ARNHOLM: No, I rather think that Mrs. Wangel has a special affinity to the sea and everything connected with it.

ELLIDA: But have you noticed how beautifully the girls have arranged everything in your honour?

WANGEL *(embarrassed):* Hm. *(Looks at his watch.)* Well, I must be getting off.

ARNHOLM: Is this really in my honour—?

ELLIDA: Certainly. You don't think we do this sort of thing every day? Ugh—how stiflingly hot it is under this roof. *(Goes down into the garden.)* Come down here. There's at least some air down here. *(Sits in the arbour.)*

ARNHOLM *(going to her):* I think the air's quite fresh up here.

ELLIDA: Oh, you're used to that dreadful city air. It's quite suffocating in summer, I'm told.

WANGEL *(who has also come down into the garden):* Well, Ellida, my dear, now you must entertain our good friend by yourself for a while.

ELLIDA: Have you work to do?

WANGEL: Yes, I must go to the surgery—and change my clothes, too. I shan't be long, though.

ARNHOLM *(seats himself in the arbour):* Please don't hurry yourself, my dear doctor. Your wife and I will manage to pass the time.

WANGEL *(nods):* Yes, I'm sure you will. Well—see you later. *(Goes out left, through the garden.)*

ELLIDA *(after a brief silence):* It's pleasant sitting here, don't you think?

ARNHOLM: Very pleasant, I think—now.

ELLIDA: We call this my arbour. Because I made it. Or rather, Wangel made it for me.

ARNHOLM: And this is where you like to sit?

ELLIDA: Yes, I sit here most of the day.

ARNHOLM: With the girls, I suppose.

ELLIDA: No, the girls stay on the verandah.

ARNHOLM: And Wangel himself?

ELLIDA: Oh, Wangel comes and goes. Half an hour with me, half an hour with the children.

ARNHOLM: Did you make that arrangement?

ELLIDA: I think it suits us all best. We can call across—when we have anything to say to each other.

ARNHOLM *(after a moment's thought):* When I last saw you—out at Skjoldviken, I mean— Hm. That's a long time now.

ELLIDA: At least ten years.

ARNHOLM: Yes. But when I remember you as you used to be

out there in that lighthouse—the old priest used to call you "The Heathen" because your father had given you the name of a ship instead of an honest Christian name, he used to say—

ELLIDA: Yes—well?

ARNHOLM: The last thing on earth I could have imagined would have been that I should ever see you here as Mrs. Wangel.

ELLIDA: Yes, then Wangel, was still—the girls' mother was alive. Their real mother, I mean.

ARNHOLM: Yes, of course. But even if he hadn't been—even if he'd been a bachelor—I could never have guessed that this would happen.

ELLIDA: Nor could I. Not for a moment. Then.

ARNHOLM: Wangel is such a good man. So honourable—so good and kind to everyone.

ELLIDA (warmly and affectionately): Yes!

ARNHOLM: But he must be so very different from you, I should have thought.

ELLIDA: He is.

ARNHOLM: How did it happen then? How did it happen?

ELLIDA: Oh, my dear Arnholm, you mustn't ask me that. I couldn't begin to explain to you. And even if I could, you could never begin to understand.

ARNHOLM: Hm. (More subdued.) Have you ever told your husband anything about me? I mean of course regarding that foolish proposal I once made to you?

ELLIDA: No. Of course not. I've never breathed a word to him about that.

ARNHOLM: I'm glad. I was a little worried at the thought that you might have—

ELLIDA: Well, you needn't be. I have merely told him the truth, which is that I was very fond of you, and that you were the best and truest friend I had out there. Have you ever thought of marrying anyone else?

ARNHOLM: Never. I have remained faithful to my memories.

ELLIDA *(half jestingly):* Oh, Arnholm! Let those sad old memories rest! You ought to look round for a wife who could make you happy.

ARNHOLM: I shall have to begin soon, then, Mrs. Wangel. I'm already thirty-seven, you know.

ELLIDA: All the more reason to lose no time then. *(She is silent for a moment, then continues earnestly and in a subdued voice.)* Arnholm, my dear, listen. I want to tell you something I could never have told you—at the time—not if my life had been at stake.

ARNHOLM: What?

ELLIDA: When you made that—when you asked—what you spoke of just now—I couldn't have replied in any other way than I did.

ARNHOLM: I know. You had nothing to offer me except friendship. I know that.

ELLIDA: But you don't know that all my thoughts and feelings were already directed elsewhere.

ARNHOLM: Already?

ELLIDA: Yes.

ARNHOLM: But that's impossible! Why, you didn't even know Wangel then.

ELLIDA: I'm not speaking of Wangel.

ARNHOLM: Not Wangel? But at that time—when you were out at Skjoldviken—I can't think of anyone else you could possibly have become attached to.

ELLIDA: No, I suppose not. The whole thing was so insane.

ARNHOLM: Tell me more.

ELLIDA: All that matters is that I was already in love with someone else. Well, now you know.

ARNHOLM: But if you hadn't been in love with someone else?

ELLIDA: Yes?

ARNHOLM: Would you have replied differently to my letter?

ELLIDA: How can I tell? When Wangel came I replied differently to him.

ARNHOLM: Then why do you bother to tell me this?

ELLIDA *(rises to her feet, as though in pain):* Because I've got to have someone to confide in. No, don't get up.

ARNHOLM: Then your husband knows nothing about this?

ELLIDA: I told him from the first that I had once been in love with someone else. He has never demanded to know any more. And we've never discussed the matter. In any case the whole thing was insane. And it soon passed over—in a way—

ARNHOLM *(rises to his feet):* In a way! Not completely?

ELLIDA: Yes, yes, completely! Oh, Arnholm, it's not as you think. It's all quite inexplicable. I don't know how I could begin to tell you. You would only think I was ill or mad.

ARNHOLM: My dear Mrs. Wangel, you must and shall tell me the whole truth.

ELLIDA: Very well. I'll try. Tell me; how, as a sensible man, can you explain this? *(Glances away and breaks off.)* I'll tell you later. Someone is coming.

> LYNGSTRAND *comes down the path from the left, and enters the garden. He is wearing a flower in his buttonhole and is carrying a large and splendid bouquet, wrapped in paper and tied with ribbon. He halts and hesitates uncertainly beneath the verandah.*

ELLIDA *(comes to the edge of the arbour):* Are you looking for the girls, Mr. Lyngstrand?

LYNGSTRAND *(turns):* Ah, is that you, Mrs. Wangel? *(Raises his hat, and comes towards her.)* No, I wasn't looking for the girls, Mrs. Wangel—it was you I wanted to see. You were so kind as to suggest I might pay a visit some time—

ELLIDA: Why, yes, so I did. You are always welcome here.

LYNGSTRAND: Thank you so much. Well, seeing that it happened to be rather a special occasion here today—

ELLIDA: Oh, you know about that?

LYNGSTRAND: Yes, so I thought I'd be so bold as to ask you to accept this. *(He bows and offers her the bouquet.)*

ELLIDA *(with a smile):* But, my dear Mr. Lyngstrand, don't you think you ought to give your beautiful flowers to Dr. Arnholm yourself? It's he who—

LYNGSTRAND *(glancing uncertainly from one to the other):* Forgive me, but I don't know this gentleman. I only came because of the—the birthday.

ELLIDA: Birthday? You have made some mistake, Mr. Lyngstrand. It's nobody's birthday here today.

LYNGSTRAND *(beams happily):* Oh, I know all about it. I didn't realise it was meant to be a secret, though.

ELLIDA: What do you know all about?

LYNGSTRAND: That it's your birthday, Mrs. Wangel.

ELLIDA: Mine?

ARNHOLM: Today? Surely not?

ELLIDA *(to LYNGSTRAND):* What makes you think it is?

LYNGSTRAND: Miss Hilde let it out. I was here for a few moments earlier today. I asked the young ladies why they'd got everything to look so smart with flowers and flags—

ELLIDA: I see.

LYNGSTRAND: And Miss Hilde said: "It's because today is mother's birthday."

ELLIDA: Mother's—?

ARNHOLM: Ah! *(He and ELLIDA exchange a glance of understanding.)* Well, since this young gentleman knows, Mrs. Wangel—

ELLIDA *(to LYNGSTRAND):* Yes, since you know—

LYNGSTRAND *(offering her the bouquet again):* May I then have the honour to offer my congratulations?

ELLIDA *(taking the flowers):* It's very kind of you. Won't you come in and sit down for a minute, Mr. Lyngstrand?

ELLIDA, ARNHOLM *and* LYNGSTRAND *sit down in the* *arbour.*

This business—about my birthday—was meant to be a secret, Dr. Arnholm.

ARNHOLM: I know. It wasn't meant to be revealed to us outsiders.

ELLIDA *(puts the bouquet down on the table):* No, that's right. Not to outsiders.

LYNGSTRAND: I promise I shan't breathe a word about it to a living soul.

ELLIDA: It's really of no importance. But tell me, how are you? You're looking better than when I last saw you.

LYNGSTRAND: Yes, I think I'm making good progress. And next year, when I get down to the south—the Mediterranean, that is—if I manage to—

ELLIDA: That's arranged, the girls tell me.

LYNGSTRAND: Yes, I hope so. I've got a benefactor in Bergen who's very good to me. He's promised he'll help me next year.

ELLIDA: How did you come to meet him?

LYNGSTRAND: A most extraordinary piece of luck. I happened to go to sea once in one of his ships.

ELLIDA: Really? So you loved the sea?

LYNGSTRAND: No, not in the least. But when my mother died, my father didn't want to have me hanging round the house any longer, so he made me go to sea. Well, on the way home our ship was wrecked in the English Channel. Luckily for me.

ELLIDA: Why do you say luckily?

LYNGSTRAND: Well, it was as a result of the shipwreck that I got this chest trouble. I was such a long time in the water before they picked me up. And it was terribly cold—cold as ice. So then I had to leave the sea. Yes, it was a great stroke of luck for me.

ARNHOLM: Oh, do you really think so?

LYNGSTRAND: Why, yes. This chest of mine isn't at all dangerous. And now I can become a sculptor, which is what I really want. Clay's so beautiful—the way it takes shape beneath your fingers.

ELLIDA: What are you going to do? Mermaids? Or Vikings?

LYNGSTRAND: No, nothing like that. As soon as I can, I want to try my hand at something really big. A group. A composition.

ELLIDA: Really? What is this composition to represent?

LYNGSTRAND: Well it's got to be something I've experienced myself.

ARNHOLM: Quite right! Always stick to your own experiences.

ELLIDA: Tell us about it.

LYNGSTRAND: Well, what I have in mind is a young girl, a sailor's wife, lying asleep—but restlessly, strangely restlessly. She's dreaming. I think I'll be able to manage it so that you can see she's dreaming.

ARNHOLM: But you said a composition.

LYNGSTRAND: Yes, I'm going to have another figure. Symbolic, don't you know? Her husband, whom she's been unfaithful to while he's been away. He's been drowned—drowned in the sea.

ELLIDA: Drowned?

LYNGSTRAND: Yes. Drowned on a sea-voyage. But he came home to her all the same. One night. And there he stands by her bed, staring at her. Wet and sodden as—as only a drowned man can be.

ELLIDA *(leans back in her chair):* That's strange. Wonderfully strange. Yes. I can see it so vividly.

ARNHOLM: But for Heaven's sake Mr.—Mr.— I thought you said this composition was to represent something that had once happened to you.

LYNGSTRAND: Yes. It did happen to me. In a manner of speaking.

ELLIDA: What exactly happened, Mr. Lyngstrand?

LYNGSTRAND: We were just about to sail for home from a town called Halifax when the boatswain fell ill, and we had to leave him behind in hospital. So we signed on another fellow instead, an American. Well this new boatswain—

ELLIDA: The American?

LYNGSTRAND: Yes. One day he borrowed a bundle of old newspapers from the captain, and spent every minute he could reading them. He said he wanted to learn Norwegian.

ELLIDA: Yes! And then?

LYNGSTRAND: Well, one evening, a terrible storm blew up. All the men were on deck except the boatswain and me. He'd sprained a foot, so that he couldn't walk, I wasn't feeling well either, and was lying in my bunk. Well, there he was sitting in the cabin, re-reading one of these old newspapers—

ELLIDA: Yes, yes?

LYNGSTRAND: Well, as he's sitting there, I hear him give a kind of howl. And when I look at him, I see his face has gone as white as chalk. Then he crumples the paper together and pulls it into a thousand pieces. But he did it all so quietly. So quietly.

ELLIDA: Didn't he say anything? Not a word?

LYNGSTRAND: Not at first. But after a bit he said to himself: "Married. To another man. While I was away."

ELLIDA *(closes her eyes and says half-audibly):* He said that?

LYNGSTRAND: Yes. And, would you believe it, he said it in really good Norwegian? He must have had a wonderful ear for languages, that man.

ELLIDA: What then? What else happened?

LYNGSTRAND: Well, then this extraordinary thing happened which I shall never forget. He said, still in the same calm voice: "But mine she is, and mine she shall always be. And she will come to join me, even though I go as a drowned man to claim her."

ELLIDA *(pours herself a glass of water. Her hand trembles):* Ugh! How close it is!

LYNGSTRAND: And the way he said it made me think he would do it too.

ELLIDA: Do you know what—what has become of this man?

LYNGSTRAND: Ah, Mrs. Wangel, he's dead, I'm sure.

ELLIDA *(passionately):* Why do you think that?

LYNGSTRAND: Well, it was just after that that we got wrecked in the Channel. I managed to get into the big lifeboat with the captain and five others. The mate got into the dinghy. And the American and one other man were there with him.

ELLIDA: And nothing has been heard of them since?

LYNGSTRAND: Nothing, Mrs. Wangel. My benefactor told me this in a letter I got from him recently. That's just why I so want to—to commemorate it. His faithless girl, and the drowned man coming home from the sea to revenge himself on her. I can see them both so clearly.

ELLIDA: So can I. *(She rises.)* Come, let's go inside. Or down to Wangel. It's so suffocatingly close here. *(She goes out of the arbour.)*

LYNGSTRAND: *(who has also got up):* Yes, well, I must say thank you and be off. I just wanted to pay a little courtesy call, seeing it was your birthday.

ELLIDA: As you wish. *(Holds out her hand.)* Goodbye. And thank you for the flowers.

LYNGSTRAND *shakes her hand and exits by the garden gate.*

ARNHOLM (*gets up and goes over to* ELLIDA): I can see this has touched you deeply, Mrs. Wangel.

ELLIDA: You could put it that way. Except that—

ARNHOLM: Still, it was something you had to be prepared for.

ELLIDA: Prepared for?

ARNHOLM: Yes, surely?

ELLIDA: Prepared for someone to come back? And to come back like that?

ARNHOLM: What on earth—? Is it this business about the dead man which so disturbed you? And I thought—

ELLIDA: What did you think?

ARNHOLM: Why, naturally, I thought you were pretending. I thought you were upset because you'd found out about this secret family celebration. Your husband and his children living a life of memories from which you are excluded.

ELLIDA: Oh, no, no! I have no right to demand of my husband that he shall be wholly and entirely mine.

ARNHOLM: I think you have. You must have.

ELLIDA: Yes. No, no, I haven't. That's the point. I live a life—from which they are excluded.

ARNHOLM: You! Do you mean to say you—you aren't really fond of your husband?

ELLIDA: Yes, yes, I am! I have grown so very fond of him. That's what makes it so dreadful.

ARNHOLM: Now you must tell me what makes you so unhappy. The whole story. Please—won't you?

ELLIDA: I can't. Not now, anyway. Later, perhaps.

BOLETTE *comes out on to the verandah and descends into the garden.*

BOLETTE: Father's just finishing in the surgery. Shall we all go into the garden room?

ELLIDA: Yes, let's.

WANGEL, *who has changed his clothes, appears on the left with* HILDE *from behind the house.*

WANGEL: Well, here I am. Finished for the day! What about a nice glass of something cool, eh?

ELLIDA: Just a moment. *(She goes into the arbour and picks up her bouquet.)*

HILDE: Oh, look! All those lovely flowers! Where did you get them from?

ELLIDA: I got them from young Mr. Lyngstrand, the sculptor.

HILDE: From Lyngstrand?

BOLETTE *(uneasily):* Has Lyngstrand been here again?

ELLIDA: Yes, he came just now with these. For the birthday, you know.

BOLETTE *(nudges* HILDE*):* Oh!

HILDE *(whispers):* The cat!

WANGEL *(in an agony of embarrassment, to* ELLIDA*):* I—you—Ellida, my dear, I—

ELLIDA *(cutting him short):* Come, children. Let's put my flowers in water with the others. *(She goes up to the verandah.)*

BOLETTE *(whispers to* HILDE*):* She's awfully nice, really!

HILDE: Monkey tricks! She's only doing it to please father!

WANGEL *(up on the verandah, presses* ELLIDA'S *hand):* Thank you, Ellida. Thank you so much, my dear.

ELLIDA *(busying herself with the flowers):* You wouldn't want me to be the only one not celebrating—mother's birthday, would you?

ARNHOLM: Hm!

He goes up to WANGEL *and* ELLIDA. BOLETTE *and* HILDE *stay down in the garden.*

ACT TWO

Up on "The Prospect," a wooded height behind the town. In the background, a cairn of stones with a weathervane. Large stones arranged as seats stand around the cairn and in the foreground. Far below to the rear can be seen the outer part of the fjord, with islets and headlands. The open sea cannot be seen.

It is the half-light of a Norwegian summer night. It is reddish-gold in the air, and above the mountain peaks far away in the distance. The sound of four-part singing can be heard faintly from the slopes away down to the right.

> *Young people from the town, of both sexes, come up in couples from the right, walk, talking intimately, past the cairn and go out, left. A few seconds later,* BALLESTED *enters, acting as guide to a group of foreign tourists and their ladies. He is weighed down with shawls and bags.*

BALLESTED *(pointing upwards with his stick):* Sehen Sie, meine Herrschaften—dort there liegt anders hill. Das willen wir also climb, und so herunter—Mesdames et Messieurs, voilà une autre montaigne. Elle a une vue magnifique—il est necessaire que nous la monterons aussi— *(He leads them out left, continuing in execrable French.)*

HILDE *comes nimbly up from the right, stops and looks back. A few moments later,* BOLETTE *follows her.*

BOLETTE: Hilde, why are we running ahead of Lyngstrand like this?

HILDE: Oh, I get bored with going so slowly. Look at the way he crawls along.

BOLETTE: Oh, but you know how ill he is.

HILDE: Do you think it's very serious?

BOLETTE: I do.

HILDE: He came to consult father this afternoon. I'd like to know what he thinks about it.

BOLETTE: Father told me he's got congestion of the lungs, or something of the kind. He won't live to be old, father said.

HILDE: No, did he say that? Just as I thought!

BOLETTE: For heaven's sake don't let him suspect you know anything.

HILDE: What do you take me for? *(Half to herself.)* Look, Hans has managed to clamber up at last. Hans. He looks as though he ought to be called Hans, doesn't he?

BOLETTE *(whispers):* Behave yourself now! Please!

LYNGSTRAND *enters from the right, carrying a parasol.*

LYNGSTRAND: Please forgive me, young ladies, for lagging so far behind you.

HILDE: Have you got yourself a parasol now too?

LYNGSTRAND: It's your mother's. She said I might use it as a stick. I didn't bring one of my own.

BOLETTE: Are they still down there? Father and the rest?

LYNGSTRAND: Yes. Your father went into the refreshment hut. And the others are sitting outside listening to the music. But they're coming up here soon, your mother said.

HILDE *(stands staring at him):* You must be very tired.

LYNGSTRAND: Yes, perhaps I am a little tired. I think I'll sit down for a minute. *(Sits on a stone in right foreground.)*

HILDE *(standing in front of him):* Do you know there's going to be dancing down there by the bandstand later?

LYNGSTRAND: Yes, so I heard.

HILDE: Do you think it's fun, dancing?

BOLETTE *(who has gone to pick small flowers in the heather):* Hilde! Give Mr. Lyngstrand a chance to get his breath back!

LYNGSTRAND: Oh, yes, Miss Hilde, I should so love to dance. If only I could.

HILDE: You mean you've never learned?

LYNGSTRAND: No—I have never learned, but that wasn't what I meant. I meant I mustn't, because of my chest.

HILDE: Does it make you very unhappy, having this chest trouble?

LYNGSTRAND: Oh, no, I can't really say that. *(Smiles.)* I think it's because of that that everyone's so good and kind and—helpful to me.

HILDE: Yes. And it isn't really serious, is it?

LYNGSTRAND: Serious? Good heavens, no, not in the least. Your father made that quite clear to me.

HILDE: It'll be all right as soon as you can get away and travel.

LYNGSTRAND: Yes. It'll be all right, then.

BOLETTE *(with flowers):* Here now, Mr. Lyngstrand. These are to go in your buttonhole.

LYNGSTRAND: Why, thank you, Miss Bolette, thank you. It's really too kind of you.

HILDE *(looking down right):* They're coming now.

BOLETTE *(also looking down):* I hope they know where to turn off. Oh, they've gone wrong.

LYNGSTRAND *(gets up):* I'll run down to the turning and shout to them.

HILDE: You'll have to shout very loud.

BOLETTE: No, don't. It'll make you tired again.

LYNGSTRAND: Nonsense, it's downhill. *(Exit, right.)*

HILDE: Downhill—yes. *(Watches him.)* Now he's jumping! It hasn't occurred to him he's got to climb uphill again on the way back.

BOLETTE: Poor boy!

HILDE: If Lyngstrand asked you to marry him, would you accept him?

BOLETTE: Have you gone mad?

HILDE: I mean if he hadn't got this chest trouble, of course. And if he wasn't going to die so soon. Would you have him then?

BOLETTE: I think he'd suit you better than me.

HILDE: Me? *(Laughs.)* He hasn't a bean. Not even enough to keep himself alive.

BOLETTE: Why do you always make so much fuss of him, then?

HILDE: Oh, only because of that chest of his.

BOLETTE: I haven't noticed that you feel sorry for him.

HILDE: No, I don't really. I think it's fascinating.

BOLETTE: What?

HILDE: To listen to him saying it's not serious, and that he's going south to become an artist. He believes every word he says, and it makes him so happy. And it'll never come to anything, because he won't live long enough. Oh, I think that's so exciting!

BOLETTE: Exciting?

HILDE: Yes, I think it's exciting. I'm not ashamed to admit it.

BOLETTE: Hilde, you are a cruel little beast!

HILDE: I want to be! So there! *(Looks down.)* I say! Arnholm's not enjoying all this climbing. *(Turns.)* It's true, it's true. Do you know what I noticed at dinner?

BOLETTE: No, what?

HILDE: His hair's beginning to fall out. Here in the middle.

BOLETTE: What nonsense! It isn't true.

HILDE: It is! And he's getting wrinkles round both his eyes. Oh, Bolette, how on earth could you have fallen in love with him when he was tutoring you?

BOLETTE *(smiles):* Yes, it's strange, isn't it? I remember once I burst into tears because he said he thought Bolette was an ugly name.

HILDE: Not really? *(Looks down again.)* Oh, come and look! The Lady from the Sea's walking with him. Father's on his own. I wonder if those two are stuck on each other?

BOLETTE: You really ought to be ashamed of yourself! How can you stand there talking like that about her? Just when we're all getting on so well together—

HILDE: Oh yes? That's what you think, my girl! She'll never get on with us. She's not our sort. And we're not hers. God knows why father ever dragged her into the house! I shouldn't be surprised if she went off her head one of these fine days.

BOLETTE: Off her head? How can you say such a thing?

HILDE: It wouldn't surprise me. Her mother went mad. She died in an asylum. I know.

BOLETTE: Is there anything you don't stick your nose into? Well, don't go round talking about it. Be nice to her—for father's sake. You hear what I say, Hilde?

WANGEL, ELLIDA, ARNHOLM *and* LYNGSTRAND *come up from the right.*

ELLIDA *(pointing upstage):* Out there it lies.

ARNHOLM: Yes, that's right. It must be in that direction.

ELLIDA: Out there lies the sea.

BOLETTE *(to* ARNHOLM*):* Don't you think it's lovely up here?

ARNHOLM: Magnificent. Splendid view.

WANGEL: Yes, I suppose you've never been up here before.

ARNHOLM: No, never. In my time I don't think you could get up here. There wasn't even a footpath.

WANGEL *(indicating the cairn and stone seats):* None of all this either. It's all new—

BOLETTE: There's an even better view from Lodskollen over there.

WANGEL: Shall we go there, Ellida?

ELLIDA *(sitting on a stone, right):* I won't, thanks. You go on. I'll sit here till you come back.

WANGEL: I'll do the same. The girls can show Dr. Arnholm the way.

BOLETTE: Would you like to come with us, Dr. Arnholm?

ARNHOLM: Thank you, I'd love to. Is there a path up there too?

BOLETTE: Oh, yes. A good broad one.

HILDE: Broad enough for two people to walk arm in arm.

ARNHOLM *(looks at her):* I can well believe it, Miss Hilde. *(To* BOLETTE*)* Shall we two see if she's speaking the truth?

BOLETTE: Yes, let's.

They go out left, arm in arm.

HILDE *(to* LYNGSTRAND*):* Shall we go too?

LYNGSTRAND: Arm in arm?

HILDE: Why not? I've no objection.

LYNGSTRAND *(takes her arm and beams happily):* This is rather a lark, isn't it?

HILDE: A lark?

LYNGSTRAND: Yes, it looks just as though we were engaged.

HILDE: Haven't you ever walked arm in arm with a lady before, Mr. Lyngstrand?

They go out left.

WANGEL *(standing by the cairn):* Well, Ellida, my dear, now we have a moment to ourselves.

ELLIDA: Yes. Come and sit here beside me.

WANGEL *(sits):* How calm and peaceful it is up here. Now we can talk a little.

ELLIDA: What about?

WANGEL: About you. You and me, Ellida. We can't go on like this.

ELLIDA: What do you want instead?

WANGEL: That we should trust each other—live together as man and wife—the way we used to before.

ELLIDA: If only we could! But it's quite impossible.

WANGEL: I think I know how you feel.

ELLIDA *(passionately):* You don't! Don't say you understand me!

WANGEL: But I do. You are so honest and loyal, Ellida.

ELLIDA: Loyal. Yes.

WANGEL: You couldn't find peace or happiness in any compromise relationship.

ELLIDA: Yes. Go on.

WANGEL: You were not made to be a man's second wife.

ELLIDA: Why do you suddenly say that?

WANGEL: I have often felt it. But today I realised it fully. The children's preparations for the anniversary. You thought I was in the conspiracy, didn't you? One cannot wipe out one's memories. I can't, anyway. I'm not made like that.

ELLIDA: I know that. Oh, I know it so well.

WANGEL: No, no. To you it's almost as though the children's mother were still alive. As though she were invisibly living among us. You think my love is divided between you and her. That thought is the cause of your unrest. You feel as though there were something—indecent in our relationship. That's why you can't—why you don't want to live with me as my wife any longer.

ELLIDA: But you haven't realised it all.

WANGEL *(rises):* I know, of course, there is something else too, Ellida.

ELLIDA *(frightened):* Something else?

WANGEL: Yes. You can't stand this place. The mountains oppress you—they weigh you down. There's not enough light for you here. Not enough sky around you. Not enough strong, clean air.

ELLIDA: How right you are! Night and day, winter and summer, it fills me—this homesickness for the sea.

WANGEL: I know. *(Puts his hand on her head.)* And now my poor sick child shall go home again.

ELLIDA: What do you mean?

WANGEL: What I say. We are going away.

ELLIDA: Going away?

WANGEL: Yes. Somewhere by the open sea. Somewhere where you can find a real home. The sort of home you long for.

ELLIDA: Oh, no, my dear. You mustn't think of it. You couldn't live anywhere in the world but here.

WANGEL: That's as it may be. Do you suppose I could be happy here without you?

ELLIDA: But I am here. And I shall stay here. I am yours.

WANGEL: Are you mine, Ellida?

ELLIDA: Don't let's talk about leaving. Your life's work lies here.

WANGEL: We are leaving this place. Going away somewhere. That is settled, Ellida.

ELLIDA: But what do you hope we shall gain by it?

WANGEL: Health and peace of mind—for you.

ELLIDA: I wonder. But what about you? Think of yourself, too. What do you hope to gain?

WANGEL: You, Ellida. You again.

ELLIDA: But you can't! No, no! You can never do that, Wangel!

WANGEL: We shall have to see. If that's how you feel, there's no other solution. You've got to go. And the sooner the better. That is settled.

ELLIDA: No. Oh, no! I'd rather tell you the truth.

WANGEL: Tell me!

ELLIDA: I'm not going to let you make yourself unhappy for my sake. Especially since it can't help us.

WANGEL: You have promised you will tell me the whole truth.

ELLIDA: I will tell you as well as I can. And as truthfully as I can. Come here and sit beside me.

They sit on the stones.

WANGEL: Well, Ellida? Tell me.

ELLIDA: That day you came out to Skjoldviken and asked me to be your wife, you spoke so frankly to me about your first marriage. You told me how happy you had been.

WANGEL: Yes, I was.

ELLIDA: I know. I only want to remind you that I was just as honest with you. I told you quite openly that I had once been in love with someone else. That we had become—in a way—engaged.

WANGEL: In a way?

ELLIDA: Yes. It lasted such a short time. He went away. And I regarded it as finished and done with. I told you all this.

WANGEL: But my dear Ellida, why drag all this up? It had nothing to do with me. I've never even asked who he was.

ELLIDA: No. You're always so considerate towards me.

WANGEL *(smiles):* Anyway, I think I could have provided the name myself. Out in Skjoldviken there weren't so many people to choose from. In fact, there was only one.

ELLIDA: You—think it was Arnholm?

WANGEL: Yes. Wasn't it?

ELLIDA: No.

WANGEL: Not he? Well, then you have me baffled.

ELLIDA: Do you remember late one autumn, a big American ship came into Skjoldviken for repairs?

WANGEL: Yes. They found the captain one morning murdered in his cabin. I went out myself and did a post-mortem.

ELLIDA: Yes, I suppose you did.

WANGEL: It was the mate who killed him.

ELLIDA: You've no right to say that! It was never proved.

WANGEL: There wasn't any room for doubt. Why else should he have gone away and drowned himself?

ELLIDA: He didn't drown himself. He went away with another ship, up into the Arctic.

WANGEL *(surprised)*: How do you know that?

ELLIDA *(unwillingly)*: Oh, Wangel! That is the man to whom I was engaged.

WANGEL *(rises quickly)*: What are you saying?

ELLIDA: It was he.

WANGEL: But in heaven's name, Ellida! How could you do such a thing? Go and get engaged to a man like that! A stranger you knew nothing about! What was his name?

ELLIDA: At that time he called himself Freeman. Later, when he wrote to me, he signed himself Alfred Johnston.

WANGEL: Where was he from?

ELLIDA: Finmark, he said. Up in the Arctic Circle. But he was born in Finland. He came to Norway as a child—with his father, I think.

WANGEL: What else do you know about him?

ELLIDA: Only that he went to sea when he was very young. And that he had voyaged all round the world.

WANGEL: Nothing else?

ELLIDA: No. We never talked about him.

WANGEL: What did you talk about, then?

ELLIDA: Mostly about the sea.

WANGEL: Ah. The sea.

ELLIDA: Storms and calms. Dark nights at sea. And the sea on sunny days—we talked about that too. But mostly we talked about whales and dolphins, and seals that lie out on the islands when it's hot. And we spoke of gulls and eagles and all the other sea-birds—you know. And—isn't it strange?—when we talked about these things, I had a feeling that these sea-beasts and sea-birds were somehow of the same blood as he.

WANGEL: And—you—?

ELLIDA: I felt almost as if I were one of them too.

WANGEL: I see. So—you became engaged to him?

ELLIDA: Yes. Well, he said I should.

WANGEL: Said you should? Had you no will of your own?

ELLIDA: Not when he was with me. Oh, when I look back at it now, it all seems so impossible to understand.

WANGEL: Did you see him often?

ELLIDA: No, not very often. One day he came out to look round the lighthouse. That was how we met. After that we saw each other occasionally. But this thing happened— with the captain—and he had to leave.

WANGEL: Tell me more about that.

ELLIDA: Early one morning—I remember it was scarcely light—I got a note from him. In it he wrote that I was to come and meet him at Bratthammeren—you remember, that headland between the lighthouse and Skjoldviken.

WANGEL: I remember.

ELLIDA: I was to go out there at once, he wrote, because he wanted to talk to me.

WANGEL: And you went?

ELLIDA: I had to. Well, then he told me that he had stabbed the captain during the night.

WANGEL: He admitted it!

ELLIDA: But he had only done what had to be done, he said. What was right.

WANGEL: What was right? Why did he kill him, then?

ELLIDA: He said it was nothing for me to know about.

WANGEL: And you believed him? Just like that?

ELLIDA: Yes. It never occurred to me to do otherwise. Well,

anyway, he had to leave. But just before he said goodbye—

WANGEL: Yes? Tell me.

ELLIDA: He took out of his pocket a key-chain, and pulled a
ring off his finger, a ring he always used to wear. And he
took a little ring from my finger too, and put these two
rings on to his key-chain. Then he said that we two were
going to marry ourselves to the sea.

WANGEL: Marry—?

ELLIDA: Yes, those were the words he used. Then he threw
the chain and rings with all his strength, as far as he
could, out into the sea.

WANGEL: And you, Ellida—you let him do this?

ELLIDA: It's strange, isn't it? At the time it seemed—
ordained. But then, thank God! He went away!

WANGEL: And when he'd gone—?

ELLIDA: Oh, I soon came to my senses, of course. I saw how
mad and meaningless the whole thing had been.

WANGEL: But you said something about letters. You have
heard from him since, then?

ELLIDA: Yes, I heard from him. First I got a few short lines
from Archangel. He just said he was going over to America. And gave an address for me to reply to.

WANGEL: Did you?

ELLIDA: At once. I wrote, of course, that everything was finished between us. And that he was not to think of me any
more, just as I would never think of him again.

WANGEL: But he wrote again?

ELLIDA: Yes, he wrote again.

WANGEL: What did he say?

ELLIDA: It was just as though I had never broken with him.
He wrote affectionately and—calmly—that I was to wait
for him. He would let me know when I could come to
him. And then I was to come at once.

WANGEL: He wouldn't give you up?

369

ELLIDA: No. So I wrote again. Almost word for word as I had written before. Even more strongly.

WANGEL: He stopped writing to you then?

ELLIDA: No. No. He wrote as calmly as before. Never a word about my having broken with him. Then I realised it was useless. So I never wrote to him again.

WANGEL: And you never heard from him?

ELLIDA: Yes, I got three more letters. One from California, and then one from China. The last I got from him was from Australia. He wrote that he was going to the gold mines. Since then I've never heard a word.

WANGEL: That man must have had an extraordinary power over you, Ellida.

ELLIDA: Yes. He was a demon.

WANGEL: But you mustn't think about him any more. Only promise me that, my dearest Ellida. We are going to find a new cure for you now. A fresher air than we have here in the fjords. The cleansing, salt-heavy air of the sea. What do you say?

ELLIDA: I shall never be able to escape from it—there, any more than here.

WANGEL: Escape from it? What—my dear, what exactly do you mean?

ELLIDA: I mean the horrible, unfathomable power he has over my mind.

WANGEL: But you have freed yourself from that. Long ago. When you broke with him. All that is dead and forgotten.

ELLIDA (*rises quickly*): No. That's just it. It isn't.

WANGEL: Not forgotten?

ELLIDA: No, Wangel. It isn't forgotten. And I'm afraid it never will be.

WANGEL (*in a choked voice*): You mean you have never really been able to forget this stranger?

ELLIDA: I did forget him. But he came back to me.

WANGEL: How long ago did this happen?

ELLIDA: About three years ago now. Or perhaps a little longer. It was while I was carrying the child.

WANGEL: Ah! Then! Ellida, now I'm beginning to understand.

ELLIDA: No, my dear, you're wrong. Oh, I don't think anyone will ever be able to understand.

WANGEL: To think that for these three years you have been in love with another man! Not with me.

ELLIDA: I don't love anyone else. Only you.

WANGEL *(in a subdued voice):* Then why have you refused to live with me as my wife all these years?

ELLIDA: Because I am afraid. Afraid of the stranger.

WANGEL: Afraid?

ELLIDA: Yes, afraid. The sort of fear that only the sea can give you. Oh, Wangel, I—

The young people from the town come back from the left, wave to ELLIDA *and* WANGEL, *and go out right.* ARNHOLM, BOLETTE, HILDE *and* LYNGSTRAND *come with them.*

BOLETTE *(as they go past):* Hullo, are you still up here?

ELLIDA: Yes. It's so lovely and cool up here on the hill.

ARNHOLM: We're going down to dance.

WANGEL: Fine, fine. We'll be down in a few minutes to join you.

HILDE: Goodbye, then. See you soon.

ELLIDA: Mr. Lyngstrand—would you mind waiting a minute?

LYNGSTRAND stays. ARNHOLM, BOLETTE and HILDE go out right.

ELLIDA *(to LYNGSTRAND):* Are you going to dance too?

LYNGSTRAND: No, Mrs. Wangel, I don't think I ought to.

ELLIDA: No, better be careful. That chest of yours—it's not quite right yet, is it?

LYNGSTRAND: Not quite, no.

ELLIDA *(slowly):* How long is it now since you were on that voyage when you—?

LYNGSTRAND: When I first got this—trouble?

ELLIDA: Yes, that voyage you were telling us about this morning.

LYNGSTRAND: Oh, it must be about—wait a moment. Yes, about three years ago.

ELLIDA: Three years.

LYNGSTRAND: Perhaps a bit more. We left America in February. Then we got wrecked in March. We ran into the spring gales.

ELLIDA *(looks at* WANGEL): That was the time.

WANGEL: But, dearest Ellida—

ELLIDA: Well, we mustn't keep you, Mr. Lyngstrand. Go on down. But no dancing.

LYNGSTRAND: I won't. I'll just watch. *(Goes out right.)*

WANGEL: Ellida, why did you ask him about that voyage?

ELLIDA: Johnston was on board with him. I'm almost sure of it.

WANGEL: What makes you think that?

ELLIDA *(ignoring the question):* He'd heard I'd married someone else. While he was away. And it was—at that moment that this—came over me.

WANGEL: You mean, this fear?

ELLIDA: Yes. Suddenly I see him—in front of me. No, not quite in front—a little to one side. He never looks at me. He's just—there.

WANGEL: How does he look?

ELLIDA: The same as when I saw him last.

WANGEL: Ten years ago?

ELLIDA: Yes. Out at Bratthammeren. I see him so clearly.

On his chest there's a pin with a big bluish-white pearl.
Like a dead fish's eye. As though it was staring at me.

WANGEL: For heaven's sake! You are sicker than I thought,
Ellida. Sicker than you know.

ELLIDA: Help me! If you can. I feel it crowding in on me—
more and more.

WANGEL: And you've been in this state for three whole
years—suffering in secret—without telling me.

ELLIDA: But—I couldn't! Not till now—when I had to—for
your sake, Wangel! If I had told you all this—I should
also have had to tell you—something unspeakable.

WANGEL: Unspeakable?

ELLIDA: No, no, no! Don't ask me! Only one thing more.
One thing. Wangel—how shall we get to the bottom of—
this riddle about the child's eyes?

WANGEL: My dearest Ellida, I promise you that was entirely
your own imagination. The child had eyes exactly like
any other child's.

ELLIDA: No he hadn't. Couldn't you see? The child's eyes
changed with the sea. When the fjord was calm and
sunny, his eyes were the same. And when it was
stormy—oh, I saw it clearly enough, even if you didn't.

WANGEL *(humouring her):* Well, suppose you are right?
Suppose you are? What then?

ELLIDA *(quietly, closer):* I have seen eyes like that before.

WANGEL: When? Where?

ELLIDA: Out at Bratthammeren. Ten years ago.

WANGEL: What do you—?

ELLIDA *(whispers):* The child had the stranger's eyes.

WANGEL *(cries):* Ellida!

ELLIDA: Now perhaps you understand why I never dare live
with you as your wife again! *(She turns quickly and runs
away down the hill.)*

WANGEL *(runs after her, crying):* Ellida! Ellida! My poor,
unhappy Ellida!

ACT THREE

A corner of DR. WANGEL's *garden. The place is damp and marshy and overshadowed by large old trees. To the right can be seen the edge of a stagnant pond. A low open fence divides the garden from the footpath and the fjord beyond. On the other side of the fjord in the distance can be seen mountain ranges and peaks. It is late afternoon, approaching evening.*

> BOLETTE *is sitting sewing on a stone bench, left. On the bench lie two or three books and a sewing basket.* HILDE *and* LYNGSTRAND *are walking along the edge of the pond, both carrying fishing rods.*

HILDE *(making signs to* LYNGSTRAND*):* Don't move! I can see a big one.

LYNGSTRAND *(looking):* Where?

HILDE *(points):* Can't you see him? Down there! God Almighty, there's another! *(Glances away between the trees.)* Oh, now he's going to come and frighten them away.

BOLETTE *(looking up):* Who's coming?

HILDE: Your tutor, madame.

BOLETTE: My—?

HILDE: He's never been mine, thank heaven.

> ARNHOLM *comes through the trees from the right.*

374

ARNHOLM: Are there any fish there?

HILDE *(pointing):* Yes, one or two old carp.

ARNHOLM: Those old carp! Are they still alive?

HILDE: Yes, they're tough. But we're going to catch one of them.

ARNHOLM: You'd have a better chance out in the fjord.

LYNGSTRAND: Ah, the pond's more—more mysterious.

HILDE: Yes, it's more exciting here. Have you been in the sea?

ARNHOLM: Yes, I've just come up from the bath-house.

HILDE: I expect you stayed close to the shore.

ARNHOLM: Yes, I'm not a very good swimmer.

HILDE: Can you swim on your back?

ARNHOLM: No.

HILDE: I can. *(To LYNGSTRAND)* Let's try over there on the other bank. *(They go along the edge of the pond and out to the right.)*

ARNHOLM *(going closer to BOLETTE):* Sitting here all by yourself, Bolette?

BOLETTE: Oh, yes. I usually do.

ARNHOLM: Isn't your mother in the garden?

BOLETTE: No. She's taking a walk with father.

ARNHOLM: How is she this afternoon?

BOLETTE: I don't know. I forgot to ask.

ARNHOLM: What are those books you have there?

BOLETTE: Oh, one's something about plants. And the other's a book about geography.

ARNHOLM: Do you like reading that sort of thing?

BOLETTE: Yes, when I can find the time. But I have to do the housework first.

ARNHOLM: But doesn't your mother—your stepmother— help you with that?

BOLETTE: No, that's my job. I had to see to it during the two years when father was alone. And I've done it ever since.

ARNHOLM: But I can see you still love reading.

BOLETTE: Yes, I love reading anything I can get—anything useful. I want to know about the world. We live so outside everything here.

ARNHOLM: Don't say that, Bolette.

BOLETTE: Oh, we do. I don't think our life is very different from the life of those carp down there in the pond. The fjord lies so close, with big shoals of wild fish swimming in and out. But the poor tame carp mustn't know anything about what goes on out there. That life is not for them.

ARNHOLM: I don't think they'd be happy if they could get out into the fjord.

BOLETTE: I wonder.

ARNHOLM: Anyway, I don't think you can really say you live outside life here. Not in the summer at any rate. Nowadays your town's become a rendezvous for people from all over the world. They only pass through, of course—

BOLETTE (smiles): Oh yes. It's easy for you to laugh at us. You're just passing through.

ARNHOLM: Laugh at you?

BOLETTE: What good is it to us that the great strange world glances in here on its way up to see the midnight sun? We can't join them. We shall never see the midnight sun. We just have to go on living here in our pond.

ARNHOLM (sits beside her): Tell me, Bolette—isn't there something—something special, I mean—that you long for as you sit here?

BOLETTE: Yes—perhaps.

ARNHOLM: What? What do you long for?

BOLETTE: To get away.

ARNHOLM: That most of all?

BOLETTE: Yes. And after that—to learn. I want to know about—oh, about everything!

ARNHOLM: When I used to teach you, your father often said he would send you to the University.

BOLETTE: Oh, yes. Poor father! He says so many things. But when it comes to the point—he never gets anything done.

ARNHOLM: I'm afraid you're right. But have you ever talked to him about it? Really sat down and talked about it?

BOLETTE: No. I've never done that.

ARNHOLM: But you should! Before it's too late. Why don't you?

BOLETTE: Because I never get anything done, either. I take after father.

ARNHOLM: Hm. Don't you think you're being unfair to yourself?

BOLETTE: No. Unfortunately, father has so little time to think about me and my future. And not much inclination either. He avoids thinking about these things as much as he can. He's so occupied with Ellida—

ARNHOLM: What do you mean by that?

BOLETTE: I mean—he and my stepmother—*(quickly)* father and mother have their own life to live.

ARNHOLM: Well, all the more reason for you to get away from here.

BOLETTE: Yes, I know, I must think of myself too. Try to go somewhere—do something. When father dies, I've no one else. But, poor father! I'm afraid to leave him.

ARNHOLM: Afraid?

BOLETTE: Yes. For his own sake.

ARNHOLM: But, good heavens, your stepmother! He'll still have her.

BOLETTE: Yes, I know. But she can't do all the things mother used to do so well. There's so much this one doesn't see. Or won't see—or won't bother about. I don't know which it is.

ARNHOLM: Hm. I think I know what you mean.

BOLETTE: Poor father—he's so hopeless about some things. Perhaps you've noticed that yourself. He hasn't enough work to keep him busy all the time. And she's quite incapable of helping him. Though that's partly his own fault.

ARNHOLM: How do you mean?

BOLETTE: Oh, father only likes to see happy faces around him. We must have sunshine and happiness in the house, he says. I'm afraid he sometimes gives her medicines which aren't good for her in the long run.

ARNHOLM: Do you really believe that?

BOLETTE: Yes, I can't help it. She's so odd sometimes. *(Passionately.)* Isn't it unfair that I should have to go on living here? It doesn't do father any good, really. And I've a duty towards myself, haven't I?

ARNHOLM: Bolette, this is something we two must discuss.

BOLETTE: Oh, what's the use? I was born to stay here in the pond.

ARNHOLM: Perhaps that depends on you.

BOLETTE *(alive):* Do you think so?

ARNHOLM: It lies entirely in your own hands.

BOLETTE: You mean you'd put in a good word for me with father?

ARNHOLM: That too. But first I'd like to have a serious talk with you. *(Glances left.)* Ssh! Don't let them notice anything. We'll speak about this later.

ELLIDA *comes in from the left. She is hatless, and wears a large shawl over her head and shoulders.*

ELLIDA *(nervously excited):* Ah, it's beautiful here. Beautiful!

ARNHOLM *(gets up):* Have you been out walking?

ELLIDA: Yes. A long, long walk over the hills with Wangel. Now we're going out sailing.

BOLETTE: Won't you sit down?

ELLIDA: No, thank you. I don't want to sit.

BOLETTE *(moving along the bench):* There's plenty of room here.

378

ELLIDA *(walks about):* No, no, no. I don't want to sit. I don't want to sit.

ARNHOLM: This walk has done you good. You look so exhilarated.

ELLIDA: Oh, yes. I feel so wonderfully well. Happy; and safe. *(Looks left.)* What's that big steamer coming in there?

BOLETTE *(gets up and looks):* That must be the big English ship. Yes. The Englander.

ARNHOLM: Tying up to the buoy. Does she usually stop here?

BOLETTE: Only for half an hour. She's going further up the fjord.

ELLIDA: And then out again, tomorrow. Out into the great open sea. And far across the sea. Just imagine if one could sail with her. If one could!

ARNHOLM: Have you never been on a long sea-voyage, Mrs. Wangel?

ELLIDA: Never. Only to and fro here in the fjord.

BOLETTE *(with a sigh):* Ah, yes. We have to stick to the land.

ARNHOLM: Well, after all, this is where we belong.

ELLIDA: No, I don't think so. I think if people could only have learned from the beginning to live on the sea—perhaps even in the sea—we should be quite different now from what we are. Better—and happier.

ARNHOLM: Are you serious?

ELLIDA: Yes. I have often talked about it with Wangel.

ARNHOLM: What does he think?

ELLIDA: He thinks I may be right.

ARNHOLM *(jestingly):* Well, perhaps you are right. But what's done is done. We've taken the wrong turning and become land animals instead of sea animals, and must remain so. It's too late to alter things now.

ELLIDA: I'm afraid you're right. And I think people sense it.

They endure it, as one endures a secret sorrow. I'm sure that's the real reason why people are melancholy. I'm sure of it.

ARNHOLM: But, my dear Ellida—I haven't noticed that people are especially melancholy. On the contrary, I think most people look on life with a calm, unthinking happiness.

ELLIDA: Oh, no, that's not true. That happiness—it is like our happiness through the long, bright summer days. Behind it lies the knowledge of the advancing darkness. And the knowledge casts its shadow over people's happiness, as the drifting cloud casts its shadow over the fjord. There it lies, so bright and blue, and then suddenly—

BOLETTE: Please stop this. A few moments ago you were so happy.

ELLIDA: Yes, yes, I know. Oh, I'm just being stupid. *(Looks uneasily round.)* Why doesn't Wangel come? He promised me he would. But he's forgotten. Oh, dear Dr. Arnholm, would you go and look for him?

ARNHOLM: Of course. Gladly.

ELLIDA: Tell him he must come at once. I can't—see him.

ARNHOLM: Can't see him?

ELLIDA: You don't understand what I mean. When he's not with me, I can't remember how he looks. Then it's as though I'd lost him. It's horrible. Please go! *(She walks restlessly up and down by the pond.)*

BOLETTE *(to* ARNHOLM*):* I'll go with you. You won't know where to look.

ARNHOLM: Never mind, I can manage.

BOLETTE *(half aloud):* No, I'm worried. I'm afraid he may be aboard the ship.

ARNHOLM: Afraid?

BOLETTE: Yes. He usually goes aboard to see if there's anyone he knows among the passengers. And the bar will be open—

ARNHOLM: Ah! Well, come along, then.

ARNHOLM *and* BOLETTE *go out left.* ELLIDA *stands for a moment staring down into the pond. Now and then she talks quietly and in snatches to herself. Then, outside, beyond the garden fence,* A STRANGER *comes down the path from the left. He is dressed as though for a journey, with a travelling bag slung on a strap from his shoulder, and a Scottish cap on his head. He has bushy, reddish hair and beard.*

STRANGER *(walks slowly along by the fence and looks into the garden. Then he sees* ELLIDA, *stops, looks hard and searchingly at her, and says softly):* Good evening, Ellida.

ELLIDA *(turns and cries):* Oh, my love—have you come at last?

STRANGER: Yes, at last.

ELLIDA *(stares at him, surprised and uneasy):* Who are you? Are you looking for someone here?

STRANGER: You know I am.

ELLIDA: What do you mean? Whom have you come to see?

STRANGER: I have come to see you.

ELLIDA: Ah! *(Stares at him, staggers backwards and cries)* The eyes! The eyes!

STRANGER: You know me at last! I knew you at once, Ellida.

ELLIDA: The eyes! Don't stare at me like that. I'll shout for help.

STRANGER: Ssh! Don't be afraid! I shan't hurt you.

ELLIDA *(puts her hand over her eyes):* Don't look at me!

STRANGER *(leans his arms on the fence):* I came in the English steamer.

ELLIDA *(looks timidly at him):* What do you want with me?

STRANGER: I promised I'd come back to you, as soon as I could.

ELLIDA: Go! Go away! Don't come back! Never come back

again! I wrote to you that everything was finished between us. For ever. You know that.

STRANGER: I wanted to come before. But I couldn't. This was the first chance I got. Now I am yours again, Ellida.

ELLIDA: What do you want with me? Why have you come here?

STRANGER: You know I've come here to fetch you.

ELLIDA: But you know I'm married.

STRANGER: Yes, I know.

ELLIDA: And yet you have come to fetch me?

STRANGER: Yes.

ELLIDA (*clasps her head in her hands*): Oh, this is horrible!

STRANGER: Don't you want to come?

ELLIDA: Don't look at me like that!

STRANGER: I am asking you: "Don't you want to come?"

ELLIDA: No, no. I don't want to! I can't. I won't! (*More quietly.*) Besides, I daren't.

STRANGER (*climbs over the fence and comes into the garden*): Very well, Ellida. Just let me say one thing before I go.

ELLIDA (*wants to run away but cannot. She stands as though paralysed by fear and supports herself against a tree by the pond*): Don't touch me! Don't come near me! Stay where you are! Don't touch me!

STRANGER (*goes carefully a few paces towards her*): You mustn't be afraid of me, Ellida.

ELLIDA (*puts her hand over her eyes*): Don't look at me.

STRANGER: Don't be afraid. Don't be afraid.

DR. WANGEL *comes through the garden from the left.*

WANGEL (*as he comes through the trees*): I'm afraid I've kept you waiting a long time.

ELLIDA (*rushes to him, clings tightly to his arm and cries*): Oh, Wangel, save me! Save me—if you can!

WANGEL: Ellida, what in heaven's name—?

ELLIDA: Save me, Wangel! Can't you see him? Over there!

WANGEL *(looks):* That man? *(Goes towards him.)* May I ask who you are? And what you are doing in this garden?

STRANGER *(nods towards* ELLIDA*):* I want to talk to her.

WANGEL: What do you want with my wife? *(Turns.)* Do you know him, Ellida?

ELLIDA *(quietly):* Yes, yes!

WANGEL *(quickly):* What?

ELLIDA: It's he, Wangel! It's he! You know. The one who—

WANGEL: What? What are you saying? *(Turns.)* Are you that—Johnston, who once—?

STRANGER: You can call me Johnston if you like. It's not my name.

WANGEL: Not your name?

STRANGER: Not any more.

WANGEL: Well, what do you want with my wife? You know that—the lighthouse keeper's daughter married long ago. And perhaps you also know who is her husband.

STRANGER: Yes. I've known that for more than three years.

ELLIDA: How did you find out?

STRANGER: I was on my way home to you. I saw an old newspaper. It contained the news of the wedding.

ELLIDA *(to herself):* The wedding!

STRANGER: I thought it strange. Because when we buried the rings in the sea—that was a wedding too, Ellida.

ELLIDA *(covers her face with her hands):* Ah—!

WANGEL: How dare you?

STRANGER: Had you forgotten?

ELLIDA *(feels his eyes on her):* Don't stand there looking at me!

WANGEL *(stands in front of the* STRANGER*):* Speak to me, not to her. Since you know the situation, what is your business here? Why have you come here to see my wife?

STRANGER: I promised Ellida I'd come back to her as soon as I could.

383

WANGEL: Ellida! How dare you call my wife—?

STRANGER: And Ellida promised to wait for me until I came.

WANGEL: Kindly do not address my wife by her first name. I don't allow such familiarities here.

STRANGER: She belongs to me.

WANGEL: Belongs to you!

ELLIDA *(moves behind* WANGEL*):* He will never let me go.

STRANGER: Did she ever tell you about the two rings? Mine and Ellida's?

WANGEL: Yes. What of it? All that is finished. You got her letters. You know it is finished.

STRANGER: Ellida and I agreed that those rings should bind us as surely as any priest.

ELLIDA: But I don't want you. I never want to see you again! Don't look at me like that!

WANGEL: You must be out of your mind if you think you can come here and claim any rights because of such childish tricks.

STRANGER: Certainly I have no rights—the way you mean.

WANGEL: Then what do you want here? You surely don't think you can take her from me by force? Against her own will!

STRANGER: No. What would be the good of that? If Ellida wants to come with me, she must come of her own free will.

ELLIDA: Of my own free will!

WANGEL: And you suppose—?

ELLIDA *(to herself):* Of my own free will!

WANGEL: You must be out of your mind. Be off with you! We have nothing further to discuss with you.

STRANGER *(looks at his watch):* It's almost time for me to go aboard again. *(Takes a step towards* ELLIDA.*)* Well, Ellida. I have fulfilled my half of our pledge. *(Another step towards her.)* I have kept the promise I made you.

ELLIDA: Don't touch me! Please!

STRANGER: Think it over before tomorrow night!

WANGEL: There is nothing to think over. Get out!

STRANGER *(still addressing* ELLIDA*)*: I'm going up the fjord now with the ship. Tomorrow night I shall be here again, on my way back. I shall come to you. Wait for me here in the garden. You and I will decide this matter alone.

ELLIDA *(quietly, trembling)*: Oh, Wangel, do you hear what he says?

WANGEL: Don't worry. We know a way to prevent any such visit.

STRANGER: Goodbye then, Ellida. Till tomorrow night.

ELLIDA *(beseechingly)*: No, no! Don't come tomorrow night! Don't ever come back here again!

STRANGER: If you decide to come with me—across the sea—

ELLIDA: Don't look at me like that!

STRANGER: I only meant—be ready for the journey, Ellida.

WANGEL: Go into the house, Ellida.

ELLIDA: I can't. Help me! Save me, Wangel!

STRANGER: Think hard, Ellida. If you don't come with me tomorrow, you will never see me again.

ELLIDA: Never again?

STRANGER *(nods)*: Never again, Ellida. I shall never come to you. You will never see me. Nor hear from me, either. I shall be dead and gone from you for ever.

ELLIDA: Ah!

STRANGER: So think carefully before you decide. Goodbye. *(Turns, climbs over the fence, stops and says)* Yes, Ellida. Be ready for the journey tomorrow night. I shall be here to fetch you. *(Goes slowly and calmly out down the footpath to the right.)*

ELLIDA *(looking after him)*: Of my own free will. He said I should go with him—of my own free will!

WANGEL: Don't worry. He has gone now. You will never see him again.

ELLIDA: How can you say that? He is coming back tomorrow night.

WANGEL: Let him come. He won't see you.

ELLIDA (shakes her head): Oh, Wangel. Don't think you can stop him.

WANGEL: Yes, my dear, I can. Trust me.

ELLIDA (not listening): After he's come here tomorrow night—and gone away with his ship across the sea—

WANGEL: Yes?

ELLIDA: I wonder—will he—ever come back?

WANGEL: No, Ellida, you need never fear that. What point would there be in his coming? After hearing from your own lips that you want no more of him? The whole thing's finished and done with.

ELLIDA (to herself): Tomorrow then. Or never.

WANGEL: And even if he should come back here—

ELLIDA: Yes?

WANGEL: We know how to clip his wings.

ELLIDA: We could never do that.

WANGEL: Oh, yes, we could. If we can't keep him away from you by any other means, we shall report him for the murder of his captain.

ELLIDA (passionately): No! We know nothing about the captain's death! Nothing!

WANGEL: Nothing? But he confessed to you himself.

ELLIDA: We shall say nothing about that! If you say anything I shall deny the whole story. Don't lock him up in a prison! He belongs out there, on the open sea.

WANGEL (looks at her and sighs slowly): Oh, Ellida! Ellida!

ELLIDA (throws herself into his arms): Oh, my dear, my dearest! Save me from that man!

WANGEL (freeing himself gently): Come, Ellida. Come with me.

LYNGSTRAND *and* HILDE, *both with fishing tackle, come along the pond from the right.*

LYNGSTRAND *(going eagerly to* ELLIDA*):* I say, Mrs. Wangel, I've got some news for you!

WANGEL: What?

LYNGSTRAND: Just imagine. We've seen the American.

WANGEL: The American!

HILDE: Yes, I saw him too.

LYNGSTRAND: He walked up past the garden and went on board the big steamer.

WANGEL: How did you know that man?

LYNGSTRAND: I went to sea with him once. I was sure he'd been drowned. But here he is, alive and kicking.

WANGEL: Do you know anything else about him?

LYNGSTRAND: No. But I'm sure he must have come to revenge himself on that faithless girl of his.

WANGEL: What did you say?

HILDE: Lyngstrand wants to make a masterpiece out of him.

WANGEL: I don't understand a word—

ELLIDA: I'll explain to you later.

ARNHOLM *and* BOLETTE *come from the left down the path outside the fence.*

BOLETTE *(to the others in the garden):* Come and look! The English steamer's starting off up the fjord! *(A large ship glides slowly past in the distance.)*

LYNGSTRAND *(to* HILDE *by the fence):* He'll visit her tonight.

HILDE *(nods):* The faithless wife. Yes.

LYNGSTRAND: At midnight. I say!

HILDE: How exciting!

ELLIDA *(looking after the ship):* Tomorrow then—

WANGEL: For the last time.

ELLIDA: Oh, Wangel! Save me from myself!

WANGEL: Ellida! I feel it—there is something behind him.

ELLIDA: The tide is behind him.

WANGEL: The tide?

ELLIDA: That man is like the sea.

She goes slowly and heavily through the garden out to the left. WANGEL *walks uneasily beside her, watching her closely.*

ACT FOUR

DR. WANGEL'S *garden room. Doors right and left. In the background, between the two windows, is an open glass door giving on to the verandah. Beyond can be seen a part of the garden. Sofa with table, downstage. Right, a piano; further back, a large arrangement of flowers. In the middle of the room is a round table, surrounded by chairs. On the table, a flowering rose-tree, and other plants in pots. It is morning.*

> *At the table on the left,* BOLETTE *is seated on the sofa, embroidering.* LYNGSTRAND *is on a chair at the upstage side of the table. Down in the garden* BALLESTED *is seated, painting.* HILDE *stands beside him watching him work.*

LYNGSTRAND (*his arms on the table, sits for a moment in silence, watching* BOLETTE): That bit round the edge. It must be jolly difficult to do that bit, Miss Wangel.

BOLETTE: Oh, no, it's not so difficult. It's just a matter of counting right.

LYNGSTRAND: Counting? Do you have to count too?

BOLETTE: Yes, the stitches. Like this.

LYNGSTRAND: I say. By Jove! It's, why, it's almost like a kind of art! Can you draw too?

BOLETTE: Yes, when I have a pattern to copy.

LYNGSTRAND: Not otherwise?

BOLETTE: No, not otherwise.

LYNGSTRAND: Oh, then it isn't really an art after all.

BOLETTE: No. It's just a knack.

LYNGSTRAND: But you know, I believe you could become an artist.

BOLETTE: But I haven't any talent.

LYNGSTRAND: No, but if you could be with a real artist all the time—

BOLETTE: You think I could learn from him?

LYNGSTRAND: I don't mean through lessons. I think it would just happen little by little. Like a miracle, Miss Wangel.

BOLETTE: How very strange.

LYNGSTRAND *(after a moment):* Have you ever considered—I mean—have you ever thought seriously about marriage, Miss Wangel?

BOLETTE *(with a quick glance at him):* About—? No.

LYNGSTRAND: I have.

BOLETTE: Have you? Really?

LYNGSTRAND: Oh, yes, I think a lot about such things. Marriage especially. I've read a lot about it in books too. I think marriage must be a kind of miracle. The way a woman gradually changes her personality so as to become like her husband.

BOLETTE: Share his interests, you mean?

LYNGSTRAND: Yes, exactly.

BOLETTE: What about his ability, his talent? Could she share them too?

LYNGSTRAND: Mm? Oh, yes. I should think she could.

BOLETTE: Then you think that what a man has made himself through thought and study, all that could somehow be communicated to his wife too?

LYNGSTRAND: Yes, that too. Little by little. Through a kind of miracle. But I know that can only happen to people who really love each other and tell each other everything.

390

BOLETTE: Has it never struck you that a man might be brought over to his wife's way of thinking? Become like her, I mean?

LYNGSTRAND: A man? No, I'd never imagined that.

BOLETTE: Why not?

LYNGSTRAND: Ah, a man's got a vocation to live for. It's that that gives a man strength and purpose, Miss Wangel. He has a calling in life, a man has.

BOLETTE: All men?

LYNGSTRAND: Oh, no. I was thinking of the artist.

BOLETTE: Do you think an artist ought to get married?

LYNGSTRAND: Yes, I think so. When he finds someone he really loves—

BOLETTE: Even then, I think he ought to live just for his art.

LYNGSTRAND: Of course he must. But he can do that just as well when he's married.

BOLETTE: What about her?

LYNGSTRAND: Her?

BOLETTE: The woman he marries. What is she to live for?

LYNGSTRAND: She must live for his art, too.

BOLETTE: I'm not sure—

LYNGSTRAND: Yes, Miss Wangel, honestly, believe me. Not only because of all the honour and respect she'll get through him. But to be able to help him to create—to make his work easy for him by being with him and looking after him and keeping him happy and comfortable. I think that must be a wonderful life for a woman.

BOLETTE: You don't know how conceited you are!

LYNGSTRAND: Conceited—me? Good Heavens, if only you knew me a little better! *(Leans closer to her.)* Miss Wangel—when I am gone—which I soon will be—

BOLETTE *(compassionately):* You mustn't say such dreadful things.

LYNGSTRAND: Dreadful? What's dreadful about that?

BOLETTE: I don't understand.

LYNGSTRAND: Why, I'm going away in a month. And then in a short while I'll be going south, to the Mediterranean.

BOLETTE: That. Oh, yes, of course.

LYNGSTRAND: Will you sometimes think of me after I've gone, Miss Bolette?

BOLETTE: Yes, of course.

LYNGSTRAND *(joyfully):* Promise?

BOLETTE: Yes, I promise.

LYNGSTRAND: Cross your heart?

BOLETTE: Cross my heart. *(In a changed voice.)* Oh, but what's the point of all this? It can't lead to anything.

LYNGSTRAND: How can you say that? It would be wonderful for me to know that you were sitting here thinking of me.

BOLETTE: And then what?

LYNGSTRAND: Then? Why, I don't know—

BOLETTE: Neither do I. So much stands in the way. The whole world stands in our way, I think.

LYNGSTRAND: Well, a miracle might happen. You see, I believe I'm lucky.

BOLETTE *(warmly):* Yes! You believe that, don't you?

LYNGSTRAND: Oh, yes, I do believe it. In a year or two, when I come home again, a famous sculptor, healthy and successful—

BOLETTE: Oh, yes, we all hope you will.

LYNGSTRAND: You can be sure I shall. If you think fondly of me while I am away in the south. And now I have your word that you will.

BOLETTE: Yes, you have my word. *(Shakes her head.)* But it can't lead to anything, all the same.

LYNGSTRAND: Yes, Miss Bolette, it will mean I shall be able to work more confidently at my composition.

BOLETTE: Do you believe that?

LYNGSTRAND: Yes, I feel it inside me. And I think it would

be so inspiring for you too—sitting up here—to know that you were, so to speak, helping me to create.

BOLETTE *(looks at him):* And you?

LYNGSTRAND: I?

BOLETTE *(looks out towards the garden):* Ssh! Let's talk about something else. Dr. Arnholm's coming.

> DR. ARNHOLM *appears down in the garden, left. He stops and talks with* BALLESTED *and* HILDE.

LYNGSTRAND: Are you fond of your old teacher, Miss Bolette?

BOLETTE: Fond of him?

LYNGSTRAND: I mean, do you like him?

BOLETTE: Oh, yes. He's a fine person to have as a friend and adviser. And he's always so helpful.

LYNGSTRAND: Isn't it odd that he should never have married?

BOLETTE: Do you think it's odd?

LYNGSTRAND: Yes. Since he's said to be well off.

BOLETTE: He is well off. I suppose it hasn't been so easy for him to find someone willing to have him.

LYNGSTRAND: Why?

BOLETTE: Oh, almost all the girls he knows are old pupils of his. He says so himself.

LYNGSTRAND: Well, what's wrong with that?

BOLETTE: Good Heavens, one doesn't marry a man who's been one's teacher!

LYNGSTRAND: Don't you think it's possible for a young girl to love her teacher?

BOLETTE: Not once one's grown up.

LYNGSTRAND: I say!

BOLETTE *(warningly):* Ssh!

> BALLESTED *has meanwhile gathered his things together and is taking them away to the right in the garden.*

HILDE *is helping him.* ARNHOLM *goes up on to the verandah and comes into the garden room.*

ARNHOLM: Good morning, Bolette, my dear. Good morning, Mr.—Mr.—hm.

He gives LYNGSTRAND *an annoyed look and nods coldly to him.* LYNGSTRAND *gets to his feet and bows.*

BOLETTE *(gets up and comes over to* ARNHOLM*):* Good morning, Dr. Arnholm.

ARNHOLM: How are you today?

BOLETTE: Oh, quite well, thank you.

ARNHOLM: Is your stepmother down bathing today too?

BOLETTE: No, she's up in her room.

ARNHOLM: Not feeling well?

BOLETTE: I don't know. She's locked herself in.

ARNHOLM: Hm. Has she?

LYNGSTRAND: Mrs. Wangel was very shaken by seeing that American yesterday.

ARNHOLM: What do you know about that?

LYNGSTRAND: I told Mrs. Wangel I'd seen him walking alive past the garden.

ARNHOLM: Oh, I see.

BOLETTE *(to* ARNHOLM*):* You and father were sitting up late together last night.

ARNHOLM: Quite late, yes. We got on to something rather important.

BOLETTE: Did you get a chance to say anything to him about me?

ARNHOLM: No, Bolette, I wasn't able to get on to that. He was—preoccupied.

BOLETTE *(sighs):* Ah, yes. He always is.

ARNHOLM *(looks meaningly at her):* But later today you and I will have a serious talk about this. Where is your father now? Isn't he at home?

BOLETTE: Yes, he's probably in the surgery. I'll go and fetch him.

ARNHOLM: No, don't bother. I'll find him.

BOLETTE *(listens left):* Wait a moment, Dr. Arnholm. I think that's father coming downstairs. Yes. He must have been upstairs with her.

DR. WANGEL *comes in through the door on the left.*

WANGEL *(holding out his hand):* Arnholm, my dear fellow, are you here already? I'm delighted you've come so early. There's something more I want to talk to you about.

BOLETTE *(to* LYNGSTRAND*):* Shall we go down into the garden and join Hilde?

LYNGSTRAND: Yes, what a good idea, I'd love to.

He and BOLETTE *go down into the garden and out through the trees in the background.*

ARNHOLM *(who has watched them leave, turns to* WANGEL*):* Do you know that young man well?

WANGEL: No, not at all.

ARNHOLM: Do you approve of him seeing so much of your girls?

WANGEL: Does he? I hadn't noticed.

ARNHOLM: I think you ought to keep an eye open.

WANGEL: Yes, you're perfectly right. But, good heavens, what's a fellow to do? The girls have grown so used to looking after themselves. They won't listen to what I say, or Ellida.

ARNHOLM: Nor to her either?

WANGEL: No. Besides I can't ask her to bother about such matters. These things bore her. But this isn't what I wanted to talk to you about. Tell me—have you thought any more about this business? What I was telling you last night?

ARNHOLM: I haven't been able to think of anything else since I left you.

WANGEL: What do you think I ought to do?

ARNHOLM: My dear doctor, I think you, as a medical man, ought to know the answer better than I.

WANGEL: Ah, if only you knew how difficult it is for a doctor to diagnose for a patient who means a lot to him! Besides, this isn't any ordinary illness. No ordinary doctor can do anything in this case—nor any ordinary medicines, either.

ARNHOLM: How is she today?

WANGEL: I was up with her just now, and she seemed quite calm. But behind all her moods there's something hidden which I cannot fathom. And she's so changeable—so unpredictable. She alters so suddenly.

ARNHOLM: I suppose that's because of her mental state.

WANGEL: Not only that. She was born like that. Ellida is one of the sea people. That is really what it is.

ARNHOLM: What exactly do you mean, my dear doctor?

WANGEL: Haven't you noticed that the people who live out there by the open sea are a different race? It's almost as though they lived the same life as the sea does. Their way of thinking, feeling—they're like the tide, they ebb and flow. And they can never uproot themselves and settle anywhere else. Oh, I should have thought of all this before. I sinned against Ellida when I tried to take her away and bring her inland to this place.

ARNHOLM: Is that how you feel now?

WANGEL: More and more. But I ought to have known it from the first. In my heart I did know it. But I wouldn't let myself believe it. I loved her so much. So I put myself first. I was unforgivably selfish.

ARNHOLM: Hm—well, everyone is a little selfish in such circumstances. Though I've never noticed that fault in you, Dr. Wangel.

WANGEL (*pacing uneasily up and down*): Oh, yes, yes! And I've been selfish since, too. I am so much older than she is. I ought to have been a father to her, and a guide. I ought to have developed her mind, taught her to think clearly. But no. I never got down to it. I wanted her as she was. But then things went from bad to worse with her. And I sat here not knowing what to do. (*More quietly.*) That was why, in my—distress, I wrote to you and asked you to come and see us.

ARNHOLM (*looks at him amazed*): What? Was that why you wrote?

WANGEL: Please don't tell anyone.

ARNHOLM: But, my dear doctor, what help did you suppose I could give you? I don't understand.

WANGEL: No, I—I suppose not. I was completely on the wrong track. I thought Ellida had been in love with you, once. That she was perhaps a little fond of you still. I thought it might possibly do her good to see you again, and talk to you about her home and the old days.

ARNHOLM: Then it was your wife you were referring to when you wrote that someone here was waiting for me— longing to see me again?

WANGEL: Yes. Who else?

ARNHOLM (*quickly*): No, of course you're right. But I didn't realise.

WANGEL: Quite understandably. I was on the wrong track.

ARNHOLM: And you call yourself a selfish man?

WANGEL: Oh, I have so much to atone for. I didn't think I had the right to neglect any—anything that might possibly ease her mind a little.

ARNHOLM: How do you explain the power which this stranger has over her?

WANGEL: My dear friend, there are aspects of this case which cannot be explained.

ARNHOLM: You mean it's something that's beyond rational explanation?

WANGEL: Yes. For the time being, anyway.

ARNHOLM: Do you believe in such things?

WANGEL: I neither believe nor disbelieve. I just don't know. So I leave it at that.

ARNHOLM: Yes, but tell me one thing. This curious, horrible notion she has about the child's eyes—

WANGEL: That business about the eyes is rubbish! Rubbish! Pure imagination. Nothing else.

ARNHOLM: Did you notice the man's eyes when you saw him yesterday?

WANGEL: Certainly I did.

ARNHOLM: And you saw no likeness?

WANGEL (evasively): Good Heavens, what do you want me to say? It was quite dark when I saw him. And Ellida had talked so much about this likeness—I couldn't look at him objectively.

ARNHOLM: No, I suppose not. But—this other matter—I mean, what she says about all this anxiety and unrest that came over her just at the time when this stranger had started on his journey home?

WANGEL: That's also something she must have made herself believe, since the day before yesterday. It didn't come over her as suddenly as she pretends now. Ever since she heard from this young Lyngstrand that Johnston—Freeman—whatever he calls himself—was on his way here three years ago—in March—she's persuaded herself that these disturbances of hers started just in that month.

ARNHOLM: Isn't that true, then?

WANGEL: Not at all. The first signs came much earlier. I admit it did happen to be in March three years ago that she had a particularly bad time of it—

ARNHOLM: Then—

WANGEL: Yes, but that's easily explained by the circumstances. The condition she was in at the time.

ARNHOLM: What is one to believe?

WANGEL *(clasping his hands)*: To be unable to help her—to be unable to think of any way out—

ARNHOLM: If you could go away? Move somewhere else. So that she could live somewhere where she'd feel more at home.

WANGEL: Don't you suppose I've thought of that? I suggested to her that we should move out to Skjoldviken. But she doesn't want to.

ARNHOLM: She doesn't want to?

WANGEL: No. She doesn't think it would do any good. Perhaps she's right.

ARNHOLM: Hm. Do you think so?

WANGEL: Yes. Besides, when I think about it I don't know if I really ought to go and settle there. The children, I mean—it'd be so awful for them to have to live in such a backwater. They must live somewhere where they'll have some chance of finding a husband.

ARNHOLM: A husband? Are you beginning to think about that already?

WANGEL: Good Lord, I must consider them too. But then, on the other hand, Ellida—my poor sick Ellida—oh, my dear Arnholm, which of them am I to put first?

ARNHOLM: I don't think you need worry about Bolette— *(Breaks off.)* I wonder where she—where they've gone to?

Goes to the open door and looks out.

WANGEL *(over by the piano)*: I'd make any sacrifice—for all three of them. If only I knew what to do!

ELLIDA *comes in through the door on the left.*

ELLIDA *(as she enters, to* WANGEL*)*: Don't go out this morning, my dear.

WANGEL: No, of course I won't. I'll stay at home with you. *(Indicates* ARNHOLM, *as the latter comes over to them.)* But aren't you going to say good morning to our friend?

ELLIDA *(turns):* Oh, it's you, Dr. Arnholm? *(Holds out her hand.)* Good morning.

ARNHOLM: Good morning, Mrs. Wangel. Not swimming today as usual?

ELLIDA: No, no, no. Don't talk about that today. But won't you sit down for a moment?

ARNHOLM: No, thank you so much, not now. *(Looks at* WANGEL.*)* I promised the girls I'd join them in the garden.

ELLIDA: Heaven knows if you'll find them there. I never know where they are.

WANGEL: I think you'll find them down there by the pond.

ARNHOLM: I'll track them down somewhere. *(Nods and passes through the verandah out into the garden, right.)*

ELLIDA: What time is it, Wangel?

WANGEL *(looks at his watch):* Just past eleven.

ELLIDA: And at eleven o'clock tonight—half-past eleven—the steamer will come. Oh, if only it were all over!

WANGEL *(goes nearer to her):* Ellida, my dear—there's one thing I should like to ask you.

ELLIDA: What's that?

WANGEL: That night before last—up there on the Prospect—you said that often during these last three years you had seen him clearly, standing alive before you.

ELLIDA: Yes, I have.

WANGEL: What did he look like?

ELLIDA: What did he look like?

WANGEL: I mean how did he look when you thought you saw him?

ELLIDA: But, Wangel, you know yourself what he looks like now.

WANGEL: Did he look the same then?

ELLIDA: Yes.

WANGEL: Just the same as when you saw him yesterday evening?

ELLIDA: Yes. Just the same.

WANGEL: Then, how was it that you didn't immediately recognise him?

ELLIDA: Didn't I?

WANGEL: No. You said yourself that to begin with you had no idea who this stranger could be.

ELLIDA: Yes, of course—you're right! That was strange, wasn't it? To think I didn't recognise him at once.

WANGEL: It was only the eyes, you said—

ELLIDA: Yes—the eyes!

WANGEL: But—up on the Prospect the night before last, you said he always appeared to you looking just the same as when you last saw him. Out there ten years ago—

ELLIDA: Did I say that?

WANGEL: Yes.

ELLIDA: Then he must have looked the same then as he does now.

WANGEL: No. You painted quite a different picture of him the night before last on the way home. Ten years ago, he had no beard, you said. And different clothes. And his tiepin with the pearl—the man yesterday wore no such thing.

ELLIDA: No, that's true.

WANGEL (*looks closely at her*): Think a little harder, Ellida. Or perhaps—perhaps you can't remember any longer how he looked when he stood with you at Bratthammeren.

ELLIDA (*closes her eyes, trying to remember*): Not—clearly. Not—today I can't. Isn't that strange?

WANGEL: Not so strange. You've got a new image of him in your mind—the real one. And that shadows the old image, so that you can't see it any longer.

ELLIDA: Do you think so, Wangel?

WANGEL: Yes. And it shadows your sick imaginings too. That's why I think it is good that reality has come at last.

ELLIDA: Good? You call it good?

WANGEL: Yes. His coming may be what you need to bring you back to health.

ELLIDA *(sits on the sofa):* Wangel—come and sit here beside me. I want to try to tell you what's in my mind.

WANGEL: Yes, my dear. Do. *(Sits on a chair on the other side of the table.)*

ELLIDA: It was a great misfortune—for both of us—that you and I ever met.

WANGEL: What?

ELLIDA: Oh, yes. It was. It had to end in tragedy. After the way we came together.

WANGEL: What was wrong with that?

ELLIDA: Wangel, it's no use our going on lying to ourselves.

WANGEL: Lying?

ELLIDA: Yes. Or hiding the truth. The real truth of the matter is that you came out there and bought me.

WANGEL: Bought! Did you say bought?

ELLIDA: Oh, I wasn't any better than you. I agreed to the bargain. Left home and sold myself to you.

WANGEL: Ellida!

ELLIDA: Is there any other word for it? You couldn't stand the emptiness of your house any longer. You looked round for a new wife—

WANGEL: And a new mother for my children, Ellida.

ELLIDA: You didn't know if I was at all suited for that. You'd only spoken to me two or three times. Then you—wanted me, and—

WANGEL: Call it what you like.

ELLIDA: And I—I stood there, helpless, so completely alone. So when you came and offered to—support me for life, I—agreed.

402

WANGEL: I asked you quite frankly if you would like to share with me and the children the little I could call mine.

ELLIDA: But I shouldn't have accepted. I shouldn't have sold myself, not at any price. I wish now I'd done anything—starved—so long as I'd chosen to do so—chosen freely.

WANGEL *(gets up):* Then have these five or six years we have lived together meant nothing to you at all?

ELLIDA: Oh, no, Wangel, no! I have had everything here that anyone could wish for. But I didn't come to your home of my own free will.

WANGEL *(stares at her):* Not of your own free will? I remember. I heard that phrase yesterday.

ELLIDA: In that phrase lies everything. It opened my eyes. Now I see it all.

WANGEL: What do you see?

ELLIDA: I see that the life we two are living together is not really a marriage.

WANGEL *(bitterly):* God knows that is true. The life we are living together now is no marriage.

ELLIDA: It never has been. Not even in those first weeks. *(Stares ahead of her.)* My first—that could have been a real marriage.

WANGEL: Your first?

ELLIDA: My marriage with him.

WANGEL: I simply don't understand you.

ELLIDA: Oh, Wangel, don't let's lie to each other. And to ourselves.

WANGEL: I don't want to lie.

ELLIDA: Don't you see? We can never escape from that fact—that a promise given freely is just as binding as any marriage.

WANGEL: But, what in heaven's name—?

ELLIDA *(rises):* Let me go. Let me leave you, Wangel.

WANGEL: Ellida!

ELLIDA: Please let me go! You must believe me—it will

403

never be any different between you and me, even if I stay. Not after the way we came together.

WANGEL: So it's come to that.

ELLIDA: It had to.

WANGEL: Then our life together has not made you mine. You have never really belonged to me.

ELLIDA: Oh, Wangel—if only I could love you as you deserve to be loved. I do so want to. But I can't and I shall never be able to.

WANGEL: Divorce then? Is that what you want? A full, legal divorce.

ELLIDA: How little you understand me! I don't care about the formalities. All I want is that we two should freely agree to release each other.

WANGEL (nods bitterly): Cancel the bargain, you mean?

ELLIDA (alive): Exactly! Cancel the bargain.

WANGEL: And then, Ellida? What then? Afterwards? Have you thought how all this will seem to us then? How life will shape itself for you and me?

ELLIDA: That can't be helped. It will have to shape itself as best it can. I beg you, I pray you, Wangel—give me my freedom. Give me my full freedom again. That's all that matters now.

WANGEL: Ellida, this is a dreadful thing you are asking me to do. Let me have time to think. Let us talk about it again. Give yourself time.

ELLIDA: We have no time. I must have my freedom again today.

WANGEL: Why today?

ELLIDA: Because he is coming here tonight.

WANGEL: He? What has this stranger to do with this?

ELLIDA: I want to be free when I meet him. Free to choose for myself.

WANGEL: And then—what do you intend to do?

ELLIDA: I don't want to hide behind the fact of being another man's wife. To hide behind the pretext that I am not free to choose. Otherwise there would be no choice to make.

WANGEL: You speak of choice? Choice, Ellida? In this?

ELLIDA: Yes, I must be free to choose. To let him go—or to go with him.

WANGEL: Do you realise what you're saying? Go with him? Give your whole future into his hands?

ELLIDA: Didn't I put my whole future into your hands?

WANGEL: But he! He! An utter stranger. A man you know practically nothing about.

ELLIDA: I knew even less about you. But I went with you.

WANGEL: At least you knew what kind of life you were going to. But he! He! Think, Ellida. What do you know about him? Nothing. Not even who he is—or what he is.

ELLIDA *(to herself):* I know. It's just that that is so—demonic.

WANGEL: It certainly is.

ELLIDA: That's why I think I must go to meet it.

WANGEL *(looking at her):* Because it is demonic?

ELLIDA: Yes.

WANGEL *(comes closer to her):* Ellida, what exactly do you mean by demonic?

ELLIDA *(pauses):* The demonic—is something that appals—and attracts.

WANGEL: Attractive, too?

ELLIDA: More than anything, I think.

WANGEL *(slowly):* You are like the sea.

ELLIDA: So is this demon.

WANGEL: I have never really known you. I am beginning to realise it now.

ELLIDA: That's why you must give me my freedom! I am not the woman you wanted to marry. Now you see it yourself. Now we can part freely, with understanding.

WANGEL *(bitterly):* Perhaps it would be best for us both to part. No, I can't! You are to me—what he is to you.

405

(Pause.) If only we can get through today. We mustn't lose our heads. I dare not let you go—give you your freedom—today. I haven't the right to do that. For your own sake, Ellida, I assert my right—my duty—to protect you.

ELLIDA: Protect me? What is there to protect me against? There is no power or force outside me that threatens me. The root of that fascination lies in my own mind. What can you do against that?

WANGEL: I can help you to fight it.

ELLIDA: Perhaps—if I wanted to fight it.

WANGEL: You mean you don't?

ELLIDA: I don't know.

WANGEL: Tonight it will all be settled, Ellida.

ELLIDA: Yes! The moment of decision is so near! I must decide. For all my life.

WANGEL: And tomorrow?

ELLIDA: Tomorrow? Perhaps by then I shall have thrown away my life.

WANGEL: Your life?

ELLIDA: A whole, full life thrown away. A life of freedom. My life—and perhaps his too.

WANGEL *(more quietly, takes her wrist):* Ellida, do you love this stranger?

ELLIDA: Do I? I can't tell. I only know that for me he is—the demon—and—

WANGEL: Yes?

ELLIDA *(tearing herself free):* It's to him I feel I belong!

WANGEL *(bows his head):* I am beginning to understand.

ELLIDA: So what help can you give me against that? What advice can you give me against that?

WANGEL *(heavily):* Tomorrow he will be gone. Then the danger will be past, and I shall be willing to give you your freedom—and let you go. Then we will cancel the bargain, Ellida.

ELLIDA: Oh, Wangel. Tomorrow it will be too late.

WANGEL *(looks out towards the garden):* The children! Let us at least keep the children out of this—while we can.

> ARNHOLM, BOLETTE, HILDE *and* LYNGSTRAND *appear in the garden.* LYNGSTRAND *takes his leave of the others there and exits right. The others come into the garden room.*

ARNHOLM: Well, we've been making great plans—

HILDE: We want to go out on the fjord tonight, and—

BOLETTE: No, don't tell them.

WANGEL: We two have also been making plans.

ARNHOLM: Indeed?

WANGEL: Tomorrow, Ellida will be going away to Skjoldviken—for a while.

BOLETTE: Going?

ARNHOLM: What a good idea, Mrs. Wangel.

WANGEL: Ellida wants to go home to the sea again.

HILDE *(moves impulsively towards* ELLIDA*):* Are you going away? Are you leaving us?

ELLIDA *(startled):* But, Hilde! What is the matter with you?

HILDE: Oh, nothing. *(Half aloud, turning away.)* Go, go. By all means.

BOLETTE *(frightened):* Father, I see it in your face. You will be going away too, to Skjoldviken.

WANGEL: I? Not at all. I shall be going out there now and then to see her—

BOLETTE: But you'll come back to us?

WANGEL: Why, of course.

BOLETTE: Now and then.

WANGEL: Dear child, it's got to be. *(Goes across the room.)*

ARNHOLM *(whispers):* I'll have a word with him now, Bolette. In private. *(Goes over to* WANGEL. *They talk quietly together near the door.)*

ELLIDA *(half aloud to* BOLETTE*):* What's the matter with Hilde? She looks quite upset.

BOLETTE: Haven't you ever noticed what Hilde has been yearning for, day after day?

ELLIDA: Yearning for?

BOLETTE: Ever since you entered this house.

ELLIDA: No, no. What?

BOLETTE: One single loving word from you.

ELLIDA: Ah! Could there be a place for me in this house?

She clasps her hands to her head and stares ahead of her, motionless, as though torn by conflicting thoughts and emotions. WANGEL *and* ARNHOLM, *whispering, come back across the room.* BOLETTE *goes and looks into the adjoining room, then opens the door wide.*

BOLETTE: Father dear, the food's on the table.

WANGEL *(with forced composure):* Is it, child? Good, good! Dr. Arnholm, please! Let us go in and drink a farewell cup to—to the Lady from the Sea.

They go towards the door on the right.

ACT FIVE

DR. WANGEL's *garden, by the pond. The deepening twilight of a summer night.* ARNHOLM, BOLETTE, LYNGSTRAND *and* HILDE *in a boat, punt from the left along the bank.*

HILDE: Look, we can easily jump ashore here.
ARNHOLM: No, no, don't do that!
LYNGSTRAND: I can't jump, Miss Hilde.
HILDE: Dr. Arnholm, can't you jump either?
ARNHOLM: I'd like to avoid it if possible.
BOLETTE: Let's tie her up to the steps by the bath-house, then.

> *They punt out to the right. As they do so,* BALLESTED *comes down the footpath from the right, carrying sheets of music and a French horn. He waves to them in their boat, turns and talks to them. Their replies are heard more and more distantly, offstage.*

BALLESTED: What's that you say? Yes, of course it's because of the English steamer. It's the last time she'll be here this year. If you want to hear the concert, you mustn't play around too long in that punt. *(Shouts)* What? *(Shakes his head.)* I can't hear you.

> ELLIDA, *her shawl over her head, comes in from the left, followed by* WANGEL.

WANGEL: But, dear Ellida, I assure you—there's plenty of time yet.

ELLIDA: No, no, there isn't. He may be here any moment.

BALLESTED (*outside the garden fence*): Why, good evening, doctor! Good evening, Mrs. Wangel.

WANGEL: Oh, it's you? Is there going to be a concert here tonight?

BALLESTED: Yes. The Horn Society will—ah—hold forth. There is no shortage of festive occasions nowadays. Tonight we are playing in honour of the English ship.

ELLIDA: The English ship? Is he in sight already?

BALLESTED: Not yet. But he's coming down the fjord through the islands. We shan't get any warning. Suddenly—pouf! He'll be upon us.

ELLIDA: Yes. That is just how it happened.

WANGEL: Tonight will be the last time. He will not come again.

BALLESTED: A grievous thought, doctor. However, this is all the more reason why we wish to honour him. (*Sighs.*) Ah dear! As it says in the tragedy: "Summer's joys will soon be past and gone, and every way to the sea be locked with ice."

ELLIDA: "Every way to the sea be locked."

BALLESTED: A melancholy reflection. For these few months we have been merry children of summer. It will be hard to accept the season of darkness. For the first few weeks, I mean. Men and women can acclai—acclimatise themselves, Mrs. Wangel. Yes, indeed they can. (*He bows and exits left*).

ELLIDA (*looking out over the fjord*): Oh, God, this torture! This unbearable hour before the moment of decision!

WANGEL: You are still determined to speak with him, then?

ELLIDA: I must speak with him myself. I must choose freely.

WANGEL: You have no choice. Ellida. I won't let you choose.

ELLIDA: You can't stop me. You or anyone. You can forbid

me to go with him—if that is what I choose to do. You can keep me here by force. Against my will. But you cannot stop me from choosing—him and not you—if I should want to—if I should have to choose that way.

WANGEL: No. That I cannot stop.

ELLIDA: Don't you see? In this house I have nothing to keep me. I have no roots here, Wangel. The children are not mine. They don't love me. They never have loved me. When I go—if I go—with him, tonight—or out to Skjoldviken tomorrow—I haven't even a key to give up, or any instructions to leave behind. I have been—outside—outside everything. From the first day I came here.

WANGEL: You wanted it that way.

ELLIDA: No, I didn't. I simply let everything stay the way it was on the day I arrived. It is you who wanted it to be like this. You and nobody else.

WANGEL: I only wanted to do what I thought would make you happy.

ELLIDA: Oh, yes, Wangel, I know. But there is retribution in this. For now there is nothing to bind me here—nothing to give me strength. I feel nothing for you. You, our home, the children—nothing.

WANGEL: Yes, I realise that now, Ellida. Tomorrow you shall have your freedom again. You shall live your own life.

ELLIDA: My own life? Oh, no. The life I was born to lead ended when I came to live with you. *(Clasps her hands in anguish.)* And now—in half an hour—he will come—the man I should have remained faithful to. He is coming to ask me—for the last time—to start my life afresh. A life I can't give up. Not willingly.

WANGEL: That's why you must let me, as your husband— and as your doctor—choose for you.

ELLIDA: Yes, Wangel, I realise that. There are moments when I think the only escape, the only peace I could find would be to give myself wholly to you—and turn my back on all this. But I can't. No, I can't!

WANGEL: Come, Ellida. Let us take a little walk together.

ELLIDA: I should like to. But I daren't. He told me to wait for him here.

WANGEL: You have plenty of time yet.

ELLIDA: Have I?

WANGEL: Plenty of time.

ELLIDA: Let us go then. For a few minutes.

They go out downstage right, as ARNHOLM *and* BOLETTE *come along the upper bank of the pond.*

BOLETTE *(noticing the others as they go out):* Look!

ARNHOLM *(quietly):* Ssh! Let them go.

BOLETTE: Can you make out what has been the matter with them these last few days?

ARNHOLM: Have you noticed anything?

BOLETTE: Have I—? Of course.

ARNHOLM: Something—in particular?

BOLETTE: Yes. Lots of things. Haven't you?

ARNHOLM: Why, I don't think so—

BOLETTE: Of course you have. You just don't want to admit it.

ARNHOLM: I think it will be a good thing for your stepmother to go away for a while.

BOLETTE: Do you?

ARNHOLM: Mightn't it be a good thing for you all if she could get away now and then?

BOLETTE: If she goes to Skjoldviken tomorrow, she will never come back to us again.

ARNHOLM: What on earth makes you say that?

BOLETTE: I know it. You'll see. She will never come back here again. Not as long as I and Hilde are here, anyway.

ARNHOLM: Hilde too?

BOLETTE: Not so much her, perhaps. She's still almost a child. And she worships Ellida, in her heart, I think. But with me, it's different. A stepmother who isn't so much older than oneself—

ARNHOLM: My dear, it may not be so long before you have a chance to get away.

BOLETTE *(alive):* You really think so? Have you spoken to father?

ARNHOLM: Yes, I spoke to him, too.

BOLETTE: Well, what did he say?

ARNHOLM: Er—well, he's so occupied with other things just now, you know—

BOLETTE: What did I tell you?

ARNHOLM: I did get one thing out of him, though. You can't count on any help from him.

BOLETTE: No help?

ARNHOLM: He spoke to me quite openly about this—about how things are with him. He made it clear it would be quite impossible for him to help you financially.

BOLETTE: Why did you have to raise my hopes? Just to make a fool of me?

ARNHOLM: Dear Bolette, it depends entirely on you whether you leave or stay.

BOLETTE: Depends on me? What depends on me?

ARNHOLM: Whether you get out into the world. Get the chance to learn everything you want to learn. Live a full life. What do you say, Bolette?

BOLETTE *(clasps her hands):* Oh, dear God! But all this is impossible. If father won't—can't—then there is no one I could turn to.

ARNHOLM: Would you be prepared to accept a helping hand from your old—I mean, your former teacher?

BOLETTE: From you, Dr. Arnholm? You mean you would be willing to—

ARNHOLM: To help you? Yes. Gladly. And not only with words. Do you agree, then? Well? Do you agree?

BOLETTE: Do I agree? To be able to go away—to see the

world—to learn something—something real and worth-
while!

ARNHOLM: Yes. You have only to say the word.

BOLETTE: And you—you are prepared to help me to achieve
all this? But how can I accept such an offer from—from a
stranger?

ARNHOLM: You can accept it from me, Bolette.

BOLETTE *(takes his hands):* Yes, I think—I think I can! I
don't know why—but—oh, I could laugh and cry for joy.
I'm so happy! I am to live after all! I was beginning to fear
that life was slipping away from me.

ARNHOLM: You don't have to worry about that any longer,
Bolette. But first you must tell me frankly. Is there anything—anything—which binds you here?

BOLETTE: Binds me? No. Nothing. That is—father, in a way
of course—and Hilde too. But—

ARNHOLM: Well, you'll have to leave your father sooner or
later. And Hilde will have to go her own way some time
too. But otherwise there's nothing, Bolette? No tie of any
kind?

BOLETTE: No, none at all. I can leave here any time.

ARNHOLM: Then, Bolette, my dear—come away. With me.

BOLETTE *(clasps her hands):* Oh, dear God! If that could
only be!

ARNHOLM: You trust me, don't you?

BOLETTE: Yes, of course.

ARNHOLM: Then you are prepared to give yourself unreservedly into my hands, Bolette? You are ready to do that,
aren't you?

BOLETTE: Yes, yes, of course! You are my old teacher—I
mean, you used to be my teacher in the old days.

ARNHOLM: I—didn't mean because of that. But—I—you are
free, then, Bolette. I therefore ask you—if you could—if
you could be willing to bind yourself to me—for life.

BOLETTE *(horrified):* What are you saying?

ARNHOLM: For all your life, Bolette. Will you be my wife?

BOLETTE *(half to herself):* No, no. This is impossible. Quite impossible.

ARNHOLM: Would it be so impossible for you to—?

BOLETTE: Dr. Arnholm, you can't mean what you are saying. *(Looks at him.)* Was that what you meant when—when you offered to do so much for me?

ARNHOLM: Listen a minute, Bolette. I see I have surprised you.

BOLETTE: Such a thing—from you—how could it but surprise me?

ARNHOLM: Perhaps you are right. You couldn't know that it was because of you I came here.

BOLETTE: You came here because of me?

ARNHOLM: Yes, Bolette. Last spring I got a letter from your father. It contained a sentence, which led me to believe that your memories of—of your former tutor were tinged with more than affection.

BOLETTE: How could father write that?

ARNHOLM: He didn't mean that. But I allowed myself to imagine that in this house a young girl was sitting and waiting for the day when I should come back. No, don't interrupt me, Bolette. When a man is no longer in his first youth, such a belief—illusion, if you like—affects him deeply. At first, I felt—merely grateful—but then—I felt I must come to see you—to tell you I shared the feelings which I—deluded myself into supposing that you cherished towards me.

BOLETTE: But now—when you know that I didn't?

ARNHOLM: That doesn't help, Bolette. My feelings towards you will always be coloured by that illusion I once had. You find this difficult to understand perhaps. But that is how it is.

BOLETTE: I had never dreamed that anything like this could happen.

ARNHOLM: But now that you know it can, what do you say? Could you not agree to—yes, to become my wife?

BOLETTE: You used to be my tutor. I can't imagine ever standing in any other relationship towards you.

ARNHOLM: No, no. Well, if you feel you can't, then, let our relationship remain as it was.

BOLETTE: What do you mean?

ARNHOLM: My offer stands. I shall enable you to get away from here and see the world. To learn something. To be secure and independent. And I shall secure your future too, Bolette. In me you will always have someone you can trust. I want you to know that.

BOLETTE: But, good heavens, Dr. Arnholm, all that is impossible now.

ARNHOLM: Is that impossible, too?

BOLETTE: Of course it is. After what you have said to me—and my reply—surely you must understand that I can't accept anything from you, ever. Now.

ARNHOLM: Would you rather go on sitting here, watching life slip away?

BOLETTE: I can't bear to think about it.

ARNHOLM: Do you want to turn your back on everything you dream of? To know there's so much more in life—and never experience it? Think, Bolette. Think hard.

BOLETTE: Yes. Yes, Dr. Arnholm. That is perfectly true.

ARNHOLM: Then, later—when your father is no longer here—perhaps to stand alone and helpless in the world? Or to have to give yourself to another man for whom you might not be able to feel any affection either?

BOLETTE: Oh, yes. I see clearly enough how true all that is. Everything you say. And yet—perhaps—

ARNHOLM *(tensely):* Yes?

BOLETTE *(in two minds):* Perhaps it's not so impossible after all.

ARNHOLM: What, Bolette?

416

BOLETTE: That it might work. That I might—what you suggested just now—

ARNHOLM: You mean, you might perhaps be willing to grant me the happiness of being allowed to help you as a loyal friend?

BOLETTE: No, no, no! That would be quite impossible now. No, Dr. Arnholm. Rather take me—

ARNHOLM: Bolette! You mean—?

BOLETTE: Yes—I think—I do.

ARNHOLM: You mean, you want—to be my wife?

BOLETTE: Yes. If you still want to have me.

ARNHOLM: If I still—! *(Seizes her hand.)* Thank you! Thank you, Bolette. If I have not won your heart yet, I shall find a way to win it. Oh, Bolette! I will—carry you through life—on my hands.

BOLETTE: I shall be able to see the world. To live. You promised me that.

ARNHOLM: I will keep my promise.

BOLETTE: And learn anything I want?

ARNHOLM: I myself shall be your teacher. As I used to be, Bolette.

BOLETTE *(quietly, deep in her own thoughts):* To be free. To come out into—all that's strange. Not to have to worry about the future. Not to have to pinch and scrape—

ARNHOLM: You need never worry about such things again. That's good, isn't it, Bolette?

BOLETTE: Yes. It is good. Yes.

ARNHOLM *(puts his arm round her waist):* You will see how happy we shall be together. How calm and trusting. It will be a good life, Bolette.

BOLETTE: Yes. I begin to think— Oh yes! It must work! *(Looks out right, and frees herself sharply from his grip.)* Ssh! Don't say anything.

ARNHOLM: What is it, my dear?

BOLETTE: It's that poor— *(Points.)* Look over there.

ARNHOLM: Your father?

BOLETTE: No, the young sculptor. He's walking there with Hilde.

ARNHOLM: Oh, Lyngstrand. What's the matter with him?

BOLETTE: You know how ill he is.

ARNHOLM: If he isn't just imagining it.

BOLETTE: No. He isn't just imagining it. He hasn't got very long. Well, perhaps it's for the best.

ARNHOLM: For the best?

BOLETTE: Yes, nothing would come of his art even if— Let's go before they come.

ARNHOLM: With all my heart, Bolette.

HILDE *and* LYNGSTRAND *appear by the pond.*

HILDE: Hullo! Aren't you going to wait for us?

ARNHOLM: Bolette and I will go on ahead. *(They go out left.)*

LYNGSTRAND *(laughs quietly):* It's lovely here just at this time. Everybody going in couples. Hand in hand.

HILDE *(looking after them):* Do you know, I think he's courting her.

LYNGSTRAND: Really? Have you noticed something?

HILDE: Oh, yes. It's not difficult. When one keeps one's eyes open.

LYNGSTRAND: Miss Bolette will never accept him. I'm sure of that.

HILDE: No. She thinks he's begun to look so old. She says he'll be bald soon, too.

LYNGSTRAND: I didn't only mean that. She wouldn't have him anyway.

HILDE: Why do you think that?

LYNGSTRAND: There's someone else she's promised to wait for. And think about.

HILDE: Think about?

LYNGSTRAND: Yes, while he's away.

HILDE: You mean you?

LYNGSTRAND: Perhaps.

HILDE: Has she promised to do that?

LYNGSTRAND: Yes. She promised me. But you mustn't tell her you know.

HILDE: Cross my heart! I'll be as silent as the grave.

LYNGSTRAND: I think it was—good of her to say that.

HILDE: And then when you come back home—will you get engaged to her? And marry her?

LYNGSTRAND: Oh, no. I daren't think of that for the first few years. And when—if—I should ever be in a position to— she'll be too old for me then.

HILDE: But you want her to sit here and think of you?

LYNGSTRAND: Yes. It'll mean so much to me, don't you see? As an artist, I mean. And it wouldn't be difficult for her, as she hasn't any particular vocation. But it's nice of her to say she'll do it.

HILDE: Do you think you'll be able to work better if you know Bolette is sitting here thinking of you?

LYNGSTRAND: Yes, I think so. To know that somewhere in the world there's a lovely, silent young woman sitting quietly and dreaming of me. I think it must be so—so—I don't know how to describe it.

HILDE: Exciting?

LYNGSTRAND: Exciting? Yes! Just that! Exciting! More or less. *(Looks at her for a moment.)* You're so wise, Miss Hilde. Amazingly wise. When I come home again, you'll be about the same age as your sister is now. Perhaps you will look like her too. Perhaps you'll have the same mind as she has now. You will have become yourself and her—in one person, so to speak.

HILDE: Would you like that to happen?

LYNGSTRAND: I don't know. Yes, I think so. But now—this summer—I want you to stay just as you are—not like anyone else. Just yourself.

HILDE: Do you like me best as I am?

LYNGSTRAND: Yes, I like you very much as you are.

HILDE: Hm. Tell me, as an artist, do you think I'm right always to wear these light summer clothes?

LYNGSTRAND: Yes. I think they suit you very well.

HILDE: You think these light colours suit me?

LYNGSTRAND: Yes, I think they suit you—beautifully, I think.

HILDE: But, tell me, speaking as an artist—how do you think I would look in black?

LYNGSTRAND: In black, Miss Hilde?

HILDE: Yes, all in black. Do you think I would look good in that?

LYNGSTRAND: Black is no colour to wear in the summer time. Though, I think you would look very beautiful in black, too. Yes. Your looks would suit black perfectly.

HILDE (to herself): Black . . . up to the neck . . . black crepe all round . . . black gloves . . . and a long black veil hanging down behind.

LYNGSTRAND: If you dressed like that, Miss Hilde, I should wish myself a painter, so that I might paint you—as a beautiful young widow in mourning.

HILDE: Or a young bride in mourning?

LYNGSTRAND: Yes, that would be even better. But surely you couldn't want to dress like that?

HILDE: I don't know, really. But I think it's exciting.

LYNGSTRAND: Exciting?

HILDE: Exciting to think of. Yes. (Suddenly points left.) Oh, look!

LYNGSTRAND (looking): The big English steamer! She's right alongside.

WANGEL *and* ELLIDA *appear by the pond.*

WANGEL: No, Ellida, my dear—you're wrong, I promise you. (Sees the others.) Are you two here? That's right, isn't it, Mr. Lyngstrand—she's not in sight yet, is she?

LYNGSTRAND: The English ship?

WANGEL: Yes.

LYNGSTRAND *(pointing):* There she is, doctor.

ELLIDA: Ah! I knew it!

WANGEL: You mean she's come?

LYNGSTRAND: Come like a thief in the night, as one might say. Softly—soundlessly—

WANGEL: You must take Hilde down to the jetty. Hurry! She'll want to hear the music.

LYNGSTRAND: Yes, we are just going, doctor.

WANGEL: We'll come on in a few minutes.

HILDE *(whispers to LYNGSTRAND):* Hand in hand. What did I say?

She and LYNGSTRAND *go out through the garden, left. Horn music is audible from far out on the fjord during the following dialogue.*

ELLIDA: He's come, then. He's here. Yes, yes. I feel it.

WANGEL: You'd better go indoors, Ellida. Let me talk to him alone.

ELLIDA: Oh, it's impossible. Impossible, I tell you. *(Cries)* There he is!

THE STRANGER *enters from the left and stands on the path outside the garden fence.*

STRANGER: Good evening. Well, Ellida. Here I am again.

ELLIDA: Yes, yes. The hour has come.

STRANGER: Are you ready to go with me? Or not?

WANGEL: You can see for yourself that she is not.

STRANGER: I don't mean is she dressed for travelling? Or has she packed her bags? All she needs on the journey I have on board. I've got her a cabin too. *(To* ELLIDA*)* I am asking you if you are ready to come with me. Of your own free will.

ELLIDA *(weakly):* Don't ask me. Don't tempt me.

A ship's bell is heard in the distance.

STRANGER: That is the first warning. You must say yes or no.

ELLIDA: To decide. To decide for one's whole life! And never to be able to undo it!

STRANGER: Never. In half an hour it will be too late.

ELLIDA *(shyly and searchingly):* What makes you hold on to me so relentlessly?

STRANGER: Don't you feel, as I do, that we two belong together?

ELLIDA: You mean, because of the promise I gave you?

STRANGER: Promises bind no one. No man, no woman. I hold on to you because I cannot do otherwise.

ELLIDA *(quiet and trembling):* Why didn't you come before?

WANGEL: Ellida!

ELLIDA: Oh, this man tempts me and draws me into the unknown! All the power of the sea is gathered in this man.

THE STRANGER *climbs over the garden fence.*

ELLIDA *(takes refuge behind* WANGEL*):* What is it? What do you want?

STRANGER: I see it in your face, Ellida. I hear it in your voice. You will choose me in the end.

WANGEL *(takes a step towards him):* The choice does not lie with my wife. It is my duty to choose for her—and to protect her. Yes, protect her! If you don't leave the country and swear never to return, do you know what will happen to you?

ELLIDA: No, Wangel, no! You mustn't!

STRANGER: What will you do to me?

WANGEL: I will have you arrested as a common criminal. Now, at once, before you board the ship. I know the truth about that murder out at Skjoldviken.

ELLIDA: Wangel! How can you—?

STRANGER: I was prepared for that. *(Draws a revolver from*

his breast pocket.) So I took the precaution of bringing this.

ELLIDA *(throws herself in front of* WANGEL*):* No, no! Don't kill him! If you must kill anyone, kill me!

STRANGER: Don't worry. I don't want to kill either of you. This is for myself. I mean to live and die a free man.

ELLIDA: Wangel! Let me say this—and say it so that he hears it too! Of course you can keep me here. You have the power and the means to do so. And that is what you want to do. But my mind—my thoughts—my dreams and longings—those you cannot imprison. They strain to roam and hunt—out into the unknown—which I was born for—and which you have locked me away from.

WANGEL *(quietly, in pain):* I see it, Ellida! Little by little you are slipping away from me. Your longing for the boundless, the infinite, will end by driving your mind into darkness.

ELLIDA: Oh, yes, yes! I feel it! Like—black soundless wings—beating over me.

WANGEL: It mustn't come to that. There's no other way to save you. None that I can see. Therefore—I agree to—to cancel the bargain. Now—at once. Now you can make your choice, Ellida—in freedom.

ELLIDA *(looks at him for a moment):* Do you mean that? Do you really mean it? With all your heart?

WANGEL: Yes. I mean it—with all my heart.

ELLIDA: But, can you—can you—let me go?

WANGEL: Yes, I can. I can—because I love you so much—so very much.

ELLIDA *(quiet and trembling):* Am I so close—so very close to you then?

WANGEL: You have become—a part of me, Ellida. Through the years we have lived together.

ELLIDA: And I have been blind to all this!

WANGEL: Your thoughts were directed elsewhere. But now—now you are free for ever from me and from everything that belongs to me. Now you can go back to the life that is really yours. Now you can choose—free—on your own responsibility.

ELLIDA *(stares unseeingly at him):* Freedom—and responsibility. *(To herself)* Responsibility as well? Everything is changing—

The ship's bell sounds again.

STRANGER: Do you hear, Ellida? She is sounding for the last time. Come.

ELLIDA *(turns, gazes at him and says in a clear voice):* I cannot go with you.

STRANGER: You're not coming?

ELLIDA *(puts her arm round* WANGEL*):* I can never leave you now.

WANGEL: Ellida! Ellida!

STRANGER: Then it is finished?

ELLIDA: Yes. Finished for ever.

STRANGER: Yes. I see. There is something here stronger than my will.

ELLIDA: Your will has no power over me any longer. For me you are a dead man washed up by the sea, whom the sea will soon claim again for her own. I no longer fear you. I no longer want you.

STRANGER: Goodbye, then. *(He vaults over the fence.)* Henceforth you are no more to me than a lost ship. *(He goes out left.)*

WANGEL *(looks at her for a moment):* Ellida, your mind is like the sea. It flows and ebbs. What changed you?

ELLIDA: Don't you understand? The change came—had to come—when you let me choose freely.

WANGEL: And the unknown attracts you no longer?

ELLIDA: I no longer yearn for it, nor fear it. I have seen into the heart of it—I could have entered it—if I had chosen to do so. I was free to choose the unknown. So—I was free to reject it.

WANGEL: I begin to understand you, little by little. You think and feel in pictures and visual images. Your restless yearning for the sea—your yearning for this stranger—all that was nothing but an expression of your longing for freedom. Nothing more.

ELLIDA: Perhaps. I don't know. But you have been a good doctor to me. You discovered, and dared to prescribe, the right remedy—the only one that could have cured me.

WANGEL: When things are desperate, we doctors have to take desperate measures. But now—will you come back to me, Ellida?

ELLIDA: Yes, Wangel—my dear, faithful Wangel. Now I come to you freely, of my own choice.

WANGEL: Ellida! Ellida! We have found each other at last. Now we can live—for each other—

ELLIDA: And with our memories. Yours as well as mine.

WANGEL: Yes! Yes!

ELLIDA: And with our children, Wangel. Our two children.

WANGEL: *Our* children?

ELLIDA: They are not yet mine. But I shall win them.

WANGEL: Our children! *(He kisses her hands.)* Thank you, Ellida! Thank you.

HILDE, BALLESTED, LYNGSTRAND, ARNHOLM *and* BOLETTE *come into the garden from the left. At the same time, a number of young people from the town and summer visitors appear on the footpath outside.*

HILDE *(half aloud to* LYNGSTRAND*)*: Look at her and father! Why, they look as though they'd just got engaged!

BALLESTED *(overhearing her)*: It is summer time, little lady.

ARNHOLM *(looking at* ELLIDA *and* WANGEL*)*: The Englander is sailing now.

BOLETTE *(going to the fence):* Here's the best place to watch from.

LYNGSTRAND: The last trip of the year.

BALLESTED: Every way to the sea will soon be locked, as the poet says. A sad thought, Mrs. Wangel. And now we shall lose you too for a while. You will be off to Skjoldviken tomorrow, they tell me.

WANGEL: No. This evening we two have changed our plans.

ARNHOLM *(looking from one to the other):* You have!

BOLETTE *(comes over to them):* Father, is this true?

HILDE *(to* ELLIDA*):* Then you'll be staying with us after all?

ELLIDA: Yes, Hilde dear—if you want me to.

HILDE *(torn between joy and tears):* If—oh!

ARNHOLM *(to* ELLIDA*):* Well, this is certainly a surprise!

ELLIDA *(smiles):* Why, Dr. Arnholm, don't you remember what we two were saying yesterday? Once one has become a landsman, one can never find one's way back to the sea.

BALLESTED: Why, that's just like my mermaid!

ELLIDA: Yes, more or less.

BALLESTED: With one big difference. The mermaid died. But men and women—they can acclaim—acclimatise themselves. Yes, I assure you, Mrs. Wangel! They can acc—li—matise—themselves.

ELLIDA: If they are free, Mr. Ballested.

WANGEL: Free and responsible, Ellida.

ELLIDA *(quickly, gives him her hand):* Yes!

The big steamer glides silently out across the fjord. The music grows louder.

Little Eyolf

Introduction

Ibsen wrote *Little Eyolf* in Christiania in the summer and autumn of 1894. He was now sixty-six, and had entered into a mellow, or at any rate comparatively mellow old age. In contrast to the prickly aloofness of his early manhood in Norway and the long years of self-imposed exile in Italy and Germany, we are told that he now often gladly entered in social life, and that he especially loved the company of young people and children: it amused him, at gatherings, to take them into a corner and entertain them with talk and questioning while their parents sat jealously apart. He said to Caroline Sontum, the wife of one of his doctors, that he "felt the need to be together with young people who would accept him as a friend." He took a close interest in young writers, and enjoyed reading their manuscripts and helping them with advice. Since he had reached the age of sixty, he had usually had a young girl as his special confidante: at this time it was the young pianist Hildur Andersen. He seems, however, to have found his own generation less congenial, and to have felt a certain sense of isolation from Christiania society; and, in particular, from his wife.

He had finished *The Master Builder* in October 1892 and, as was his custom, let his mind lie fallow during the following winter, spring and summer. On 18 September 1893 he wrote to his publisher, Jacob Hegel of Gyldendal: "I have now begun to plan a new dramatic work, which it is my intention to complete during next summer.'' We hear no further reference to this in his correspondence until 22 June 1894, when he apologized to Gerda Brandes (the wife of the critic Georg Brandes) for having left a letter unanswered for three months: ''But today I must and shall write to you, for I have now begun to work seriously on my new play, and so must clear my desk and, as far as possible, my conscience of all other commitments.''

We do not know the exact day on which he began, for the pages of his preliminary draft have not survived, but he completed Act 1 on 10 July. The next day he began Act 2, and a fortnight later, on 25 July, he was able to write to Hegel: ''Yesterday I completed the second act of my new play, and have already today begun work on the third and last act. So I hope to have the final version completed in good time. This of course means that I cannot think of taking any summer holiday this year. But I don't need one. I am very content here, and am happiest when I am working at my desk.'' The third act he completed on 7 August; in other words, each of the last two acts took him (in draft) exactly a fortnight. During the fortnight which he spent on Act 3 he seems also to have found time to make some alterations to Acts 1 and 2, but he proceeded to revise the whole play so thoroughly that over two months elapsed before he was ready, on 13 October, to send the play to the printer.

A comparison of the preliminary draft of *Little Eyolf* with Ibsen's final version is particularly revealing. William Archer summed up the main differences in one of his best critical passages:

''Revision amounted almost to re-invention; and it was the re-invention that determined the poetic value of the play. The poet's original idea (though he doubtless knew very well that this would not be final) was simply to study a rather commonplace wife's jealousy of a rather commonplace child. The lameness of Eyolf proves to have been an afterthought; and as Eyolf is not lame, it follows that the terrible cry of 'The crutch is floating' was also an afterthought, as well as the almost intolerable scene of recrimination between Allmers and Rita as to the accident which caused his lameness. We find, in fact, that nearly everything that gives the play its depth, its horror and its elevation came as an afterthought. The suggestion of the 'evil eye' motive is of the very slightest. Instead of the exquisite beauty of the final scene in its ultimate form, we have a page of almost conventional sentimentalizing over Eyolf's continued existence in the hearts of his parents. Instead of telling her the wonderful tale of his meeting with Death in the mountains, Alfred reads to Rita the poem which Ibsen had written as a first hint for *The Master Builder*. * In no case, perhaps, did revision work such a transfiguration as in *Little Eyolf*.''

As usual, Ibsen changed the names of his characters sev-

---

*They dwelt, those two, in so cosy a house
  In autumn and winter weather.
  Then came the fire—and the house was gone.
  They must search the ashes together.

For down in the ashes a jewel lies hid,
  Whose brightness the flames could not smother,
  And search they but faithfully, he and she,
  'Twill be found by one or the other.

But even though they find it, the gem they lost,
  The enduring jewel they cherished—
  She ne'er will recover her vanished faith—
  Nor he the joy that has perished.

(A. G. Chater's translation)

The only change Ibsen made when he inserted the poem into the first draft of *Little Eyolf* was to substitute "peace" for "faith" in the penultimate line.

eral times as he progressed with his draft. His original cast
list reads as follows:

> HARALD BORGHEJM
> JOHANNE, his wife.
> RITA, his sister.
> ALFRED, his son, aged 11.
> EJVIND ALMER, a road-engineer.
> MISS VARG [i.e. WOLF], Johanne's aunt.

But by the time father and son make their first appearance
(the early pages of the draft are missing), Harald Borghejm
has become Haakon Skjoldhejm, an established and famous
author now working on his masterpiece. Then, as he is
speaking of his determination to abandon his book and ded-
icate himself to his son, he becomes Dr. Alfred Almer, then
Allmer, and finally, still in Act 1, Allmers. (Ibsen had been
intending for some time to create a character with the Christian name of Alfred, for he had originally given that name to
Rosmer, and then to Ragnar Brovik in *The Master Builder*.)

True to his usual custom, he switched the names of the
characters as he wrote. Thus Johanne changes to Andrea and
then to Rita. As she drops the name of Andrea her sister-in-
law (formerly Rita) takes it over, and it is not until Act 3 that
the latter becomes Asta. When the father appropriates his
son's name of Alfred, a kind of general post takes place; he
passes on his old surname of Borghejm to the engineer, who
in turn passes on his Christian name, Ejvind, to the son. (At
the beginning of this preliminary draft, the engineer and the
sister are already engaged.)

The character of Asta may have been based on Ibsen's
sister-in-law, Marie Thoresen. Ibsen had long cherished a
warm affection for her; like Asta, she was a schoolteacher,
and as long ago as 1863 he had written her a poem entitled
"With a water-lily"—the flower which, at the end of Act 2,

Asta gives to Allmers as a remembrance. The idea of Eyolf's lameness probably sprang from a casual remark which Ibsen put into the boy's mouth in his preliminary draft. Responding to his father's suggestion that they should go together to the mountains next summer, Eyolf (or, as Ibsen called him at this stage, Alfred) asks nervously: "But might I not easily fall and be crippled?" It is possible that Eyolf may be a portrait, conscious or unconscious, of Ibsen himself as a child—the ugly and undersized boy who felt cut off by his temperament from the other village children—and the mock soldier's uniform may reflect Ibsen's old feeling of guilt at not having volunteered to fight for the Danes against the Germans in the Schleswig-Holstein war of 1864.

The Rat Wife is also probably a memory from his childhood in Skien. Her cryptic reference to her sweetheart whom she drowned is clarified in the earlier version:

ALFRED (EYOLF): Why did you leave him?

MISS VARG: Because he had gone away from me. [I loved him so dearly.] Far, far away over the salt waves. But I drew him and drew him home to me again. I almost had him. But then my grasp failed. He was gone for ever.

This passage carries a strong echo of the relationship between Ellida and the Stranger in *The Lady from the Sea,* and it may have been the obviousness of the similarity that caused Ibsen to delete it.

Allmers is another of those "heroes" torn between the demands of his own sensuality and what he feels to be his calling whom Ibsen portrayed so repeatedly in his plays (Brand, Eilert Lœvborg, Solness, Rubek); unlike them but like Rosmer, Gregers Werle, and Earl Skule in *The Pretenders,* he is crippled and rendered impotent by a sense of guilt. Rita is, with the possible exception of Hedda Gabler, the most memorable of those unsatisfied and demanding wives whom we find in every play which Ibsen wrote after his meeting with Emilie Bardach in 1889 (Aline Solness, Gunhild Borkman, Maja Rubek). She is, one might say, Hedda with money and a child; her remark in Act 1 about the possibility of seducing Borghejm from Asta ("So much the better—if I took him from someone else!") had in fact been put by Ibsen into Hedda's mouth four years earlier, though he deleted the line in revision.

The theme of an attraction between half-brother and half-sister had already been explored in *Ghosts* (Oswald and Regina). Professor Didrik Arup Seip has remarked that the major cause of Allmers's feeling of guilt lies not in Eyolf's lameness, nor in his relationship to Rita, but in his relationship to Asta, and that his realization of the truth of this relationship, though almost unbearably painful, acts on him like a cure.

Little Eyolf was published by Gyldendal of Copenhagen on 11 December 1894. It had already received the usual public reading in London to secure copyright (at the Haymarket Theatre on 3 December), and was staged for the first time at the Deutsches Theater in Berlin on 12 January 1895. Three days later it was performed in Christiania (at the Christiania Theater), and before the month was out it had also been produced in Bergen, Helsinki and Gothenburg. Milan and Vienna saw it in February, Copenhagen and Stockholm in March. Later that spring it was presented in Chicago and Paris, where Lugné-Poe played Allmers.

London had to wait another eighteen months to see *Little Eyolf* for it was not staged there until 23 November 1896. It had, however, already aroused considerable interest in its printed form. Two years earlier, almost to the day, Henry James had written to Elizabeth Robins, the American actress who was largely responsible for its ultimate presentation:

434

"Heinemann has lent me the proofs of the 2 first acts of the Play—the ineffable Play—and I can't stay my hand from waving wildly to you! It is indeed immense—indeed and indeed. It is of a rare perfection—and if 3 keeps up the tremendous pitch of 1 and 2 it will distinctly stand at the tiptop of his achievement. It's a masterpiece and a marvel; and it *must* leap upon the stage. . . . The inherent difficulties are there, but they are not insurmountable. They are on the contrary manageable—they are a matter of tact and emphasis—of art and discretion. The thing will be a big *profane* (i.e. Ibsen and non-Ibsen *both*) success. The part—*the* part—is Asta—unless it be the Rat-hound in the Bag! What an old woman—and what a Young!"

But three days later, in a letter of apology for having talked indiscreetly about the play "in the despair of a dull dinner—or after-dinner—at Sir Alfred Lyall's," he wrote to Miss Robins:

"I fear, in truth, no harm can be done equal to the harm done to the play by its own most disappointing third act. It came to me last night—and has been, to me, a subject of depressed reflection. It seems to me a singular and almost inexplicable drop—dramatically, *representably* speaking. . . . The worst of it is that it goes back, as it were, on what precedes, and gives a meagreness to that too—makes it less interesting and less significant. . . . I don't see the meaning or effect of ·Borghejm—I don't see the value or final *function* of Asta. . . . I find the solution too simple, too immediate, too much a harking back, and too productive of the sense that there might have been a stronger one. . . . My idea that Asta was to become an active, *the* active agent is of course blighted." However, he admitted: "Really uttered, *done,* in the gathered northern twilight, with the flag flown and the lights coming out across the fjord, the scene might have a real solemnity of beauty—and perhaps that's

435

all that's required!!'' But, he concluded: ''I fear Allmers will never be thought an actor manager's part.''

James's objections to the third act were, in general, shared by his contemporaries, and by the next generation of readers and theatre-goers. In recent years, however, there has been a growing body of opinion that this act, if properly understood and adequately interpreted, is by no means meagre and that the solution is not, as James thought it, too simple. Supporters of the modern view hold that Ibsen, when he wrote this act, did not envisage it as a happy ending. Devoting themselves to charity, sharing their ''gold and green forests'' with the poor, will not provide the answer and the peace which Alfred and Rita are seeking. They have reached rock-bottom; but unless they can prove that they have undergone a genuine change of heart, and are prepared to grapple with the realities of life, this will be no solution but merely another, more plausible, but equally insidious ''life-lie.'' They are only at the beginning of their long climb to salvation.

My own belief is that the third act, like the two that precede it, is among the greatest that Ibsen ever wrote, and that in it he achieved exactly what he set out to achieve, namely, to reveal the interior of what, in *Brand,* thirty years before, he had called ''the Ice Church''—the interior of a human soul in which love has died—so that, in Rita's words, all that is left to her and Allmers is to ''try to fill that emptiness with something. Something resembling love.''

Little Eyolf is the most subtle and elusive of all Ibsen's plays. There are several reasons for this elusiveness besides the false belief in the ''happy ending,'' which, if it is played that way, vitiates much of what has gone before. One is that James's fears concerning the unwillingness of established actors to play Allmers have been proved only too true. ''How,'' asked Bernard Shaw in his review of the first English performance of the play in 1896, ''could he recommend himself to spectators who saw in him everything they are ashamed of in themselves?'' And James Agate, writing of the performance at the Arts Theatre in 1930, concluded: "The character is deadly anyhow, and should be relegated to the index of the unactable." The character of Allmers is in fact only deadly if, as is common practice, it is romanticized. A romanticized Allmers and a happy ending are burdens that no production of *Little Eyolf* can hope to survive.

A third consideration which has, until recently, hampered appreciation of the play is its frankness about sex. In this context it is instructive to analyse the reactions of the London press to the productions of 1896, 1928 and 1958. *The Times* expressed itself in the following terms about the 1896 production:

"A perplexing phantasmagoria which still less than the majority of its predecessors deserves the name of a public entertainment. . . . Propriety forbids one to analyse. . . . None of the characters appear quite sane. . . . A set of irresponsible people moved by unaccountable impulses and addicted to fantastic views of duty. There is no knowing what they will do next. They are not amenable to the rules of ordinary human nature. . . . Terribly depressing and lugubrious society. . . . One does not breathe freely until one has escaped from the atmosphere of the theatre into the open air. Gloom, depression, and a sense of the remoteness of the action from all living human interests overcome the spectator, whose abiding impression of the play is that of having seen, in a dream, the patients of a madhouse exercising in their yard."

In 1928 *The Times* saw the play somewhat differently. Analysing the production at the Everyman Theatre, its critic wrote:

"This play is seldom acted, yet how wonderfully actable even a moderately good performance shows it to be. . . . It must then be from its subject that the ordinary playgoer shrinks. He is rarely in the mood to enjoy the 'iron-mouthed' Ibsen's condemnation of just the kind of conjugal love that romantic writers bestow on those whom they destine to live happily ever after. It is a natural hesitancy, but the ordinary playgoer misses much by his unwillingness to risk the possibility of pain, even a queer exhilaration.''

By 1958 public opinion was beginning to catch up with *Little Eyolf.* The production at Hammersmith that spring coincided with the West End presentation of Tennessee Williams's *Cat on a Hot Tin Roof,* and the critics were not slow to compare the two plays, as the following extracts show:

"It is hard to see why *Little Eyolf* has so long been left out of the Ibsen repertory. . . . Fresh and pungent, a rare and exciting treat. . . . Its subject is a marriage and it takes that marriage apart about as frankly and twice as truthfully as, say, Tennessee Williams takes apart the marriage of Brick and Maggie the Cat, and it is (written though it was in 1894) just as modern if not more so. . . . The effect is terrific.''

T. C. Worsley in the *New Statesman*

"This magnificent play . . . so frank about sex that it makes Tennessee Williams look like pap for infants.''

John Barber in the *Daily Express*

"A rich, rare, late Ibsen.''

Kenneth Tynan in the *Observer*

"A masterpiece which is rarely done but which is immensely more rewarding to see than to read.''

Alan Dent in the *News Chronicle*

"A great modern drama which wipes the smile off your face and puts the fear of God into your heart before you can say Tennessee Williams.''

Alan Brien in the *Spectator*

"This great play's haunting moral beauty. . . . A post-Freudian generation will surely marvel at the justness and truth with which this pre-Freudian master picks his symbols."

Philip Hope-Wallace in the *Manchester Guardian*

"A horrifying experiment in vivisection, conducted with deadly skill."

Eric Keown in *Punch*

But even when public opinion has caught up with the play, and the ending is understood, and Allmers is played with the conflict between sensual imagination on the one hand, and intellect plus morality on the other, which the part, like that of Rosmer, demands, two difficulties remain. One is the title. *Little Eyolf* is a fine title when one has read or seen the play, but is not, either in English or in Norwegian, a title likely to lure people into a theatre. Yet one hesitates to rename it simply because, when one has read or seen the play, one despairs of ever finding any other title which could so perfectly pinpoint the twin horns of the dilemma on which the two chief characters find themselves impaled. The final obstacle, with due diffidence, is that of translation. *Little Eyolf* is incomparably the most elusive and difficult of all Ibsen's plays to translate, not excluding *Brand*. Ibsen's characters, especially in his later plays, are inhibited by a deep sense of guilt which makes them evasive in their speech, but none are as evasive as Allmers and Rita, who spend their time circling round a subject which they dread to talk about yet cannot escape from. If one renders these passages too directly, the play becomes a melodrama; if, on the other hand, one takes refuge behind cloudy word-combinations, as, with the greatest respect, Archer did, the thread of the argument gets lost. It is, for example, evident from the reviews of the 1896, 1928, 1930 and even 1945 productions that many of the critics had not the faintest idea that the shock of Eyolf's fall has rendered Allmers sexually impotent, and unless this fact is made absolutely clear to the audience they can only feel a very restricted sympathy with him.

However, the English public has at last been persuaded to appreciate *Brand,* ninety-four years after Ibsen wrote it, and perhaps it is not too much to hope that before too long they may be allowed to see a production of *Little Eyolf* which will establish it as one of the old master's supreme achievements.* Nowhere else does he probe so mercilessly into the complexities of human minds and relationships; it is like a long, sustained and terrifying operation. On the occasion of its first production in England in 1896, William Archer wrote: "I rank the play beside, if not above, the very greatest of Ibsen's works, and am only doubtful whether its soul-searching be not too terrible for human endurance in the theatre."

I again gladly acknowledge my debt to Mr. Casper Wrede for much minute and invaluable criticism in connection with the translation.

MICHAEL MEYER

---

*Since these words were written, two such productions have taken place (see page 442).

CHARACTERS

ALFRED ALLMERS, a man of property; also of letters; some-
time supply teacher
RITA, his wife
EYOLF, their son, aged 9
ASTA ALLMERS, Alfred's younger half-sister
BORGHEJM, an engineer
THE RAT WIFE

The action takes place on Allmers's estate, by a fjord in
western Norway, a few miles outside town.

This translation of *Little Eyolf* was performed on B.B.C. Television on 19 July 1982. The cast was:

ALFRED ALLMERS	Anthony Hopkins
RITA	Diana Rigg
ASTA	Emma Piper
EYOLF	Timothy Stark
RAT WIFE	Peggy Ashcroft
BORGHEJM	Charles Dance

Directed by Michael Darlow

On 13 January 1985, it was performed at the Lyric Theatre, Hammersmith. The cast was:

ALFRED ALLMERS	Ronald Pickup
RITA	Diana Rigg
ASTA	Cheryl Campbell
EYOLF	Steven Kember/Nigel Harman
RAT WIFE	Anne Dyson
BORGHEJM	Paul Moriarty

Directed by Clare Davidson

ACT ONE

A handsome and expensively appointed garden room, full of furniture, flowers and plants. Upstage, glass doors open on to a verandah, with a broad view over the fjord. Wooded mountain ranges in the distance. In each of the side walls, there is a door; the one on the right is a double door, set upstage. Downstage right is a sofa, with loose cushions and rugs. Chairs and a small table at the corner of the sofa. Downstage left, a larger table with armchairs around it. On the table stands an open portmanteau. It is early on a summer morning; the sun is shining warmly.

> RITA ALLMERS *stands at the table, facing left, unpacking the portmanteau. She is a handsome, blonde, Junoesque woman of about 30, dressed in a light-coloured house-coat.*

> *After a few seconds,* ASTA ALLMERS *enters through the door on the right, dressed in a light-brown summer suit, with hat, jacket and parasol. Under her arm she carries a large, locked portfolio. She is slim, of middle height, with dark hair and deep, serious eyes. She is about 25.*

ASTA *(in the doorway):* Good morning, Rita, my dear.

RITA *(turns her head and nods):* Why, Asta! Fancy seeing you here so early! What brings you all this way from town?

ASTA *(puts her things on a chair by the door):* I felt I had to come out and see Eyolf today. Little Eyolf. And you, Rita. *(She puts her portfolio down on the table by the sofa.)* So I caught the steamer and—here I am.

RITA *(smiles):* And, quite by accident, you happened to meet someone you knew—a friend—on board?

ASTA *(calmly):* No, as a matter of fact I didn't. *(Sees the portmanteau.)* Why, Rita, what's that?

RITA *(continues unpacking):* Alfred's portmanteau. Don't you recognize it?

ASTA *(happily, going over to her):* You mean Alfred has come home?

RITA: Yes, would you believe it? He arrived quite unexpectedly by the night train.

ASTA: So that was it. That was what brought me here. But hadn't he written to say he was coming? A postcard, even?

RITA: Not a word.

ASTA: Not even a telegram?

RITA: Yes—it arrived an hour before he did. Short and to the point. *(Laughs.)* Isn't that just like him, Asta?

ASTA: Yes. That's his way. He always was secretive.

RITA: Well, it makes it all the more wonderful to have him home again.

ASTA: I know how you feel.

RITA: A whole fortnight before I was expecting him.

ASTA: And he's well and happy? Not depressed?

RITA *(closes the portmanteau and smiles at* ASTA*):* He looked quite transformed as he came in through the door.

ASTA: He must have been tired, surely?

RITA: Tired? He was ready to drop. Poor darling, he'd come most of the way on foot.

ASTA: That mountain air must have been too sharp for him.

RITA: I don't know. I haven't heard him cough once since he got back.

ASTA: There you are! The doctor was right after all to advise him to go on that walking tour.

RITA: Yes, I suppose so, but— You don't know what a dreadful time this has been for me, Asta. I haven't been able to bring myself to talk about it. And you've hardly ever been out to see me.

ASTA: I should have come more often. But—

RITA: No, no—you had your school work to attend to in town. I know. *(Smiles.)* And our pioneer, our builder of roads—he's been away too, hasn't he?

ASTA: Oh, stop it, Rita.

RITA: Very well. The pioneer is dismissed. Oh, but Asta, how I've missed Alfred! How empty it's been, how desolate! Just as though someone had died here.

ASTA: Rita! He's only been away six or seven weeks—

RITA: Ah, but you must remember that Alfred has never been away from me before. Not even for a day. In all the ten years we've been—

ASTA: But Rita, that's just why I thought it was time he got away this year. He ought to have gone walking in the mountains every summer. That's what he ought to have done.

RITA *(smiles):* Ah, it's easy for you to talk. If I were as sensible as you are, I would have let him go before now—perhaps. But I couldn't, Asta. I couldn't. I felt somehow that if I once let him go, I might never get him back again. You can understand that, can't you?

ASTA: No. But then I don't have anyone I'm afraid of losing.

RITA *(teasingly):* Really? No one at all?

ASTA: Not that I know of. *(Quickly.)* But, tell me, Rita, where is Alfred? Asleep?

RITA: Asleep? Not he! He got up this morning just as early as ever.

ASTA: He can't have been all that tired, then.

RITA: He was last night, when he arrived. But now he's had Eyolf in with him for—oh, at least an hour.

ASTA: Poor, pale little child! Is he going to be made to study all day again?

RITA *(shrugs her shoulders)*: Well, you know Alfred wants it that way.

ASTA: Yes, but I think you ought to try to stop him.

RITA *(a trifle impatiently)*: Well, really, I can't interfere in these things. Alfred is better qualified to understand these matters than I am. What else would you have Eyolf do? He can't run about and play like other children.

ASTA *(firmly)*: I shall speak to Alfred about it.

RITA: Yes, my dear, you do that. Ah, here they are!

> ALFRED ALLMERS, *in a summer suit, enters through the door on the left, leading* EYOLF *by the hand.* ALLMERS *is a slim, delicately built man of 36 or 37, with gentle eyes, thinning brown hair and beard, and a serious, thoughtful expression.* EYOLF *wears a suit cut like a uniform, with gold braid and buttons with lions on them. He is lame, and limps with a crutch under his left arm. His leg is paralysed. He is undersized and looks frail, but has fine, wise eyes.*

ALLMERS *(lets go of* EYOLF, *comes forward happily and stretches out both his hands to* ASTA*)*: Asta! Asta, my dearest! Are you out here? It's good to see you so soon.

ASTA: I felt I had to. Welcome home.

ALLMERS *(clasps her hands)*: Thank you.

RITA: Doesn't he look splendid?

ASTA *(looking intently at him)*: Wonderful. Wonderful. Your eyes—so sparkling. You must have done a lot of writing while you've been away. *(In sudden excitement.)* Have you—finished the book?

ALLMERS: The book? *(Shrugs his shoulders.)* Oh, that.

ASTA: I thought it would go easily once you could get away and be alone.

ALLMERS: I used to think so, too. But it didn't turn out that way. If I must confess the truth, I have not written a line.

ASTA: You haven't written—?

RITA: Oh! So that's why I found all those blank sheets of paper in your bag.

ASTA: But my dear Alfred, what on earth have you been doing all this time?

ALLMERS: Walking and thinking. Thinking. Thinking.

RITA *(puts her arm round his shoulders)*: Thinking a little of us too, I hope.

ALLMERS: Yes, of course. A lot. Every day.

RITA *(lets go of him)*: Well then, everything is as it should be.

ASTA: But did you do no work at all on the book? You look so happy and—contented. We don't often see you like that—I mean, when your work's not going well.

ALLMERS: Yes, I know. I have been so stupid. Thinking is what matters. What one can manage to put down on paper is insignificant.

ASTA: Insignificant!

RITA *(smiles)*: Have you gone mad, Alfred?

EYOLF *(looks trustingly up at him)*: No, father. What you write is important.

ALLMERS *(smiles and strokes the boy's hair)*: Yes, my son. If you say so. But I tell you, there is one who will come after me and who will do these things better.

EYOLF: Who will that be? Oh, tell me!

ALLMERS: Give him time. He will show himself.

EYOLF: But what will you do when he comes?

ALLMERS: I shall return to the mountains.

RITA: Shame on you, Alfred!

ALLMERS: To the high peaks and the great wide spaces.

EYOLF: Father, don't you think I shall soon be well enough to come with you?

ALLMERS *(ill at ease):* Perhaps, perhaps, my boy.

EYOLF: I think it would be nice if I too could climb mountains.

ASTA *(quickly, changing the subject):* How smart you look today, Eyolf.

EYOLF: Do you think so, aunt?

ASTA: Yes. Is it for your father's sake that you've put your new clothes on?

EYOLF: Yes. I asked mother to let me. I wanted father to see me in them.

ALLMERS *(aside, to* RITA*):* You shouldn't have given him that kind of suit.

RITA *(aside):* But he begged me so. Again and again. He gave me no peace.

EYOLF: Father, Borghejm has given me a bow. Isn't it wonderful? And he's taught me to shoot with it.

ALLMERS: Yes, that really is a good idea, Eyolf.

EYOLF: Next time he comes, I'm going to ask him to teach me to swim, too.

ALLMERS: To swim? Why do you want to learn that?

EYOLF: All the other boys can swim. I'm the only one who can't.

ALLMERS *(moved, puts his arm round the boy's shoulders):* You shall learn anything—anything you want to learn, you shall.

EYOLF: Shall I tell you what I most want to learn, father?

ALLMERS: What? Tell me.

EYOLF: Most of all I should like to be a soldier.

ALLMERS: Ah, little Eyolf, there are so many other things better than that.

EYOLF: Yes, but when I grow big I must be a soldier. You know that.

ALLMERS: Yes, yes. We shall see.

ASTA *(sits at the table, left)*: Eyolf! Come over here and I'll tell you something.

EYOLF *(goes over to her)*: What is it, aunt?

ASTA: What do you think, Eyolf? I have seen the Rat Wife.

EYOLF: What? Have you seen the Rat Wife? Oh, no, it's not true!

ASTA: Yes, it is. I saw her yesterday.

EYOLF: Where did you see her?

ASTA: On the road, outside the town.

ALLMERS: I saw her too, out in the countryside.

RITA *(seated on the sofa)*: Perhaps we shall see her too, then, Eyolf.

EYOLF: Aunt, isn't it strange that she should be called the Rat Wife?

ASTA: People call her that because she goes round the country and drives away all the rats.

ALLMERS: I believe her real name is Mother Lupus.

EYOLF: Lupus? That means a wolf, doesn't it?

ALLMERS *(strokes him affectionately on the head)*: What a lot of things you know, Eyolf.

EYOLF: Then perhaps it may be true after all that she turns into a werewolf at night. Do you think it is, father?

ALLMERS: No, I don't think so. Now, why don't you go out and play in the garden?

EYOLF: Oughtn't I to take some of my books with me?

ALLMERS: No, no more books from now on. Off you go down to the shore and play with the other boys.

EYOLF *(embarrassed)*: No, father. I don't want to go down and play with them today.

ALLMERS: Why not?

EYOLF: Because of my clothes.

ALLMERS *(frowns):* Do they make fun of—of your fine clothes?

EYOLF *(evasively):* No, they wouldn't dare to do that. If they did I should beat them.

ALLMERS: Well, then, why—?

EYOLF: I don't like them. And they say I can never become a soldier.

ALLMERS *(with suppressed anger):* Why do they say that?

EYOLF: I think they envy me. They're so poor, father, that they have to go barefoot.

ALLMERS *(quietly):* Ah, Rita. How this gnaws at my heart!

RITA *(rises to calm him):* Now, now, now!

ALLMERS *(grimly):* These boys shall know one day who is the master down there.

ASTA *(listens):* Someone is knocking.

EYOLF: It must be Borghejm!

RITA: Come in!

> THE RAT WIFE *comes softly in through the door on the right. She is a little, thin, shrivelled old woman, grey-haired, with sharp, piercing eyes, wearing an old-fashioned flowered dress, with a black bonnet and a black cloak with tassels. She carries a large, red umbrella, and from her arm a black bag dangles on a string.*

EYOLF *(clutching* ASTA'*s skirt, whispers):* Aunt! This must be her!

RAT WIFE *(curtseys at the door):* Begging your pardon—have your honours any troublesome thing that gnaws here in this house?

ALLMERS: Have we—? No, I don't think so.

RAT WIFE: Ah. I'd be glad to rid you of it, if there was any gnawing thing that troubled you.

RITA: We understand. But we have nothing like that in this house.

RAT WIFE: That's a great pity. For I'm on my round, and who knows when I shall pass this way again? Ah, but I'm tired.

ALLMERS *(indicates a chair):* Yes, indeed, you look tired.

RAT WIFE: Poor little creatures. Everyone hates them. After them the whole time. It oughtn't to be tiring, helping them, being kind to them. But it drains a body's strength.

RITA: Sit down and rest yourself, old woman.

RAT WIFE: Thank you, gracious lady. A thousand thanks. *(She sits on a chair between the door and the sofa.)* The whole night I've been about my business.

ALLMERS: Have you? Where?

RAT WIFE: Over on the islands. *(Chuckles.)* The people there sent for me. They didn't want to. But they had no choice. They had to bury their teeth in the sour apple. *(Looks at EYOLF and nods.)* Sour apple, little master. Sour apple.

EYOLF *(involuntarily):* Why did they have to—

RAT WIFE: Have to what, little master?

EYOLF: Bury their teeth in the sour apple.

RAT WIFE: Why, because they couldn't get anything to fill their bellies with. Because of the rats and all the hungry little baby rats, you understand, young master.

RITA: Poor, wretched people! Were they so plagued by them?

RAT WIFE: Plagued? *(Laughs.)* Thousands of them, swarming, teeming. *(Smiles with quiet satisfaction.)* Up in the beds they crawled and crept the whole night long. They plopped down into the milk churns. And over the floors they hissed and rustled, this way, that way.

EYOLF *(aside, to ASTA):* I never want to go there, aunt.

RAT WIFE: But then *I* came—I and another. And we took them all away with us. The sweet, small creatures. We made an end of every one of them.

EYOLF *(shrieks):* Father! Look! Look!

RITA: For God's sake, Eyolf, what's the matter?

451

EYOLF *(points):* Something's struggling in her bag!

RITA *(goes left, with a scream):* Ugh! Get rid of her, Alfred!

RAT WIFE *(laughs):* Ah, dear lady, don't be afraid of such a harmless little creature.

ALLMERS: What have you got there?

RAT WIFE: It's only Mopsemand. *(Unfastens the strings of her bag.)* Come up from your darkness, my little lovely.

> *A small dog with a broad, black nose sticks its head out of the bag.*

RAT WIFE *(nods and beckons to* EYOLF*):* Don't be afraid, my little wounded soldier. Come close and stroke him. He won't bite you. Come and stroke him. Come and stroke him.

EYOLF *(close to* ASTA*):* No. I daren't.

RAT WIFE: Doesn't my young master think Mopsemand has a lovely, gentle face?

EYOLF *(points, amazed):* Him?

RAT WIFE: Yes, dearie, him.

EYOLF *(half to himself, staring intently at the dog):* I think he has—the most horrible face I have ever seen.

RAT WIFE *(closes her bag):* You'll change your mind, dearie. You'll change your mind.

EYOLF *(draws close to her, and strokes the bag lightly):* And at the same time he's beautiful. Beautiful.

RAT WIFE *(solicitously):* But just now he's so tired and full of aches and pains, the poor creature. So dreadfully tired he is. *(Looks at* ALLMERS.*)* It drains a body's strength—that kind of game.

ALLMERS: What game?

RAT WIFE: Why—*(laughs)*—follow my leader.

ALLMERS: Ah—and is this dog of yours the one who lures and leads them?

RAT WIFE *(nods):* Mopsemand and I, we lead them. We work together, he and I. Easiest thing in the world, you'd think, to watch us. I just tie a string to his collar and lead him three times round the house. While I do this, I play on my pipe. And when they hear me play, up they have to come from the cellars, down from the lofts, out of all their dark holes and crannies—all of them, bless their little hearts.

EYOLF: And then he bites them all to death?

RAT WIFE: No. We just go down to the boat, he and I. And they come after us. The big grown ones, and their little darlings with them.

EYOLF: And then? What happens?

RAT WIFE: Well, we draw away from the land. I pull at the oars, and play on my pipe. And Mopsemand swims behind me. *(Her eyes flash.)* And all the little creatures that crept and crawled, they follow us further and further out to the deep waters. They have to.

EYOLF: Why do they have to?

RAT WIFE: Because they don't want to. Because they're so afraid of the deep water—that's why they have to swim out to it.

EYOLF: And then they drown?

RAT WIFE: Every single one. *(More softly.)* And then they've all the dark and quiet and peace they could wish for, little angels. Down there they sleep so sweet, so long a sleep. All the little creatures men hate and persecute. *(She gets up.)* In the old days I needed no Mopsemand. I used to lure them myself. Alone.

EYOLF: What did you lure?

RAT WIFE: Men. One specially.

EYOLF: Who? Oh, tell me!

RAT WIFE *(smiles):* Why, my sweetheart, little lady's man.

EYOLF: Where is he now?

RAT WIFE *(spitefully):* Down among the rats. *(Amiably again.)* But now it's time for me to be about my business again. *(To* RITA*)* Are you sure you've no work for me to-day? I could get it done at once.

RITA: No, thank you, I don't think we need your services to-day.

RAT WIFE: You think so? Well, one can never be sure. If you should happen to remember anything that nibbles and gnaws, creeps and crawls, just send for me and Mopse-mand. Fare ye well!

She goes out through the door, right.

EYOLF *(to* ASTA*):* Now I've seen the Rat Wife, too!

RITA goes out on to the verandah and fans herself with her handkerchief. A moment later EYOLF slips unnoticed out through the door on the right.

ALLMERS *(takes the portfolio from the table by the sofa):* Is this your portfolio, Asta?

ASTA: Yes, I've got some of those old letters in it.

ALLMERS: Oh, our family letters?

ASTA: Don't you remember? You asked me to go through them while you were away.

ALLMERS *(pats her head):* Did you really manage to find the time?

ASTA: Yes. I did some of it here and some at home. In town.

ALLMERS: Thank you. Did you find anything of interest in them?

ASTA *(casually):* Oh, one always finds something of interest in old letters. *(More quietly, serious.)* The ones in the portfolio are my mother's.

ALLMERS: You must keep them, of course.

ASTA *(with an effort):* No, I'd like you to look through them too, Alfred. Some time—later. I haven't brought the key of the portfolio with me today.

ALLMERS: Never mind, my dear. I shan't want to read your mother's letters.

ASTA *(looks pointedly at him):* One quiet evening I will tell you something they contain.

ALLMERS: Yes, do that. But keep your mother's letters. You haven't so many reminders of her.

Hands the portfolio to ASTA. *She takes it and puts it on the chair, under her overcoat.* RITA *comes back into the room.*

RITA: Ugh! That horrid old woman! She's brought the smell of death into the house.

ALLMERS: She was rather horrible, wasn't she?

RITA: I felt quite ill while she was in the room.

ALLMERS: You know, I can understand that power of compelling and drawing things that she spoke of. Being alone in the mountains, up on those huge, open spaces—one feels that power.

ASTA *(glances sharply at him):* What has happened to you, Alfred?

ALLMERS *(smiles):* Happened?

ASTA: Something has happened. You're changed. Rita knows it, too.

RITA: Yes. I knew at once. But that's good, isn't it, Alfred?

ALLMERS: I hope so. Something good must come from it.

RITA: Something happened to you while you were away. Don't deny it. I can see it.

ALLMERS *(shakes his head):* Nothing happened *to* me. But—

RITA *(tensely):* But—?

ALLMERS: *In* me, something happened. A kind of transformation.

RITA: Oh, God!

ALLMERS *(pats her hand reassuringly):* Only for the better, Rita dear. Believe me.

RITA *(sits on the sofa):* Now you must tell us all about it. Absolutely everything.

ALLMERS *(turns to* ASTA*):* Yes. Let's sit down, and I'll try to tell you. As well as I can.

He sits on the sofa beside RITA. ASTA *brings forward a chair and sits on it near him. Short pause.*

RITA *(looks expectantly at him):* Well?

ALLMERS: When I look back on my life—the road I have taken—these past ten years, it seems almost like a fairy-tale, or a dream. Don't you think so, Asta?

ASTA: Yes, I think so. In many ways.

ALLMERS *(continues):* When I think what we were, Asta. Two orphans—without a penny.

RITA *(impatiently):* Oh, that's so long ago.

ALLMERS *(not listening):* And now I sit here, comfortable, prosperous. Able to follow my calling; to work and study, just as I please. *(Stretches out his hand.)* And all this unbelievable, unlooked-for happiness we owe to you, my dearest Rita.

RITA *(half in jest, half in spite of herself, smacks his hand):* Now that's enough of that silly talk!

ALLMERS: I mention this only as a kind of preamble.

RITA: Well, let's take it as read.

ALLMERS: Rita—don't think it was the doctor's advice that drove me up to the mountains.

ASTA: Not the doctor?

RITA: What was it, then?

ALLMERS: I couldn't find peace to write any more.

RITA: No peace? But, my dear, who disturbed you?

ALLMERS *(shakes his head):* No one disturbed me. I just came to feel that I was really misusing—well—no, neglecting—my true gifts. That I was wasting time.

ASTA *(her eyes wide):* In writing?

ALLMERS *(nods):* Don't you see—I wasn't put here just to write. There must be something I can *do* as well.

RITA: And that was what you were brooding over?

ALLMERS: Yes. Mostly.

RITA: Then that's why you've been so discontented with yourself these last months. And with us, too. Oh, yes you were, Alfred.

ALLMERS *(looking straight ahead):* I sat there bent over my desk, writing, day after day. Nights as well. Writing and writing my great, thick book on "The Responsibility of Man." Hm!

ASTA *(puts her hand on his arm):* But, my dear—that book is your life's work.

RITA: Yes, you've said so often enough.

ALLMERS: It was going to be. Or so I thought. From the time I grew up. *(With a warm expression in his eyes.)* Then you made it possible for me to devote myself to it, my dearest Rita.

RITA: What nonsense you talk!

ALLMERS *(smiles at her):* You with "your gold and your green forests"—

RITA *(half smiling, half vexed):* If you go on talking like that I shall smack you!

ASTA *(stares at him, worried):* But the book, Alfred?

ALLMERS: Somehow it began to seem less and less important. And the claim of higher duties began to fill my mind.

RITA *(takes his hand, her eyes radiant):* Alfred!

ALLMERS: I am thinking of Eyolf, my dear.

RITA *(lets go his hand):* Oh. Eyolf.

ALLMERS: He is always in my mind. Since that tragic fall from the table— And especially now that we know he can never be cured—

RITA: But you do everything you can for him, Alfred.

ALLMERS: As a schoolmaster, perhaps. But not as a father. From now on I want to be a father to Eyolf.

RITA *(stares at him and shakes her head):* I don't think I quite understand you.

ALLMERS: I mean I am going to do everything in my power to help him to come to terms with the irrevocable, and live with it.

RITA: But, Alfred, thank God I don't think Eyolf feels so deeply about it.

ASTA *(emotionally):* Yes, Rita. He does.

ALLMERS: Yes; you may be sure he feels it deeply.

RITA *(impatiently):* But, Alfred, what more can you do for him?

ALLMERS: I want to try to reveal the potential of the dreams which are dawning in his childish mind. To nurture those high hopes so that they flower and come to fruition. *(With increasing ardour, rising to his feet.)* I want to do more than that. I want to help him to shape his ambitions towards goals that lie within his reach. As he is now, he longs only for the things he can never attain. I want to put happiness within his grasp.

He paces once or twice up and down the room. ASTA *and* RITA *watch him.*

RITA: Shouldn't you take these things more calmly, Alfred?

ALLMERS *(stands at the table on the left and looks at them):* Eyolf shall take up my life's work. If he so wishes. Or he may choose to attempt something which shall be completely and entirely his. Perhaps that would be best. In any case, I shall write no more.

RITA *(rises):* But, Alfred dearest—can't you work both for yourself and for Eyolf?

ALLMERS: No! Impossible! In this matter, I cannot divide myself. Therefore I prefer to yield. Eyolf shall be the one of our family to fulfil himself. And it shall be my task to bring him to self-fulfilment.

ASTA *(has risen and goes over to him):* It has been a hard struggle for you, Alfred. To come to this decision.

ALLMERS: It has. Here, at home, I would never have been

able to conquer myself. I would never have been able to force myself to renounce anything. Not in this house.

RITA: Was that why you went away this summer?

ALLMERS *(his eyes shining):* Yes! I climbed up into an infinite solitude. I saw the sun rise above the mountain tops. I felt—nearer the stars—almost as if I understood them, and belonged with them. Then I was—able to do it.

ASTA *(looks at him sadly):* But will you never carry on with "The Responsibility of Man"?

ALLMERS: No, never. I have told you I cannot divide myself between two tasks. I shall fulfil my ideal of human responsibility through my own life.

RITA *(with a smile):* Do you really believe you will be able to stay faithful to such high ideals in this house?

ALLMERS *(takes her hand):* With your help, Rita. *(Stretches out his other hand.)* And with yours, Asta.

RITA *(withdraws her hand):* Then you can divide yourself, after all.

ALLMERS: But, my dearest—

> RITA *turns away from him and goes to the french windows. There is a quick tap on the door and* BORGHEJM *comes briskly in. He is a young man of thirty-odd, with a bright, cheerful face and an easy, upright bearing.*

BORGHEJM: Good morning, good morning, Mrs. Allmers. *(Stops short with delight as he sees* ALLMERS.*)* Well, well! What's this? Home again already, Mr. Allmers?

ALLMERS *(shakes his hand):* Yes. I came last night.

RITA *(gaily):* His leave was up, Mr. Borghejm.

ALLMERS: Rita's joking.

RITA *(comes towards them):* Joking? It's the truth. His leave had expired.

BORGHEJM: You keep your husband on a tight rein, Mrs. Allmers.

RITA: I insist on my rights. In any case, everything has to come to an end some time.

BORGHEJM: Oh, not everything—I hope. Good morning, Miss Allmers.

ASTA *(avoiding his eyes):* Good morning.

RITA *(looks at* BORGHEJM*):* Not everything, did you say?

BORGHEJM: I do believe there is at least one thing in this world which need not come to an end.

RITA: I see. You're thinking of love, and that kind of thing.

BORGHEJM: I am thinking of all that is lovely and unforgettable—

RITA: And that will never end? Yes, let us hope so for all our sakes.

ALLMERS *(goes over to them):* I suppose you will soon have finished this road you've been building here?

BORGHEJM: I have finished it. Yesterday. It's taken a long time. Thank heaven that came to an end!

RITA: And that's why you are so cock-a-hoop this morning?

BORGHEJM: Yes.

RITA: Well, I must say—!

BORGHEJM: What, Mrs. Allmers?

RITA: That's not very nice of you, Mr. Borghejm.

BORGHEJM: Oh? Why not?

RITA: Well, it means you won't be seeing very much more of us.

BORGHEJM: No, that's true. I hadn't thought of that.

RITA: Still, I suppose you'll be able to visit us now and then.

BORGHEJM: I'm afraid that won't be possible. For a long time.

ALLMERS: Oh? Why not?

BORGHEJM: I've just been given an important new contract which I have to start work on at once.

ALLMERS: No, have you? *(Presses his hand.)* I'm delighted to hear it.

RITA: Congratulations, Mr. Borghejm, congratulations.

BORGHEJM: Sssh! I'm not meant to be talking about it yet. But I can't keep it to myself. It's a big road that's to be built up in the north. Mountains to negotiate. Extraordinary obstacles to overcome. *(Exclaims)* Oh, it's a marvellous life to build new roads!

RITA *(smiles and looks teasingly at him):* Is it just this new road that brings you out here to see us today in such high spirits?

BORGHEJM: No, not only that. The whole future seems so full of hope and promise.

RITA *(in the same tone as before):* Perhaps there's something even more marvellous lying ahead?

BORGHEJM *(glances at* ASTA*):* Who knows? When fortune comes, she comes like the spring floods. *(Turns to* ASTA.*)* Miss Allmers, shall we two take a little stroll together? As usual?

ASTA *(quickly):* No. No, thank you. Not now. Not today.

BORGHEJM: Ah, please! Just for a few minutes. I've so many things I want to say to you before I go.

RITA: Something else you mustn't talk about yet, perhaps?

BORGHEJM: I—er—

RITA: Well, things that cannot be talked about may sometimes be whispered. *(Aside to* ASTA*)* Go with him, Asta.

ASTA: But, Rita—

BORGHEJM *(pleadingly):* Miss Asta—remember this will be our last walk together.

ASTA *(takes her hat and parasol):* Well, let us take a short stroll in the garden, then.

BORGHEJM: Thank you—thank you!

ALLMERS: You might keep a look out for Eyolf while you're down there.

BORGHEJM: Eyolf? Why, yes. Where is Eyolf today? I've brought something for him.

ALLMERS: He's playing somewhere down there.

461

BORGHEJM: Really? So he's started to play now? He usually just sits indoors reading.

ALLMERS: I'm going to change all that now. I want him to spend a lot of time out of doors.

BORGHEJM: Quite right! Let him have his share of the free air too, poor little fellow! Good God, the best thing we can do in this blessed world is to play. I sometimes think our whole life is a game. Come, Miss Asta.

BORGHEJM *and* ASTA *go out on to the verandah and down into the garden.*

ALLMERS *(stands looking after them)*: Rita, do you think there is anything between those two?

RITA: I don't know what to think. I used to believe there was. But Asta's been behaving so strangely these last weeks—almost as though she'd become a stranger to me.

ALLMERS: Really? While I've been away, you mean?

RITA: Yes, these last weeks.

ALLMERS: You don't think she's really interested in him?

RITA: Not seriously. Not with her heart and soul—ruthlessly. No, I don't think she's seriously interested in him now. *(Looks searchingly at him.)* Would it upset you if she was?

ALLMERS: Not upset me, exactly. I can't deny that it would worry me a little, though.

RITA: Worry you?

ALLMERS: Remember I am responsible for Asta. And for her happiness.

RITA: Nonsense! Responsible? Asta isn't a child. She's old enough to know whom to choose for herself, I should have thought.

ALLMERS: Yes, let us hope she is, Rita.

RITA: I see no harm in Borghejm.

ALLMERS: No, my dear, neither do I. Rather the reverse. And yet—

RITA *(continues):* And I should be very happy to see him and Asta married.

ALLMERS *(not pleased):* Would you? Why?

RITA *(with increasing emotion):* Because she'd have to go far away with him, and then she could never come and visit us again!

ALLMERS *(stares amazed at her):* What? You mean you want to be rid of Asta?

RITA: Yes, Alfred, yes!

ALLMERS: But why—?

RITA *(throws her arms passionately round his neck):* Yes! Then I would have you to myself at last! No—not even then! Not to myself! *(She begins to cry hysterically.)* Oh, Alfred, Alfred! I can't let you go!

ALLMERS *(frees himself gently):* Rita, my dear. Be reasonable.

RITA: No, I don't want to be reasonable! I only want you! Nothing else, in all the world! *(Throws herself again round his neck.)* I want you, you, you!

ALLMERS: Let me go! You're strangling me!

RITA *(releases him):* I wish I could! *(She looks at him with flashing eyes.)* Oh, if only you knew how I have hated you—

ALLMERS: Hated me?

RITA: Yes. When you sat alone in there, brooding over your work. Deep into the night. *(Complainingly.)* So long, and so late, Alfred. Oh, how I've hated that work of yours!

ALLMERS: But now I am finished with it.

RITA *(laughs jarringly):* Yes. And now you are preoccupied with something even more hateful.

ALLMERS: Hateful? You call our child hateful?

RITA *(violently):* I do! For what he has done to us! Your book had no face, no voice, but this child is a living wall between us. [*(Her voice rises.)* I won't stand for it, Alfred! I won't stand for it, I tell you!

ALLMERS *(looks steadily at her, then says quietly):* Sometimes you almost frighten me, Rita.

RITA: Sometimes I frighten myself. Don't rouse the demon in me, Alfred.

ALLMERS: In heaven's name—do I do that?

RITA: Yes! When you destroy what is most sacred between us.]

ALLMERS: Rita, be reasonable. It's your child—our only child—we're talking about.

RITA: The child is only half mine. *(Bursts out)* But you—you shall be mine—all mine—only mine! I demand it. It's my right.

ALLMERS *(shrugs his shoulders):* My dear Rita, it's no use demanding. These things can only be given freely.

RITA: And from now on you are unable to do that?

ALLMERS: Yes. I must divide myself between Eyolf and you.

RITA: But if Eyolf had never been born?

ALLMERS *(defensively):* That would have been different. Then I would have had only you to love.

RITA *(quietly trembling):* Then I wish to God I had never borne him!

ALLMERS: Rita! You don't know what you're saying!

RITA: I gave birth to him in unimaginable pain. But I endured it gladly—for your sake.

ALLMERS *(warmly):* Yes, yes. I know you did.

RITA: But that's over and done with. I want to *live.* With you. Just you and I. I can't be just a mother. Eyolf's mother and nothing else. I will not, I tell you—I cannot. I want to be everything to you. To you, Alfred.

ALLMERS: But you are, Rita. Through our child—

RITA: Oh! Sickening, stale phrases! No, that's not for me. I was made to bear your child; but not to act the mother to it. You must take me as I am, Alfred.

ALLMERS: But you were always so fond of Eyolf.

RITA: I pitied him. Because you gave him no love or kindness; made him read until his eyes ached; hardly spent an hour with him.

ALLMERS *(nods slowly):* I was blind. I had not yet come to realize—

RITA: But now you have?

ALLMERS: Yes; at last. Now I see that the highest duty open to me in this world is to be a true father to Eyolf.

RITA: And to me? What are you going to be to me?

ALLMERS *(gently):* I shall go on loving you, Rita. With all my soul. *(He tries to take her hands.)*

RITA *(avoids him):* I'm not interested in your soul! I want you—all of you—to myself—the way it used to be in those first, few, unforgettable years— *(Viciously.)* I will never let myself be fobbed off with the scraps of love.

ALLMERS *(gently):* Surely there is enough happiness to share between the three of us?

RITA *(contemptuously):* Then you can't want much. *(Sits at the table, left.)* Listen.

ALLMERS *(comes closer):* Well? What is it?

RITA *(looks up at him with a dull glow in her eyes):* When I got your telegram last night—

ALLMERS: Yes?

RITA: I dressed in white—

ALLMERS: Yes. I noticed you were wearing white when I arrived.

RITA: I let down my hair—

ALLMERS: It smells so sweetly—

RITA: So that it streamed down over my back and shoulders—

ALLMERS: I know. I know. Oh, you were beautiful, Rita.

RITA: I put rose-coloured shades over both lamps. We were alone—just you and I awake in the whole house. And there was champagne on the table.

ALLMERS: I didn't have any.

RITA *(bitterly):* True; you didn't. "The champagne stood there, but who raised his glass?" As the poet said.

She gets up from the armchair, goes as though tired to the sofa and half sits, half lies on it.

ALLMERS *(goes across and stands in front of her):* I [was full of serious thoughts. I] needed to talk to you about our future. Above all, about Eyolf.

RITA *(smiles):* And so you did, my dear.

ALLMERS: No. I wasn't able to. You started to undress yourself.

RITA: Yes. And while I undressed myself, you talked about Eyolf. Remember? You asked me how little Eyolf's stomach was.

ALLMERS: Rita!

RITA: And then you lay down in your bed. And slept like a child.

ALLMERS *(shakes his head):* Rita.

RITA *(lies down full length and looks up at him):* Alfred?

ALLMERS: Yes?

RITA: "The champagne stood there, but who raised his glass?"

ALLMERS *(in a hard voice):* I left it—untouched.

He turns from her and goes to the french windows. RITA lies for some seconds motionless, her eyes closed.

RITA *(suddenly leaps to her feet):* But let me tell you something, Alfred.

ALLMERS *(turns at the window):* What?

RITA: Don't be too sure of yourself.

ALLMERS: Sure of myself?

RITA: You take things too much for granted. You're too sure that you have me.

ALLMERS *(comes closer):* What do you mean?

RITA *(with trembling lips):* I have never been unfaithful to you, Alfred—even in my thoughts—not for a moment—

ALLMERS: I know, Rita. I know you so well—

RITA *(with flashing eyes):* But if you should turn your back on me—

ALLMERS: Turn my back on you? I don't understand what you mean—

RITA: You don't know what I might do if—

ALLMERS: If?

RITA: If I should ever believe that you no longer cared for me—loved me as you used to do—

ALLMERS: But, my dearest Rita—people change with the years—and it must happen to us also—it does to everyone.

RITA: Not to me. And I won't have any change in you either. I couldn't stand it. I want to keep you all to myself.

ALLMERS *(looks troubled at her):* Your jealousy is terrible—

RITA: I can't change. I am what I am. *(Threateningly.)* If you divide yourself between me and anyone else—

ALLMERS: Well?

RITA: I would have my revenge on you, Alfred.

ALLMERS: How could you have your revenge?

RITA: I don't know. Yes. I do know.

ALLMERS: How?

RITA: I would throw myself into the arms of the first man who comes along.

ALLMERS *(looks warmly at her, and shakes his head):* That you could never do—my proud, faithful Rita!

RITA *(puts her arms round his neck):* Oh, you don't know what I could do, if you stopped loving me.

ALLMERS: Stopped loving you? How can you say such a thing?

RITA *(half laughing, lets him go):* I could, for example, spread my nets for that builder of roads who is walking in our garden.

ALLMERS *(relieved):* Thank heavens! For a moment I thought you were being serious.

RITA: So I am. Why not him? As well as the next man?

ALLMERS: But—! In any case, he's already—

RITA: So much the better! If I took him from someone else. That's exactly what Eyolf has done to me.

ALLMERS: How can you say that Eyolf has done that?

RITA *(points her finger at him):* You see! You see! As soon as you even mention Eyolf's name, your voice becomes soft and trembles. *(Threateningly, clasping her hands together.)* Oh, I could almost wish—!

ALLMERS *(looks at her, frightened):* What would you wish, Rita?

RITA *(violently, moves away from him):* No, no, no! I won't tell you. Ever.

ALLMERS *(goes closer to her):* Rita, I beg of you, for both our sakes—do not let yourself be tempted to anything evil.

BORGHEJM *and* ASTA *come up from the garden. Both are disturbed, but controlled. They look serious and downcast.* ASTA *remains on the verandah.* BORGHEJM *comes into the room.*

BORGHEJM: Well, Miss Allmers and I have taken our last walk together.

RITA *(looks at him in surprise):* You won't be—taking a longer journey?

BORGHEJM: I shall, yes.

RITA: Alone?

BORGHEJM: Yes, alone.

RITA *(glances at* ALLMERS*):* You hear that, Alfred? *(Turns to* BORGHEJM*.)* I wouldn't mind betting some evil eye has played you a trick here.

BORGHEJM *(stares, amazed):* Evil eye?

RITA *(nods):* Yes.

468

BORGHEJM: Do you believe in the evil eye, Mrs. Allmers?

RITA: I am beginning to. Or anyway in the evil that lies in a child's eye.

ALLMERS *(shocked, whispers):* How can you—?

RITA *(half aloud):* It is you who are making me like this, Alfred.

Confused shouts and screams are heard in the distance, down by the water.

BORGHEJM *(goes to the french windows):* What is that noise?

ASTA *(on the verandah):* Look at all those people running out on the jetty.

ALLMERS: What is it? *(Glances out.)* Those guttersnipes up to something again, I suppose.

BORGHEJM *(shouts down from the verandah):* Hi, you boys! What's going on down there?

Several voices are heard simultaneously, making indistinct reply.

RITA: What are they saying?

BORGHEJM: They say a child has been drowned.

ALLMERS: A child drowned?

ASTA *(uneasily):* A little boy, they say.

ALLMERS: But they can all swim.

RITA *(cries suddenly in fear):* Where is Eyolf?

ALLMERS: Don't worry. Eyolf's playing in the garden.

ASTA: No. He wasn't when we were there.

RITA *(clasps her hands to her head):* Don't let it be him!

BORGHEJM *(listens and shouts down):* Whose child is it, did you say?

Indistinct voices are heard. BORGHEJM *and* ASTA *utter a suppressed cry and run down through the garden.*

ALLMERS *(in anguish):* It isn't Eyolf. It isn't Eyolf, Rita.

RITA *(on the verandah, listening):* Hush! Be quiet! Let me

hear what they are saying. *(She listens for a moment, then gives a dreadful scream and turns back into the room.)*

ALLMERS: What did they say?

RITA *(sinks down into the armchair):* They said: "The crutch is floating."

ALLMERS *(stunned):* No! No!

RITA: Eyolf! Eyolf! Oh, God! They must save him!

ALLMERS *(distraught):* They must, they must! So precious a life! So precious a life!

He runs down through the garden.

ACT TWO

A small, narrow glen in the forest on ALLMERS'S *estate, down by the shore. On the left, old, tall trees lean out over the scene. Down the slope in the background a stream gushes, losing itself among the stones on the edge of the wood. A path winds alongside the stream. To the right stand a few trees, through which the fjord can be seen. In the foreground can be seen the corner of the boathouse, with a boat drawn up. Beneath the old trees on the left stands a table, with a bench and a few chairs, all made of slender birchwood. It is a heavy day, pregnant with rain, and with low, drifting clouds.*

> ALFRED ALLMERS, *dressed as before, is seated on the bench, with his arms resting on the table. His hat lies in front of him. He is motionless, staring abstractedly out over the water. After a few moments,* ASTA ALLMERS *comes down the path. She is carrying an open umbrella.*

ASTA *(comes quietly up to him):* You ought not to sit here in this grey weather, Alfred.

> ALLMERS *nods slowly.*

ASTA *(shuts her umbrella):* I've been looking for you for such a long time.

471

ALLMERS *(expressionlessly):* Thank you.

ASTA *(moves a chair and sits next to him):* Have you been sitting here long? The whole time?

ALLMERS *(does not at first reply. Then he says):* No. I don't understand it. It seems so—impossible. All this.

ASTA *(puts her hand on his arm):* Poor Alfred.

ALLMERS *(stares at her):* Has it really happened, Asta? Or have I gone mad? Or am I dreaming? Oh, if only it were a dream! How beautiful if I could wake up now!

ASTA: I wish I had the power to wake you.

ALLMERS *(stares out over the water):* How merciless the fjord looks today. Lying there so heavy . . . drowsy. Lead-grey, with flashes of yellow . . . reflecting the rain-clouds.

ASTA: Alfred, you mustn't sit here staring at the fjord.

ALLMERS *(not listening):* On the surface, yes. But deep down, there is the undertow.

ASTA *(frightened):* For God's sake don't think of that!

ALLMERS *(looks mildly at her):* You think he lies out here, don't you, Asta? But he doesn't. You needn't fear that. Remember how strong the current is here. Out to the open sea.

ASTA *(throws herself sobbing over the table, her hands covering her face):* Oh God! God!

ALLMERS: That is why little Eyolf has been taken so far—far away from us now.

ASTA: Don't talk like that, Alfred.

ALLMERS: You can work it out, you're so clever with figures. Twenty-eight hours, twenty-nine—let me see, let me see.

ASTA *(screams and puts her hands over her ears):* Alfred!

ALLMERS *(presses his fist hard against the table):* But can you see the meaning of it?

ASTA: Of what?

ALLMERS: Of what has been done to me and Rita.

ASTA: The meaning of it?

ALLMERS *(impatiently):* Yes, the meaning. There must be some meaning in it. Life, creation, providence—have they no meaning, no purpose at all?

ASTA: Oh, Alfred, how can we tell the purpose of these things?

ALLMERS *(laughs bitterly):* No, no, indeed. Perhaps it's all haphazard. Things take their own course, like a wrecked ship drifting. Perhaps that's how it is. It seems so, anyway.

ASTA *(quietly):* What if it only seems?

ALLMERS *(sharply):* Oh? Perhaps you can give me a better answer? For my part, I see none. *(More gently.)* Here is Eyolf, on the threshold of discovering life. Potent with promise—such rich promise. He was to fill my life with pride and joy. And then it only needs a crazy old hag to come to the house and dangle a dog in a sack—

ASTA: But, Alfred, we don't know for certain *how* it happened.

ALLMERS: Oh, yes. We know. The boys saw her row out over the fjord. They saw Eyolf standing alone on the end of the jetty, staring after her. Suddenly he—seemed to become giddy. And then he fell—and disappeared.

ASTA: I know. But—

ALLMERS: She dragged him down into the deep. I'm sure of it.

ASTA: But, my dear—why should she?

ALLMERS: Exactly. Why should she? It can't be retribution; there's nothing to atone for. Eyolf never did her any harm. Never shouted abuse at her, never threw a stone at her dog. He had never set eyes on her or the dog before yesterday. So it can't be retribution. How senseless it is; how absolutely meaningless, Asta. And yet it seems to serve the purposes of providence.

ASTA: Have you talked about this with Rita?

ALLMERS *(shakes his head):* I seem to find it easier to talk to you about it. As about everything else.

ASTA takes her sewing things and a small package wrapped in paper from her pocket. ALLMERS sits watching her abstractedly.

ALLMERS: What's that you have there, Asta?

ASTA *(takes his hat):* Only some crape.

ALLMERS: Is it necessary?

ASTA: Rita asked me to do it. May I?

ALLMERS: I see. By all means. *(She begins to sew the crape on to his hat.)* Where is Rita?

ASTA: Walking in the garden, I believe. Borghejm is with her.

ALLMERS *(mildly surprised):* Oh? Is Borghejm out here today?

ASTA: Yes. He came by the noon train.

ALLMERS: Oh, I didn't expect him to take the trouble.

ASTA *(as she sews):* He was very fond of Eyolf.

ALLMERS: Borghejm is good and loyal.

ASTA *(warmly):* Yes. You are right. He is loyal.

ALLMERS *(looks at her):* You are fond of him, aren't you?

ASTA: Yes. I am fond of him.

ALLMERS: But you can't—make up your mind to—?

ASTA *(cuts him short):* Oh, Alfred, don't let's talk about it.

ALLMERS: Very well. Only—tell me why—

ASTA: Oh, no, please don't ask me, Alfred. It's too distressing for me to talk about. Here, your hat's ready.

ALLMERS: Thank you.

ASTA: Now give me your left arm.

ALLMERS: Are you going to put crape on that, too?

ASTA: It's usual.

ALLMERS: As you wish.

She moves her chair closer to him and begins to sew crape on to his left sleeve.

ASTA: Keep your arm still. Otherwise I shall prick you.

ALLMERS *(with a little smile):* This is like old times.

ASTA: Yes, isn't it?

ALLMERS: You used to sit like this mending my clothes when you were a little girl.

ASTA: I wasn't very good at it.

ALLMERS: I remember, the first thing you ever sewed for me was a piece of black crape.

ASTA: Oh?

ALLMERS: On my student cap. When father died.

ASTA: Did I really? I don't remember.

ALLMERS: Of course not. You were only a child then.

ASTA: Yes, I was only a child.

ALLMERS: Then, two years later—when your mother died— you sewed a big black band on my arm.

ASTA: I thought you ought to have one.

ALLMERS *(pats her hand):* Yes, yes, quite right. And afterwards, when we two were left alone in the world—have you finished already?

ASTA: Yes. *(She gathers her sewing things together.)* It turned out to be a happy time for us after all, Alfred. Just the two of us.

ALLMERS: Yes, it did. It was a hard struggle, though.

ASTA: It was for you.

ALLMERS *(livelier):* It was a struggle for you too, Asta. *(Smiles.)* Dear, faithful—Eyolf.

ASTA: Oh, don't remind me of that nonsense.

ALLMERS: If you had been a boy, you would have been called Eyolf.

ASTA: If—yes. But then when you went to the university— *(She smiles involuntarily.)* To think you could have been so childish.

ALLMERS: *I* was childish?

ASTA: Yes, now I look back on it. You were ashamed of not having any brother, only a sister.

475

ALLMERS: No, it was you who were ashamed.

ASTA: A little, perhaps. I felt—I don't know—somehow sorry for you.

ALLMERS: Yes, you must have done. You got out the old clothes I'd worn as a boy—

ASTA: Your best Sunday clothes. Do you remember that blue blouse? And the knee breeches?

ALLMERS *(his eyes linger on her):* How well I remember how you looked! When you put them on and walked round in them.

ASTA: I only did it when we were alone at home together.

ALLMERS: How solemn we were, and how seriously we took ourselves! And I would always call you Eyolf.

ASTA: Alfred, you haven't said anything about this to Rita, have you?

ALLMERS: I believe I mentioned it to her once, yes.

ASTA: Oh, Alfred! How could you?

ALLMERS: You know how it is. One tells one's wife everything—practically everything.

ASTA: I suppose one does.

ALLMERS *(as though suddenly waking, clasps his forehead and leaps to his feet):* Good God! How can I sit here and—!

ASTA *(rises concerned):* What is it?

ALLMERS: I almost forgot him. I forgot him—completely.

ASTA: Eyolf?

ALLMERS: I was sitting here, absorbed in my memories. And he wasn't there.

ASTA: No, Alfred, you're wrong! Litle Eyolf was there, in everything we said.

ALLMERS: He was not. He slipped right out of my mind. Out of my thoughts. I didn't see him for a moment while we were talking. All that while I forgot him completely.

ASTA: You must have some rest from your grief.

ALLMERS: No, no. That is just what I mustn't have. I have

476

no right to it; and no heart for it, either. *(Walks across, right.)* There is no place for me but the place where he lies, drifting down there in the dark.

ASTA *(goes after him and holds him back):* Alfred! Alfred! Don't go near the fjord.

ALLMERS: I must go to him. Let me go, Asta. Let me get to the boat.

ASTA *(in terror):* No, Alfred, no! Don't go near the fjord!

ALLMERS *(yielding):* No, no; I won't. Just leave me alone.

ASTA *(leads him back to the table):* You must let your mind rest, Alfred. Come and sit down with me again.

ALLMERS *(is about to sit on the bench):* Very well. As you wish, Asta.

ASTA: No, not there.

ALLMERS: Yes, let me sit here.

ASTA: No. When you sit there, you look over the— *(Presses him down on to a chair, facing left.)* Like that, now. That's better, isn't it? *(Sits on the bench.)* Now. Let's go on with what we were talking about before.

ALLMERS *(breathing audibly):* It was good to forget these sorrows for a moment.

ASTA: You must forget, Alfred.

ALLMERS: But don't you think me weak and unfeeling to be able to do so?

ASTA: Oh, no! One cannot circle round the same thought for ever.

ALLMERS: I can't, anyway. Before you came down to me just now, I was sitting here tormented by this haunting, gnawing grief—

ASTA: Yes?

ALLMERS: And then—can you believe it, Asta?—hm—

ASTA: What?

ALLMERS: In my agony, I suddenly found myself wondering what there was going to be for dinner today.

ASTA *(soothingly):* As long as it gave you comfort—

ALLMERS: Comfort? Yes, that is what I seemed to find. *(Reaches out his hand to her across the table.)* What a blessing I have you, Asta. It gives me such joy. Joy—in my sorrow—

ASTA *(looks seriously at him):* Your greatest joy should be Rita.

ALLMERS: Of course. But Rita is not of my blood. It is not the same as having a sister.

ASTA *(tensely):* Is that how you feel, Alfred?

ALLMERS: Yes. Our family is—something apart. *(Jokingly.)* Our Christian names always begin with a vowel. Do you remember how we used to talk about it? And all our relations are equally poor. And we all have the same eyes.

ASTA: But—I—

ALLMERS: Ah, Asta, you are your mother's child. You don't really look like one of us. Not even like father. And yet—

ASTA: Yet—?

ALLMERS: I was thinking that our life together has somehow made you and me resemble each other—mentally, I mean.

ASTA *(moved):* No, Alfred. It's I who've grown to resemble you. I owe everything to you—everything I value in the world.

ALLMERS *(shakes his head):* You owe me nothing, Asta. On the contrary—

ASTA: Yes, Alfred. I owe you everything. You should know that. No sacrifice has been too great—

ALLMERS: Sacrifice! What nonsense you talk, Asta. I have simply—loved you. Ever since you were a small child. *(Short pause.)* Besides, I always felt there was so much I had to make amends for. Not so much for what I'd done, as for father.

ASTA: Father—! What do you mean?

ALLMERS: Father was never very kind to you.

ASTA: You mustn't say that.

ALLMERS: It's true. He never loved you. As he should have done.

ASTA *(defensively):* Perhaps not as much as he loved you. But that was only to be expected.

ALLMERS: He was often unkind to your mother, too. During their last years together.

ASTA *(quietly):* You must remember mother was so very much younger than he.

ALLMERS: Do you think they weren't suited to each other?

ASTA: I think perhaps not.

ALLMERS: And yet father was always so kind and generous to everyone else—

ASTA *(quietly):* Mother wasn't always as she should have been.

ALLMERS: Your mother?

ASTA: Perhaps not always.

ALLMERS: To father?

ASTA: Yes.

ALLMERS: I never noticed anything.

ASTA *(rises, trying not to cry):* Oh, Alfred. Let the dead rest in peace. *(She crosses right.)*

ALLMERS *(rises):* Yes, let them rest. *(Clasps his hands.)* But the dead will not give us peace. Day and night they haunt us.

ASTA: It will seem less painful as time goes by.

ALLMERS: It must—mustn't it? But how I shall survive these first, ghastly days, I cannot imagine.

ASTA *(puts her hands on his shoulders):* Go up to Rita. I beg you.

ALLMERS *(frees himself):* No, no! Don't ask me to do that! I can't, don't you understand? I can't! *(More calmly.)* Let me stay here with you.

ASTA: All right. I won't leave you.

ALLMERS *(takes her hand and holds it tightly):* Thank you.

(Glances out for a moment across the fjord.) Where is my little Eyolf now? *(Smiles bitterly.)* Can you answer me that, my big, wise Eyolf? *(Shakes his head.)* No. No-one in the whole world can tell me that. I know only the one dreadful certainty, that I no longer have him.

ASTA *(glances up left, and withdraws her hand):* They are coming now.

RITA *comes down the path, with* BORGHEJM *following her. She is wearing dark clothes, with a veil over her face. He carries an umbrella.*

ALLMERS *(goes to meet her):* How are you, Rita?

RITA *(walks past him):* Need you ask?

ALLMERS: Why have you come down here?

RITA: Only to look for you. What are you doing?

ALLMERS: Nothing. Asta came down to sit with me.

RITA: Yes, but what were you doing before Asta came? You've been away from me the whole morning.

ALLMERS: I've been sitting here, looking out over the water.

RITA *(shudders):* How can you?

ALLMERS *(impatiently):* I prefer to be alone now.

RITA *(walking about restlessly):* Sitting in the same spot like a statue.

ALLMERS: I have no reason to go anywhere.

RITA: I can't stand it anywhere. Least of all here. With the fjord lapping one's feet.

ALLMERS: That's why I sit here. Because it is so near the fjord.

RITA *(to* BORGHEJM*):* Don't you think he should come up with the rest of us?

BORGHEJM *(to* ALLMERS*):* I think it would be better for you.

ALLMERS: No. Let me stay where I am.

RITA: In that case I shall stay with you.

ALLMERS: As you please. You stay too, Asta.

480

ASTA *(whispers to* BORGHEJM*):* Let's leave them alone together.

BORGHEJM *(nods):* Miss Allmers, shall we take a stroll along
the shore? For the very last time?

ASTA *(takes her umbrella):* Yes, let us.

> ASTA *and* BORGHEJM *go out together behind the boat-
> house.* ALLMERS *walks around for a little, then sits
> down on a stone under the trees, downstage left.*

RITA *(comes closer and stands in front of him with her hands
folded):* Alfred, is it possible that we have lost Eyolf?

ALLMERS: We must accustom ourselves to the thought.

RITA: I can't. I can't. That dreadful sight—I shall never forget it as long as I live.

ALLMERS *(looks up):* What sight? What have you seen?

RITA: I didn't see it myself. Only heard about it. Oh!

ALLMERS: Tell me.

RITA: I went with Borghejm down to the jetty—

ALLMERS: Why did you go there?

RITA: I wanted to question the boys about how it had happened.

ALLMERS: We know.

RITA: We know more now.

ALLMERS: What?

RITA: It isn't true that he disappeared at once.

ALLMERS: They say that now?

RITA: Yes. They say they saw him lying on the bottom.
Deep down in the clear water.

ALLMERS *(bitterly):* And they didn't save him?

RITA: I don't suppose there was anything they could do.

ALLMERS: They can swim. All of them.

RITA: They say he lay on his back. With his eyes wide open.

ALLMERS: With his eyes open? And quite still?

RITA: Yes, quite still. Then something came and carried him
out towards the sea. They called it the undertow.

ALLMERS *(nods slowly):* And that was the last they saw of him?

RITA: Yes.

ALLMERS: And no one will ever see him again.

RITA: Day and night I shall see him lying there.

ALLMERS: With his eyes wide open.

RITA: Yes. With those huge, open eyes. I can see them. I can see them now.

ALLMERS *(rises slowly and looks quietly but menacingly at her):* Were they evil eyes, Rita?

RITA *(turns pale):* Evil?

ALLMERS *(goes close to her):* Were they evil eyes staring up from the sea bed?

RITA *(shrinks from him):* Alfred!

ALLMERS *(follows her):* Answer me! Were the child's eyes evil?

RITA *(screams):* Alfred! Alfred!

ALLMERS: Now it is as you wished, Rita.

RITA I? What did I wish?

ALLMERS: That Eyolf should be out of the way.

RITA: Never for one moment did I wish that! I wished that he might not stand between us—yes—but—

ALLMERS: Well, he won't now, will he?

RITA *(quietly, to herself):* Perhaps now more than ever. *(Shudders.)* Oh, that dreadful sight!

ALLMERS *(nods):* Yes. The evil eye of a child.

RITA *(shrinks away from him fearfully):* Alfred! Leave me alone. You frighten me. I've never seen you like this before.

ALLMERS *(hard and cold):* Grief makes one cruel.

RITA *(frightened but still defiant):* Yes. It has made me so too.

ALLMERS *goes right, and looks out over the fjord.* RITA *sits at the table. Short pause.*

482

ALLMERS *(turns his head towards her)*: You never loved him. Not really.

RITA *(cold and controlled)*: Eyolf would never allow me to make him wholly mine.

ALLMERS: Because you never wanted him.

RITA: You are wrong. I did want him. But someone stood between us. From the first.

ALLMERS *(turns so that he stands facing her)*: You mean I stood between you?

RITA: Oh, no. Not in the beginning.

ALLMERS *(goes closer)*: Who, then?

RITA: His aunt.

ALLMERS: Asta?

RITA: Yes. Asta stood like a wall between Eyolf and me.

ALLMERS: You feel that?

RITA: Yes. Asta made him hers—right from the time it happened. The accident—

ALLMERS: If she did, she did it out of love.

RITA *(violently)*: Exactly. And I am not prepared to share with anyone. Not in love.

ALLMERS: You and I ought to have shared him. In love.

RITA *(looks scornfully at him)*: We? If it comes to that, you never really loved him either, Alfred.

ALLMERS: *I* never loved him?

RITA: No. You were only in love with your book. About—responsibility.

ALLMERS *(firmly)*: I was—preoccupied with that, it is true. But I gave it up. For Eyolf's sake.

RITA: But not because you loved him.

ALLMERS: What do you mean?

RITA: You gave it up because you were eaten up with self-distrust. You had begun to doubt whether you had any great calling to live for after all.

ALLMERS *(searchingly)*: Did I give you any cause to think that?

RITA: Oh, yes—in small things. And then you needed something new. I dare say I wasn't enough for you any longer.

ALLMERS: It is the law of change, Rita.

RITA: That was why you wanted to make poor little Eyolf into a child prodigy.

ALLMERS: That's not true. I wanted to make him—happy. That is all.

RITA: But not because you loved him. Look into yourself. *(With a certain shyness.)* And think of all that you have buried there, and would like to forget.

ALLMERS *(avoids her eyes):* You're trying to avoid the issue.

RITA: So are you.

ALLMERS *(looks thoughtfully at her):* If you are right in what you are thinking, our child never really belonged to us.

RITA: No. We never loved him.

ALLMERS: And yet we sit here bitterly mourning his loss.

RITA *(bitterly):* Yes. Isn't it odd? That we are sitting here mourning a little stranger boy.

ALLMERS: Rita, for God's sake! Don't call him a stranger!

RITA *(shakes her head):* We never won his love, Alfred. Neither you, nor I.

ALLMERS: And now it's too late. Too late. *(With sudden violence.)* It's you who are guilty!

RITA *(rises):* I?

ALLMERS: Yes! It's your fault that he became what he was! It's your fault he couldn't save himself when he fell into the water!

RITA *(defensively):* Alfred! Don't blame me for that!

ALLMERS: I do, I do! You know it's true! It was you who left that helpless baby unattended on the table—

RITA: He lay there so comfortably among the cushions. And slept so sweetly. And you had promised to keep an eye on him.

ALLMERS: That's right. *(Lowers his voice.)* And then you came—and tempted me in to you.

RITA *(defiantly):* Be a man and admit that you forgot the child, and everything else!

ALLMERS *(with suppressed fury):* By God, you are right! *(More quietly)* I forgot the child. In your arms.

RITA: Alfred—that's vile!

ALLMERS *(quietly):* In that moment, you condemned little Eyolf to death.

RITA: You too! You too! If I am guilty, so are you!

ALLMERS: Oh, very well, if you wish. We are both guilty. So there was retribution in Eyolf's death after all.

RITA: Retribution?

ALLMERS *(more controlled):* Yes. A judgement on you and me. Now we have what we deserve. While he lived, our cowardly, furtive consciences would not let us love him because we could not bear to look at the—thing he carried—

RITA *(quietly):* The crutch.

ALLMERS: Yes. That. And what we call our loss, our grief, is merely the gnawing of our consciences. Nothing more.

RITA *(helplessly):* Alfred—this can only lead us into despair—perhaps beyond—into madness. We can never undo what has been done.

ALLMERS *(in a quieter mood):* I dreamed of Eyolf last night. I thought I saw him coming up from the jetty. He could run like other boys. Nothing had happened to him. Nothing at all. This stifling existence was only a dream, I thought. Oh, Rita, how I praised and thanked— *(Stops himself.)*

RITA: Whom?

ALLMERS *(evasively):* Whom?

RITA: Whom did you praise and thank?

ALLMERS: I told you, I was dreaming—

RITA: That God in Whom you do not believe?

ALLMERS: It just happened like that. I was asleep, I tell you.

RITA: You should not have sowed the seeds of doubt in me, Alfred.

ALLMERS: Would I have done better to let you continue through life believing in empty illusions?

RITA: It would have been better for me. I should at least have been able to turn somewhere for comfort. Now I have nowhere.

ALLMERS *(looks at her closely):* If you were given the choice now—if you could follow Eyolf to—to where he now is—

RITA: Yes?

ALLMERS: If you could be sure you would find him again. Know him—understand him—

RITA: Yes, yes?

ALLMERS: Would you leap the gulf to join him? Leave all this? Renounce life? Would you do that, Rita?

RITA *(quietly):* You mean—now?

ALLMERS: Yes. Today. Now. Answer me. Would you?

RITA *(hesitantly):* Oh, I don't know, Alfred. I think I would choose to stay here with you for a while.

ALLMERS: For my sake?

RITA: Yes. Only for your sake.

ALLMERS: But afterwards? Would you? Answer me.

RITA: Oh, what can I say? You know I could never leave you. Never.

ALLMERS: But suppose I were to go to join Eyolf—and suppose you knew for sure that you would meet both him and me there? Then would you come to join us?

RITA: I should like to. With all my heart. But—

ALLMERS: But—?

RITA: I don't think I could. No, no—I simply couldn't. No, not even for the promise of heaven.

ALLMERS: Neither could I.

RITA: No, Alfred. You couldn't do it either, could you?

ALLMERS: No. This is where we belong. Here on earth. Living.

RITA: Yes. Here is the kind of happiness we understand.

ALLMERS: Oh, happiness—happiness—

RITA: You mean we shall never find happiness again? But suppose—? No. I daren't say it.

ALLMERS: Say it, Rita, Say it.

RITA *(hesitantly):* Couldn't we try to—? If only we could forget.

ALLMERS: Forget Eyolf?

RITA: No. Forget ourselves. Our guilt.

ALLMERS: Is that what you want?

RITA: Yes. If it's possible. *(In a sudden outburst.)* I can't bear this much longer, Alfred. Can't we find something to make us forget?

ALLMERS: What?

RITA: We could travel. Go far away.

ALLMERS: Go away? You are never happy anywhere but here.

RITA: Well, we could invite people here. Keep open house. Throw ourselves into some activity which would deaden—

ALLMERS: That kind of life is not for me. No, rather than that I would try to take up my work again.

RITA *(acidly):* Your book? Which has stood for so many years between us?

ALLMERS *(slowly, looking coldly at her):* There will always be something between us now.

RITA: Why?

ALLMERS: Who knows whether huge child-eyes do not watch us night and day?

RITA *(softly, shuddering):* Alfred!

ALLMERS: Our love has been a consuming fire. Now it has burned itself out.

RITA: Burned out!

ALLMERS *(in a hard voice):* It is already burned out in one of us.

RITA *(as though turned to stone):* And you dare say that to me!

ALLMERS *(more gently):* It is dead, Rita. But something has taken its place—a sharing of guilt and remorse—a sharing in which there is perhaps a new beginning—a resurrection—

RITA *(violently):* Resurrection! What do I care about resurrection!

ALLMERS: Rita!

RITA: I am flesh and blood! I cannot drowse my life away like a fish! To be walled up for the rest of my life in a cell of guilt and remorse! With a man who is no longer mine, mine, mine!

ALLMERS: It had to end some time, Rita.

RITA: Had it to end like this? A love that began as consumingly as ours did?

ALLMERS: My first feeling for you was not love, Rita.

RITA: What was it, then?

ALLMERS: Fear.

RITA: That I can understand. But if that was so, how did I manage to win you?

ALLMERS: You were so—so consumingly beautiful, Rita.

RITA: Was it only that? Answer me, Alfred. Was there nothing else?

ALLMERS *(reluctantly):* Yes. There was something else.

RITA: I can guess what it was. "My gold and my green forests," I think you called them. Aren't I right, Alfred?

ALLMERS: Yes.

RITA: How could you? How could you do it?

ALLMERS: I had Asta to think of.

RITA: Oh, yes—Asta! So it was Asta who brought us together!

ALLMERS: She knew nothing. She has no inkling of it even now.

RITA: None the less, it was Asta. *(Smiles scornfully.)* No. It
   was little Eyolf. Yes, Alfred. Little Eyolf.

ALLMERS: Eyolf?

RITA: You used to call her Eyolf, didn't you? I seem to remember you telling me so once—in a secret moment.
   (Comes closer.) Do you remember that terrifyingly beautiful moment, Alfred?

ALLMERS *(shrinks from her):* I remember nothing! I don't
   want to remember!

RITA *(following him):* It was that moment when your other
   little Eyolf became a cripple.

ALLMERS *(supports himself against the table):* The retribution.

RITA: Yes. The retribution.

   ASTA *and* BORGHEJM *come back past the boathouse.
   She has some water-lilies in her hand.*

RITA *(controlled):* Well, Asta. Have you and Mr. Borghejm
   said everything you had to say to each other?

ASTA: Oh, yes—I think so.

   *She puts down her umbrella and lays the flowers on a
   chair.*

BORGHEJM: Miss Allmers has been very quiet during our
   walk.

RITA: Really? Alfred and I have said enough to each other—

ASTA *(looks tensely from one to the other):* Yes?

RITA: To last us for the rest of our lives. Come now, let's go
   up to the house. Alfred and I need company from now on.
   We can't be alone now.

ALLMERS: You two go ahead. Asta, I must have a word with
   you.

RITA: Indeed? Well, come with me then, Mr. Borghejm.

   RITA *and* BORGHEJM *go out.*

ASTA: Alfred, what's been happening?

ALLMERS: I can't stand it here any longer.

ASTA: Here? You mean with Rita?

ALLMERS: Yes. Rita and I cannot go on living together.

ASTA *(shakes his arm):* Alfred, you mustn't say such dreadful things.

ALLMERS: It is true. Living together makes us evil and cruel.

ASTA: I'd never realized—

ALLMERS: Nor had I. Until today.

ASTA: And now you want to—yes, what do you want, Alfred?

ALLMERS: To get away from this place. Far away from it all.

ASTA: And live on your own?

ALLMERS *(nods):* Yes. As I used to.

ASTA: But you can't live alone.

ALLMERS: I did once.

ASTA: You mean in the old days? But then you had me with you.

ALLMERS *(tries to take her hand):* Yes, Asta. And now I want to come home to you again.

ASTA *(avoids his hand):* To me? No, no, Alfred. That's quite impossible.

ALLMERS: Because of Borghejm?

ASTA *(emotionally):* No, you are wrong. It's not because of him.

ALLMERS: I am glad. Then I return to you, my dear, my dearest sister. I must come home to you to be cleansed and purified from my life with—

ASTA: Alfred! It's a sin—

ALLMERS: No. I have sinned against her. But not in this. Remember, Asta? Do you remember how our life used to be? Was it not one long ecstasy of dedication?

ASTA: Yes, Alfred. But we can't relive the past.

ALLMERS *(bitterly):* You mean my marriage has unfitted me for that kind of life?

ASTA *(calmly):* No, I don't mean that.

ALLMERS: Then let us live again as we used to.

ASTA *(firmly):* We cannot do that, Alfred.

ALLMERS: We can. Love between brother and sister is the one relationship which does not obey the law of change.

ASTA *(quietly, trembling):* But if that should turn out not to—be our relationship?

ALLMERS *(amazed):* Not our—? What do you mean?

ASTA: My mother's letters—the ones in the portfolio—

ALLMERS: Well? What of them?

ASTA: Read them—when I have gone.

ALLMERS: Why?

ASTA *(with an effort):* Well, you'll find that—

ALLMERS: Yes?

ASTA: That I have no right to bear your father's name.

ALLMERS: Asta!

ASTA: Read the letters. Then you will see. And understand—and perhaps be able to forgive—my mother too.

ALLMERS: I don't understand this. I can't credit it. Asta! You mean you're not—?

ASTA: You are not my brother, Alfred.

ALLMERS *(quickly, defiantly, looking her in the eyes):* Well? What difference does that make? None at all.

ASTA *(shakes her head):* It changes everything, Alfred. Our relationship is not that of brother and sister.

ALLMERS: But it is still sacred. It will always remain sacred.

ASTA: Now it must obey the law of change.

ALLMERS *(looks searchingly at her):* You mean—?

ASTA *(quietly, warmly):* Please don't say anything more. My dearest—my dearest! *(She takes the flowers from the table.)* Do you see these water-lilies?

ALLMERS *(nods slowly):* They are the sort that shoot up to the surface from the depths.

491

ASTA: I gathered them from the lake. Where it flows out into the fjord. *(Holds them out.)* Would you like them, Alfred?

ALLMERS *(takes them):* Thank you.

ASTA *(with tears in her eyes):* Take them as a last greeting from—from little Eyolf.

ALLMERS *(looks at her):* From Eyolf out there? Or from you?

ASTA *(quietly):* From us both. *(She takes her umbrella.)* Come. Let us go up to Rita.

She goes up the path.

ALLMERS *(takes his hat from the table and whispers):* Asta. Eyolf. Little Eyolf—!

He follows her up the path.

ACT THREE

A shrub-covered mound in ALLMERS's *garden. In the background, a sheer cliff, with a railing along its edge and steps on the left leading down. A broad view over the fjord lying deep below. Close by the railing stands a flagstaff, with a line but no flag. In the foreground on the right is a summer-house, covered with creepers and wild vine. A bench stands outside it. It is late summer evening; the sky is clear. Dusk is falling.*

> ASTA *is seated on the bench, her hands in her lap. She is wearing outdoor clothes and hat; her parasol is at her side, and she carries a small travelling-bag slung from her shoulder on a strap.*

> BORGHEJM *climbs up backstage left. He, too, carries a travelling-bag slung from his shoulder, and a rolled-up flag over his arm.*

BORGHEJM (*catches sight of* ASTA): Ah, here you are.

ASTA: I thought I would sit here and look out over the fjord for the last time.

BORGHEJM: How lucky for me I came here too.

ASTA: Have you been searching for me?

BORGHEJM: Yes. I wanted so much to get the chance to say *au revoir*. Not goodbye, I hope.

ASTA (*smiles*): You are very persistent.

BORGHEJM: You have to be to be a road-builder.

ASTA: Did you see anything of Alfred? Or Rita?

BORGHEJM: Yes, I saw them both.

ASTA: Together?

BORGHEJM: No. Apart.

ASTA: What are you going to do with that flag?

BORGHEJM: Mrs. Allmers asked me to come and hoist it.

ASTA: Hoist it—now?

BORGHEJM: To half-mast. Let it hang there night and day, she said.

ASTA *(sighs):* Poor Rita. And poor Alfred.

BORGHEJM *(busying himself with the flag):* Have you really the heart to leave them? I ask because I see you are dressed for a journey.

ASTA *(in a low voice):* I have to go.

BORGHEJM: Of course, if you must—

ASTA: You are going tonight, too?

BORGHEJM: Yes. I, too, must go. I shall be catching the train. Will you be on it?

ASTA: No. I shall be taking the steamer.

BORGHEJM: *(with a glance at her):* Ah. Different ways, then?

ASTA: Yes.

She sits watching him while he hoists the flag to half-mast. When he has finished he goes over to her.

BORGHEJM: Miss Asta—you cannot imagine how deeply little Eyolf's death grieves me.

ASTA *(looks up at him):* I know it does.

BORGHEJM: It hurts so much. You see, it's not in my nature to mourn.

ASTA *(turns her eyes towards the flag):* Time will heal it. As it heals all things. All sorrows.

BORGHEJM: All? Do you believe that?

ASTA: They pass like summer showers. When you are far away from here, then—

BORGHEJM: It will have to be very far.

ASTA: And you have your big new road to think about.

BORGHEJM: Yes. But no one to help me with it.

ASTA: Of course you will.

BORGHEJM *(shakes his head):* No one to share the excitement and the joy of the work. And that's what one wants to share.

ASTA: What about the sweat and the toil?

BORGHEJM: Ah—that one can endure alone.

ASTA: But the joy must be shared?

BORGHEJM: Yes. What is the use of finding happiness if one cannot share it with anyone?

ASTA: Perhaps you are right.

BORGHEJM: Of course one can enjoy happiness alone for a while. But not for long. No, happiness can only be felt by two.

ASTA: Two? Why not three, or five, or ten?

BORGHEJM: Ah—that's a different sort of happiness. Miss Asta—couldn't you bring yourself to share the joys and triumphs of life—and the sweat and toil, too—with just one person?

ASTA: I have tried it—once.

BORGHEJM: Have you?

ASTA: Yes. All the years my brother—all the years Alfred and I lived together.

BORGHEJM: Oh, your brother? But that's quite different, surely. I would call that peace rather than happiness.

ASTA: Anyway, it was wonderful.

BORGHEJM: There, now! Even that seemed wonderful! But suppose now—just suppose he had not been your brother—

ASTA *(almost rises, but controls herself):* Then we would never have lived together. I was a child at the time. And he was little more than a child.

495

BORGHEJM *(after a moment):* Were they so wonderful, those years?

ASTA: Yes. Oh, yes. They were.

BORGHEJM: You had moments of real happiness and exhilaration?

ASTA: Oh, yes. So many. So many.

BORGHEJM: Tell me about them, Miss Asta.

ASTA: Oh, they were only little things.

BORGHEJM: Such as?

ASTA: Such as the time Alfred won his scholarship to the University. He'd done so well. And when he got a post at a school. Or when he was working at his thesis. And read it to me. And then later it got printed in a periodical.

BORGHEJM: Yes, I can imagine it must have been a good life. Brother and sister, sharing each other's happiness. *(Shakes his head.)* I don't know how your brother ever brought himself to let you go.

ASTA: He got married, you know.

BORGHEJM: That must have been difficult for you.

ASTA: Yes, At first. I thought I'd lost him.

BORGHEJM: But luckily you hadn't.

ASTA: No.

BORGHEJM: All the same, how could he? Marry, I mean. When he could have gone on living with you.

ASTA *(to herself):* The law of change, I suppose.

BORGHEJM: The law of change?

ASTA: It's Alfred's phrase.

BORGHEJM: Pah! A stupid law. I don't believe in it.

ASTA *(rises):* Not now, perhaps. You may come to believe in it in time.

BORGHEJM: I? Never! *(Earnestly.)* But listen to me, Miss Asta—be sensible for once—about all this, I mean—

ASTA *(interrupts him):* Please, please don't let's discuss it any further.

BORGHEJM: Yes, Asta! I can't let you go as easily as that.

Your brother has chosen his own way of life. He is quite happy without you. He does not even miss you. Then this—this thing happened which altered everything for you—

ASTA *(starts):* What do you mean?

BORGHEJM: The death of his child. What did you think I meant?

ASTA *(recovers her composure):* Little Eyolf. Yes.

BORGHEJM: Now there is nothing to keep you here any longer. No little crippled child who needs your love. No duties, nothing—

ASTA: Mr. Borghejm, please! Don't make it so hard for me.

BORGHEJM: I must. I would be mad if I did not. Any day now I shall leave town. I may not have an opportunity to see you there before I go. I may not see you again for years. Who knows what may happen before we meet again?

ASTA *(smiles):* So you are afraid of the law of change?

BORGHEJM: Oh, no I'm not! *(Laughs bitterly.)* In any case, what change have I to be afraid of? In you, I mean. It's clear you don't really care for me.

ASTA: You know I do.

BORGHEJM: Not enough. Not the way I want you to. *(More violently.)* In God's name, Asta—Miss Asta—can't you see how wrong you're being? Just over the horizon a whole lifetime of happiness may be laying in wait for us— and we are simply letting it lie there. Don't you think we're going to regret it, Asta?

ASTA *(quietly):* I don't know. I only know that we have to let it lie there waiting.

BORGHEJM: Then I must build my road alone?

ASTA *(warmly):* Oh, if only I could share it with you—the work and the joy—

BORGHEJM: Would you? If you could?

ASTA: Yes. I would.

BORGHEJM: But you can't?

ASTA *(looks down):* Would you be content with only half of me?

BORGHEJM: No. I must have all of you.

ASTA *(looks at him and says quietly):* Then I cannot.

BORGHEJM: Then goodbye, Miss Asta.

He turns to go. ALLMERS *climbs up from the back, left.* BORGHEJM *pauses.*

ALLMERS *(as he reaches the top of the steps, points and says quietly):* Is Rita down there in the summer-house?

BORGHEJM: No, there's no one here but Miss Asta.

ALLMERS *comes forward.*

ASTA *(goes towards him):* Shall I go down and look for her? And get her to come up here?

ALLMERS: No, no, no—don't bother. *(To* BORGHEJM*)* Did you hoist the flag?

BORGHEJM: Yes. Your wife asked me to. That was why I came up here.

ALLMERS: And you're leaving us tonight?

BORGHEJM: Yes. Tonight I really am leaving you.

ALLMERS *(with a glance at* ASTA*):* You have found a good travelling companion, I trust?

BORGHEJM *(shakes his head):* I am travelling alone.

ALLMERS *(startled):* Alone?

BORGHEJM: Quite alone.

ALLMERS *(abstractedly):* Oh, really?

BORGHEJM: And I shall stay alone.

ALLMERS: It is terrible to be alone. The thought of it chills my blood.

ASTA: But Alfred, you are not alone.

ALLMERS: That can be terrible too, Asta.

ASTA *(uneasily):* Don't talk like that.

ALLMERS: But if you are not going with—why not stay out here with me and Rita?

ASTA: No, Alfred, I can't. I must go back to town now.

ALLMERS: But only to town, Asta. You hear?

ASTA: Yes.

ALLMERS: And promise me you'll come out here soon again.

ASTA *(quickly):* No, I can't promise that. Not for a while.

ALLMERS: As you wish. We'll meet in town, then.

ASTA: But Alfred, you must stay here with Rita now.

ALLMERS *(turns to* BORGHEJM*):* I think you're probably lucky to be travelling alone.

BORGHEJM: What on earth do you mean?

ALLMERS: You never know whom you may meet. On the journey.

ASTA: Alfred!

ALLMERS: The right travelling companion. When it's too late.

ASTA *(quietly, trembling):* Alfred! Alfred!

BORGHEJM *(looks from one to the other):* What do you mean? I don't understand—

> RITA *climbs up from the back, left.*

RITA: Why are you all leaving me?

ASTA *(goes to meet her):* You said you wanted to be alone—

RITA: I know. But I daren't. It's getting so dark. I seem to see huge open eyes staring at me.

ASTA *(gently):* What if they are, Rita? You shouldn't be afraid of those eyes.

RITA: I don't know how you can say that.

ALLMERS *(urgently):* Asta, I beg you. Please. Stay here— with Rita.

RITA: Yes. And with Alfred, too. Please stay, Asta.

ASTA *(fighting with herself):* Oh! I would so gladly—

RITA: Well then, stay. Alfred and I cannot face our grief alone. Our bereavement.

ALLMERS: Why not say the gnawing of our consciences?

RITA: Whatever you call it—we two can't face it alone. Asta, I beg you with all my heart. Stay here and help us. Be to us what Eyolf was.

ASTA *(shrinks):* Eyolf!

RITA: You'd like her to stay, wouldn't you, Alfred?

ALLMERS: If she can, and if she wants to.

RITA: You used to call her your little Eyolf, didn't you? *(Takes* ASTA's *hand.)* From now on you shall be *our* Eyolf, Asta. Eyolf, as you used to be.

ALLMERS *(controlling his emotion):* Stay—and share our life, Asta. With Rita. With me. Your—brother.

ASTA *(withdraws her hand and says with decision):* No. I can't. *(Turns to* BORGHEJM.*)* When does the steamer leave?

BORGHEJM: Any minute now.

ASTA: Then I must go aboard. Are you coming with me?

BORGHEJM: Am I—? Yes, yes, yes!

ASTA: Come along, then.

RITA *(slowly):* Oh. I see. Well, then of course you can't stay with us.

ASTA *(throws her arms round* RITA's *neck):* Thank you, Rita. For everything. *(Goes over to* ALLMERS *and clasps his hand.)* Goodbye, Alfred. Goodbye.

ALLMERS *(quietly):* What is this, Asta? Are you running away?

ASTA: Yes, Alfred. I am.

ALLMERS: From me?

ASTA *(whispers):* From you—and from myself.

ALLMERS *(shrinks):* Ah—!

ASTA *hurries out.* BORGHEJM *waves his hat and follows her.* RITA *leans against the porch of the summer-house.* ALLMERS *walks to the railing and stands there, looking down. Pause.*

ALLMERS *(with forced composure):* Here's the steamer, Rita. Come and look.

RITA: I dare not look at it.

ALLMERS: Dare not?

RITA: No. It has a red eye. And a green eye also. Great glaring eyes.

ALLMERS: You know they are only lanterns.

RITA: They will always be eyes to me. They stare and stare out of the darkness. And—into the darkness too.

ALLMERS: Now she is coming alongside.

RITA: Where will they be mooring her this evening?

ALLMERS *(comes near her):* At the jetty, as usual, my dear—

RITA *(draws herself up):* How can they moor her there?

ALLMERS: You know they have to.

RITA: But it was there that Eyolf—! How can they do it?

ALLMERS: Life is pitiless, Rita.

RITA: People are pitiless. They don't consider anyone. Neither the living nor the dead.

ALLMERS: You're right. Life goes on, just as if nothing had happened.

RITA: Nothing has happened. To the rest of the world. Only to you and me.

ALLMERS *(his pain reawakening):* Rita—how meaningless it was, your pain in bearing him. For now he is gone—without a trace.

RITA: Only the crutch was saved.

ALLMERS: Be quiet! I never want to hear that word!

RITA: I can't bear the thought that he's gone from us.

ALLMERS *(coldly and bitterly):* You managed well enough without him while he was alive. Whole days would pass without your seeing him.

RITA: Only because I knew I could see him any time I wanted.

ALLMERS: Yes. That's how we wasted the few years we had with little Eyolf.

RITA *(listens):* Listen, Alfred. It's tolling again.

ALLMERS *(glances out over the fjord):* That's the steamer sounding its bell. It is ready to leave.

RITA: I don't mean that bell. All day this bell's been ringing in my ears. Ah! There it is again!

ALLMERS *(goes to her):* You are mistaken, Rita.

RITA: No. I hear it so clearly. It sounds like a funeral bell. Slowly—slowly. Always the same words.

ALLMERS: Words? What words?

RITA *(nods in time with the syllables):* "The–crutch–is–float–ing. The–crutch–is–float–ing." Surely you can hear it?

ALLMERS *(shakes his head):* I hear nothing. There is nothing to hear.

RITA: Oh, you can say what you like. I hear it clearly.

ALLMERS *(looks out over the railing):* Now they are aboard, Rita. Now the ship is steaming towards town.

RITA: Can't you hear it? "The–crutch–is—float–ing. The–crutch—"

ALLMERS *(comes towards her):* You mustn't stand here listening to something that isn't there. I tell you, Asta and Borghejm are aboard now, and on their way. Asta has gone.

RITA *(glances timidly at him):* Then you will soon be gone too, Alfred?

ALLMERS *(quickly):* What do you mean?

RITA: You will be following your sister.

ALLMERS: Has Asta said anything to you?

RITA: No. But you told me yourself that it was for Asta's sake you married me.

ALLMERS: Yes. But you have bound me to you. By the years we have lived together.

RITA: Ah! In your eyes I am not so—so consumingly beautiful as I was once.

502

ALLMERS: Perhaps the law of change will hold us together, in spite of everything.

RITA *(nods slowly):* A change is taking place in me. Oh, God! It hurts me so!

ALLMERS: Hurts?

RITA: Yes. Like a birth.

ALLMERS: That is what it is. A birth. Or a resurrection. A transition. To another way of living.

RITA *(stares sadly ahead of her):* Yes. But it means the wreck of all life's happiness.

ALLMERS: In that wreck lies our victory.

RITA *(violently):* Oh—words! Good God, we are human! Flesh and blood!

ALLMERS: We are also kin with the sea and the sky, Rita.

RITA: You, perhaps. Not I.

ALLMERS: You too. More than you know.

RITA *(takes a step towards him):* Tell me, Alfred. Couldn't you think of taking up your work again?

ALLMERS: That work you hate so much?

RITA: I am humbler now. I am ready to share you with your book.

ALLMERS: Why?

RITA: So that I may keep you here. Near me.

ALLMERS: I can be of little help to you, Rita.

RITA: But perhaps I could help you.

ALLMERS: To work, you mean?

RITA: No. To live.

ALLMERS *(shakes his head):* I have no life left to live.

RITA: To endure the years that remain, then.

ALLMERS *(almost to himself):* I think it would be best for both of us if we were to part.

RITA: Whom would you go to? Asta?

ALLMERS: No. Not Asta. I shall never see her again.

RITA: Where, then?

ALLMERS: Up into my solitude.

RITA: The mountains?

ALLMERS: Yes.

RITA: But these are only day-dreams, Alfred. You couldn't live up there.

ALLMERS: Perhaps. But that is where I long to go. To the mountains.

RITA: Why?

ALLMERS: I want to tell you something.

RITA: Something that happened to you up there?

ALLMERS: Yes.

RITA: Something you kept from Asta and me?

ALLMERS: Yes.

RITA: Oh, why do you keep everything to yourself? You shouldn't.

ALLMERS: Sit down and I'll tell you.

RITA: Yes. Tell me.

She sits on the bench by the summer-house.

ALLMERS: I was alone up there. In the heart of the high mountains. Suddenly I came to a large, desolate lake. And I had to cross that lake. But I couldn't, for there was no one there, and no boat.

RITA: What happened then?

ALLMERS: I went all alone, with no one to guide me, into a side valley. I thought that way I might be able to push forward over the heights and between the peaks, and so come down on the other side of the lake.

RITA: And you got lost?

ALLMERS: Yes. I lost all sense of direction, for there was no kind of road nor path there. I walked all day—and all night, too. I began to think I would never find my way back.

RITA: I know your thoughts were with us.

ALLMERS: No; they were not. It was strange. Both you and Eyolf had drifted far, far away from me. And Asta too.

504

RITA: Then what were you thinking about?

ALLMERS: Nothing. I struggled along the deep crevasses, exulting in the peace and serenity of being in the presence of death.

RITA *(jumps to her feet):* It's horrible! How can you use such words about it!

ALLMERS: But that was how I felt. I had no fear. I felt that Death and I walked side by side like two good fellow-travellers. It all seemed so natural. So logical. In my family we do not live to be old—

RITA: Don't talk any more about it, Alfred. You are alive.

ALLMERS: Yes. Quite suddenly, I found I was there. On the other side of the lake.

RITA: That must have been a night of terror for you, Alfred. But now that it's over, you won't admit it.

ALLMERS: That night resolved me. I turned back and came home. To Eyolf.

RITA *(quietly):* Too late.

ALLMERS: Yes. For my fellow-traveller came and claimed him. And then he suddenly seemed loathsome—and life too—this damned existence we dare not tear ourselves away from. We are earthbound, Rita, you and I.

RITA: Yes! You're the same, aren't you? *(Comes towards him.)* Oh, let us live our lives together. As long as we can.

ALLMERS *(shrugs his shoulders):* Live? *(Laughs.)* What for? Our lives are empty wastes. Whichever way I look.

RITA: Oh, Alfred. Sooner or later you will leave me. I feel it. I can see it in your eyes. You will leave me.

ALLMERS: You mean, when my fellow-traveller comes for me?

RITA: No. Worse. Of your own free will. Because it's only when you are here with me that your life is meaningless. Answer me! Isn't that what you think?

ALLMERS *(looks her in the eyes):* And if I do?

Angry, spiteful voices are heard raised against each other in a hubbub from far below. ALLMERS *goes to the railing.*

RITA: What's that? *(Cries)* Oh, they've found him!

ALLMERS: He will never be found.

RITA: Then why are they shouting?

ALLMERS *(comes forward):* They're only fighting. As usual.

RITA: Down by the shore?

ALLMERS: Yes. The whole of that damned village ought to be cleared. Now the men have come home—drunk, of course. Someone's beating his children. Listen to them yelling! And his wife shouting for someone to save them—

RITA: Oughtn't we to get someone to go down and help them?

ALLMERS: Help them? They were the ones who let Eyolf drown. No, let them perish—as they let Eyolf perish.

RITA: You mustn't talk like that, Alfred. Or even think it.

ALLMERS: How else can I think? All those old shacks ought to be demolished.

RITA: What would happen to those poor people!

ALLMERS: They'd have to go somewhere else.

RITA: And the children?

ALLMERS: Does it matter where they lead their miserable lives?

RITA *(quietly, reproachfully):* You are making yourself hard, Alfred.

ALLMERS: I have a right to be hard. A duty.

RITA: A duty?

ALLMERS: My duty towards Eyolf. He must not lie unavenged. So. There it is, Rita. I advise you to think it over. Have the village levelled to the ground—when I am gone.

RITA: When you are gone?

ALLMERS: At least it will give you something to occupy yourself with. And you'll need that.

RITA *(with decision):* You're right. I shall need something. But can you guess what I am going to do? When you are gone.

ALLMERS: Well? Tell me.

RITA: The moment you leave me, I shall go down there and bring all those poor, neglected children up to this house.

ALLMERS: What do you want them here for?

RITA: I want to make them mine.

ALLMERS: You!

RITA: Yes. From the day you leave they shall all live here. As if they were mine.

ALLMERS: In our little Eyolf's place?

RITA: Yes. They shall live in Eyolf's room—look at his books—play with his toys.

ALLMERS: But this is absolute madness. There's no one in the world less suited than you to such work.

RITA: Then I shall have to teach myself. Work; and learn.

ALLMERS: If you really mean this, Rita, a great change must indeed have taken place in you.

RITA: It has, Alfred. You have seen to that. You have left me empty, and I must try to fill that emptiness with something. Something resembling love.

ALLMERS *(stands in thought for a moment, looking at her):* It's true we haven't done much for those poor people down there. Have we?

RITA: We haven't done anything for them.

ALLMERS: Hardly thought of them.

RITA: Not with compassion, anyway.

ALLMERS: We who had the gold and the green forests.

RITA: We closed our doors to them. And our hearts, too.

ALLMERS *(nods):* No wonder they wouldn't risk their lives to save little Eyolf.

RITA *(quietly):* Ask yourself, Alfred. Are you sure—quite sure—we would have risked ours?

ALLMERS: Rita! Can you doubt it?

RITA: Oh, Alfred. We are so earthbound, you and I.

ALLMERS: Well, what do you intend to do for these wretched children?

RITA: To begin with, I shall have to try to make life less hard for them.

ALLMERS: If you can do that, Eyolf will not have been born in vain.

RITA: And will not have been taken from us in vain.

ALLMERS *(looks at her):* Don't deceive yourself, Rita. You are not doing this out of love.

RITA: No. I'm not. Not yet, anyway.

ALLMERS: Why are you doing it, then?

RITA: I have so often heard you talking to Asta about human responsibility—

ALLMERS: That book you hated so much.

RITA: I hate it still. But I sat there and listened to you talking. And now I want to try to carry on from there—in my own way.

ALLMERS *(shakes his head):* For the sake of that unfinished book.

RITA: No. I have another reason. *(Quietly, with a sad smile.)* I want to placate the eyes that stare at me.

ALLMERS *(looks at her):* Will you let me stay with you, Rita?

RITA: Would you like to?

ALLMERS: Yes. If I was sure that I could help you.

RITA *(hesitantly):* You would have to go on living here.

ALLMERS *(quietly):* Let us see if we cannot make it work.

RITA *(almost inaudibly):* Yes, Alfred. Let us see.

Both are silent for a few moments. Then ALLMERS *walks over to the flagstaff and hoists the flag to the top.*

RITA *stands by the summer-house watching him quietly.*

ALLMERS *(comes back to her):* We have a long day ahead of us, Rita.

RITA: You will see. A Sunday calm will fall on us now and then.

ALLMERS *(quietly, moved):* Then, perhaps, we shall sense their spirits beside us.

RITA *(whispers):* Spirits?

ALLMERS: Yes. Perhaps they will come to visit us. The ones we have lost.

RITA *(nods slowly):* Our little Eyolf. And your big Eyolf, too.

ALLMERS: Perhaps now and then, on our way, we shall catch a glimpse of them.

RITA: Where shall we look, Alfred?

ALLMERS *(his eyes meet hers):* Upwards.

RITA: Yes. Upwards.

ALLMERS: Up towards the mountains. Toward the stars. And the great silence.

RITA *(stretches out her hand towards him):* Thank you.

Note on the Translations

Rosmersholm and *Little Eyolf* are two exceptionally difficult plays to translate. They abound in the kind of weighted and evasive dialogue that is the hallmark of Ibsen's later plays, from *The Wild Duck* onwards; the characters are continually saying one thing and meaning another, and the dialogue must enable the actors, as in the Norwegian, to express both the surface and the hidden meaning. Ibsen's leading characters are, almost without exception, inhibited by a deep sense of guilt, and for much of the time they speak evasively, like the characters of Joseph Conrad. Suddenly there is an exchange of knife-thrusts; then they return to their evasions. If the dialogue in these passages is flattened out and made too direct, the states of mind and actions of the characters become insufficiently motivated, and we miss the sense of what A. B. Walkley, writing about *Rosmersholm* in 1891, called, in a Wordsworthian phrase, "the obstinate questionings of invisible things."

The dialogue of *Little Eyolf* is especially elusive. Apart from the usual problem of creating a style which will convey the changes from evasiveness to directness without losing homogeneity or dropping into obscurity or flatness, a particular difficulty which this play poses is that of following Ibsen's subtle changes of pace. No one knew better than he the art of pacing his dialogue; to read any of his mature plays in the original is like watching an orchestra obey the beat of a conductor, and correct pacing is more essential to the translation (and staging) of *Little Eyolf* than to those of any other play he wrote.

After *Little Eyolf*, *Peer Gynt* is the most difficult of Ibsen's plays to translate, because the style is continually changing. Although it is written in rhyme throughout, Ibsen employed half a dozen different measures. In the first three acts, where Peer is a peasant of twenty, the language resembles nothing so much as that of *The Playboy of the Western World*, with its ebullience, naïveté and extravagant imagery. In the fourth act, Peer is a middle-aged man of the world, and talks in a pretentious, would-be epigrammatical style like a character from one of Aldous Huxley's early novels; while the fifth act is—I had almost said Shakespearian, but that is not quite accurate; the conception is Shakespearian, but the style remains racy and colloquial; its characteristic quality, as Archer observed, is its vernacular ease and simplicity, so that when one reads the play in Norwegian one has no feeling of incongruity between the various sections. As with *Brand*, a free verse, with broken rhythms, seemed the only answer, apart from certain passages which demand rhyme.

Wherever I have had to choose between maintaining the rhythm and using the most effective phrase, I have not hesitated to prefer the latter. As long as each section is controlled by a general overall rhythm, the individual phrase or line can, and indeed, I believe, should break out of it. This translation was originally much more regular; a good deal of valuable fragmentation took place during rehearsal.

The text is presented complete and unabridged. Cuts made for the 1962 Old Vic production are indicated by square brackets.

The final 'e' is always pronounced in Norwegian names, like an abbreviated '-er'. Thus, Aase ('Awse'), Lunde, Ronde, Grane, etc., are all bisyllabic.

The Lady from the Sea is, in general, simply written; for most of the time, the characters, even Ellida, say what they mean. The main problems here, in addition to those mentioned at the foot of page 510, are those which confront a translator when tackling any Ibsen play: lifting the language when Ibsen lifts it, and differentiating between the characters' various modes of speech. Ibsen was a close observer of speech idiosyncrasies; he remarked, for example, that people tend to speak differently in the morning from the way they do in the evening. "Before I write one word," he told M. G. Conrad, the German editor of *Die Gesellschaft,* "I must know the character through and through, I must penetrate into the last wrinkle of his soul. I always proceed from the individual; the stage setting, the dramatic ensemble, all of that comes naturally and causes me no worry, as soon as I am certain of the individual in every aspect of his humanity. But I have to have his exterior in mind also, down to the last button, how he stands and walks, how he bears himself, what his voice sounds like. Then I do not let him go until his destiny is fulfilled."

On another occasion, Ibsen explained his method in more detail:

As a rule, I make three drafts of my plays, which differ greatly from each other—in characterisation, if not in plot. When I approach the first working-out of my material, it is as though I knew my characters from a railway journey; one has made a preliminary acquaintance, one has chatted about this and that. At the next draft, I already see everything much more clearly, and I know the people roughly as one would after a month spent with them at a spa; I have discovered the fundamentals of their characters and their little peculiarities; but I may still be wrong about certain essentials. Finally, in the last draft, I have reached the limit of my knowledge; I know my characters from close and long acquaintance—they are my intimate friends, who will no longer disappoint me; as I see them now, I shall always see them.

As with all the plays, I have not modernised Ibsen's dialogue, but have tried to translate it into a language common to the period in which the plays are set and to the present. I have, however, retained certain turns of phrase which look Victorian on the printed page but have proved effective in the theatre when spoken by an actor or actress in nineteenth-century costume in a nineteenth-century room. I have deleted some stage directions, mainly adjectives and adverbs which suggest a style of acting which would strike a modern audience as somewhat melodramatic.

I gladly acknowledge my thanks to Mr. Casper Wrede for much invaluable advice and criticism in connection with the translations of *The Lady from the Sea* and *Little Eyolf*.

ABOUT THE AUTHOR

HENRIK IBSEN, widely regarded as the founder of modern drama, was born in Skien, Norway in 1828 into a family of prosperous merchants. His father's business failed suddenly while Ibsen was still a young boy, and Ibsen was forced to work as an apothecary's assistant. After six years of humiliating poverty, Ibsen entered the university, and in 1850 he was asked to join the new National Theater, where he wrote and directed plays and designed productions. His plays were not admired, the National Theater went bankrupt, and Ibsen, forced to live on the charity of friends and a government travel stipend, emigrated to Italy.

It was not until 1866, when *Brand* was published to critical acclaim and *Peer Gynt* to even greater praise, that Ibsen began to gain recognition as a playwright. The next decade was a fertile one. Ibsen's dramas of social and family life attracted more attention, and *A Doll's House* was produced to international admiration, though it aroused controversy for its unromantic portrayal of marriage and its realistic depiction of the tensions between husband and wife. Ibsen's next play, *Ghosts* (1881), which dealt frankly with free love and venereal disease, was violently attacked as indecent. His succeeding plays, among them such acknowledged masterpieces as *The Wild Duck* (1884) and *Hedda Gabler* (1890), were met with bafflement and disdain, the artistic establishment accusing Ibsen of being relentlessly pessimistic and unnecessarily obscure. In 1891, Ibsen returned to Norway, where he lived until his death from a stroke in 1906. He never lived to see the recognition that would one day place him among the greatest dramatists of Western Literature.

ABOUT THE TRANSLATOR

Michael Meyer is one of the leading Ibsen scholars of his generation. He was born in London in 1921 and educated at Oxford. He has lived extensively in the Scandinavian countries and taught English literature at Upsala University in Sweden. In addition to his translation of *The Plays of Ibsen,* available in four volumes from Washington Square Press, he has written a biography of Ibsen, translated the plays of Strindberg, and, most recently, written a biography of Strindberg. He currently resides in London.